CRUSADING AND THE OTTOMAN THREAT

Crusading and the Ottoman Threat, 1453–1505

NORMAN HOUSLEY

OXFORD
UNIVERSITY PRESS

OXFORD
UNIVERSITY PRESS

Great Clarendon Street, Oxford, OX2 6DP,
United Kingdom

Oxford University Press is a department of the University of Oxford.
It furthers the University's objective of excellence in research, scholarship,
and education by publishing worldwide. Oxford is a registered trade mark of
Oxford University Press in the UK and in certain other countries

© Norman Housley 2012

The moral rights of the author have been asserted

First Edition published in 2012

Impression: 1

All rights reserved. No part of this publication may be reproduced, stored in
a retrieval system, or transmitted, in any form or by any means, without the
prior permission in writing of Oxford University Press, or as expressly permitted
by law, by licence or under terms agreed with the appropriate reprographics
rights organization. Enquiries concerning reproduction outside the scope of the
above should be sent to the Rights Department, Oxford University Press, at the
address above

You must not circulate this work in any other form
and you must impose this same condition on any acquirer

British Library Cataloguing in Publication Data

Data available

Library of Congress Cataloging in Publication Data

Data available

ISBN 978–0–19–922705–1

Printed in Great Britain by
MPG Books Group, Bodmin and King's Lynn

Links to third party websites are provided by Oxford in good faith and
for information only. Oxford disclaims any responsibility for the materials
contained in any third party website referenced in this work.

For Ravi: another one to put on the shelf

Preface

I am grateful to the University of Leicester for granting me a full year of study leave in 2009–10, and to All Souls College Oxford for a visiting fellowship during the same year. Amongst the numerous colleagues who have helped me to form and refine my ideas and arguments, particular thanks are due to Iulian Damian, Dan Ioan Mureşan, Alexandru Simon, Benjamin Weber, and the contributors to my volume of essays *Crusading in the Fifteenth Century: Message and Impact*. Christopher Dyer provided helpful stylistic suggestions and Jen Moore's copy-editing skills were invaluable.

Norman Housley

Contents

List of Abbreviations	xi
1. Introduction	1
1.1 Recent historiography	1
1.2 The sources	7
1.3 The trajectory of events	10
1.4 The structure of the analysis	16
2. Underpinnings: antagonisms and allegiances	18
2.1 Christianity and Islam: the Turks	18
2.2 The Holy Land and the Orthodox Christians	26
2.3 Catholic Europe: the universal and the particular	34
2.4 *Antemurale* states	40
2.5 *Item tu Sixte canis, iam amicus Turcorum*: criticism, challenges, and alternatives to papal authority	50
3. Strategy, mobilization, and control	62
3.1 Strategic perceptions and planning	62
3.2 The papal *curia*: memory and methods	71
3.3 The search for unity: crusading congresses and diets	74
3.4 Synergizing self-interest: crusading leagues and subsidies	83
3.5 *Unum tandem remedium*: leading from the front	96
4. Recruitment and finance	100
4.1 *Crucesignati* and fifteenth-century crusading	100
4.2 Volunteerism and military service in Hungary	107
4.3 Pius II, Perault, and volunteer service	119
4.4 Crusade taxation and the funding shortfall	127
5. Communication	135
5.1 The Franciscan Observants and preaching: the pattern of involvement	136
5.2 The Franciscan Observants and preaching: individuals, techniques, and themes	145
5.3 Orations	159
5.4 Printing	167
6. Indulgences and the crusade against the Turks	174
6.1 *Ea bulla, quam cruciatam dicimus*: the character and administration of crusade indulgences	175

    6.2 Popularity and returns   187
    6.3 Control and retention   197

7. Conclusion   211

Bibliography   217
Index   235

List of Abbreviations

AE	*Annales ecclesiastici*
AIRCRUV	*Annuario dell'Istituto Romeno di Cultura e Ricerca Umanistica di Venezia*
AM	*Annales minorum*
AR	*Ausgewählte Regesten*
AS Oct	*Acta Sanctorum Octobris,* X (Brussels, 1861)
BF	*Bullarium Franciscanum*
CFC	Norman Housley, ed., *Crusading in the Fifteenth Century: Message and Impact* (Basingstoke, 2004)
CLMAR	Ivan Supičič, ed., *Croatia in the Late Middle Ages and the Renaissance: A Cultural Survey* (London and Zagreb, 2008)
CTO	Hubert Houben, ed., *La conquista turca di Otranto (1480) tra storia e mito,* 2 vols (Galatina, 2008)
DBI	*Dizionario biografico degli Italiani* (Rome, 1960–)
DS	*Diplomatarium svecanum*
ETR	Bodo Guthmüller and Wilhelm Kühlmann, eds, *Europa und die Türken in der Renaissance* (Tübingen, 2000)
FHR	János M. Bak and Béla K. Király, eds, *From Hunyadi to Rákóczi: War and Society in Late Medieval and Early Modern Hungary* (New York, 1982)
LdM	*Lexikon des Mittelalters,* 10 vols (Munich, 1980–99)
MCH	*Mathiae Corvini Hungariae regis epistolae ad Romanos pontifices datae et ab eis acceptae*
MDE	*Magyar Diplomacziai Emlékek. Mátyás Király Korából 1458–1490*
MGH SRG	*Monumenta Germaniae Historica, Scriptores rerum Germanicarum*
MKL	*Mátyás Király Levelei. Külügyi Osztály*
ML	*Matthias and his Legacy: Cultural and Political Encounters between East and West,* ed. Attila Bárány and Attila Györkös (Debrecen, 2009)
NC	Martin Nejedlý and Jaroslav Svátek, eds, *La Noblesse et la croisade à la fin du Moyen Âge (France, Bourgogne, Bohême)*, Les Croisades tardives, 2 (Toulouse, 2009)
OEEH	Franz Fuchs, ed., *Osmanische Expansion und europäischer Humanismus* (Wiesbaden, 2005)
PG	*Patrologia graeca*
Pius II	Zweder von Martels and Arjo Vanderjagt, eds, *Pius II 'el più expeditivo pontifice': Selected Studies on Aeneas Silvius Piccolomini (1405–1464)* (Leiden and Boston, 2003)

PNTM	R.N. Swanson, ed., *Promissory Notes on the Treasury of Merits: Indulgences in Late Medieval Europe* (Leiden and Boston, 2006)
QFIAB	*Quellen und Forschungen aus italienischen Archiven und Bibliotheken*
RISNS	Rerum Italicarum Scriptores, nova series
RK	Erich Meuthen, ed., *Reichstage und Kirche* (Göttingen, 1991)
SP	Arturo Calzona and others, eds, *Il sogno di Pio II e il viaggio da Roma a Mantova* (Florence, 2003)
VMH	*Vetera monumenta historica Hungariam sacram illustrantia*, ed. Theiner
VMP	*Vetera monumenta Poloniae et Lithuaniae gentiumque finitimarum historiam illustrantia*, ed. Theiner

1
Introduction

In the half century that followed the fall of Constantinople in 1453 Christian Europe experienced a sustained attempt to expel the Ottoman Turks from the continent by crusading means. The energies of some of the Church's most talented and creative individuals focused on how best to employ the mechanisms of crusade to mobilize Christian resources. The activity that resulted was far-reaching and immense. Numerous crusading bulls, adapting templates and language that in many cases had their origins in the thirteenth century, were issued by the papal *curia*. The cross was preached across the whole of Europe and indulgences were distributed with the goals of recruiting soldiers, providing shipping and war equipment, and raising cash. Large-scale measures of taxation were attempted both of churchmen and, more controversially, of the laity. No great crusade came about, but both the scale of the efforts involved and their impact on contemporaries' income and lives are undeniable. This was the last substantial attempt by the Church to persuade the faithful to take collective military action, on the basis of their religious beliefs, to defend shared values and achieve common goals.

It is inadequate to dismiss these programmes as anachronistic and therefore doomed to fail. Although the practice of crusading had originated in a different world, it was malleable: there were grounds for believing that it could be updated to meet changing social and economic circumstances, and tailored in response to volatile strategic scenarios and evolving operational demands. Nor were contemporaries unreceptive to the message that lobbyists for the crusade were sending out. Europe's crusading past provided inspiration and example. Christians generally retained a strong propensity to manage and portray their conflicts in religious terms. Many humanists, the period's most dynamic and ambitious cultural group, advocated a crusade against the Turks, and they brought a sophisticated and appealing new rhetoric to bear on it. And crusade enthusiasts were willing to embrace technological advances, above all printing, that might be harnessed to their cause. This was not the last gasp of a dying movement, but a big and resonant project.

1.1 RECENT HISTORIOGRAPHY

In the past twenty years the study of crusading in fifteenth-century Europe has benefited from a surge of interest on the part of scholars.[1] In four respects recent

---

[1] For publications to 1990, see Norman Housley, *The Later Crusades, 1274–1580: From Lyons to Alcazar* (Oxford, 1992), 469–74.

historiography has added substantially to our knowledge. In the first place, there has been a cluster of reassessments of regional impacts and initiatives. Most importantly, since the end of the Cold War a new generation of scholars, particularly those based in Hungary and Romania, has clarified the interactions between western Europe's courts and centres of power in Hungary, Transylvania, Moldavia, and Albania.[2] For the most part these exchanges were military and economic in character, but there was also an ecumenical dialogue between Catholic and Orthodox clerics, especially after the council of Florence in 1439. There is a case for arguing that after 1453 crusading can be regarded, for the first time in its history, as an inclusively Christian activity rather than an exclusively Catholic one. Participation, both actual and projected, spanned the breadth of the Balkans from the Adriatic to the Black Sea.

Away from Europe's frontline states, the espousal of crusading by the ducal court of Burgundy has been clarified by Jacques Paviot and the response to crusading appeals in the Scandinavian lands has been investigated by Janus Møller Jensen.[3] The problematic position of the Czechs following the compromise settlement at Basel is receiving attention: an important development given that so much of papal policy in our period was informed by an awareness of the unresolved Hussite question and the utraquists' search for allies.[4] The Europe-wide spectrum of views about and approaches towards crusade has also been elucidated by the published volumes

---

[2] See in particular, publications by Damian, Mureşan, Schmitt and Simon, as follows. Iulian Mihai Damian, 'La *Depositeria della Crociata* (1463–1490) e i sussidi dei pontefici romani a Mattia Corvino', *AIRCRUV*, 8 (2006), 135–52; id, 'La disfatta di Solgat (Crimea) e i suoi echi nei trattati d'arte militare rinascimentale', *Ephemeris* (forthcoming); and id, '*Sub crucis vexillo*: il re e la crociata', in *Between Worlds* (forthcoming). Dan Ioan Mureşan, 'Girolamo Lando, titulaire du patriarcat de Constantinople (1474–1497), et son rôle dans la politique orientale du Saint-Siège', *AIRCRUV*, 8 (2006), 153–258; id, 'La croisade en projets. Plans présentés au Grand Quartier Général de la croisade—le Collège des cardinaux', forthcoming; and id, 'Les *Oraisons contre les Turcs* de Bessarion: propaganda de la croisade au *Große Christentag* de Ratisbonne (1471)', forthcoming. Oliver Jens Schmitt, 'Skanderbeg als neuer Alexander. Antikerezeption im spätmittelalterlichen Albanien', in *OEEH*, 123–44. Alexandru Simon, 'The Use of the "Gate of Christendom". Hungary's Mathias Corvinus and Moldavia's Stephen the Great, Politics in the late 1400s', *Quaderni della Casa Romena*, 3 (2004), 205–24; id, 'The Hungarian Means of the Relations between the Habsburgs and Moldavia at the End of the 15th Century', *AIRCRUV*, 8 (2006), 259–96; id, 'Anti-Ottoman Warfare and Crusader Propaganda in 1474: New Evidence from the Archives of Milan', *Revue roumaine d'histoire*, 46 (2007), 25–39; id, 'Antonio Bonfini's *Valachorum regulus*: Matthias Corvinus, Transylvania and Stephen the Great', in *Between Worlds [I], Stephen the Great, Matthias Corvinus and their Time*, ed. László Koszta and others (Cluj-Napoca, 2007), 209–26; id, 'The Arms of the Cross: The Christian Politics of Stephen the Great and Matthias Corvinus', in *Between Worlds [I]*, 45–86; id, 'The Limits of the Moldavian Crusade (1474, 1484)', *AIRCRUV*, 9 (2007), 273–326; id, 'The Walachians between Crusader Crisis and Imperial Gifts (mid 1400' and early 1500')', *AIRCRUV*, 9 (2007), 141–94; id, 'The Ottoman-Hungarian Crisis of 1484: Diplomacy and Warfare in Matthias Corvinus' Local and Regional Politics', in *ML*, 405–36; and id, and Cristian Luca, 'Documentary Perspectives on Stephen the Great and Matthias Corvinus', *Transylvanian Review*, 17 (2008), 85–114. The forthcoming proceedings of a conference on Matthias Corvinus held at Cluj/Napoca in 2008 will contain a number of important essays.

[3] Jacques Paviot, *Les ducs de Bourgogne, la croisade et l'Orient (fin XIVe siècle–XVe siècle)* (Paris, 2003); Janus Møller Jensen, *Denmark and the Crusades 1400–1650* (Leiden and Boston, 2007).

[4] See Martin Nejedlý, 'Promouvoir une alliance anti-turque, éviter une croisade anti-hussite: un noble tchèque en mission diplomatique. Le témoignage de l'écuyer Jaroslav sur l'ambassade à Louis XI en 1464', in *NC*, 163–84; and František Šmahel, 'Antoine Marini de Grenoble et son Mémorandum sur la nécessité d'une alliance anti-turque', in *NC*, 205–31.

that have emanated from Daniel Baloup's research programme *Les Croisades tardives: Conflits interconfessionnels et sentiments identitaires à la fin du Moyen Âge en Europe*. One of the most impressive features of Baloup's programme has been its comprehensiveness. This will make it easier for scholars to relate the anti-Turkish crusade not just to other crusading that was occurring at the same time—above all in Iberia and North Africa—but also to alternative trends that promoted conversion and *convivencia*.

A second area of advance is the relationship between humanism and crusading. James Hankins paved the way for this by publishing a series of important texts accompanied by a commentary that set the humanist reaction to the Turks within a much more nuanced context than anybody had previously done.[5] Nancy Bisaha explored the full range of humanist responses to the Ottoman Turks, showing that their engagement with the subject was instrumental in creating a self-consciously 'European' or 'civilized' identity.[6] Margaret Meserve similarly examined how the image of the Turk was created in Renaissance Europe, with particular reference to the Turks' supposed ethnic roots and historic origins.[7] As these scholars and others have shown, the humanist response was far from straightforward: outlooks varied and were shaped by events as well as by the differing aspirations and backgrounds of individuals. Much of the value of the best collections of essays and conference papers derives from an editorial strategy of incorporating as full a range of viewpoints as circumstances permit. Hence the collections edited by Bodo Guthmüller and Wilhelm Kühlmann,[8] and by Franz Fuchs,[9] usefully complement the focused monographs by Bisaha and Meserve. Other useful recent collections have been those edited by Zweder von Martels and Arjo Vanderjagt,[10] and by Arturo Calzona,[11] on Aeneas Sylvius Piccolomini, who as Pope Pius II (1458–64) must be credited with completing the synthesis of traditional crusading ideas with the new humanist discourse. Hubert Houben has published a collection that reassesses the Ottoman occupation of Otranto in 1480.[12] This was an event second only to 1453 in terms of its impact on contemporaries. Indeed, for Italian humanists it was the fall of Otranto, rather than Constantinople, that constituted their '9/11 moment', when the full extent of the Turkish threat hit home and their perspective on it shifted from witness to victim.[13] The real 9/11 has exercised a palpable impact on research into the interface between the Turks and the humanists: it has both reinforced the need for sensitivity when analyzing the intersections of religious and cultural difference in the past, and it has given research into that subject a sharper relevance. Thus far the great crusades to the Holy Land (1095–1291) have

---

[5] James Hankins, 'Renaissance Crusaders: Humanist Crusade Literature in the Age of Mehmed II', *Dumbarton Oaks Papers*, 49 (1995), 111–207.
[6] Nancy Bisaha, *Creating East and West: Renaissance Humanists and the Ottoman Turks* (Philadelphia, 2004).
[7] Margaret Meserve, *Empires of Islam in Renaissance Historical Thought* (Cambridge, Mass., 2008).
[8] *ETR.* [9] *OEEH.* [10] *Pius II.* [11] *SP.* [12] *CTO.*
[13] See Gabriella Albanese, 'La storiografia umanistica e l'avanzata turca: dalla caduta di Costantinopoli alla conquista di Otranto', in *CTO*, 1.319–52; and Francesco Tateo, 'Letterati e guerrieri di fronte al pericolo turco', in his *Chierici e feudatari del Mezzogiorno* (Bari, 1984), 21–68.

appeared more pertinent to public discussions about interfaith relations than resistance to the advance of the Turks in the fifteenth century. But Bisaha has made a strong argument for the case that the later period is at least as germane to contemporary debate, because of the way the ideology that she and others have identified migrated to the New World.

A third area of recent advance has been the highlighting of contributions made by a series of individuals who in the past have been wholly neglected or underestimated. When the author planned this book, it was conceived as a study of three fifteenth-century churchmen: Giovanni da Capistrano (1386–1456), Piccolomini (1405–64), and Raymond Perault (or Peraudi) (1435–1505). These individuals will have large parts to play in the pages that follow, but the crusading project that they tried so hard to promote now looks much more like a collective exercise. The relief of Belgrade in 1456 was without question the period's greatest crusading success, and in large part it was due to Capistrano's charisma and leadership. But in terms of underlying preaching techniques, it makes sense to assess Capistrano in conjunction with the activities of a substantial group of his fellow Franciscan Observants, including Jacopo delle Marche, Roberto Caracciolo da Lecce, Bartolomeo da Camerino, and Angelo Carletti. Each of these individuals has received some attention, though less than they deserve. As for Perault, his extraordinary career has become easier to assess as we have gained a better understanding of other promoters of indulgences. One such was Marinus de Fregeno, whose career has been elucidated by Klaus Voigt.[14] Another was the Augustinian Johannes von Paltz, who worked with and admired Perault. Paltz's voluminous writings about indulgences and their management have been edited and analyzed by Berndt Hamm.[15] Birgit Studt has demonstrated the need for a longer perspective, given that the papal legates during the Hussite crusades of the 1420s and early 1430s anticipated much of what Perault later tried to achieve, by linking crusade preaching with pastoral concerns.[16] That said, arguably the most valuable insights into Perault's preaching campaigns have come from the interest that students of religion, including Erich Meuthen, Bernd Moeller, and Wilhelm Winterhager, have shown in the controversy about the popularity of indulgences and the doctrine of salvation by works during the pre-Reformation generation.[17] This has enabled us to locate Perault's

---

[14] Klaus Voigt, 'Der Kollektor Marinus de Fregeno und seine "*Descriptio provinciarum Alamanorum*"', *QFIAB*, 68 (1968), 148–206.

[15] Johannes von Paltz, *Werke, 2: Supplementum Coelifodinae*, ed. Berndt Hamm, Spätmittelalter und Reformation. Texte und Untersuchungen, 3 (Berlin and New York, 1983); Berndt Hamm, *Frömmigkeitstheologie am Anfang des 16. Jahrhunderts. Studien zu Johannes von Paltz und seinem Umkreis* (Tübingen, 1982).

[16] Birgit Studt, *Papst Martin V. (1417–1431) und die Kirchenreform in Deutschland* (Cologne, 2004).

[17] Erich Meuthen, 'Reiche, Kirchen und Kurie im späteren Mittelalter', *Historische Zeitschrift*, 265 (1997), 597–637; Bernd Moeller, 'Die letzten Ablaßkampagnen. Der Widerspruch Luthers gegen den Ablaß in seinem geschichtlichen Zusammenhang', in Hartmut Boockmann and others, eds, *Lebenslehren und Weltentwürfe im Übergang vom Mittelalter zur Neuzeit. Politik—Bildung—Naturkunde—Theologie* (Göttingen, 1989), 539–67; id, 'Die frühe Reformation als Kommunikationsprozeß', in

modus operandi in a more convincing and rounded way, as one conspicuous thread in a large tapestry of devotional stimulus.

As for Piccolomini, recent investigation of his contemporaries has brought into question the significance of his contribution to the crusade. His reputation, which in 1992 appeared robust, has proved vulnerable to critical reassessment from a number of directions. There is much interest in the crusading activity of his immediate predecessor, Calixtus III. It was Calixtus who created an infrastructure of preaching and collection that would serve the dual purpose of taking the crusading message as far afield as possible, while raising sufficient resources to permit a financially debilitated papacy to contribute as fully as its contemporaries expected and its self-respect demanded. Arguably Calixtus showed a greater appreciation of the importance of naval power than his successor would, laying the foundations for what under Paul II and Sixtus IV would constitute the most striking direct papal contributions to the struggle: the despatch of squadrons of war galleys to the East. It is hard not to associate this with origins: Calixtus was Valencian, Paul Venetian, and Sixtus Ligurian, while Pius originated from inland Siena. The ideas and insights of a number of Piccolomini's less well-known contemporaries, men such as Rodrigo Sánchez de Arévalo and Girolamo Lando, have been examined.[18] Most importantly, Cardinal John Bessarion appears more impressive and influential than he was previously given credit for.[19] My view is that the emergence from partial or total obscurity of this cluster of activists and thinkers has the effect of highlighting rather than diminishing the distinctiveness of what Piccolomini/Pius wrote and did. But it is now apparent that he worked within a circle, which gradually hardened into a team; after the Pope's death its members managed for a number of years to sustain the crusading momentum despite growing indifference at the centre. The existence of this cluster of like-thinking churchmen seems to have been a feature of the years immediately following the fall of Constantinople: by the time Bessarion died in 1472 it had waned, and the impression given by the sources is that in the 1490s Perault was carrying the flame virtually alone in terms of unflawed commitment to the crusade. This is not to say that the interaction of so many enthusiasts in the 1450s and 1460s was an unmixed blessing for the

---

Hartmut Boockmann, ed., *Kirche und Gesellschaft im Heiligen Römischen Reich des 15. und 16. Jahrhunderts* (Göttingen, 1994), 148–64; Wilhelm Ernst Winterhager, 'Ablaßkritik als Indikator historischen Wandels vor 1517: Ein Beitrag zu Voraussetzungen und Einordnung der Reformation', *Archiv für Reformationsgeschichte*, 90 (1999), 6–71.

[18] See Wolfram Benziger, *Zur Theorie von Krieg und Frieden in der italienischen Renaissance. Die Disputatio de pace et bello zwischen Bartolomeo Platina und Rodrigo Sánchez de Arévalo und andere anläßlich der Pax Paolina (Rom 1468) entstandene Schriften* (Frankfurt a.-Main, 1996), updating Richard H. Trame, *Rodrigo Sánchez de Arévalo, 1404–1470: Spanish Diplomat and Champion of the Papacy* (Washington D.C., 1958); Mureşan, 'Girolamo Lando'; id, 'La croisade', forthcoming; and id, 'Les Oraisons', forthcoming.

[19] See for example Concetta Bianca, *Da Bisanzio a Roma. Studi sul cardinale Bessarione* (Rome, 1999), and the forthcoming studies by Mureşan ('La croisade' and 'Les Oraisons'). Ludwig Mohler, *Kardinal Bessarion als Theologe, Humanist und Staatsmann. Funde und Forschungen,* 3 vols (Paderborn, 1923–42), remains fundamental. Manselli offers a good introduction (Raoul Manselli, 'Il cardinale Bessarione contro il pericolo turco e l'Italia', *Miscellanea francescana*, 73 (1973), 314–26).

crusading cause. They shared the goal of bringing about the expulsion of the Turks from Europe, but there was much disagreement among them about how it could best be achieved.

The last major area of advance has been the role and approach of the papal *curia*. Establishing a credible perspective on the Renaissance papacy is a prerequisite for a balanced assessment of anti-Turkish crusading endeavours.[20] It was no longer viable for the papal *curia* to pursue a crusading programme with the ambition and confidence of its predecessor in the thirteenth and fourteenth centuries. The papacy's weaknesses in the post-conciliar period have been reaffirmed by many of the regional studies referred to above. There have been useful accounts of the way the papal *curia*'s bureaucracy operated outside Italy, including Christiane Schuchard's analysis of the papal collectorates.[21] But most striking have been contributions to the functioning of the central organs of government, the *curia* as a centre of diplomacy, and the relationship between the Pope and the College of Cardinals.[22] It is the last of these, for example, that has enabled us to make a more convincing appraisal of the formation, status, and operation of the *depositeria della crociata*. The papal viewpoint is of course to be found in the inexhaustible documentation that resides in the Vatican Archives and the Archivio di Stato di Roma. These and other sources have made it possible to construct detailed narratives of papal crusading activity. Although it is more than a century old and not without confessional bias, Ludwig Pastor's *History of the Popes* gives a good deal of attention to crusading and retains much value. In the 1970s Kenneth Setton, focusing on papal policy towards the East, produced a more up-to-date narrative, incorporating much new archival material from the Vatican, Venice, and other Italian archives.[23] But neither Pastor nor Setton tried to analyze their evidence. That has now been done by Benjamin Weber, who has also brought to bear a large amount of new archival evidence in support of his arguments. Weber's thesis, soon to be published by the École française de Rome, is an indispensable source of information and clarifies in numerous respects the view that the papal *curia* espoused about how crusading against the Turks ought to be managed.[24]

---

[20] Nicole Lemaitre, 'La Papauté de la Renaissance entre mythes et réalités', in Florence Alazard and Frank la Brasca, eds, *La Papauté à la Renaissance* (Paris, 2007), 13–34, offers a useful introduction to the issues.

[21] Christiane Schuchard, *Die päpstlichen Kollektoren im späten Mittelalter* (Tübingen, 2000).

[22] See Peter Partner, 'Papal Financial Policy in the Renaissance and Counter-Reformation', *Past & Present*, 88 (1980), 17–62; Marco Pellegrini, 'A Turning-Point in the History of the Factional System in the Sacred College: The Power of Pope and Cardinals in the Age of Alexander VI', in Gianvittorio Signorotto and Maria Antonietta Visceglia, eds, *Court and Politics in Papal Rome, 1492–1700* (Cambridge, 2002), 8–30; and Christine Shaw, 'The Papal Court as a Centre of Diplomacy from the Peace of Lodi to the Council of Trent', in Florence Alazard and Frank la Brasca, eds, *La Papauté à la Renaissance* (Paris, 2007), 621–38.

[23] Kenneth M. Setton, *The Papacy and the Levant (1204–1571)*, 4 vols (Philadelphia, 1976–84).

[24] In view of its imminent publication, references to Weber's book will cite chapter, section, and sub-section.

1.2 THE SOURCES

In any phase in its long history, crusading makes unusually large demands on its students in the variety and volume of the sources that it requires them to master. Official documentation issued by the authorities of Church and state constitutes a corpus of relevant evidence about how armies were mobilized and maintained, but that is seldom more than the tip of the iceberg. Sermons, preaching manuals, and other devotional works illustrate modes of communication as well as the way churchmen liked to depict crusading. Poems, songs, wills, and memoirs help us to reconstruct the thinking of the laity. For the expeditions themselves we usually possess narratives and letters, and often consolatory or polemical texts that were composed in the wake of failure. *Mutatis mutandis*, most of these types of source are represented for the period studied in this book. A text such as Lampo Birago's *Strategicon adversus Turcos* has its counterpart in the range of tracts written about recovering the Holy Land in the late thirteenth and early fourteenth centuries,[25] and even Pius II's *Commentarii* has precedents of a kind in Villehardouin and Joinville.[26] But there are also substantial differences from the sources encountered when studying the period 1095–1400, and these are worth noting.

First, there is the enormous increase in quantity that we would expect to encounter in the later fifteenth century. The most striking example is the *Regesta Imperii*, the compilation of sources for German history, which contains more than 21,000 summaries of documents for the reign of Maximilian, covering the period 1493–1504.[27] Compiling these entries—which sometimes run to several thousand words each and are fully accessible online—was a remarkable contribution to scholarship on the part of Hermann Wiesflecker and his research students. It deserves the highest praise.[28] As the *Regesta Imperii* well illustrate, there is a shift in emphasis towards documentary sources. With certain exceptions (1456 and 1463–4 being the obvious ones) most planned crusading in this period did not materialize, so campaign literature of the sort so well known from earlier generations becomes relatively scarce.[29] To compensate, we have a substantial increase in those types of source that inform us of the whole process of promoting crusades.

---

[25] See Agostino Pertusi, 'Le notizie sulla organizzazione amministrativa e militare dei Turchi nello "Strategicon adversus Turcos" di Lampo Birago (c. 1453–1455)', *Studi sul medioevo cristiano offerti a Raffaello Morghen*, 2 vols (Rome, 1974), 2.669–700. Iulian Damian is preparing a full edition of Birago's text.

[26] The literature on the *Commentarii* is immense: the essays by Lacroix (Jean Lacroix, 'I Commentarii di Pio II fra storia e diaristica', in Luisa Rotondi Secchi Tarugi, ed., *Pio II e la cultura del suo tempo* (Milano, 1991), 133–49); von Martels (Zweder von Martels, '"More Matter and Less Art". Aeneas Silvius Piccolomini and the Delicate Balance between Eloquent Words and Deeds', in *Pius II*, 205–27); and Pozzi (Mario Pozzi, 'La struttura epica dei Commentari', in Luisa Rotondi Secchi Tarugi, ed., *Pio II e la cultura del suo tempo* (Milan, 1991), 151–62) form a useful introduction to the issues.

[27] *AR*.

[28] I have used the *AR* when they paraphrase unpublished sources; checking *AR* texts against originals in the case of published sources reveals an admirable degree of accuracy.

[29] Even in the case of a frontline power like Hungary, documentary sources contain more detail about campaigning than narrative ones, though it is often tendentious.

Diplomatic exchanges, transmission of orders, and the records of assemblies (congresses and diets) are the most obvious ones.[30] Projects and plans such as Birago's are another. And a third is the accounts that were kept and submitted by collectors, relating to their preaching campaigns.[31]

Collectors' accounts usually survive because once they had been vetted they were stored in the papal archives. Their abundance and their richness of detail foster hopes that we can form a comprehensive picture of how much money was raised, and thus assess the ability of contemporaries to meet the fiscal demands that crusading posed. Such hopes are easily dented once we encounter the selectivity and omissions that characterize many of the accounts. We do get a fuller picture of crusade finance than is possible for earlier expeditions, but it is still far from being a complete one. A similar issue attends the 'briefs' (*breve*), the concise and business-like letters that were mainly used by the Popes in this period to get their policies carried out. To anybody familiar with papal crusading policy in the thirteenth and fourteenth centuries, the briefs come as a revelation. They seem to take us to the heart of the governmental machine as it translated policy into action. But of course this too can be deceptive. Briefs are selective in what they cover, mainly illustrating problems and even then just the ones that the *curia* thought it had a chance of resolving. They rarely inform us when success was achieved.[32] The survival of collections of briefs is haphazard and it can be misleading. In relation to crusading, we possess many for Calixtus III and they have been paraphrased or fully edited several times. As a result, we can analyze Calixtus's management of the implementation of his programme to an exceptionally detailed level.[33] By contrast, the loss of Paul II's briefs for 1464–6 constitutes a serious obstacle to gauging how he handled the follow-through of Pius II's programme.[34] Chance survival gives us Sixtus IV's briefs from August 1481 to August 1482, which may be compared with the situation under Calixtus III, though their content is rather less flattering to Sixtus's reputation.[35] The fact remains, however, that the briefs sometimes give us a different perspective on the *curia*'s activities: one that valuably complements the bulls, the correspondence of cardinals such as Jacopo Ammannati Piccolomini and rulers such as Lorenzo de' Medici, and, above all, the reports that were sent from the *curia* and elsewhere by diplomatic envoys of the Italian powers.

---

[30] For example, the *Deutsche Reichstagsakten*, which are a mine of information but are regrettably slow to appear in print.

[31] Two excellent collections covering Sweden and the Low Countries are *DS* and *Codex documentorum sacratissimarum indulgentiarum Neerlandicarum*, ed. Paul Fredericq (The Hague, 1922).

[32] An exception may have been Calixtus III's practice of thanking his collectors for doing their job well: though it is possible that he did this because he might have to use their services again.

[33] *Acta Albaniae Vaticana. Res Albaniae saeculorum XIV et XV atque cruciatam spectantia*, ed. Ignatius Parrino, Studi e testi, 266 (Città del Vaticano, 1971); *Il 'Liber brevium' di Callisto III. La crociata, l'Albania e Skanderbeg*, ed. Matteo Sciambra and others (Palermo, 1968).

[34] Giovanni Soranzo, 'Sigismondo Pandolfo Malatesta in Morea e le vicende del suo dominio', *Atti e memorie della r. deputazione di storia patria per le provincie di Romagna*, ser. 4, 8 (1917–18), 211–80, at 211–12.

[35] Ludwig Pastor, *The History of the Popes*, Engl. tr., vols 2–6, 5th/7th edns (London, 1949–50), 4.344 note; Joseph Schlecht, *Andrea Zamometić und der Basler Konzilsversuch vom Jahre 1482*, 2 vols (Paderborn, 1903), 1.5–6.

Introduction 9

The dispatches of these envoys, together with the instructions that they were following, form arguably the period's most detailed and revealing source. In her study of Pius II, Barbara Baldi relied heavily and profitably on the Milanese dispatches.[36] Like any evidence they have the capacity to mislead. Envoys could be ill-informed, their judgement could be poor, or they might place a false interpretation on what they were reporting. Even when they were reporting rumour without distorting it to their own or their recipient's advantage, it remained rumour. But rumour helped to shape policy, and the diplomatic interweaving that made up so much of crusading hopes and aspirations in this period derived from a mixture of perceived self-interest, half-correct information, and attempts to predict what was going to happen. This becomes clear from the way Venice steered its approach towards Pius II's Mantua congress in 1459, when the republic's deep unwillingness to be dragged into a costly war against the Turks had to be balanced against its anxiety not to alienate the Pope or cede an advantage to an Italian rival.[37] The same volatility characterized Germany in the 1490s and during Perault's legation there in 1501–4. The numerous reports that Cardinal Leonello Chiericati sent back to Alexander VI illuminate the divergence between the Pope's public stance on the crusade and the policy that he and his legate were following on Italian matters. And the equally rich reports sent to Venice by Zaccaria Contarini some years later provide an unparalleled insight into the quagmire of conflicting issues that Perault had to contend with.

In any case, envoys did sometimes function as simple reporters, passing on to us as well as to their employers information which we would otherwise not possess. One good example is a letter sent to the Milanese envoys Otto de Carretto and Cico Simonetta in July 1464 by an agent called Paganino who had been entrusted with the job of lobbying for amendments to papal decrees levying crusade taxes at Genoa. The letter is revealing on how business was transacted during Pius's fateful journey to Ancona. It shows the Pope discussing the exact wording to be employed, but it also highlights the mediatory role that was played by Pius's friend Gregorio Lolli. At one point Lolli wonders how a phrase that refers to Genoese crusading taxes safeguarding their own interests can be justified, given that Francesco Sforza's troops will be fighting in Albania. Paganino's astute reply is that the weakening of Turkish power in one area will weaken it indirectly in others, including those where Genoa's rights were at risk. Milanese interests make progress but it takes time; Lolli undertakes to communicate Paganino's arguments to Pius but only when the opportunity arises. While none of this is earth-shattering, it does constitute a useful view from the inside of Pius's decision-making at work.[38]

---

[36] Barbara Baldi, *Pio II e le trasformazioni dell'Europa cristiana* (Milan, 2006).
[37] See Giovanni Battista Picotti, *La dieta di Mantova e la politica de' Veneziani* (Trent, 1912; facs. edn, Trent, 1996), updated by Michael Mallett in 'Venezia, i Turchi e il papato dopo la pace di Lodi', in *SP*, 237–46.
[38] *Ungedruckte Akten zur Geschichte der Päpste vornehmlich im XV., XVI. und XVII. Jahrhundert, erster Band: 1376–1464*, ed. Ludwig Pastor (Freiburg i.-Breisgau, 1904), 306–9, no 196.

1.3 THE TRAJECTORY OF EVENTS

The anti-Turkish crusade was given great impetus by news of the fall of Constantinople, and most subsequent developments came about in response to other threats and advances on the part of the Turks. In a sense, therefore, the Ottoman sultanate played the role of offstage protagonist.[39] But the response to the Turkish advance was conditioned primarily by the political situation in the West, and crusading programmes were in practice the outcome of an interaction between the two areas. Since the remainder of this study will be analytical, this is a good point at which to outline some of the most important events and determining features of this interaction. It makes sense to divide the outline into four phases.

1453–64

The capture of Constantinople by Mehmed II in May 1453 provided a framework for some key themes of the crusading message that was fashioned in the years that ensued; especially the growth and aggressive intent of Ottoman military power, Christianity's retreat from the lands where it had originated and flourished, and Turkish brutality. But strategically, what mattered most was the fact that in 1453 the Christian frontier with the Turks was already hundreds of miles further west. The Turks had overrun Thrace, Bulgaria, Macedonia, and much of Serbia and Albania, and inflicted heavy defeats on the Hungarians and their allies at Varna in 1444 and Kosovo in 1448. Notwithstanding its overall control of the seas, Venice was starting to suffer from Turkish naval raids on its Greek possessions, and the tribal leader George Kastriote (Iskanderbeg), who was rallying resistance against the Turks in Albania, only just managed to hold onto his principal fortress of Krujë in 1450. It was these successes in the west that freed the new sultan's hands to focus on taking the Byzantine capital after his accession in 1451. In turn, his conquest of Constantinople enabled him to renew the westwards drive, though his first major venture, an attempt to take the Danubian fortress at Belgrade in 1456, resulted in probably the worst defeat of his entire reign. For a strong army, commanded by Mehmed in person, was routed by the Hungarians, directed by Janos Hunyadi, and an army of crusading volunteers recruited and led by the Franciscan friar Capistrano.

Christian success at Belgrade was in part due to the energetic activity of Pope Calixtus III, who throughout his reign (1455–8) displayed an unflagging dedication to using crusade as a means of combating the Turks. In addition to supporting Capistrano's work in Hungary, Calixtus equipped and funded a squadron of galleys that achieved notable successes in the eastern Mediterranean in 1457. Pope Pius II, who succeeded Calixtus, already had considerable expertise in crusading affairs and

---

[39] For recent analysis of the sultanate see in particular Colin Imber, *The Ottoman Empire 1300–1481* (Istanbul, 1990); id, *The Ottoman Empire, 1300–1650: The Structure of Power* (Basingstoke, 2002); Cemal Kafadar, *Between Two Worlds: The Construction of the Ottoman State* (Berkeley Calif., 1995).

he carried forward his predecessor's work. Pius was convinced that frontline powers such as Hungary, Bosnia, and Albania must be supported by their co-religionists. He summoned a congress to meet at Mantua in 1459 with the goal of organizing a large and broad-based crusade, which would consist of coordinated operations on land and at sea. The Mantua congress was an event of central significance. Its troubled history and the reported exchanges that have survived provide us with much of our best evidence about attitudes towards the Turkish issue and the promotion of a crusade. Substantial political obstacles to a united crusade, notably the French claim to the kingdom of Naples and the fragmentation of the Holy Roman Empire, were given a thorough and sometimes heated airing. Pius drove his congress to a conclusion which, at least as represented in his own summing-up, offered prospects for the crusade coming about. But it is unlikely that anybody failed to see through the smokescreen, and Mantua's failure became a big obstacle to belief in a crusade that would bring together the whole of Catholic Europe.

Even while Pius's congress was in session, Mehmed was pursuing his programme of conquest. He overran the Peloponnese in 1458–60, Serbia in 1458–9, and Bosnia in 1463. These astonishing advances (and there were others in the east) at least made it possible for Pius II to adapt his crusading strategy to one of an alliance of threatened frontline states. Venice, which reluctantly went to war against Mehmed in 1463, and Hungary under its young king Matthias Corvinus, formed the natural core of the alliance, and the hope was that they would be assisted by Pius, the crusading enthusiast Philip the Good of Burgundy, and any other state that the Pope could persuade to meet its Mantua obligations. In the winter of 1463–4, using this alliance as his military backbone, and resolved to accompany the expedition in person, the Pope had the crusade preached across Europe. His plan was to embark with his army at Ancona in June 1464. In the early months of 1464 there was an excited response to the prospect of a crusade that would include the Pope, and thousands of volunteers made their way to the Italian peninsula. But Pius's plan was foiled by a failure to make the logistics work, by French pressure on Philip of Burgundy (which gave the aged duke the excuse he needed to stay at home), and by the Pope's own failing health. Leaving Rome for Ancona later than planned, Pius died at the port in August, and both army and fleet melted away.

1464–81

There is a quality of altruistic commitment to the years 1453–64 that marks them out as not just distinctive but unique. This commitment radiated from the reigning Popes and their entourages of enthusiasts, while the response to Capistrano's preaching to relieve Belgrade, and to Pius II's preaching campaign of 1463–4, demonstrates that beyond the prevarication and duplicity that dominated the stage at Mantua, there existed a broader potential for response to appeals. After 1464, on the other hand, the commitment at Rome became questionable, and, if the potential persisted, it found no outlets to match these earlier ones. This did not mean that during the four decades that followed Pius II's demise the anti-Turkish crusade was in decline, let alone that mere lip service was paid to it. For political reasons alone this was not a viable option. Papal authority was under constant challenge from lay rulers and exponents of conciliarism, and it was not in the interests of Pius's successors to neglect the crusade, even when it represented a diversion from other concerns. More importantly, Mehmed II continued to pursue his headlong programme of expansion. His conquest of Bosnia in 1463 meant that only Croatia stood between the Turks and the northern Adriatic, and in 1466–7 the sultan drove Iskanderbeg out of Albania. Pope Paul II (1464–71) did not share his predecessor's enthusiasm for anti-Turkish crusading, instead focusing on the internal threat that he believed was posed by George Podiebrad of Bohemia. But when news arrived of the Turkish capture of Negroponte (Venice's great fortress in Euboea) in July 1470, Paul and his successor Sixtus IV (1471–84) recognized the need for a major initiative. Legates were despatched to secure help from Europe's courts and the imperial diet. Oratory reached an intensity not experienced since the 1450s and it displayed some awareness of how the strategic situation had moved on. Negroponte had been the most important Christian possession remaining in the Aegean Sea and its loss was the worst setback since 1453. It was also a clear demonstration of Ottoman naval ambition and potential.

This stop-go response on the part of the *curia* continued for the remainder of the 1470s. In 1475 the sultan captured Caffa, the Genoese port in the Crimea, and in 1479 the Albanian fortress town of Shkodër (Scutari). An exhausted Venice made peace with Mehmed in 1479, ending a sixteen-year war. The following year saw a double blow: one Turkish army besieged Hospitaller Rhodes while another landed in Apulia, where it captured Otranto. The Knights of St John successfully defended Rhodes but Otranto was still under Turkish occupation when in May 1481 Mehmed died while setting out on his latest campaign. Four months later combined action by the Pope and King Ferrante of Naples restored Otranto to Christian hands. This alliance between Sixtus IV and Ferrante ran counter to the current grain of Italian politics in which they were enemies; a contemporary commented that if it had not been the Turks who had taken Otranto, Sixtus would have been delighted by Ferrante's defeat there.[40] It would be inaccurate to say that Sixtus turned his back on the crusade any more than Paul had done. He persisted with Paul's strong reaction to the fall of Negroponte, sending a substantial war fleet to the East in 1472. The Pope responded to overtures from the Akkoyunlu sultan, Uzun Hasan, Mehmed II's most dangerous adversary in the east. He grasped the strategic importance of Moldavia, which absorbed much Ottoman energy in the late 1470s. There were understandable reasons for not giving more support to Venice as the republic soldiered on with its war against Mehmed. King Matthias was, by this point, more interested in fighting the Habsburgs than the Turks. But there can be no doubt that a contraction of ambition had occurred.[41] It contrasted sharply with Sixtus's handling of the machinery of preaching and collection that

---

[40] Sigismondo de' Conti, *Le Storie de' suoi tempi*, 2 vols (Rome, 1883), bk 3, ch 5, 1.109.
[41] Oscar Halecki strikes the right balance in his overview, 'Sixte IV et la Chrétienté orientale', in *Mélanges Eugène Tisserant, vol. II. Orient chrétien, première partie*, Studi e testi, 232 (Città del Vaticano, 1964), 241–64.

Calixtus III and Pius II had created or adapted. Sixtus was a Franciscan and he possessed a sound grasp of this machinery's potential. In his preaching of indulgences for the Rhodes and Otranto campaigns, following the 1475 Jubilee, the Pope worked to make indulgences a more profitable business. It was in this respect that significant advances were made, which was bound to be problematic when there was no matching military programme.

1481–94

In the fourteen years that followed Mehmed's death the situation in the Ottoman Empire did not cease to shape crusading plans, but it now did so in a more roundabout way: through the person of Sultan Djem (Cem). Djem, Mehmed's younger son, had fought his brother Bayezid for the succession and after his defeat had sought refuge on Rhodes. Pius II had incorporated a similar pretender (the *turchetto*, or little Turk) into his crusade planning, and thinking about Djem followed a familiar pattern: that if the prince were to accompany a crusading army to the East then his former followers would flock to his banner, fragmenting the Turkish opposition. The Hospitallers sent Djem to France, from where he was transferred in 1489 to the custody of Pope Innocent VIII (1484–92) at Rome. For Bayezid II, Djem was one reason for not renewing his father's aggressive programmes in the West. Bayezid was in any case less warlike and fear of internal revolts made him wary of renewing the financial strain that his father's ceaseless campaigning had placed on his subjects. The new sultan could not avoid war: both Ottoman ideology and the frontier tensions created by Mehmed's thirty years of conquest made that impracticable. But he directed his attention northwards to Moldavia and the Black Sea ports, and southwards, where the Ottomans fought their first major war against the Mamluk sultanate between 1485 and 1491.

The 1480s were paradoxical. Following thirty years in which the initiative had lain with a great Islamic power, Bayezid's relative quiescence coincided with the series of campaigns in which Ferdinand of Aragon and Isabella of Castile conquered Granada (1482–91). Both Sixtus IV and Innocent VIII complied with demands that the Granada war be construed and waged as a crusade, demands that they could hardly turn down given the historic assimilation of crusading practices into the *Reconquista*. The financial apparatus that had been refined in association with the anti-Turkish crusade was applied to the Granada campaigns where it proved to be of fundamental importance. There is no denying the contrast between the successes of crusading in southern Iberia and its failure when attempts were made to use it against the Turks. It is one of the core questions that lie behind this book. For instance, it is hard not to believe that the reported successes of Ferdinand and Isabella shaped Innocent VIII's thinking when he decided to capitalize on Djem's arrival in Rome in 1489 by convening a congress of European powers. It is interesting, though probably coincidental, that these gatherings form an approximately decennial pattern: Innocent's 1490 congress followed the Mantua congress of 1459, meetings at Rome and at Regensburg (the *Große Christentag*) in 1471, and ambassadorial discussions at Rome in the wake of the Otranto occupation in 1480. The 1490 congress proved no more productive than these predecessors. The excuse cited was the death of Matthias, but that was no more than a fig leaf; it is more likely that Innocent's congress simply ran out of steam.

1494–1505

Since the Peace of Lodi of 1454 the rivalries of Italy's major states had impacted substantially on planning for a crusade. The papacy's own standing and goals in peninsular politics affected not just its own commitment to pursuing an anti-Turkish crusading programme, but also its readiness to ally with and support Italian powers that had a particularly strong stake in such a programme. Naples and Venice were the obvious examples of this latter point. More positively, the leagues that were formed to maintain the peace secured at Lodi were looked to as potential frameworks for organizing a common Italian contribution towards the crusade, though in practice the tendency for the leagues to become alliances directed against excluded states subverted such inclusive and altruistic goals. Progress against the Turks came to depend largely on the approaches that were pursued by individual Popes: to a remarkable extent, Pius II proved successful in preventing his crusading and Italian policies from colliding, but Sixtus IV was incapable of doing so, even when he was confronted by a crisis as serious as the Otranto occupation.[42] Despite such disappointments, Italy seemed to be the most promising environment for active crusade planning throughout the four decades after Lodi. This was partly because the peninsula's vulnerability to Ottoman attack created much genuine anxiety and partly because there was no challenger for the role of Europe's crusading protagonist: for all the lustre of their crusading pasts, France, Germany, and Iberia offered fewer prospects than Italy did. The kings of France were preoccupied with containing Burgundian ambitions, Frederick III was too weak to do more than assert his good intentions, and Iberia was distant and disunited.

By 1494 this scenario had been transformed. The trigger for change was Charles the Bold's death at the battle of Nancy in 1477. The dismantling of the Burgundian state after Nancy enabled the Valois kings of France to resume their ambitions in Italy, while Habsburg dynastic might was amplified by the absorption of the Low Countries between 1477 and 1489. Finally, the conquest of Granada freed Spanish energies for intervention in the kingdom of Naples. From one angle, the Italian wars that ensued, starting with Charles VIII's invasion of Italy in 1494, were confirmation of the internecine strife that had plagued attempts to promote a crusade since 1453, indeed well before that date. What caused the anti-Turkish crusade to become interwoven with the three-cornered contest between France, the Habsburg lands, and Spain was the simultaneous renewal of Ottoman aggression. In the mid-1490s Bayezid sponsored large-scale raiding in Croatia, Hungary, and Transylvania, and following Djem's death in 1495 the sultan began planning

---

[42] See the analysis by Francesco Somaini, 'La curia romana e la crisi di Otranto', in *CTO*, 1.211–62.

further conquests. The sultan consolidated his hold over Moldavia and in 1499 went to war with Venice. Ottoman naval power had been enormously augmented since the war of 1463–79 and the republic was no longer a match for the Turks: it suffered a series of disastrous defeats which robbed it of its remaining Greek possessions, and in 1503 its envoys, together with those of its ally Hungary, concluded a humiliating peace with Bayezid's agents.

It is possible to argue that once the Italian wars had begun, the crusade became little more than a reference point in the exchange of propaganda between the great powers and, for that matter, the papacy too. The pervasive corruption and barely concealed dynasticism of Pope Alexander VI (1492–1503) do nothing to detract from the appeal of such an argument. Alexander's lurid deficiencies as Pope all too easily get in the way of a balanced assessment of the way he handled the Turkish problem. It is easy to forget Cardinal Rodrigo Borgia's accomplishments as an administrator, and the fact that he attended the congress of Mantua in 1459 and was at Pius II's side at Ancona in 1464. When his approach towards the crusade is compared with those of Calixtus and Pius, as many similarities as differences emerge. His alliance with Venice and Hungary in 1501 was modelled on Pius's in 1463; and he spent heavily on galleys in the East.[43] But, while he was willing to continue such strands of papal policy, Alexander, like Sixtus IV and Innocent VIII, gave the impression of going through the motions when it came to larger initiatives. It is very hard to take his grand schemes seriously. Nor is this just an issue of personalities. Following the failure experienced at Mantua in 1459 and reiterated at Rome in 1490 the *curia* was caught on the horns of a dilemma; it could not ignore expectations that it should rise to its responsibility to rally Christendom, but it knew that the exercise was futile. Escaping this dilemma was all the harder because all three of the great powers now fighting for dominance in Italy also made use of their crusading traditions in their incessant jousting for the moral high ground. In 1494, for example, it was impossible for Alexander to avoid handing Prince Djem over to Charles VIII, who claimed to be en route to fight Bayezid once he had taken rightful control over Naples.

Nonetheless, the anti-Turkish crusade programme was more than a network of contested responsibilities, rhetoric, and assertions. An infrastructure of preaching and collection had been created, and in October 1500 Alexander sent Cardinal Perault to the Holy Roman Empire to preach the crusade in association with the Jubilee indulgence. There is every reason to credit Perault with the conviction that a substantial expedition could be brought into being. He set his sights on a stable peace between Germany and France, followed by the mobilization of a great crusade to bolster beleaguered Hungary and Venice. The legate's painful struggle to bring this about, which lasted from 1501 to 1504, was the last phase in the project to revive the crusade that had been initiated half a century earlier. In these terms, Perault is a more important as well as a more appealing figure than the Pope who

---

[43] Michael Mallett, *The Borgias: The Rise and Fall of a Renaissance Dynasty* (London, 1969), 109–256, provides a sound assessment of Alexander's character and reign.

appointed him. Despite his convictions, talent, and energy, Perault proved unable to bring his anti-Turkish programme to fruition. Militarily, the setback was not disastrous, because after concluding peace with Hungary and Venice in 1503 Bayezid II again turned his attention to the east. But when Perault died in 1505 he was under no illusions about the seriousness and implications of his failure in Germany. It constituted final confirmation that hopes of regenerating the crusade as the means of uniting Christian Europe against the Turks had been misplaced.

1.4 THE STRUCTURE OF THE ANALYSIS

It is logical to begin with a chapter on premises, the range of hostilities and allegiances that encouraged hopes that the crusade could be made to work, but whose inherent tensions also militated strongly against it. At the heart of the crusade was an assumed antagonism between Christianity and Islam. There was no problem in identifying the enemy, but the nature of the threat that he posed was subject to some major rethinking, both in terms of what lay behind it and of what was at stake. Some contemporaries reflected on the relationship between the anti-Turkish crusade and the earlier struggle for the Holy Land, while others gave thought to the role that could be played within military planning by Orthodox Christian populations and their rulers. The crux issue, however, was how to deal with particularism and self-interest among Catholic rulers. To this there were some creative responses. The papal *curia* worked its way towards a view of a European community of powers whose interests were complementary: hence if each power played its part properly it would be serving the common good. The most striking offshoot of this view was *antemurale* (bulwark) thinking, the impact of which was most noticeable in the cases of Hungary and Venice. The problem was that while some elements in this way of construing the make-up of the Christian *respublica* demonstrated a pragmatic acceptance of change, it still rested on an interpretation of papal authority that contemporaries found unacceptable. In virtually every respect, therefore, it encountered rejection and subversion. The anti-Turkish crusade, which was intended to defuse or even make positive use of Europe's particularistic tendencies, instead demonstrated their unstoppable momentum and its centrifugal effect.

The next chapter will address issues of strategy and mobilization. It is undeniable that the range of strategic questions addressed by lobbyists was impressive and their responses could be clever and imaginative; ranging from the integration of naval and land operations to full-scale alliance with non-Christian powers that were hostile towards the Ottoman sultanate. But reality was more challenging. Again and again, initiating action proved to be crushingly difficult, whether it was attempted by convening congresses or diets, by organizing leagues and systems of subsidizing military activity, or by the Pope himself assuming the lead role. In bringing expeditions into being it proved impossible to circumvent underlying disagreements about authority, in addition to the variety of organizational and financial difficulties that derived from the project's inherent military challenges.

The question of resources—human and financial—lies at the heart of these challenges. Analysis of this topic in Chapter 4 will start with the role that voluntary service played. Did enthusiasts and planners want their contemporaries to take the cross or had volunteer service become incompatible with their overriding goal, which was fielding an effective and sustained military response? We shall see that contemporaries did take the cross, sometimes in considerable numbers. How was their contribution managed? If the way forward was to fund a crusade principally on the basis of taxation, from whom and how was the money to be raised, and what were the implications for relations between Church and state?

Chapters 5 and 6 will focus on communication and indulgences. These were areas where old and new can be seen interacting in particularly revealing ways. Most of the work of communicating the crusading message was still done through preaching, and the most effective campaigns were handled by the Franciscan Observants. For the most part their preaching was ably managed and it produced results. But the friars could only operate if rulers or their envoys had been won over to the cause, and set-piece orations delivered in the new humanistic style were considered to be crucial in achieving this. It is natural to ask how such orations differed from sermons. Printing too was starting to impact on the delivery of the crusading message, in a variety of ways that ranged from indulgence receipts to disseminating polemical exchanges. Finally, the crucial role that was played by marketed indulgences will be placed centre stage. This is the obvious topic with which to end the book because indulgences constituted the most important impact that the anti-Turkish crusade programme exerted on pre-Reformation Europe. Given the problems involved in raising money for the crusade through taxation, it is arguable that contemporaries were bound to consider whether essential resources might be assembled through the promotion of indulgences in the most intense and systematic fashion. But the issue was not just one of persuading the faithful to part with their money; the donated cash and goods had also to be safeguarded and used for correct purposes. In this discussion the central figure will be that of Perault, though earlier developments will be examined in order to place Perault's techniques and work in proper perspective.

2
Underpinnings: antagonisms and allegiances

2.1 CHRISTIANITY AND ISLAM: THE TURKS

There could be no better introduction to the image of the Turks that underpinned crusading against them than the bull which Nicholas V issued in response to the fall of Constantinople in 1453.[1] *Etsi ecclesia Christi* addressed the threat with admirable concision from three key perspectives. Historically, the disaster was the latest blow inflicted on Christianity by the followers of Mohammed, who had already overrun the East, Egypt, and North Africa. Eschatologically, this pattern of defeat fulfilled John's prophecy of the dragon in Revelation 12 and 13, with the consoling implication that God would not desert his people. Individually, the threat was associated with the ambitions of Sultan Mehmed, 'the second Mohammed'.[2] Comparison with the bulls which Alexander VI issued for his crusade programme in 1500 shows that Nicholas V's approach had proved its durability, allowing for the facts that Bayezid II had replaced his father as Satan's standard-bearer and that Rome itself, 'this sweet city, in which Peter's see is located', was now under threat.[3] At the same time there is no doubt that by this point each of the three reference points mapped out almost half a century earlier had been substantially developed.

Apocalyptic thinking was one of the period's most characteristic features and the Turkish advance was thoroughly assimilated into it. In papal crusading appeals its expression rarely went beyond passing references to Revelation 12/13, but popular literature explored the theme much more vigorously and it is likely that crusade sermons did so as well.[4] And on at least one occasion there was a well-attested wave of apocalyptic excitement which had the potential to dovetail with crusading efforts. This occurred in eastern Flanders in the spring of 1501 and was probably stimulated by the recent preaching of Alexander VI's Jubilee. On 18 May Johannes de Horne, the bishop of Liège, wrote a detailed report to Maximilian on what had happened. He described the miraculous appearance in churches, houses, and in the open air of red and black crosses, which were witnessed on the clothing of both married and unmarried women. Most were ordinary crosses though some took the

---

[1] For reception generally of the fall of Constantinople see Erich Meuthen, 'Der Fall von Konstantinopel und der lateinische Westen', *Historische Zeitschrift*, 237 (1983), 1–35.
[2] *AE*, 9.616–17, ad ann. 1453, nos 9–11, at 616.
[3] Johann Burchard, *Liber notarum*, ed. Enrico Celani, 2 vols, RISNS 32, pt 1, 2.220–4 (= *AR*, no 14158), with quote at 221; *AR*, no 14472.
[4] Ottavia Niccoli, *Prophecy and People in Renaissance Italy*, tr. L.G. Cochrane (Princeton, 1990); Marjorie Reeves, ed., *Prophetic Rome in the High Renaissance Period* (Oxford, 1992).

form of the eight-pointed cross associated with the Order of the Holy Sepulchre; recently drops of blood too had been seen. Horne related the phenomenon to the emperor-elect's plan for a crusade, referring to similar phenomena at the time of Charlemagne, and adding the cautionary note that in the past miracles such as these had sometimes been divine warnings against negligence; a warning that was wasted on Maximilian. The bishop reported that at Malhorne, near Limburg, a young woman of nineteen had experienced visions of the Virgin Mary, who urged penance. Crosses and visionary alike had been thoroughly investigated and there was no sign of fraud. Throughout the region people were responding with solemn prayers, processions, and pilgrimages.[5] The chronicler Jean Molinet added further details: recurrent sightings of armed men riding through the sky above Jerusalem, a comet shaped like a sword, supernatural voices counselling flight. Molinet was aware that crosses had appeared in the sky during the preaching of the Fifth Crusade, but his most telling addition showed that the days had long gone when crosses,[6] comets, freakish celestial activity, and visions could function as straightforward stimuli to action. This addition was a report of rumours that a Turkish army was on its way to support Naples against the French.[7] Nonetheless, when Maximilian applied himself late in 1503 to promoting a crusade, he tried to make capital out of what had happened two years previously. As a warning and portent of God's anger, he claimed, this mass apparition of crosses was even more significant than the spread of syphilis.[8]

The attention paid to Mehmed II in 1453 afforded more scope for development, especially when taken in conjunction with the people and structures at the sultan's command. Responding to the fall of Negroponte, in December 1471 Sixtus IV overtly linked Mehmed's goals of conquering Rome and destroying Christianity to both his personal qualities and the resources at his disposal. Mehmed was strong, greedy, ambitious, skilled at war, in the prime of life, and physically tough; and he had access to a bottomless reservoir of money, soldiers, and war material.[9] There was only so much mileage to be got out of dissecting the psychology of Mehmed (or his successors), and it was two broader themes that received more attention in the writings of apologists. These were the genetically programmed brutality of the Turks and the innate bellicosity of their system. Attributing Turkish cruelty to an innate and systemically cultivated lack of humanity deriving from their Scythian origins was clearly important to informed contemporaries. It is conspicuous in the accounts given of the massacres that the Turks perpetrated at Negroponte and Otranto.[10] The

---

[5] Marino Sanuto, *I diarii*, ed. R. Fulin and others, 58 vols (Venice, 1879–1903), 4.137–40 (= *AR*, no 15362).

[6] The fullest treatment of the various crosses in 1501 is D. Iohannes Nauclerus, *Chronica… ab initio mundi usque ad annum Christi nati M. CCCCC* (Cologne, 1579), 1120–2 (= *AR*, no 15363).

[7] *AR*, no 15200.

[8] *Volumen rerum germanicarum novum libri V*, ed. Johannes Philippus Datt (Ulm, 1698), 214–17, *Modus cruciatae Sancti Georgii* (= *AR*, no 17881), at 215. See also Winterhager, 'Ablaßkritik', 51–2.

[9] *AE*, 10.520, ad ann. 1471, nos 72–3; also in *DS*, 544, no 1407.

[10] Bessarion, 'Ad principes Italiae de Christianorum clade in Chalcide Euboeæ… orationes', *PG*, 161.641–76, at 665; *Gli umanisti e la guerra otrantina. Testi dei secoli XV e XVI*, ed. Lucia Gualdo Rosa and others (Bari, 1982).

effect was to introduce an element of ethnicity to the rationale behind anti-Turkish crusading, though it never became dominant. Religious identity, with its presupposition of choice, continued to be the deciding factor: in his famous *Letter to Mehmed* (1461), Pius II argued that a single drop of baptismal water would 'make you the greatest, most powerful and illustrious man of all who live today'. The Pope was offering Mehmed the prospect of attaining all his political ambitions in Europe if he would just become a Christian.[11] And six years earlier, in a rare *ius in bello* comment, the same writer advocated the humane treatment of defeated Turks. Even though it sprang from pragmatism—the enemy should not be driven to fight with the courage of the desperate—this was still, in a roundabout way, to acknowledge a common humanity.[12] Similarly, it was claimed that the period's greatest crusade preacher sought not the death of the Turks but their defeat and conversion.[13]

More insightful than the *topos* of Turkish savagery is the analysis of their military prowess and limitations that was provided most fully by Cardinal John Bessarion in his response to the fall of Negroponte. The two orations that Bessarion wrote on this occasion have been hailed as a breakthrough, and they certainly acquired an influential audience through their rapid printing and dissemination. In his first oration (*De periculis imminentibus*) he outlined the trajectory of Turkish power, pointing to its accelerating increase over periods of 130, 40, and 17 years. Moving on to the sultanate's profile, he argued that there was a causal link between Mehmed's aggression and the nature of the resources that he controlled. The point was that because the sultan's troops were paid from the public purse, he had to keep them occupied. He was not following a rationally conceived strategy; in particular, the fiscal balance sheet did not add up because many of his conquests did not justify the expense involved. Rather, Mehmed fought because he had to sustain his own position: 'He invades the lands of others so as not to lose his own.' Not only was the sultan disliked by his own familiars, he also had neighbours in Asia who were constantly watching out for signs of weakness. This analysis provided the answer to a familiar crusade conundrum, that emphasizing the need for action entailed highlighting the enemy's might, which had a counterproductive effect by inducing despair. In contrast, Bessarion's approach did not simply stress the Juggernaut's inherent weaknesses; it also demonstrated the existence of potential allies in the form of domestic opposition and Muslim rivals. This was a significant advance.[14]

---

[11] Aeneas Sylvius Piccolomini, *Epistola ad Mahomatem II*, ed., with translation and notes, Albert R. Baca (New York, 1990), 17, 122. The letter's purpose is still under debate: see most recently Nancy Bisaha, 'Pope Pius II's Letter to Sultan Mehmed II: A Reexamination', *Crusades* 1 (2002), 183–200; Benjamin Weber, 'Conversion, croisade et œcuménisme à la fin du Moyen-âge: encore sur la lettre de Pie II à Mehmed II', *Crusades* 7 (2008), 181–99.

[12] *Pii II orationes*, ed. Joannes Dominicus Mansi, 3 vols (Lucca, 1755–9), 1.287–306, no 14 (*In hoc florentissimo*), at 301.

[13] Giovanni da Tagliacozzo, 'Relatio de victoria Belgradensi', in *AM*, 12.750–96, at 784.

[14] Bessarion, 'Ad principes Italiae...orationes', 651–9. The gist of Bessarion's argument was repeated by Perault in 1501: see Victor Felix von Kraus, *Das Nürnberger Reichsregiment, Gründung und Verfall, 1500–1502* (Innsbruck, 1883), 229.

Initially, Bessarion's second Negroponte oration (*De discordiis sedandis*) seems less promising. In its opening pages he rehearsed the need for peace in Italy and moved through the familiar sequence of justice, necessity, and facility (the last being the grounds for believing that military action would succeed). But 'facility' led Bessarion to embark on some revealing detail about the military weaknesses of the Turks. Even Pius II had been content to ascribe Turkish victories to their numbers alone, which meant that Europeans could defeat them provided they fielded sufficient troops. Like Asiatic armies throughout history, they placed their trust in quantity, not quality. Bessarion took the discussion to a more sophisticated plane, accurately categorizing the Turkish troops as *akinjis*, janissaries, and *sipahis*. He claimed that the *akinjis*, who made up the majority of the Turkish army, were an undisciplined rabble, men who followed the standard for plunder rather than for religion or wages. Because they deserted easily if things got tough, defeating them presented no great problem.[15] The paid army—70,000 strong—was a tougher prospect, but there was a solution. Only the 15,000 or so janissaries were household troops. The remainder, the *sipahis*, were maintained by tribute paid by the provinces. They were the sultan's Achilles's heel because their revenue only lasted for four months. Before the fall of Constantinople they had been observed selling their horses, arms, and equipment to raise the money to get home. So the trick was to call Mehmed's bluff by compelling his army to remain in the field beyond these four months. He would have to resort to treasury money to pay his *sipahis*, but the Ottoman treasury was incapable of supporting both janissaries and *sipahis*. Ottoman forces would therefore shrink to dimensions that European skill and religious devotion could comfortably handle. King Ladislas V of Hungary had defeated them with just 14,000–18,000 troops.[16]

These two texts throw up issues that have a broader frame of reference. One is assessing the extent of Bessarion's originality. It is tempting to ascribe the pragmatism and specificity that we encounter to their author's Byzantine origins, ranging from the cardinal's familiarity with wisdom accumulated over the centuries about how best to manage encroaching barbarian threats, to his own store of anecdotes (the observed plight of *sipahis*) and collections of data (Ottoman revenues). Possibly the cardinal was aware of the need to counter the criticism that his analysis was a condescending Byzantine tutorial: he ruefully admitted that the Greeks at Constantinople had been as guilty as anybody of putting self-interest before the common good.[17] But by 1471 Bessarion had been moving for years in circles at both Rome and Venice that placed value on a strategically informed approach to the Ottoman threat; the interactions between members of those circles were

---

[15] For a nuanced and acute analysis of the *akinjis* see Konstantin Mihailović, *Memoirs of a Janissary*, tr. Benjamin Stolz (Ann Arbor, 1975), 177–81.

[16] Bessarion, 'Ad principes Italiae...orationes', 659–69. Reality did not differ radically from Bessarion's analysis: John F. Guilmartin, 'Ideology and Conflict: The Wars of the Ottoman Empire, 1453–1606', in Robert I. Rotberg and Theodore K. Rabb, eds, *The Origin and Prevention of Major Wars* (Cambridge, 1989), 149–75; Rhoads Murphey, 'Ottoman Military Organisation in South-Eastern Europe, *c.* 1420–1720', in Tallett and Trim, eds, *European Warfare*, 135–58.

[17] Bessarion, 'Ad principes Italiae...orationes', 668.

constant. The views of the Milanese humanist Lampo Birago overlap with much of the content of Bessarion's second oration: did Bessarion learn from Birago or Birago from Bessarion?[18] A second issue springs from the fact that in the period following these orations crusading lobbyists began to show markedly more interest in forging alliances with Islamic powers and Ottoman pretenders, most importantly Uzun Hassan and Sultan Djem. Did theory inspire action or vice versa? It is possible that they were unconnected. A third issue, arguably the most challenging, is the temptation we face to invest texts like these with more significance than, say, collections of atrocity stories or prophecies of Turkish conquests, because we appreciate the strategic awareness and sophistication of the former, and rapidly tire of the repetitive and formulaic character of the latter. The fact that we find a particular text rewarding to read does not mean that contemporaries did. This is not just because tastes change, but also because the portrayal of the Turk in crusading texts had to serve a number of different purposes: they could be advisory, exhortatory, consolatory, or homiletic.

We saw that in the three reference points mapped out by Nicholas V's *curia* in 1453, the sultanate's eschatological function and the vaunting ambitions of its young ruler were set alongside an appreciation of the historical significance of Constantinople's fall. It is in the theme of endangered Europe that the distinctive character of anti-Turkish crusading is most clearly to be located. It was rooted in the conviction that crusade was a natural response on the part of the Church to Turkish attacks on Christians, which found expression as early as the mid-fourteenth century in bulls of Clement VI.[19] But the differences in the fully fledged anti-Turkish crusade are hard to exaggerate, and they lie in two related spheres: the geographical shift towards an embattled Christian heartland and the identification of this heartland with values that were civilized as well as religious. The first of these was arguably the greatest achievement of Pope Pius II, who interpreted the significance of Constantinople's fall to Mehmed as Christianity's retreat to a corner (*angulum*) of the world.[20] Both before and after he became Pope, Pius made much of the theme of retreat, including the loss of all but one of the early Church's five patriarchal sees. What remained of Christendom was in essence Europe, so it was to the defence of a defined space and its inhabitants that Pius summoned the faithful. The goal of a crusade was 'the liberation of Europe', as Venice put it in 1465.[21] Barbara Baldi emphasized that Pius's exposition of the Europe theme gained credibility from his own experience, with its unique synergy of learning, travel, and familiarity with the political workings of so many European powers, especially those that lay along the German-Italian axis. His *De Europa*, a virtuoso survey of the continent's political landscape, is at first glance only tangentially related to the anti-Ottoman struggle, but in a deeper sense it has a pervasive relevance to the

---

[18] Pertusi, 'Le notizie'. [19] *VMH*, 2.660–2, no 986.
[20] For antecedents see Cesarini at Basel, 1434: *Monumenta conciliorum generalium seculi decimi quinti*, ed. Kaiserliche Akademie der Wissenschaften in Wien, 3 vols (Vienna, 1857–86), 2.299–316, at 315.
[21] *MDE*, 1.342–4, no 212.

subject: he was mapping out, in as much detail as one man could command, the terrain that Christians were being called to arms to protect.[22]

Crusading lobbyists clung to the belief that the more convincingly they could characterize the threat to this heartland, the more chance they had of securing action. This meant identifying anticipated points of attack and the openings that they would create for the Turks. In the years following 1453 the attention of many commentators was drawn to the Peloponnese. In the immediate wake of Constantinople's fall Bessarion predicted that the region would be the sultan's next target.[23] He lobbied vigorously and effectively for it to receive assistance on the basis of its wealth and strategic location.[24] The issue of priorities was unavoidable and rivals for resources had to learn the language of pressure points. In 1459 Bessarion portrayed the Peloponnese as the bridge for Crete, Italy, Sicily, and Albania (Illyricum).[25] Five years later Matthias Corvinus of Hungary advocated help for Bosnia on the basis that its recovery was a matter of concern for 'not just Europe's corners or peripheries but its heartlands (*precordia*)'.[26] By then it was apparent that Bosnia would have to compete with Greece and the Mediterranean. It was a tension that resonated throughout Pius II's crusade programme, making it hard even today to be certain where the Pope was planning to take his recruits in the summer of 1464. From this point of view at least, crusade as response to disaster made things easier: the call to arms was anchored in the perceived strategic threat generated by Ottoman victory. Hence the fall of Negroponte in 1470 was depicted as opening the door to Italy: echoing the Venetians' reaction to events, Bessarion argued that burgeoning Turkish sea power enabled them to attack the peninsula by sea from Avlona (Vlorë, Appollonia) in Albania, as well as overland through Friuli.[27] As earlier with the Peloponnese, Bessarion got it right: it was from Avlona that the Turks captured Otranto in 1480,[28] causing Sixtus IV to set the port's capture as his goal when he envisaged taking the war to the Turks after Otranto's recapture.[29] Twenty years later, Bayezid II's capture of Modon and Coron was similarly depicted as opening up the path to Apulia, or the coastlands around Ancona.[30]

The Turks' capture of Negroponte, Otranto, even Modon and Coron, were watershed events: their significance, in themselves or by implication, was easily demonstrated. By contrast, the raids launched on a regular basis from Bosnia into

---

[22] Aeneas Sylvius Piccolomini, *De Europa*, ed. Adrian van Heck, Studi e testi, 398 (Città del Vaticano, 2001); Barbara Baldi, 'Enea Silvio Piccolomini e il *De Europa*: umanesimo, religione e politica', *Archivio storico italiano*, 598 (2003), 619–83; Gherardo Ortalli, '*Europa-christianitas*. Tra Giorgio di Trebisonda e Enea Silvio Piccolomini', in Giancarlo Andenna and Hubert Houben, eds, *Mediterraneo, mezzogiorno, Europa. Studi in onore di Cosimo Damiano Fonseca*, 2 vols (Bari, 2004), 2.783–97. More generally see Barbara Baldi, 'Il problema turco dalla caduta di Costantinopoli (1453) alla morte di Pio II (1464)', in *CTO*, 1.55–76; Johannes Helmrath, 'Pius II. und die Türken', in *ETR*, 79–137.

[23] Mohler, *Bessarion*, 3.475–7, no 29.   [24] Ibid. 3.490–3, no 39.
[25] Ibid.   [26] *MKL*, 1.48, no 36, and see too 43–4, no 35.
[27] Bessarion, 'Ad principes Italiae…orationes', 654. Cf. *MDE* 2.59–60, no 35, in relation to Durazzo.
[28] Franz Babinger, *Mehmed the Conqueror and his Time*, ed. William C. Hickman, tr. Ralph Manheim (Princeton, 1978), 390–1.
[29] *BF*, NS3.766–8, no 1516.   [30] Kraus, *Reichsregiment*, 227.

Croatia, Carniola, and Styria had a more attritional effect. A big raid like that in 1480 could be highly destructive, leading to agitated discussion and lobbying in Austrian provincial assemblies and imperial diets.[31] But it did not have the shock effect of the disasters further south. It is revealing that when the papal collector, Marinus de Fregeno, wrote to Bishop Albert of Lübeck and his chapter in August 1472 to recruit their assistance in preaching indulgences, he placed the recent raids within a twofold context. On the one hand, he related them to Christian losses as far away as Antioch, establishing a trajectory that was geographically and chronologically broad, akin to the one deployed by recent Popes when they reviewed Turkish advances. On the other hand, he claimed that the raids had the specific purpose of creating a depopulated zone around Bruneck (Brunico). Turkish control of the area would be secured by a hilltop garrison, cutting the trunk road that linked Bavaria to Venice via the Brenner Pass, and allowing future raiding parties to ride northwards into Germany without having to worry about being attacked in the rear.[32] It is interesting but not surprising that the Italian Marinus had command of such specific information; seven years later he wrote a highly detailed *Descriptio provinciarum Alamanorum* for Cardinal Auxias de Podio, the legate whom Sixtus sent to the Nürnberg diet.[33] As in the cases of Negroponte and Otranto, emphasizing the Ottoman danger entailed crediting the Turks with a remarkable finesse in their strategic planning. Placed alongside their resources and savagery, it made a strong case for action, or so it was hoped.

Ever since Clement VI's bulls of 1343, the crusading response to the Turks had been couched in terms of the physical threat they posed to Christians. But there is no doubt that the fully fledged anti-Ottoman crusade incorporated broader values. This applies above all to the embrace of crusading by the humanists, some of whom envisaged the Ottoman threat as fully in cultural terms as in religious ones. Famously, Aeneas Sylvius Piccolomini portrayed the sack of Constantinople as a second death for Homer and Plato.[34] Humanists were convinced that Ottoman victory would mean the extinction of a revival of letters which had only just got into its stride. But some distinctions are necessary. In the first place, crusading's central frame of reference was by definition a religious one and it is widely accepted that a distinct shift in approach took place in Piccolomini's own depiction of anti-Turkish crusading once he became Pope.[35] Secondly, the spread of humanism beyond Italy remained patchy; indeed Johannes Helmrath has shown that anti-Turkish oratory was instrumental in advancing the use of humanist rhetoric at the imperial diets, with Piccolomini taking the lead in this respect in 1454–5.[36] Piccolomini himself sensed that he could not take the importance of humanism for granted, arguing somewhat tortuously that soldiers needed scholars to set down

---

[31] Babinger, *Mehmed*, 400; *Notes et extraits pour servir à l'histoire des croisades au XVe siècle*, ed. Nicolae Iorga, 6 series (Paris and Bucharest, 1899–1916), 4th and 5th ser. *passim*. The consequences of such raids are reflected in *BF*, NS3.544, no 1112 (1478), 729–30, no 1440 (1481).
[32] *DS*, 554–7, no 1416.   [33] Voigt, 'Kollektor', 169.
[34] See Baldi, 'Il problema turco', 62–8, esp. note 24, for the evolution of this famous text.
[35] Nancy Bisaha, 'Pope Pius II and the crusade', in *CFC*, 39–52, 188–91.
[36] Johannes Helmrath, 'The German *Reichstage* and the crusade', in *CFC*, 53–69, 191–203.

their deeds in writing for the sake of posterity.[37] Undoubtedly, the association could be close between the spread of humanist learning, promotion of the crusade, and the development of printing, as Margaret Meserve and Dan Mureșan have shown in the case of the diffusion of Bessarion's Negroponte orations.[38] But in some parts of Europe where the spread of the crusading message achieved a respectable impact, such as the Scandinavian lands, humanism had yet to make its mark.[39] And in others, such as Hungary, it was confined to a few islands of learning in an ocean of backwardness.[40] This means that the association of the Turks with barbarism—a polar opposite of Christian values—should not be construed in narrowly humanist terms. We have to watch out for the seductive appeal of a Piccolomini or a Bessarion.

It is arguable that the *topos* of the Turks as barbarians should be interpreted in ways that are culturally broader. Contemporaries seem to have accepted the claim so often made by Popes and preachers that the goal of the Ottomans was to destroy the Christian religion. There was one interesting dissenting voice: the Carthusian Vinzenz of Aggsbach displayed hostility towards Calixtus III's crusade in 1456 on the basis that since the Turks did not expect their subjects to convert, the war against them was a purely secular matter. 'Undoubtedly the war should be proclaimed by those kings and princes concerned to protect their position (*status*), rather than by churchmen.'[41] But he was exceptional and, while arguments *ex silentio* are by definition questionable, it seems fair to say that Europeans believed that Turkish rule entailed loss of faith, and could not imagine losing their faith without losing the rest of their social fabric.[42] This made it credible to couch crusading appeals in terms of the defence of faith, family, hearth, and home, even if the response to such appeals so often proved to be disappointing. Certain well-publicized features of the Ottoman system facilitated this: notably the *devshirme* practice of tithing the most promising children in conquered territories, the absolute power wielded by the sultan, the deployment of destructive and enslaving *akinji* raiding parties to wear down resistance, and the tactical use of atrocities to induce garrisons to surrender. When the Croatians appealed for help in September 1493, following their disastrous defeat by the Turks, they were astute in emphasizing that their army had been trying to free Christian captives whom the Turks were herding back to Bosnia.[43] It was not that Christians rose above such behaviour, rather that

---

[37] Aeneas Sylvius Piccolomini, *Opera omnia* (Basel, 1571; facs. edn, Frankfurt a. M., 1967), 678–89 (*Constantinopolitana clades*), at 681–2.

[38] Margaret Meserve, 'Patronage and Propaganda at the First Paris Press: Guillaume Fichet and the First Edition of Bessarion's Orations against the Turks', *Papers of the Bibliographical Society of America*, 97 (2003), 521–88; Mureșan, 'Les *Oraisons*', forthcoming.

[39] Jensen, *Denmark*.

[40] Marianna D. Birnbaum, *Janus Pannonius, Poet and Politician* (Zagreb, 1981).

[41] Joachim W. Stieber, *Pope Eugenius IV, the Council of Basel and the Secular and Ecclesiastical Authorities in the Empire: the Conflict over Supreme Authority and Power in the Church* (Leiden, 1978), 338–9.

[42] cf. Erik Fügedi, 'Two Kinds of Enemies—Two Kinds of Ideology: The Hungarian-Turkish Wars in the Fifteenth Century', in Brian Patrick McGuire, ed., *War and Peace in the Middle Ages* (Copenhagen, 1987), 146–60.

[43] *AR*, nos 2764, 2777.

the information that circulated about the enemy's misdeeds, both at home and abroad, was rarely at odds with the *imago turci* that was disseminated by the advocates of crusading. The image of 'turkishness' that emerged was robust enough for contemporaries to label as 'turkified' those rulers and lords who departed from what were viewed as acceptable standards of behaviour by Christians. In Hungary in 1514 it generated some extraordinary inversions of argument and practice when a crusade against the Turks turned into a social revolt.[44]

2.2 THE HOLY LAND AND THE ORTHODOX CHRISTIANS

The anti-Ottoman crusade was promoted by the Church in defence of Catholic Europe, but for a number of reasons, rhetorical, strategic, and spiritual, it could not be confined within those parameters. First, it enjoyed a relationship to the 'classical' crusades to the Holy Land (1095–1291) in terms of inspiration. Crusading against the Ottoman Turks had its own back story before 1453, but its most important campaigns, Nicopolis (1396) and Varna (1444), had been disastrous defeats which at best could provide object lessons in avoiding future failure. Janos Hunyadi's victories against the Turks offered more promising material and, from 1456 onwards, the relief of Belgrade was a success, the scale and miraculous nature of which could be compared with the greatest crusading victories of the past.[45] But Hunyadi and Belgrade were hardly household names, so it is not surprising that the heroes of the Holy Land crusades, especially the first crusaders, were so frequently cited as inspirational exemplars to take up arms against the Turks.[46] The incessant roll-calling of Godfrey of Bouillon, Bohemund, and other heroes of early crusading was a promotional response to the draining away of popular enthusiasm lamented by lobbyists, recognition that a crust of scepticism had formed that had to be pierced by any means possible if action was to follow. So it made sense to tailor the exemplars who were cited to the audience being addressed: at Mantua in 1459 Pius II referred to assorted Charleses, Pippins, Henries, Ottos, Fredericks, and Conrads when exhorting the German envoys, and galley fleets that had been despatched to Syria and (on the Fourth Crusade) to Constantinople, when he was trying to stir the Venetians into action.[47]

Citing past crusading to the Holy Land was one thing; bringing the contemporary holy places into a strategic relation to anti-Ottoman crusading quite another.

---

[44] Norman Housley, 'Crusading as Social Revolt: The Hungarian Peasant Uprising of 1514', *Journal of Ecclesiastical History*, 49 (1998), 1–28.

[45] Norman Housley, 'Giovanni da Capistrano and the Crusade of 1456', in *CFC*, 94–115, 215–24.

[46] Dieter Mertens, '*Claromontani passagii exemplum*: Papst Urban II. und der erste Kreuzzug in der Türkenkriegspropaganda des Renaissance-Humanismus', in *ETR*, 65–78; Robert Black, *Benedetto Accolti and the Florentine Renaissance* (Cambridge, 1985), 226–40.

[47] *Sacrorum conciliorum nova et amplissima collectio*, ed. G.D. Mansi, vols 32, 35 (Paris, 1902), 35.110, 112–13.

On the whole, the defence of Europe was not configured with the recovery of Jerusalem. It would have been extraordinary if contemporaries, who were perfectly well aware that the holy places were under occupation by the Mamluk sultanate, had believed that defeating the Ottomans would have any impact on the situation further south. In the 1440s the goal of recovering Jerusalem made occasional appearances in papal bulls: it featured in the commission of Alberto da Sarteano to preach the crusade in May 1443, but not in the papal tenth levied four months earlier, when we would expect Eugenius IV to use every argument available.[48] After 1453 it vanished almost entirely, with one glaring exception, which was Calixtus III. It is tempting to ascribe Calixtus's obsession with recovering Jerusalem to the excitement generated by the relief of Belgrade. And there is no doubt that for Calixtus, as for Giovanni da Capistrano, that event was construed as a divine signal (*tempus acceptabile*) for the recovery of the Holy Land.[49] But the Pope's outlook preceded the events of 1456: shortly after his accession the new Pope notified the Franciscan Observants assembled at Bologna that he was intent on 'recovering the city of Constantinople, and pursuing and attacking the infidels'. They were to choose six brethren to take on the task of preaching 'in various provinces of the world'.

> Moreover, given that our campaign against the barbaric infidels will, with the help of the Lord of hosts, enter the regions of the Holy Land, you should use your diligence to bring this to the attention of those of your brethren who are stationed in the Holy Land, in strict confidence, so that those who feel unprepared or too weak to embrace martyrdom can get away.[50]

In June 1456, again before the relief of Belgrade took place, the Pope issued a general call to recover the Holy Land.[51] News of the Christian success that summer certainly excited Calixtus further. August saw him writing to the archbishop of Arras that 'our inviolable faith gives us certain hope that we shall not just recover Constantinople, but liberate Europe, Asia, and the Holy Land'[52]; optimism that he reiterated two months later when he wrote that, notwithstanding Hunyadi's death, he planned to achieve 'victory not just against the most wicked Turk but also against every type (*genus*) of unbeliever'.[53] In December the Pope took the first steps towards an alliance with the king of Ethiopia; he sent gifts of relics accompanied by a letter containing three references to Jerusalem and awash with hopes and fears.[54] Such aspirations continued into 1457 and in 1458 they surfaced in documents referring to the congress that Calixtus planned to convene to discuss his crusade.[55] We have to assume that a Calixtine equivalent of Mantua would have been closer than Pius's to the general councils that had met at Lyons (1245 and

---

[48] *Epistolae pontificiae ad concilium Florentinum spectantes*, pt 3, ed. George Hofmann (Rome, 1946), 68–75, no 261, 80–3, no 265, at 81.
[49] See *AS Oct*, 383–4, for Capistrano's exhortations in August 1456.
[50] *BF*, NS2.13, no 27.   [51] *BF*, NS2.99, no 180.
[52] *VMH*, 2.280–1, no 443.   [53] *BF*, NS2.117, no 210.
[54] *BF*, NS2.120–2, no 225.   [55] *VMH*, 2.310, no 479, 312, no 481, 314, no 482.

1274) and Vienne (1311–12), to the extent that its ultimate goal would have been advertised as the recovery of the Holy Land.

How should we interpret Calixtus's reiterated goal of recovering the Holy Land? Several possible explanations suggest themselves. The first is that he was simply in rhetorical overdrive; but that is hard to reconcile either with the number of his statements or with their extended period of delivery. A second possibility is that this focus on the Holy Land was tactical, pitched at making more palatable Calixtus's heavy taxation of the Church. The Pope was acutely aware of the burden that his crusading squadron had entailed, above all for the clergy, who faced incessant demands for financial support. But, to an even greater extent than in 1443, the threat posed by the Turks was sufficient in itself to validate such demands, and past experience indicated that promising more than there was any chance of delivering was more hazardous than underselling the cause. It is unlikely that the Pope would so lightly have disrupted Franciscan missionary activity in the Holy Land; and he must have known that if he set unrealizable goals he was running the risk of his congress becoming a laughing stock from the start. More plausible is the argument that this Valencian Pope suffered from the 'Spanish syndrome': an inferiority complex springing from Iberia's relatively undistinguished showing in the Palestinian crusades, which drew his attention away from the Turks towards the Holy Land. It is possible, though improvable, that this helped to shape his attitude; certainly he relied heavily on Iberian crusading terminology, above all the use of the word *cruzada* itself. But the strongest interpretation is an eschatological one. The Pope's reflection on the meaning of Constantinople's fall led him to the conclusion that his generation was living through a supreme crisis in Christian history. This belief was strengthened by the welcome news of successes at Belgrade and Mytilene, and in Albania. The tide was turning and, as so often in prophecy, the worst disaster (i.e. 1453) would prove to be the prelude to the greatest victory. 'Never before has such an opening or opportunity been offered not just to defeat the Turk and recover both Constantinople and the Holy Land, but to wipe out (*exterminande*) the sect of Mohammed.'[56] It was this that made it worthwhile expending the extra effort, despite the complaints that his measures and methods were generating.

It is worth reflecting on the legacy of this brief resurgence of the Holy Land programme, or more accurately its lack of one. Calixtus's successor and admirer, Pius II, did not sustain the Holy Land references, a shift in policy that was the more remarkable given Pius's continuation of much other Calixtine methodology, including heavy taxation of clerics. The recovery of the Holy Land did not feature on the Mantua agenda and Pius seems to have been largely immune to the appeal of eschatological thinking. For him crusading against the Turks was for the most part associated with political, financial, and military measures, undertaken in defence of an embattled Europe. He envisaged the central spine of that defence as the German-Italian lands, working with a series of bulwark-states in the Balkans and advance posts such as Rhodes in the eastern Mediterranean. It was a clear, concrete

---

[56] *VMH*, 2.312, no 481.

approach based on a fund of personal experience and a shrewd, if flawed, assessment of the military situation. The glory and devotion of Christendom's crusading past held important places in the repertoire of arguments and images that the Pope hoped would stir contemporaries into life. But it is significant that, to Pius, the most important crusading term associated with the Holy Land, *passagium*, was largely of philological and antiquarian interest.[57] In such a scenario, with adroit use of the Jubilee adding to Rome's prominence as a shrine centre and pilgrimage destination, growing emphasis on Turkish access to Rome and the peninsula generally, the increasing engagement of Italian humanists in promoting the crusade, and not least a succession of four Italian Popes, it is hard to avoid the impression of a *translatio Terrae Sanctae* to Italy. The next non-Italian Pope, Calixtus's nephew, Alexander VI, was the last person likely to revive his uncle's mystical and eschatological approach. In 1496 he assured King Constantine of Georgia, whose envoy he had received at Rome, that he was constantly reflecting on how to recover the lost patriarchal sees in the East, but given his track record such assertions carried scant credibility.[58]

If the anti-Ottoman crusade represented contraction from the viewpoint of recovering Jerusalem, for the Orthodox it brought aspirations towards inclusivity. Formal Church union had been achieved at the council of Florence in 1439 and, in the years leading up to the catastrophe at Varna in 1444, it generated altruistic fraternity in the way papal and Hungarian circles depicted the promotion of anti-Turkish crusading. Sympathy for the sufferings of the Orthodox population is conspicuous in the oration that Cardinal Giuliano Cesarini gave at Basel in 1434 and in a major crusading statement by Eugenius IV of 1443, in which the Orthodox were described as 'carved from the same clay as ourselves, formed from the same elements, and most importantly, joined to us by the same religion and faith'.[59] A detailed and emotionally charged commentary on Turkish cruelty, Bartolomeo da Giano's letter to Alberto da Sarteano of 1438, described the suffering and enslavement inflicted on the Orthodox peoples of the Balkans side by side with those committed against Catholics.[60] Most striking is the so-called Act of Nrem: a short document issued by Wladislas I during the 1444 campaign in which the king called on the Turkish garrisons stationed along his line of march to withdraw to Anatolia. Wladislas proclaimed his war to be one of liberation, fought to release the Greeks and Bulgarians, fellow Christians who had recently rejoined the western Church, from Turkish subjection.[61] The king may have hoped to rekindle the enthusiasm with which the subject populations had greeted his troops during the Long March of 1443. The assistance they gave to the Hungarians on that occasion

---

[57] For detail on this, see Norman Housley, 'Pope Pius II and Crusading', *Crusades* 11 (2012), forthcoming.
[58] *VMP*, 2.258–9, no 287.
[59] *Epistolae pontificiae*, 68–75, no 261, at 73. Stressing common humanity was not pure altruism: the pope pointed out that what the Greeks had suffered, the Latins could as well.
[60] Bartolomeo da Giano, 'Epistola de crudelitate Turcarum', in *PG*, 158.1055–68.
[61] *Codex epistolaris saeculi decimi quinti*, ed. A Sokołowski and others, 3 vols (Cracow, 1876–94), 2.451–2, no 303.

was so notable that it provoked Sultan Murad into annulling their status as *zimmis*: that is, protected non-Muslims.[62]

In the case of both Orthodox and Catholics, this excitement died down after Varna and old resentments resurfaced. As so often in the past, union proved highly unpopular among the Orthodox laity, and reactions to 1453 showed that Catholic churchmen had to overcome their own suspicions. Shock at Constantinople's conquest was accompanied by an undercurrent of grecophobia that attributed the city's fall to the sinfulness of its inhabitants, displayed, for example, in a letter that Piccolomini wrote on Calixtus III's behalf to King Ladislas V of Hungary in 1457.[63] We have already witnessed Bessarion acknowledging that the Greeks had contributed to their own downfall by failing to pool their resources for the common good and, in an encyclical written ten years almost to the day after the disaster of 1453, the patriarch promoted a rigorously Unionist position: only adherence to Florence could rescue the Greeks from Turkish rule.[64] Both Bessarion and Girolamo Lando, who was titular patriarch from 1474 to 1497, were fervently committed not just to liberating their flock but also to persuading the free Orthodox to enter a crusading alliance; but neither would compromise on the terms of union.[65]

The background noise of suspicion and resentment persisted for many years after 1453. It was strongly in evidence in the Hungarian activities of Capistrano. The friar's apologist, Giovanni da Tagliacozzo, made his hero voice the conviction that during the hour of crisis that was Mehmed's siege of Belgrade, all non-Catholics should be welcomed as allies. 'Whether they are Serbs, schismatics, Wallachians, Jews, heretics, even unbelievers, if they stand alongside us in this tempest, we shall embrace them in friendship.'[66] Serbs, above all, were welcome because they were such skilled fighters on water.[67] But the circumstances of 1456 were exceptional: at other times even a dedicated lobbyist for the crusade like Capistrano could not avoid taking action against people who were suspected of heretical belief, and he regarded devout Orthodox as potential converts. His reputation went before him: in 1455 the town fathers of Lippa, a strategic stronghold in western Transylvania, asked him to come and preach there because there were 'many pagans, schismatics and unbelievers' whom he could convert.[68] Even when arguing the case for crusading assistance for the Greeks and Serbs to Calixtus III in 1455, Capistrano could not help commenting that they were suffering 'through God's disposition or at least permission, because of their erroneous and schismatic beliefs'.[69] A few days after the Raab diet of June 1455 Capistrano wrote a detailed letter to the Pope complaining about the errors of the Serbs, who were also impeding conversion

---

[62] Imber, *The Ottoman Empire*, 124.

[63] *Aeneae Silvii Piccolomini Senensis opera inedita*, ed. Josephus Cugnoni (Rome, 1883; facs. edn, Farnborough, 1968), no 60, p. 131.

[64] Mureşan, 'Girolamo Lando', 161.   [65] Ibid. *passim*.

[66] Tagliacozzo, 'Relatio', 761, cit. Housley, 'Giovanni da Capistrano', 104.

[67] Tagliacozzo, 'Relatio', 761.

[68] *AM*, 12.302. Cf. Johannes Hofer, *Johannes Kapistran: Ein Leben im Kampf um die Reform der Kirche*, 2 vols (rev. repr., Heidelberg,1964–5), 2.357–8.

[69] *AM*, 12.285–7.

work among the heretical Bosnians.[70] And in a letter that is undated but was probably written in 1456, Calixtus III expressed concern to Cardinal Juan Carvajal about complaints reaching Rome that Capistrano was forcibly rebaptizing Greeks, burning their churches and generally treating the Hungarian Orthodox worse than the Turks did. Given the damage this would do to Christian resistance to the Turks, the Pope found the reports hard to credit, but he asked his legate to make enquiries since, as he tactfully put it, 'all things have their time'.[71]

At this point the Peloponnese presented a different set of issues. We have seen that in the 1450s and 1460s this region was central to much thinking about how best to stem the Turkish advance, and Bessarion integrated these concerns with his promotion of the interests of surviving members of the Palaeologos dynasty. Silvia Ronchey has emphasized that the cardinal was helped by a series of marriages between the Palaeologoi and many of the most prominent Italian families, beginning with that between Theodore II of Mistra and Cleope Malatesta in the mid-1420s. Ronchey has ascribed a remarkably ambitious plan to Bessarion, 'un vero e proprio piano di salvataggio di Bisanzio' that would tie in these dynastic links (or 'alleanza italo-bizantina') with the mobilization of the Catholic world through the mechanism of crusade. Adapting the suggestions of other scholars, Ronchey has argued that Piero della Francesca's masterpiece, *The Flagellation of Christ*, is a coded representation of the Bessarion project, depicting its principal protagonists, with the tortured Christ representing Constantinople.[72] Plans to send an expeditionary force to the Peloponnese (Morea) in 1459, the arrival in Rome of the exiled despot Thomas in 1461, followed by the (similarly exiled) head of St Andrew the following year, and the guardianship of Thomas's daughter Zoe, also known as Sophie, following his death in 1465, can be construed as elements in a Latin-Greek *rapprochement*. Greeks were coming to the Catholic West in substantial numbers at this time and their contributions to a spectrum of activities were impressive.[73] The repercussions of this interest in the Peloponnese and its Palaeologan rulers were wide-ranging, but a number of motivations and influences were involved and it remains difficult to distinguish between them with confidence. It is plausible that Bessarion was a faithful lobbyist for the Palaeologoi, but reductionist to portray his entire crusade programme revolving around the restoration of the dynasty. Even it if did, it is improbable that the cardinal persuaded Pius II that this approach should take priority over any others. Pius was always highly pragmatic, willing to press into service any rhetorical device that lay to hand, whether it was the imperial claims of Despot Thomas at Mantua in 1459 or the resonant symbolism of

---

[70] *Acta Bosnae potissimum ecclesiastica*, ed. Euzebije Fermendžin (Zagreb, 1892), 224–6, no 954; Hofer, *Kapistran*, 2.353–4.

[71] *BF*, NS2.89, no 162.

[72] Silvia Ronchey, 'Malatesta/Paleologhi. Un'alleanza dinastica per rifondare Bisanzio nel quindicesimo secolo', *Byzantinische Zeitschrift*, 93 (2000), 521–67. These arguments are expanded in her book, *L'Enigma di Piero. L'ultimo bizantino e la crociata fantasma nella rivelazione di un grande quadro* (Milan, 2006).

[73] Jonathan Harris, *Greek Emigrés in the West 1400–1520* (Camberley, 1995), 189.

St Andrew's head fleeing from Turkish-occupied Patras to join that of his brother, St Peter, at Rome in 1462.

In 1472 Zoe was married to Ivan III ('the Great') of Moscow; the expenses involved being met from the funds of the papal *depositeria della crociata*. It is possible to see in this match the realization of Bessarion's project of perpetuating the Palaeologan dynasty, incorporating it in the ideology of Muscovy constituting a 'Third Rome'.[74] The possibility arose of creating a grand anti-Ottoman coalition stretching from Muscovy to the lands of Uzun Hassan in Persia, particularly since the death of George Podiebrad in March 1471 offered the hope of the papal *curia* extricating itself from the Bohemian imbroglio. Given the repeated failure of Catholic rulers to respond to appeals, most recently the four legations despatched by Sixtus IV in the wake of Negroponte's fall, the lure of creating alliances of eastern powers is understandable. But if Bessarion and others really believed that it would be possible to enlist Russian support against the Turks, they were soon disappointed. After she arrived in Moscow Zoe reverted to her baptismal Orthodoxy. The Russians had vigorously rejected church union and the geo-political scenario militated against Russian involvement in crusading plans. In this context, the death of the great bridge-builder, Bessarion, in 1472 and the Orthodox Church's rejection of union the same year, were incidental. For it was almost inevitable that the north's two great expansionist powers, Muscovy and Poland-Lithuania, would become enemies rather than allies. The Ottoman conquest of Caffa in 1475, establishment of a vassal-khanate in the Crimea in 1478, and conquest of Moldavia's seacoast in 1484, raised concerns at both Cracow and Moscow but did not alter the situation. For both powers, such events were overshadowed by Muscovy's conquest of Novgorod in 1478.[75] Moscow needed a stable southern frontier and it regarded the khanate as a natural ally against the Lithuanians and Poles. In the 1490s Russian ambitions in the Baltic region brought them into a collision course with the papacy as the Catholic powers responded with appeals to Rome for help. In 1496 the Swedish regent, Sten Sture, was given indulgences to repel Russian attacks on Finland.[76] At the same time, the Livonian master of the Teutonic Knights tried to gain access to the proceeds of indulgences granted on the basis of Maximilian's planned *Romzug*/crusade. It would not be long before the Order was plunged into a disastrous and financially draining war with Muscovy.[77]

The prospects for bringing Moldavia into a crusading coalition seemed more promising.[78] In 1473, just at the point when the hopes entertained of Muscovy were being dashed, self-styled 'Duke' Stephen the Great rebelled against the Turks, ending a period of subjection to the sultanate that had started in 1456. It is possible that Stephen was influenced by his wife Maria Assanina Palaeologina, whom he had married in 1472. The opportunity presented itself of a new crusading front

---

[74] Ronchey, 'Malatesta/Paleologhi', 559–66.   [75] Halecki, 'Sixte IV', 241–64.
[76] *VMP*, 2.262, no 290. See also Thomas Lindkvist, 'Crusades and Crusading Ideology in the Political History of Sweden, 1140–1500', in *Crusade and Conversion on the Baltic Frontier 1150–1500*, ed. Alan V. Murray (Aldershot, 2001), 119–30, at 126–9.
[77] *AR*, no 7005.   [78] See the numerous studies by Alexandru Simon.

on the Lower Danube; and Moldavians, who were familiar with Ottoman tactics, would pose a more dangerous threat to the sultan than Polish or Hungarian armies. It is not surprising that Sixtus IV was eager to capitalize on this, especially after Stephen's troops won a significant victory at Vaslui in January 1475. The arrival at Rome of standards captured at Vaslui made a welcome change from the usual flow of bad news, which in 1475 included the Turkish conquest of the Genoese port of Caffa. On 9 April 1476 the Pope made one of the period's most extraordinary grants to Stephen. He conceded the Jubilee indulgence to believers in Moldavia who carried out a specified devotional programme and placed cash in the Catholic church at Baia. The proceeds were to go exclusively to Stephen for the Turkish war and the concession was extended to the cathedral churches at Akkerman (Cetatea Albă) in January 1477.[79] It is clear from wording used by Sixtus that the initiative for the two grants came from Stephen. He was facing a big Ottoman attack and the terminology reflected his clever portrayal of his principality as Christendom's outlying defensive zone, an 'outer redoubt' that shielded the Hungarian *antemurale* from harm. Alexandru Simon has shown that Stephen was well versed in the period's crusading discourse and his advisers must have reckoned the Jubilee grant to be worth having. The identity of the penitents and donors referred to in the bulls is less certain. Moldavia had a sizeable population of Catholics from Hungary, Germany, and Poland. Other beneficiaries were presumably converts: in 1461 the Observants had claimed great success in Moldavia, securing concessions on hearing confessions by the neophytes because there was no parish infrastructure there.[80] As Mureşan has pointed out, the unusually elaborate historical preamble to the 1476 bull was an excellent way of explaining the close connection between the indulgences and papal authority.[81] Stephen's political ambitions are murky, but he may have hoped that Rome's praise and support would help him establish Moldavia as an independent power, *de facto* or *de iure*.

Opposition to the Turks failed to bring the assistance from the Catholic world that was hoped for and needed. Venice, which strongly encouraged Stephen's diplomatic approaches to Rome, made peace with Mehmed in 1479; and without the republic's mediation his relations with the *curia* quickly cooled. Neither Hungary nor Poland was prepared to assist Stephen, each calculating that his humiliation by the Turks would enable it to assert its protection over Moldavia on favourable terms. The *curia* did not dare invest too heavily in an Orthodox prince, especially in the light of Hungary's sensitivity about Moldavia's status and suspicions at Buda that Stephen would muscle in on its demands for papal support (which he did). The fall of Otranto boosted Stephen's credit at Rome because Moldavia, like Albania earlier, was seen as a valuable drain on Ottoman resources, but it brought the *vaivode* no additional help: on the contrary, the *curia*'s priority was the recovery of the Apulian port. In 1484 Stephen suffered the disastrous loss of his entire Black Sea littoral, including the ports at Kilia and Akkerman, and his anti-Ottoman

---

[79] *VMH*, 2.449–51, no 634, 452–3, no 636.
[80] *BF*, NS2.497–8, no 955.
[81] Mureşan, 'Girolamo Lando', 206–7.

policy quickly ran into the sand. The military situation became muddled: in 1497 Stephen made use of Hungarian and Ottoman troops to repel a Polish invasion that had been promoted as a crusade to recover the lost ports.

This disappointment was typical of the situation in the Balkans and Greek world. In 1443 the assistance that the Bulgarians gave to the Hungarians during their 'Long March' was substantial enough to impress their co-religionists and infuriate their Turkish rulers. But would they have risen again if another such expedition had materialized? The Serb, Konstantin Mihailović, who was captured by the Turks in 1455 and served in their army until 1463, reported that the Ottomans were worried that they would, and some crusading enthusiasts continued to factor Christian uprisings into their planning.[82] It was a favourite topic of Pius II, as when he addressed his supporters amongst the cardinals in March 1462.[83] At the end of 1481, on the other hand, Matthias poured cold water on the idea that Bayezid II was facing grave internal problems. Where, he asked Cardinal Gabriele Rangoni sceptically, were the so-called Christian revolts that people were always talking about?[84] An answer might have been that following Turkish reprisals for what they had done in 1443, the subject population would only rebel if they saw their co-religionists arriving in force and, since this failed to happen, neither Ottoman fears nor Christian hopes were put to the test. For all the vision and intelligence shown by advocates of *rapprochement*, like Bessarion and Lando, it became clear that freeing this region from Ottoman control could only be done by mobilizing Catholic Europe. The question was: would the pattern of allegiances and antagonisms prevailing *within* the Catholic community prove more conducive to crusading than the one outside it?

2.3 CATHOLIC EUROPE: THE UNIVERSAL AND THE PARTICULAR

The argument underpinning the whole fabric of anti-Ottoman crusading ideology was that the Turks threatened every Christian believer and all the states that made up the *respublica Christiana*. It was this that made a united response both necessary and appropriate. The mass of the population would contribute on an individual basis, mainly through personal service or financial donations, while their rulers would work in conjunction with the Pope to coordinate that response, providing military structure and leadership. Though apparently straightforward, this approach contained irresolvable tensions. In the first place, was contribution obligatory or

---

[82] Mihailović, *Memoirs*, 147, 169. For Mihailović see Stephen Turk Christensen, 'The Heathen Order of Battle', in Stephen Turk Christensen, ed., *Violence and the Absolutist State: Studies in European and Ottoman History* (Copenhagen, 1990), 75–135. Jean Germain was optimistic in 1451: C. Schefer, ed., 'Le discours du voyage d'oultremer au très victorieux roi Charles VII, prononcé, en 1452 [sic] par Jean Germain, évêque de Chalon', *Revue de l'orient latin*, 3 (1895), 303–42, at 330–1.
[83] *Pii II Commentarii rerum memorabilium que temporibus suis contigerunt*, 7.16, ed. Adrian van Heck, 2 vols, Studi e testi, 312–13 (Città del Vaticano, 1984), 1.460–3.
[84] *MKL*, 2.191–5, no 103.

voluntary? The *curia* took the position that supporting the crusade was so important that it represented a religious obligation for everybody. Christians who failed to assist the crusade placed their own salvation in jeopardy.[85] A robust written response to criticism of Calixtus III's indulgences for the crusade emphasized the duty of the faithful to contribute as 'a prerequisite for salvation' (*de necessitate salutis*). Anybody who refused to respond to this 'general obligation' was deficient in charity, and the Pope's call to crusade was as valid as if it issued directly from the mouth of Christ or St Peter.[86] In this and similar texts, including Rodrigo Sánchez de Arévalo's *De remediis afflictae Ecclesiae* of 1470, which he dedicated to Bessarion, a number of themes interwove: advocacy of crusade, defence of indulgences, and rejection of conciliarism.[87] But the idea of a *generalis obligacio* to crusade remained controversial, at odds not just with reality but with the historically voluntary nature of taking the cross. This led to some extraordinary bluster, as when Pius II asserted in January 1460 that his 'plenitude of power' (*plenitudo potestatis*) gave him the right to tax all Christians for the crusade without reference to their rulers.[88] In essence, a religious obligation was being manufactured, or at least extrapolated from less questionable ones, to handle the intractable financial problems that crusading raised. As in the parallel case of papal attempts to tax lay people for the Holy Land crusade, notably the Saladin tithe for the Third Crusade, religious and public duties were being confused. We shall see that in the late fifteenth century, as in the late twelfth, the laity perceived the confusion and rejected the tax.

Secondly, did the Turkish threat in reality affect everybody? When a Pope asserted, as Sixtus IV did in March 1472, that those who campaigned against the Turks would be fighting 'for the defence of the Catholic faith, for their country (*patria*), for their children and wives',[89] he was using strongly personalized rhetoric in relation to an allegedly universal cause. Lobbyists were fond of the Horatian quote 'Nam tua res agitur, paries cum proximus ardet' (bk 1, ep. 18): that is, it is your business when your neighbour's house is ablaze. But this became less relevant the further away the burning house was and, although Raymond Perault assured the dean and chapter of Utrecht in 1502 that the Turkish threat concerned their city as much as it did the Austrians and Hungarians, all parties knew that the truth was otherwise.[90] Everybody was not, as the doge of Venice claimed in 1470, 'in the same boat'.[91] The sceptic's reply to Sixtus's call to arms in 1472 was that the time to fight would be when the Turks really *were* threatening one's own home, wife, and children. That riposte was an old one: the poet Rutebeuf had cited it as a response to appeals on behalf of the Holy Land two centuries earlier.[92] And in religious, moral, strategic, and pragmatic terms, an arsenal of counter-arguments lay

---

[85] *AE*, 9.617, ad ann. 1453, nos 9–11; Piccolomini, *Opera omnia*, 922.
[86] *Notes et extraits*, 6th ser., 155–68. [87] Ibid. 4th ser., 279–82.
[88] *Sacrorum conciliorum*, 32.265–6. [89] *AE*, 10.525, ad ann. 1472, nos 2–3.
[90] *Codex documentorum*, 417–21, no 290, at 418.
[91] Margaret Meserve, 'News from Negroponte: Politics, Popular Opinion and Information Exchange in the First Decade of the Italian Press', *Renaissance Quarterly*, 59 (2006), 440–80, at 453.
[92] Rutebeuf, *Œuvres complètes*, ed. Edmond Faral and Julia Bastin, vol. 1 (Paris, 1959), 476, stanza 20, lines 156–60.

to hand. Practising charity by taking up arms in defence of fellow believers, who were being killed, enslaved, and oppressed by the Turks, was a core Christian virtue which had been embedded within crusading ideology from the start.[93] There would be no moral case for a prince facing Turkish attack to appeal to other powers for assistance if he had earlier failed to answer similar appeals from others. It made sense for princes to support frontline Christians because Turkish *libido dominandi* was so powerful that they would not stop advancing until they were defeated.[94] In a particularly shrill development of this theme, Perault asked the German diet in July 1501 where they planned to seek refuge once the Turks had reached the German heartlands; maybe they would gather at Lübeck to sail off to England, Ireland, or the Orkneys?[95] And fighting at a distance saved one's own lands from the inevitable damage of war. As Maximilian put it in December 1501, it was far preferable to take up arms 'for the faith and for the protection of other Christians and for glory', than to fight 'not just for the faith but also for country, hearth, children, wives, freedom, and life itself', thereby incurring 'warfare, massacre, arson, destruction, and captivity'.[96] Although it entailed turning Sixtus IV's *pro patria* theme on its head, Maximilian's point was a shrewd one, and together with the other arguments it made up a well-rounded case that rested on solid scriptural, classical, and practical foundations.

The trouble was that while the first counter-argument (charity) derived from religious values, the others hinged on self-interest. In moral terms, crusading was unbeatable as a cause: whatever legitimacy lay behind a prince's war against his fellow believers was trumped by war for Christ.[97] But when it came to practical issues, the points just made could be overturned or checkmated by stronger ones, including some that the authors would avoid expressing openly. To take the obvious example, Italian powers concerned about Venice's mainland expansion were delighted to see the republic suffering territorial, commercial, and financial losses at the hands of the Turks. Overall, they might be more afraid of the Turks than of Venice, but the policy they followed constituted a good example of the 'prisoner's dilemma', in which altruistic collective action promises the best long-term dividend, but the short-term rewards of self-interest prove irresistible. In a roundabout way, and with uncharacteristic naivety, Pius II acknowledged the problem when he reassured Francesco Sforza that he could safely leave Milan to lead a crusade against the Turks because his main enemy, Venice, stood to gain from the expedition; it is not hard to imagine the duke's reaction.[98] In practice, if Pius gained Venetian

---

[93] Jonathan Riley-Smith, 'Crusading as an Act of Love', *History*, 65 (1980), 177–92.
[94] Or, in arguments directed at Italian rulers, until they had added Old Rome to New Rome among their possessions: *Codex diplomaticus partium regno Hungariae adnexarum*, ed. L. Thallóczy and A. Antal, vol. 2 (Budapest, 1907), 209–10, no 278.
[95] Kraus, *Reichsregiment*, 231.
[96] Gebhard Mehring, 'Kardinal Raimund Peraudi als Ablaßkommissar in Deutschland 1500–1504 und sein Verhältnis zu Maximilian I.', in *Forschungen und Versuche zur Geschichte des Mittelalters und der Neuzeit. Festschrift Dietrich Schäfer* (Jena, 1915), 334–409, doc. no 4, 394–6, at 395, para 5.
[97] E.g. Piccolomini, *Opera omnia*, 843 (written for Calixtus III to Frederick III, 1457): 'sit iustissima tua causa, at iustius est pro Christo pugnare'.
[98] *Pii II orationes*, 3.113–14.

support for the crusade, he lost Milan's, and *vice versa*.[99] Hence the conundrum, lamented by the estates of Carinthia in 1477, that on the Second and Third Crusades the dukes of Bavaria had travelled all the way to Anatolia and Armenia with Conrad III and Barbarossa, yet their descendants would not come to the assistance of their neighbours, even when there was clear advantage to them.[100] A religious case that rested on arguments like these was fundamentally flawed.

These were serious problems, though it would be wrong to overplay their subversive effect. Then, as always, people managed to live with contradictions. There was a parallel in the normative ban on commerce with Muslims, which was affirmed every Holy Thursday in the bull *In coena domini*, yet was incessantly flouted, or circumvented, through the papacy's own practice of granting extended licences to trade.[101] Crusading ideology had always contained tensions, starting with the imperfect synergy of holy war and pilgrimage in Pope Urban II's 1095 Clermont appeal. And from Urban onwards every crusade enthusiast, lobbyist, and preacher had learnt to match his arguments and appeals to the particular audience that he was addressing. Circumstances were crucial and there was a telling demonstration of what this meant in practice in Hungary in June 1456. Cardinal Carvajal yielded to Hunyadi's request that Capistrano should not go to Vienna on the grounds that he was still needed in Hungary. The point was that the legate had earlier judged that self-interest rendered Capistrano's powers of persuasion surplus to requirements 'in Hungary's lower regions, believing as we did that the Hungarians there could easily be stirred up to fight by your [i.e. Hunyadi's] authority, their own misfortunes and fear of the Turks'. Hence it would be more profitable to have Capistrano working for the crusade at the imperial court.[102] On occasion we can see the requests made of people who were asked for help being tailored to their location. In 1455 Calixtus instructed his preachers in central Italy to include assistance of a non-military kind, 'for the preparation or launching of the crusade or the provision of other personal services', amongst the contributions for which they could grant indulgences.[103] In the following year the Pope allowed one of his preachers, who was assembling hull timber, masts, and sail yards for the papal galleys, to issue indulgences for helping with their transportation.[104] And when Pius II despatched preachers to the provinces of the Papal State at the end of 1463 he included grain among the list of acceptable donations, knowing that it would come in handy for an expedition that would be embarking at Ancona.[105]

Hungary in 1456 and central Italy in the 1450s and 1463–4 were special cases, where immediate and specific needs were uppermost in shaping both responsiveness to the crusading message and the form that the response assumed. In more

---

[99] Baldi, *Pio II*, 239–41, though as she notes (247), French pressure on Milan early in 1464 forced the duke to make an eleventh-hour commitment to help Pius's crusade.
[100] *Notes et extraits*, 5th ser., 14–15.
[101] See the important study by Stefan Stantchev, *Embargo: The Origins of an Idea and the Implications of a Policy in Europe and the Mediterranean, ca. 1100–ca. 1500*, PhD University of Michigan, 2009, esp. ch. 6.
[102] *AM*, 12.384.   [103] *BF*, NS2.58–9, no 109.
[104] Ibid. NS2.123, no 230.   [105] *AM*, 13.310–12.

distant lands the range of factors affecting how people reacted was broader. Sometimes they were chiefly political. The French position on the crusade was inextricably interwoven with Valois ambitions in Italy, whether these were nurtured by the royal court or by the cadet house of Anjou. The uncompromising stance adopted by France's envoys at the Mantua congress illustrates this well,[106] and while relations reached their lowest point during Pius II's reign, there was not much improvement thereafter. The fact was that however much individual French men and women were unsettled by news of Ottoman advances and Turkish atrocities, it was rarely possible to draw on their services or money because the monarchy did not back the idea, except when it suited the Neapolitan project.[107] It is possible that they did not even hear much about it in their churches: Amnon Linder noted that whereas surviving evidence for Clement V's liturgical promotion of the Holy Land crusade in 1308 has a 'predominantly French character', such sources shrink dramatically in the fifteenth century.[108] By 1500 it was becoming clear that, notwithstanding all the kudos attached to the *Gesta Dei per Francos* image, there was a natural synergy between France's diplomatic interests and those of the Ottomans.

Germany presents a radically different picture. In southern Germany Calixtus III's adaptation in 1456 of the Clementine material for use against the Ottomans (and later the Hussites) met with an appreciative response. As Linder put it, 'war liturgy against the Infidel was infinitely more relevant to the populations living along the Danube than to those on the Seine or the Thames'.[109] At the same time *Turcica*, that is to say newsletters, prophecies, sermons, and miscellaneous reportage about the Turks, began to pour off the printing presses, feeding a market that was simultaneously appalled and fascinated by the bad news arriving from the Balkans.[110] Diet after diet debated the fact that the frontline was moving towards Germany. In November 1501 Maximilian claimed that Regensburg might become a frontline city, in the event that the Turks overran both Hungary and Poland. He conjured up the nightmare of an alliance between infidel Turks and heretical Hussites, in which case the whole empire would have to assist the Bavarian city against the threat. To some extent this was a characteristic exercise in bluff: Maximilian was playing up Regensburg's importance because he favoured that town as the seat for the imperial administration (*Reichsregiment*) headed by his principal enemy, Berthold von Henneberg, whose agents and supporters preferred Frankfurt.[111] But by 1501 Turkish incursions in Maximilian's Austrian lands had reached such a level that a threat to Bavaria was no longer pure fantasy. Despite this, Germany's range of princes, who held most of the effective power, refused to act; and though they sheltered behind the excuse that a general mobilization of Christian Europe was

---

[106] *Sacrorum conciliorum*, 32.251–5.
[107] Jean-François Lassalmonie, 'Louis XI, Georges de Poděbrady et la croisade', in *NC*, 185–203.
[108] Amnon Linder, *Raising Arms: Liturgy in the Struggle to Liberate Jerusalem in the Late Middle Ages* (Turnhout, 2003), 125, 187.
[109] Ibid. 126 (quote), 186–9, and see also 364–5 for discussion of impact.
[110] *Turcica: Die europaische Türkendrucke des XVI. Jahrhunderts, I. Bd, MDI–MDL*, ed. Carl Göllner (Bucharest, 1961).
[111] *AR*, no 12713.

called for, their underlying attitude was most likely that Maximilian's hereditary Austrian lands (*Erbländer*) should look after themselves.

One major reason for the unresponsiveness of the imperial diets was growing suspicion of papal motives. As Erich Meuthen emphasized, the message suffered from the shrinking credibility of the messenger.[112] At Mantua, and the series of diets in 1460 where Cardinal Bessarion attempted to secure movement on commitments made by imperial envoys at the congress, the viewpoint was expressed that the crusade was a device for extracting German money and exporting it to Rome. In 1460 Bessarion argued forcefully and plausibly against this prejudice. Recent historians have concluded that it was not true that the German lands provided more cash for the *curia* than others did. But it certainly contributed to Bessarion's own failure and decades later the same prejudice constituted an obstacle that Peraut in turn had to negotiate.[113] His chief apologist, Johannes von Paltz, argued ingeniously that Germany would be materially better off after Peraut's preaching 'because indulgences lead to divine reconciliation, which brings an end to the food shortages and conflicts generated by sinfulness, and depriving lands of their specie. Other things being equal, money and prosperity generally increase once famine and warfare cease'.[114] Pius II's spirited exchange of views with Martin Mair on the economic balance sheet of Germany's long relationship with Rome is revealing on the tangled issues that were bound to emerge once contemporaries went beyond bland generalities about the unity of the *respublica Christiana* and engaged in hardcore cost-benefit analysis. Such issues were sensitive as well as complex: in his response to Mair, the Pope came close to saying that the Church had civilized the Germans, an attitude that stoked the fires of German resentment towards the stream of Italians who crossed the Alps to collect their money.[115] Pius wrote at a point when Tacitus's text, *Germania*, had just been rediscovered and this fuelled his argument about the process by which the Germans had been brought into civilization. Although, it has been pointed out that this classic text did not have to impact in a negative way on Germany's reception of crusading appeals: in the oration that he composed for the Regensburg *Große Christentag* of 1471, Giannantonio Campano cited Tacitus in his praise for the valorous and (he hoped) inspirational ways of the Germans' forebears.[116]

In a typically gloomy assessment of the situation written in 1481, when the preaching of the indulgences for Rhodes had generated 'a thousand excesses', Bishop Georg of Chiemsee warned Cardinal Francesco Piccolomini that in

---

[112] Meuthen, 'Reiche'.

[113] Norman Housley, '*Robur imperii*: Mobilizing Imperial Resources for the Crusade against the Turks, 1453–1503', in *Partir en croisade à la fin du moyen âge: financement et logistique*, ed. Daniel Baloup, forthcoming.

[114] Johannes von Paltz, *Werke, 2: Supplementum Coelifodinae*, 78.

[115] Piccolomini, *Opera omnia*, 836–9, no 369. Cf. his 'De ritu, situ, moribus et conditione Germaniae, descriptio', ibid. 1034–86.

[116] J. Blusch, 'Enea Silvio Piccolomini und Giannantonio Campano: Die unterschiedlichen Darstellungsprinzipien in ihren Türkenreden', *Humanistica Lovaniensia*, 28 (1979), 78–138, esp. 80–2, 92.

Germany 'charity and devotion towards the Holy See have grown cold'.[117] By 1500 German national feeling was defining itself in a way that was implicitly anti-Roman. Here lay the heart of the dichotomy between universalism and particularism. Pius and many other enthusiasts for the crusade accepted growing national differences and tried to harness patriotism by emphasizing different qualities. Allegedly, Germany was wanted for the crusade, as Pius stressed and Campano reaffirmed, because it produced such fine warriors. In the process, commonality could all too easily become no more than a cliché, while a roll-call of national strengths was easily inverted to become one of stereotypical weaknesses, as when Pius II, frustrated and caught off guard by French opposition during his arduous journey to Ancona in 1464, assailed 'French fickleness'.[118] Most dangerously, the papal *curia*, which naturally saw itself both as standing at the centre and as above particularism, could be regarded as just another player in the European cast. We shall address the dangers of this later; for the moment it is important to register the constant stress created by the attempt to square the circle.[119]

2.4 *ANTEMURALE* STATES

The most sustained way in which those involved in crusade planning tried to resolve the tension between the universal and the particular was by cultivating the ideology of the bulwark or *antemurale*. The idea itself was straightforward. While the whole of Christendom was threatened by Turkish might and ambition, there were certain frontline states that bore the brunt of the assault and, for that reason, had a moral claim on the military and financial support of their co-religionists; support which would be solicited on their behalf by the papal *curia*. There was nothing new about *antemurale* rhetoric: the Byzantine Empire had been viewed as Christendom's rampart against the barbarians and the image had been transferred to Hungary and, to a lesser extent, Poland in the thirteenth and fourteenth centuries in the context of the Mongol incursions and their aftermath.[120] But for two reasons the situation in the fifteenth century heightened the attractions of the rhetoric, particularly in the case of Hungary.[121] The first reason was the *topos* that the Ottoman advance was inexorable, 'like the sea, which never increases nor decreases, and it is of such nature: it never has peace but always rolls'.[122] The second was contemporaries'

---

[117] Schlecht, *Zamometić*, 2.98–9, no 78.
[118] *Ungedruckte Akten*, 296–303, no 193, esp. 298–300 ('quelli cervelli francesi, pieni de legereza e de instabilità').
[119] On this topic see also Diana M. Webb, 'Italians and Others: Some Quattrocento Views of Nationality and the Church', in Stuart Mews, ed., *Religion and National Identity* (Oxford, 1982), 243–60.
[120] Nora Berend, *At the Gate of Christendom: Jews, Muslims and 'Pagans' in Medieval Hungary, c. 1000–c. 1300* (Cambridge, 2001), 163–71; Paul W. Knoll, 'Poland as *antemurale Christianitatis* in the late Middle Ages', *Catholic Historical Review*, 60 (1974), 381–401.
[121] In Poland the situation was much less favourable: see Angelo Tambora, 'Problema turco e avamposto polacco fra Quattrocento e Cinquecento', in Vittore Branca and Sante Graciotti, eds, *Italia, Venezia e Polonia tra Medio Evo e Età Moderna* (Firenze, 1980), 531–49; Natalia Nowakowska, 'Poland and the Crusade in the Reign of King Jan Olbracht, 1492–1501', in *CFC*, 128–47, 227–31.
[122] Mihailović, *Memoirs*, 191.

grasp of the strategic role that was played by strongholds, rivers, and mountain ranges. This perception was common to both sides. In striking passages, Konstantin Mihailović, perhaps echoing what he had heard from his Ottoman captors as much as from any Christian milieu, pointed to the fortresses of Belgrade, Kilia, and Akkerman, together with the four rivers Danube, Sava, Drava, and Tisza, as pressure points in the Christian defensive system. In particular, Mihailović claimed, the Ottomans believed that they would only make major gains once they had succeeded in taking the three fortresses.[123] There was a general appreciation, confirmed by the Turkish sieges of 1440 and 1456, that Belgrade, which lay at the confluence of the Danube and Sava, possessed unrivalled strategic significance; its harbour sheltered ships that could patrol the whole frontier and move troops along it quickly and with ease. On the Christian side, a strong attraction of *antemurale* rhetoric was that it could be absorbed into the period's political rivalries, as a cluster of frontline states deployed the discourse to their advantage. The process is best examined with reference to two such states, which between them dominated *antemurale* debate throughout the half century after 1453: Hungary in relation to the long Balkan frontier, stretching from the Adriatic to Turnu Severin, and Venice at sea and through its fortified bases in the eastern Mediterranean.

Medieval Hungary was no stranger to *antemurale* language, but during the long reign of Matthias Corvinus (1458–90) the set of ideas that it encapsulated was applied with virtuosity to sustain and justify a foreign policy of dazzling range.[124] Most of the relevant material for this comes from the royal correspondence. As Marianna Birnbaum put it, the royal letters 'are to be viewed as the first important evidence of a sophisticated humanist court in Hungary'.[125] Despite the upheavals that had marked Hungary's domestic politics since Wladislas I's death at Varna in 1444, from the start of Matthias's reign his chancery proved capable of matching the refinement of its counterparts at Rome, Venice, and Vienna. Particularly important was the role within the chancery of the king's tutor, János Vitéz (c. 1408-72) and Vitéz's nephew, Janus Pannonius (1434–72). These two humanists were central figures in Hungary's Renaissance.[126] The king needed to exploit their talent to the limit because his military achievements against the Turks fell far short of what might have been expected given the threat to his lands, not to speak of the spectacular hopes that were invested in him at the start of his reign by Calixtus III. He did respond vigorously to Mehmed II's conquest of Bosnia in 1463, retaking Jajce late in the year and establishing marcher zones around it and Srebrenica.[127] But thereafter he undertook little offensive warfare against the Turks. In 1468 he carried out a decisive turn to the north, first invading Hussite Moravia in association with his adoptive father, Frederick III, then becoming embroiled in

[123] Ibid. 133, 197, and see also Simon, 'The Use of the "Gate of Christendom"', 223.
[124] See Norman Housley, 'Matthias Corvinus and Crusading', in *Between Worlds IV: Matthias Corvinus and His Time*, forthcoming.
[125] Birnbaum, *Janus Pannonius*, 126.
[126] Tibor Klaniczay, 'Hungary', in Roy Porter and Mikuláš Teich, eds, *The Renaissance in National Context* (Cambridge, 1992), 164–79.
[127] See Tomislav Raukar, 'Croatia within Europe', in *CLMAR*, 7–38, at 28–9.

warfare with Poland over the Bohemian crown lands. But his most serious conflict was with Frederick himself and this was successful, at least in terms of Matthias's own reign: the apogee of the king's military career was probably his review of his 28,000-strong army at Wiener Neustadt (Frederick's beloved Austrian residence) following its capture in August 1487.[128] Matthias did not entirely neglect the southern frontier after 1464. A powerful Turkish raid into central Hungary in 1474 compelled him to form an alliance with Stephen of Moldavia with the result that the king's Transylvanian subjects helped Stephen win his great victory at Vaslui in 1475. A year later Matthias himself took the field to besiege the Turkish stronghold at Šabac, 30 miles west of Belgrade on the southern bank of the Sava. Between 1479 and 1481 the king reacted forcefully to raids in Transylvania and Croatia, but generally he maintained peaceful relations with Bayezid II.[129]

Historians have passed harsh judgements on Matthias's handling of the Turkish issue. Pál Engel, while paying credit to the attention the king bestowed on his frontier defences, commented adversely on his preference for maintaining the status quo: 'By far the most important aspect of Hungarian foreign policy, namely the defence against the Ottomans, had been permanently relegated to the background.'[130] It is not hard to find contemporaries who agreed with this. Concluding his memoir/treatise under Matthias's successor Wladislas II, Konstantin Mihailović criticized the late king for getting tied up in warfare against the Czechs and Austrians, though he blamed the Pope and emperor for this as well. The point for Mihailović was that Hungary and Poland constituted Christendom's best hope against the Turks, a hope reinforced by the fact that Wladislas II was also king of Bohemia, as well as the brother of the Polish king, John Albert.[131] The Polish chronicler, Jan Długosz (1415–80), wrote that a 1471 conspiracy to replace Matthias with a Polish prince was driven in part by shock at royal neglect of the frontier in favour of the Bohemian intervention, hyperbolically expressed through the assertion that if the Poles refused to help out, the conspirators would call in the Turks, 'for they would rather obey a barbarian than a shameful king and cruel tyrant'.[132] It is not surprising that southern Hungarians and Croatians, including Vitéz and Pannonius, shared this disappointment; Pannonius becoming one of the conspirators against Matthias in 1471.[133] It was perhaps these internal tensions

[128] The classic study of the conflict between Matthias and Frederick is Karl Nehring, *Matthias Corvinus, Kaiser Friedrich III. und das Reich. Zum hunyadisch-habsburgischen Gegensatz im Donauraum* (Munich, 1975).

[129] For detail see Pál Engel, *The Realm of St Stephen: A History of Medieval Hungary, 895–1526*, tr. Tamás Pálosfalvi (London, 2001), 306–9. See also Attila Bárány, 'Matthias's European Diplomacy in the 1480s', in *ML*, 363–92; Gyula Rázsó, 'Hungarian Strategy against the Ottomans (1365–1526)', in *XXII. Kongress der Internationalen Kommission für Militärgeschichte: Acta 22* (Vienna, 1997), 226–37; Benjamin Weber, 'La croisade impossible: Étude sur les relations entre Sixte IV et Mathias Corvin (1471–1484)', in Bernard Doumerc and Christophe Picard, eds, *Byzance et ses périphéries. Hommage à Alain Ducellier* (Toulouse, 2004), 309–21.

[130] Engel, *Realm*, 306.

[131] Mihailović, *Memoirs*, 197.

[132] Jan Długosz, *Annals* (= *Annales seu cronicae incliti regni Poloniae*), ad ann. 1471, tr. Maurice Michael, with commentary by Paul Smith (Chichester, 1997), 578.

[133] Miroslav Kurelac, 'Croatia and Central Europe during the Renaissance and Reformation', in *CLMAR*, 41–62, at 46–7.

that led Matthias to take over the drafting of so many of his own letters from 1471 onwards. According to Birnbaum, about 75 per cent of royal letters for the decade 1471–81 can be attributed to the king.[134] In these documents, Matthias's assertiveness, self-belief, and ambition are constantly on display; qualities which were registered by papal envoys in their reports of interviews with the king at the very end of his reign.[135]

In the period stretching from the twelfth to the fourteenth centuries the normative argument used by rulers who were slow to keep promises to crusade had been that their Christian rivals stood in their way and that, once these conflicts had been settled, the military needs of the Holy Land would be addressed. Matthias's position, based on an *antemurale* status which the papal *curia* never ceased emphasizing,[136] went far beyond this. It comprised a number of linked arguments. First, the king embraced in full both Hungary's special military role and the expectations that were held of him as a son of the great Hunyadi. Throughout his life he depicted himself as the selfless athlete of Christ, devoting his own energy and the resources of his kingdom to the defence of Christendom. Rivals like George Kastriote (Iskanderbeg) were put firmly in their place: if Matthias was to report his victories as fully as the Albanian did, he assured the Pope in 1465, he would never stop writing.[137] Naturally, the king and his advisors had a sound grasp of how best to characterize Hungary's role in relation to the Turkish threat. When circumstances warranted it, Matthias was willing to reach beyond the *antemurale* idea and portray his lands as a springboard for offensive warfare. Capitalizing on the brief excitement that followed the death of Mehmed II, he complained in August 1481 that the Austrian partisanship of Sixtus IV's legate, Orso Orsini of Theano, was robbing him of the 10,000 cavalry that the imperial diet had promised for the war against the Turks: with such a strong force, he claimed, he could have reached Constantinople.[138] This piece of sheer bravado echoed the claim that his father had made to Capistrano in 1455 that if he was provided with an army of 100,000 men, properly equipped, he could drive Mehmed out of Europe in three months.[139]

Normally realism prevailed and the king and his apologists focused on the defensive roles played by the southern strongholds. These they characterized with some finesse. Writing in 1465 to the envoys he had sent to Italy (including Pannonius), Matthias pictured Mehmed judging his life's work to be incomplete until he had managed to take Belgrade and Jajce: the former being the door to Hungary, Poland, and Bohemia, the latter to Dalmatia, Istria, Italy, and Germany.[140] And eleven years later, when lobbying the Pope on the king's behalf during his bold attempt to take Šabac with a winter siege, Gabriele Rangoni, royal counsellor and bishop of Eger, presented a colourful image of the fortress as Mehmed's right eye,

---

[134] Birnbaum, *Janus Pannonius*, 126. [135] Esp. *VMH*, 2.521–30, no 718.
[136] As shown by the collection *Hungary as 'Propugnaculum' of Western Christianity: Documents from the Vatican Secret Archives (ca. 1214–1606)*, ed. Edgár Artner and others, (Budapest and Rome, 2004).
[137] *MKL*, 1.105–12, no 77.
[138] Ibid. 2.159–60, no 92, 161–2, no 93. See also *MCH*, 181–4, no 136.
[139] *AM*, 12.293. [140] *MKL*, 1.82–4, no 62.

which enabled him to keep a foot firmly fixed on the Christian throat. Šabac, Rangoni maintained, was even more important for Mehmed than Smederevo, located to the east, because the garrison at Belgrade generally managed to contain the depredations of the Turks who used Smederevo as their jumping-off point; by contrast, raiding parties that gathered at Šabac could take their pick of victims, for Slavonia, Croatia, Carniola, Carinthia, and Styria were all within striking distance of this impressively located fortress.[141] This emphasis on the lands bordering the Sava due west of Belgrade naturally appealed to the Hasburgs; in a printed circular in 1493 Maximilian referred to Belgrade and Croatia as the two pressure points: should either give way, the Turks would water their horses in the Rhine.[142]

The most important point of the exercise was securing additional financial resources for the bulwark. In August 1481 Matthias observed that the reason why his envoys were finding it hard to get an audience with the Pope might well be Sixtus's assumption that they came clutching the usual begging bowl. Absolutely not, the king blustered; he was perfectly capable of defending his own lands without outside help.[143] But this was the exact opposite of his normal approach, which consisted of loudly rattling the bowl. Matthias argued repeatedly that the Hungarian war effort was on the point of collapse, that Hungary must have assistance, and that it was not enough just to cede him money from within his own lands. Proceeds from preaching the Jubilee indulgence within Hungary, he asserted in 1476 during his trying siege of Šabac, would not stretch to supporting ten armed men for a year.[144] This may not be as hyperbolic as it sounds, for the king kept a close eye on detail. Just a month before proudly announcing that he had no need of outside support, he was complaining about changes to the terms of the Jubilee indulgence: the removal of the second occasion on which recipients could be granted the indulgence (i.e. on their deathbed) would reduce take-up, particularly as it was included in the Rhodes indulgence which was also being preached.[145] *A fortiori*, it was unacceptable that any Hungarian money should be channelled elsewhere. So in early 1479 Matthias complained indignantly to Rangoni, whom Sixtus had raised to cardinal in 1477, because he had committed thousands of gold pieces from the revenues he was still entitled to collect in Eger as his contribution to a fleet that Sixtus wanted to prepare in Italy. This was intolerable and the king was minded to cancel Rangoni's exemption from providing troops for the royal host 'in accordance with the kingdom's longstanding custom'.[146] Late in 1481 Matthias wrote caustically to Rangoni, who had made the mistake of complaining about his losses during the campaign to recover Otranto. His inconveniences, the king wrote, were minor by comparison with the sufferings borne by those who fought on Hungary's frontier.[147] Ever the martyr, the king complained to the Venetian envoy in 1475 that others who failed to saddle a single horse for the sake of

---

[141] *Codex diplomaticus*, 388–90, no 519.
[142] *AR*, no 158. For Croatia as *antemurale* see Franjo Šanjek, 'The Church and Christianity', in *CLMAR*, 245–7.
[143] *MKL*, 2.159–60, no 92, 161–2, no 93. [144] *MCH*, 104–8, no 81.
[145] *MKL*, 2.139–44, no 79, at 141–2. [146] Ibid. 1.425–6, no 284.
[147] Ibid. 2.191–5, no 103.

Underpinnings: antagonisms and allegiances 45

the faith received more than he, who struggled unremittingly, on the edge of Christendom, to keep the Turk at bay.[148]

Occupation of the moral high ground, at which Matthias became a magisterial practitioner, served diplomatic as well as financial purposes. He went so far as to remind Sixtus IV that it was a bad idea for the Pope to alienate him because he was one of his few supporters,[149] and to criticize Venice, at the end of the republic's sixteen-year war against the Turks, for coming to terms with the infidel.[150] With Venice cravenly giving in, he wrote, he would have no option but to give the Turks free passage through his lands to reach their prey.[151] But his most enduring target was the man whose coronation as Holy Roman Emperor obliged him *ex officio* to take charge of Christendom's war effort against the Turks. It was therefore the more shocking that through his incessant opposition to Matthias's foreign policy, Frederick III impeded Hungary's ability to respond to the Ottoman threat. Amongst the numerous complaints along these lines, a letter that the king wrote to Sixtus IV on 6 November 1480 describing the escalating fighting in Bosnia typifies his stance. Matthias described how he had pursued a Turkish raiding party which had been devastating Styria, one of Frederick's lands, but had moved too fast to be caught. While camped by the Sava, Matthias had received news of a splinter group that was raiding Croatia. He pounced on them and, out of 3,000 raiders, barely 200 escaped his clutches. The king then assembled a larger force to invade Turkish territory, only to hear that Frederick, as usual, was attacking his rear. After splitting his forces, despatching the more lightly armed troops to raid Turkish lands, he received Sixtus's letters urging him to campaign against them. Matthias would act in accordance with papal prompting, setting aside private interests in favour of 'the public matter of the faith' (*pro publico fidei negotio*), but he must have support against the disruptive Frederick, in addition to subsidies from Rome.[152] A few weeks later he sent Sixtus a further letter, this time trumpeting the capture of Vrhbosna (Sarajevo), which he claimed was one of Mehmed II's four most prized possessions. Out of eleven encounters with the Turks in 1480, none of them fought against fewer than 3,000 men, he laid claim to ten successes.[153] It is hard to see how he could have squeezed more kudos from the situation, or used it more adroitly to blacken Frederick's name.

But Matthias's handling of *antemurale* rhetoric shows that it could be taken in unorthodox directions. We know that at the time he wrote these letters to Sixtus IV, Matthias was allowing the Turks safe passage through his lands to attack Frederick's territories: indeed in 1480 he lodged a complaint with the sultan about the Turkish commander who was pillaging Croatia while returning from Styria.[154] Naturally Frederick appealed to the Pope to prevent it.[155] Matthias was quite capable of

---

[148] Ibid. 1.320, no 225.   [149] *MCH*, 104–8, no 81.
[150] *MCH*, 141–4, no 112, esp. 143, 'Quis enim non detestetur et doleat Romanum pontificem illis adherentem socium et confederatum dici, qui Christiani nominis hostibus socii, censuarii et subditi existunt?'
[151] *MKL*, 1.471–4, no 320, at 472.   [152] *MCH*, 148–52, no 116.
[153] Ibid. 154–8, no 118.   [154] *MKL*, 2.388–90, no 247.
[155] *Hungary as 'Propugnaculum'*, no 111. See too Schlecht, *Zamometić*, 2.6–11, no 3, at 7 (1478 claim by Frederick).

justifying this 'open door' policy in terms of Frederick's alleged commitment towards undermining Hungary's *antemurale* mission, but his preferred approach, as in 1480, was to assume the injured martyr stance, i.e. that despite the emperor's many injuries to Matthias, the king was doing all he could to protect Frederick's neglected flock. In November 1483, for instance, he reported to Sixtus IV that he had routed a party of Turks who were returning from raids into Carniola and Styria. He had sent home Frederick's captured subjects—10,000 strong, mainly women and children—even though a strict application of the *ius in bello* entitled him to keep them.[156] In 1481 Matthias dropped hints that he would be justified in using Turkish assistance to defend his lands against Frederick's aggression. The latter, he claimed, was the more outrageous because Frederick was siphoning off a substantial military support package that the imperial diet had intended for Matthias.[157] In a brusque exchange of views with the papal legate in June 1489 Matthias was frank both about letting the Turks through and about allying with them.[158]

It is tempting to regard Matthias's crusading apologias with suspicion and undeniably his special pleading could be brazen. But it is noteworthy that at least one contemporary legal expert who was also a crusading enthusiast, Rodrigo Sánchez de Arévalo, regarded alliances with infidel powers by frontier rulers like Matthias as legitimate in extreme circumstances.[159] The king's overall position was coherent, provided one accepts the underlying premise that royal policy was driven not just by dynastic claims and the pursuit of honour but also by dedication to the Christian cause, the two converging in the advantages to Christendom of a strong *antemurale*. His conviction and self-assurance certainly came to rest on unrivalled experience. By the 1480s Matthias had been facing the Ottoman threat for over two decades. He had worked with five Popes and had successfully withstood Mehmed II's onslaught. Most significantly, in 1464 he had been let down by the failure of Pius II's project, to whose grandiose programme he had subscribed; and his reaction to Innocent VIII's Rome congress shows him at his most sceptical about the prospect of a truly international crusade materializing. By that point he had convinced himself that his tried and tested methods of containment were the most effective ones. After all, Bayezid was now directing his energies northwards against Moldavia. Typically, Matthias argued that the best thing to do with Djem was to send him to Buda to be deployed in order to further that strategy. In Matthias's eyes the Pope was too subject to the demands made on him by powerful rulers to exercise balanced judgement. Matthias by contrast was free of such leverage, besides being shaped by birth, training, experience, and inclination to be Christ's athlete. So his view of what was best for the faith was the purer one of the two. At least one contemporary text, Andreas Pannonius's *Libellus de virtutibus Matthiae Corvino dedicatus* of 1467, encouraged this self-image with its eulogistic treatment.[160]

---

[156] *MCH*, 210–13, no 166. [157] Ibid. 256–7, no 206.
[158] *VMH*, 2. 521–30, no 718, and for Angelo's mission see 515–17, no 711.
[159] Benziger, *Zur Theorie von Krieg und Frieden,* 159, 161.
[160] Andreas Pannonius, 'Libellus de virtutibus Matthiae Corvino dedicatus', in *Irodalomtörténeti Emlékek*, 1 (Budapest, 1886), 1–133. See also Z.J. Kosztolnyik, 'Some Hungarian Theologians in the Late Renaissance', *Church History*, 57 (1988), 5–18, at 7.

There are both similarities and differences between this outlook and Venice's handling of its *antemurale* status. The similarities reside in the vocabulary deployed and in the focus on pressure points which, once captured, would open up a pathway for the Turks.[161] The closest Venetian equivalent to Belgrade was its island fortress at Negroponte, and Venice's response to its fall in 1470 showed the republic's sensitivity to the universal/particular dichotomy. In a comparatively short letter to Sforza conveying the news in August, the doge referred to *Italia* nine times, whereas the word did not feature at all some weeks later in a report sent to the republic's envoy at the imperial court.[162] When Modon fell in 1500 there was little to add except that the threat had come even closer; there was evidence that Brindisi was next on the Turkish hit list and the resulting war would be fought 'in Italy's heartlands, and around the altars of St Peter'.[163] These similarities aside, however, Venice's *antemurale* status seems to have been less embedded in the republic's diplomacy and political culture than it was in the case of Hungary. There are a number of possible explanations for this. The most obvious one is that the core metaphor was less suited to Venice's overseas possessions (the *Stato da Màr*) than it was to Hungary's long Danubian frontier, or indeed that of other *antemurale* zones such as Albania and Moldavia. Secondly, the papal *curia* had a much more fraught relationship with Venice than it did with Hungary. It was willing to proclaim Venice's role as an *antemurale* state when the latter was at war with the Turks (1463–79 and 1499–1503), but it avoided bestowing on Venice the ongoing kudos of being Christendom's bulwark. From Rome's perspective, Venice as often as not impeded the crusade through its encroachments on papal lands and claims. In February 1487 the orator, Leonello Chiericati, listed the occasions when Pope and doge had stood side by side for the cause of the faith, going back as far as Calixtus II in the early twelfth century;[164] but four years previously Sixtus IV had accused the republic of fighting an unjust war 'against God and men' over Ferrara.[165] The city had been the target of a crusade in 1309 and in 1504 Julius II channelled the proceeds of Perault's German preaching against it.[166] More generally, the republic's engagement in trade with the Turks, and its exceptional reluctance to fight them, acted as constraints on the credibility of an image that demanded at least a reasonable consonance with reality. Irrespective of its king's shortcomings as a crusading protagonist, Hungary was a frontline state whose people faced intermittent raiding, the demographic and economic impact of which necessitated royal interventions.[167]

---

[161] For the reality behind the rhetoric see Simon Pepper, 'Fortress and Fleet: The Defence of Venice's Mainland Greek Colonies in the Late Fifteenth Century', in David S. Chambers and others, eds, *War, Culture and Society in Renaissance Venice: Essays in Honour of John Hale* (London and Rio Grande, 1993), 29–55.
[162] *MDE*, 2.186–8, no 131, 189–90, no 133.   [163] *Notes et extraits*, 5th ser., 301–3.
[164] Sigismondo de' Conti, *Le storie*, 1.426, no 11.   [165] Ibid. 1.418, no 8.
[166] Housley, *Later Crusades*, 243; *AR*, nos 20965, 21139–40.
[167] E.g. *MKL*, 2.50–2, no 33. Kurelac, 'Croatia', 51–3, provides some detail on population movements in Croatia.

Venice's ambivalent relationship with the anti-Ottoman crusade was not helped by persistent rumours of complicity. Examples are legion. A Sforza envoy at the Burgundian court reported in 1455 on suspicions that Venice was supplying the Turks with arms.[168] A story circulated about 600 Venetians fighting for the sultan at Belgrade in 1456, of whom 300 were captured and beheaded by Hunyadi, and their captain skinned alive.[169] In 1469 another Sforza envoy reported stories of Venetian plotting to set the Germans against the Turks to their own profit.[170] The most tenacious example of this *legenda negra* has proved to be Venetian culpability for the Ottoman capture of Otranto in 1480, which some contemporaries insisted on attributing to Venetian advice, prompting, and assistance.[171] The Venetian response to that event illustrates one of the republic's biggest problems: the ease with which its neutrality could be construed as cooperation with the Turks. Its refusal to be dragged into a league to recover Otranto did not just encourage Venice's diehard enemies; even less hostile contemporaries viewed it as characteristically unhelpful, ignoring the fact that Venice had only recently emerged from a sixteen-year war with the sultan.[172] In February/March 1494 the republic denied Maximilian ship transports to carry his troops and supplies across the Adriatic to Croatia on the grounds that it dared not offend the sultan, who was certain to hear about it. Maximilian responded coldly that he could not see how any Venetian agreement with the Turk could be so strict that it had effectively to seal off the Adriatic in this way.[173] It was not long since that Matthias had opened the door to Turks en route to attack the subjects of Maximilian's father; now the region's other leading *antemurale* was shutting the door to Christians on their way to fight the Turks. Another factor that fed the rumour-mill was the hatred felt by so many Italians for the republic. A papal nuncio in England in 1472, Pietro Aliprandi, may have exaggerated when he wrote that the whole world would like to see the Venetians drowned in their canals because they were worse than the Turks, but the sentiment was certainly deeply rooted in Italy, to the concern of Venice itself.[174] Nicolai Rubinstein showed that the creation of the *terraferma*, Venice's commitment to the maintenance of a standing army, and the consistency that its republican institutions bestowed on its foreign policy, combined to generate fears that the Venetians nurtured ambitions that were scarcely less threatening than those of the Ottomans. The ingenuity of the Sforza chancellery created the myth that Venice dreamt of a *renovatio romani imperii*, but even without such hyperbole it was clear that distrust of Venice was strong enough to render impracticable any hopes of Italian cooperation except *in extremis*.[175]

---

[168] *Carteggi diplomatici fra Milano Sforzesca e la Borgogna*, ed. E. Sestan, 2 vols, Fonti per la storia d'Italia, 140–1 (Rome, 1985–7), 1.23–6, no 2.
[169] *Notes et extraits*, 4th ser., 349.   [170] *Carteggi diplomatici*, 1.258–61, no 164.
[171] Sigismondo de' Conti, *Le storie*, bk 3, ch 5, 1.110. In general see Ermanno Orlando, 'Venezia e la conquista turca di Otranto (1480–1481). Incroci, responsabilità, equivoci negli equilibri europei', in *CTO*, 1.177–209. Remarkably, the charge of complicity continues to be reproduced, e.g. Kurelac, 'Croatia', 55.
[172] Somaini, 'La curia romana', 223–4, 240–2.   [173] *AR*, no 433 and see also nos 446, 479.
[174] *Carteggi diplomatici*, 1.285–7, no 177; Sanuto, *I diarii*, 3.842 (= *AR*, no 14447).
[175] Nicolai Rubinstein, 'Italian Reactions to Terraferma Expansion in the Fifteenth Century', in John R. Hale, ed., *Renaissance Venice* (London, 1973), 197–217. See too Lassalmonie, 'Louis XI', 195.

It is possible that Venice's reputation as a potential crusading state never recovered from the serious damage inflicted in 1459–60 by the way it managed its response to the Mantua congress. We shall consider the detailed arguments deployed in the next chapter; here it is enough to note that Venice's position at the congress was just as cogent as the one that supported Matthias's interpretation of Hungary's *antemurale* role. Concerned though the republic was about Mehmed's conquest of the Peloponnese, it did not believe that Pius's congress would be successful and therefore placed a premium on preserving its neutrality. Beside which, there was as always the peninsular angle to consider: excluded from the Milan-Rome-Naples axis that largely formed Pius II's Italian policy, Venice was bound to look towards France, and this aggravated its marginalization. The problem was that this stance inevitably struck contemporaries as both negative and self-seeking. Given Pius's intense disappointment at Venetian policy, it would be understandable if he momentarily embraced the anti-Venetian sentiments emanating from Sforza's court, because there was a general consensus bordering on truism that a crusade could only succeed if it involved operations on land and at sea. So Venice's adamantine refusal to engage came close to destroying his project. In 1463, when the sheer range of Mehmed's offensive designs realigned Venetian interests, the city was fortunate to play host to Bessarion. The cardinal-legate's sympathy for the republic's position and his high credit rating at Rome enabled him to repair some of the damage that Venetian behaviour four years earlier had done to their relations with Pius II.[176]

The problem they now faced, as they commented in June 1465, was their lack of a land frontier with the Turks.[177] This made it very difficult to make the best use of their naval superiority. So, while being jealously protective of the management of the conflict at sea, they accepted their dependence on *protégés* and allies to inflict substantial damage on the sultan's war-making capacity. For some years the advantages of Christendom's two leading *antemurale* states fighting together, one on land and the other at sea, were so apparent that the republic patiently persisted in trying to make the Hungarian coalition work after it had become clear that Matthias had lost interest in Bosnia and turned to fight elsewhere. Even without subsidizing Matthias, the burden to the republic of spreading its military spend in this way was enormous. In June 1467 Venice complained that in addition to the expenses of its own fleet, and its land forces in the Peloponnese and at Negroponte, it was sending foot soldiers to Albania, fortifying its various ports, and subsidizing Iskanderbeg.[178] But the *antemurale*'s unique character and military profile gave it no choice but to subsidize others. The same pattern recurred in the war of 1499–1503, when the republic came to see the only hope of victory residing in military partnership with Maximilian. The fact that this came to nothing, and that the republic's relations with the emperor-elect proved just as frustrating as those with Matthias had been,

---

[176] Mohler, *Bessarion*, 3.516–22, nos 52–3. In his discussions with the Milanese envoy Pius effectively described his alliance with Venice as circumstantial, but this may have been intended to assuage Sforza's fears: Baldi, *Pio II*, 242.
[177] *MDE*, 1.335–6, no 207.   [178] Ibid. 2.59–60, no 35.

confirmed the wisdom of the normative neutrality that had proved so offensive at Mantua.[179]

2.5 *ITEM TU SIXTE CANIS, IAM AMICUS TURCORUM*: CRITICISM, CHALLENGES, AND ALTERNATIVES TO PAPAL AUTHORITY

Antemurale powers like Venice and Hungary formed their own opinions about the character and direction that a crusade should take and they expressed them robustly. We have seen that Matthias in particular was assertive in his letters and, in his heated conversations with papal envoys, he used language that bordered on abuse. But Matthias could mount no challenge to Rome's control of the crusade; he was too dependent on it and he was aware that, for all its shortcomings and vacillation, papal policy formed a useful pillar of his rule. He would not even listen to the overtures of anti-papalists like Podiebrad, rightly judging that that there was more to be got from supporting Rome than from backing Prague. Others did challenge the papacy's *dirigiste* role in attempts to generate crusading against the Turks and they created at least one formal alternative to papal control over the crusade, as well as several initiatives that represented substantive inroads into the papal position. Behind almost all the flak of criticism that was directed against the Popes there loomed the threat, open or covert, of a revival of conciliarism, deployed either as a genuine programme for reform of the Church or as leverage in the service of a less altruistic goal.

It is important to place such criticism in proper perspective. Attacks on the Church's shortcomings were commonplace and they included critiques of Rome's corruption, abuses, and failure or slowness in promoting the crusade. Divine punishment for this constituted one recurrent theme in the way Ottoman successes were interpreted and the Popes got used to hearing sermons in which reform and crusade were linked. In that way criticism was domesticated and its sting extracted.[180] Criticism made outside this controlled environment was another matter. And at times we can detect what amounted to challenges, as high-ranking clerics who were dedicated to the cause of crusade saw that the Pope was moving away from it and took such steps as they could to counteract it. Was this new? Undoubtedly we owe the visibility of such resistance to the increased volume of sources depicting the views and activities of such men, especially when they were cardinals.[181] But there may be other reasons. For a period of some decades following Martin V's election in 1417, the *curia* was a genuinely oligarchic government in which the

---

[179] For the impact of the two wars on Venice's economy see Freddy Thiriet, *La Romanie vénitienne au Moyen Âge. Le développement et l'exploitation du domaine colonial vénitien (XIIe–XVe siècles)* (Paris, 1959), pt 3 *passim*.

[180] E.g. Paolo Toscanella's hard-hitting Ascension Day sermon of 1482: Schlecht, *Zamometić*, 2.138–47, no 116.

[181] Above all the dispatches of envoys, which assisted Baldi in identifying the supporters and opponents of Pius II's approach toward Naples: Baldi, *Pio II*, 183.

cardinals were able and willing to create oppositional factions. More concretely, the formation around Calixtus III and then Pius II of a group of cardinals dedicated to the crusade, and its recognition by Paul II in the context of monitoring expenditure from Pius II's *depositeria della crociata,* formally created a lobby group for the Turkish crusade, the influence of which can be traced through to Bessarion's death in 1472, arguably even further if we include the activities of Lando.[182] The group almost certainly persuaded Paul at the start of his reign to issue what amounted to a manifesto. He declared his intention of carrying forward Pius II's programme at the opening of a letter in which he dispatched Lando to Hungary to make use of crusading subsidies to hire troops and combine their service in the field with those of men who had taken the cross under Pius.[183]

We might expect Paul's decision four years later to redirect the target of his crusading ambitions to Podiebrad's Bohemia to have met with resistance from this anti-Turkish crusade lobby, but none has come to light and two key members of the lobby, Bessarion and Carvajal, became important executives of this renewed application of force to the Bohemian problem.[184] Both men had played central roles in the papal abrogation of the Basel Compacts in 1462.[185] In some ways their acquiescence is puzzling, because Paul's shift to a policy of simply containing the Turks while focusing on Bohemia was much more radical and sustained than earlier challenges to the prioritization of the Ottoman threat, such as Calixtus's war against Jacopo Piccinino in 1455[186] and Pius's hostility towards Sigismondo Malatesta. It may be that they were convinced that the stalled momentum of the Turkish crusade was largely due to Podiebrad's incessant diplomatic manoeuvrings and that the crusade would only become viable once he was crushed: his designs on the title of emperor of Constantinople would certainly have alarmed the philo-Palaeologan Bessarion. Matthias was eager to become the military arm of this reoriented papal policy, so there was no criticism from one of the two most affected frontline powers: indeed, two letters written on 2 October 1465, one backtracking on the Turks and the other embracing with joy the prospect of combat in Bohemia, made Matthias's hopes crystal clear.[187] As for the other key *antemurale*, Venice was embroiled in a cluster of disputes with this (ironically) Venetian Pope, and by 1468 it had given up hope that Paul would do much to help out against the Turks.[188]

---

[182] Mureşan, 'Girolamo Lando'; Damian 'La *Depositeria*', 135–52.
[183] *VMH*, 2.398–9, no 572.
[184] Damian, 'La *Depositeria*', 148.
[185] Otakar Odložilík, *The Hussite King: Bohemia in European Affairs 1440–1471* (New Brunswick, NJ, 1965), 130–4.
[186] Alan Ryder, *Alfonso the Magnanimous: King of Aragon, Naples and Sicily 1396–1458* (Oxford, 1990), 410–16, highlighted the damaging effects of Calixtus's antagonism towards Piccinino on his ability to work with Alfonso of Aragon.
[187] *MKL*, 1.105–12, no 77, 112–14, no 78, esp. 114, 'Sive ergo in Bohemos, sive in Turcos opus est, ecce Mathias simul et Hungaria, quantumcumque mee et regni mei vires se extendunt, supra omnes apostolice sedi et vestre beatitudini devote manent, eternumque manebunt.'
[188] Ian Robertson, 'Pietro Barbo-Paul II: *Zentilhomo de Uenecia e Pontifico*', David S. Chambers and others, eds, *War, Culture and Society in Renaissance Venice: Essays in Honour of John Hale* (London and Rio Grande, 1993), 147–72, at 163.

The fall of Negroponte placed Paul II in an embarrassing position, forcing him to give credence to Matthias's boast that he could take on both heretics and Turks.[189] Nonetheless, it was not his Bohemian crusade but his successor's Italian wars that raised hackles, in part because the nepotistic means that Sixtus employed were one of the most scandalous features of the reign. The crusading lobby that dated back to Pius's days expired with Bessarion's death, though the old man bequeathed a forthright statement of his views about the scale and imminence of the Ottoman threat in his *Orationes*. But Lando was prepared to show his disapproval when the Pope turned against Lorenzo de' Medici in 1478, provoking official Venetian censure in 1479 and again in 1480 when he openly sided with Lorenzo. On 7 July 1480 Lando was banished from Venetian territory 'for having spoken ill of the Pope' and sought refuge in Crete. As Mureşan has suggested, it is unlikely to be coincidental that this was the point when Rome's hopes of alliance with the Orthodox were waning. But Lando did not stay in exile for long. During the winter of 1482–3 Venice itself became the target of papal hostility. In May 1483 Sixtus placed the republic under interdict, ignoring representations from lobbyists including Cardinal Marco Barbo, patriarch of Aquileia, who emphasized the importance of Venice's *antemurale* status. Back from Crete, Lando initiated and steered through the republic's response in June: after taking extensive legal advice the city appealed to a future general council, which would be presided over by Lando. In the meantime Lando took it upon himself to suspend the Pope's sentence. It is likely that Lando's stance in the summer of 1483 was partly inspired by patriotic feeling and, perhaps, by chagrin at his failure to secure a cardinalate; nonetheless, coming from a titular patriarch of Constantinople with an outstanding track record of engagement with the anti-Turkish crusade, such a statement of intent carried serious implications. Venice was successful in getting its response secretly posted in prominent locations in Rome, including the door of St Peter's, causing such disturbances that Sixtus ordered the negligent night watchmen to be executed.[190]

One reason why Sixtus reacted so harshly to Venice's coup in getting its response publicized was that its appeal to a general council came just a year after a related, though more eccentric, incident at Basel. This pointed to broad currents of concern and also demonstrated that, for a Pope who made as many political enemies as Sixtus did, it was dangerous to lay yourself open to the charge of neglect. The protagonist at Basel was a Croatian Dominican called Andrija Jamometić (Andrea Zamometić). He was a former envoy of Frederick III and since 1476 titular archbishop of Granea (Krajina, in northern Albania). In Basel cathedral on the feast day of the Annunciation (25 March) 1482 he denounced the Pope for a long list of crimes ranging from heresy to murder. They included a number of crusade-related charges, notably a secret alliance with Mamluk Egypt, preferring wars in Italy to promoting a crusade, and 'permitting' the occupation of Otranto. In sum, Sixtus was a friend of the Turks: *Item tu Sixte canis, iam amicus Turcorum*. Jamometić

---

[189] *VMH*, 2.421, no 600, and cf. 418–21, nos 595–6, 598–9.
[190] Mureşan, 'Girolamo Lando', 224–7, 238; *Venice: A Documentary History, 1450–1630*, ed. David Chambers and Brian Pullan (Oxford, 1992), 220.

therefore proclaimed a general council that would assemble at Basel.[191] The purging of this disastrous Pope, the reform of the Church, and the crusade were construed as interlocked items on his council's agenda.[192] The man's origins, titular see, and, above all, the frustrations he had gone through in trying to promote a crusade during his diplomatic missions to Rome, combined to make him particularly sensitive to Sixtus's disappointing track record on crusading, though there were other causes for his extraordinary behaviour. As with Lando, they included bitterness at being denied promotion to cardinal; a status that Jamometić blithely awarded himself. He had made no secret of his views about Sixtus's court, for which he had suffered imprisonment in Castel Sant'Angelo in 1481. Even though welcomed, for reasons of prestige and economic advantage, by his host city, his council would have got nowhere had Lorenzo de' Medici, Sixtus's main enemy, not shown enough interest to send an envoy, Baccio Ugolini, to discuss it with Jamometić. It was ominous that Frederick III did not immediately denounce his former envoy and, with a Neapolitan army threatening Rome and plague breaking out in the city, for a few weeks in the spring and summer of 1482 Sixtus's pontificate seemed to be at risk. But Jamometić secured no firm backers, Frederick leant on Basel to withdraw its support, and Sixtus was able to contain the damage; Jamometić was arrested and found hanged in his prison cell in 1484.[193]

Whereas Jamometić's Basel 'proclamation' in 1482 was short lived and bears the hallmarks of a farce, Perault's dealings with Alexander VI were protracted as well as highly revealing about the dilemma facing a crusading enthusiast shackled to a deeply corrupt Pope who was intent on using the crusade almost exclusively to further Italian policies which were clearly dynastic in nature. When Alexander was elected in 1492 Perault's experience on the anti-Turkish crusade was already profound; he had preached for the crusade with distinction in Germany in 1486–8 and 1489–90. Alexander could not resist Maximilian's demand that Perault be given a cardinal's hat in the appointments that he made in September 1493. Nobody, Maximilian assured the Pope at the end of the year, was more dedicated to the crusade or more expert on the issue of the Turks than the new cardinal.[194] When the crisis of the French invasion broke out a year later Perault's zeal for a crusade combined with his patriotic loyalty to incline him to give credence to Charles VIII's manifesto claims. At the same time he harboured no illusions about the Pope: when the French crusade programme was publicized in November Perault was circulating documents showing that Alexander had conducted secret negotiations with the sultan.[195] Perault was no agent or dupe of the French and, while

---

[191] Schlecht, *Zamometić*, 2.36–41, no 20.   [192] e.g. ibid. 2.66–8, no 46, 80–1, no 55.

[193] Schlecht, *Zamometić*, passim; Jürgen Petersohn, *Kaiserlicher Gesandter und Kurienbischof, Andreas Jamometić am Hof Papst Sixtus' IV (1478–1481): Aufschlüsse aus neuen Quellen* (Hannover, 2004). The fullest account of the episode is in Pastor, *History*, 4.358–63, where Jamometić is called Zuccalmaglio. For the Croatian background see Šanjek, 'The Church and Christianity', in *CLMAR*, 227–58, esp. 227, 252–3, 256.

[194] *AR*, no 273.

[195] *AR*, no 3184. Johannes Schneider, *Die kirchliche und politische Wirksamkeit des Legaten Raimund Peraudi (1486–1505)* (Halle, 1882), 38ff., elucidates Perault's position.

the authenticity of his documents about Alexander's dealings with Bayezid remains in question, the cardinal's character makes it highly unlikely that he fabricated them himself. His priorities were clear and in July 1495 the archbishop of Cologne astutely observed that if the Pope were to give him a crusade legation and control over the money he raised, he would forget all about supporting the king of France.[196] In the meantime, however, he was bound to take offence at Alexander's diplomatic manoeuvrings against Charles, especially the Pope's use of the crusade as camouflage. Open resistance at the *curia* was futile since the College of Cardinals had lost most of its power and deposition was impracticable.[197] As early as 1480 the group of eight cardinals who were *deputati alle provvisioni contra il Turco* by Sixtus IV during the Otranto crisis, exercised a purely executive role.[198] So throughout the later 1490s Perault worked away at restoring peace between Charles and Maximilian for the greater good of the crusade,[199] while Alexander worked equally hard to feed their hostility, with the goal of expelling the French from Italy.

The man caught in the crossfire was Leonello Chiericati, bishop of Concordia, one of the period's most accomplished diplomats and orators.[200] Chiericati was papal nuncio in Germany from 1495 to 1499. His contributions towards the Turkish crusade were scarcely less impressive than Perault's and his experience of German politics dated back to the legatine mission led by Marco Barbo in 1472, in response to the fall of Negroponte. He was an astute, intelligent man and a keen observer. In January 1498, when political business was slack, he sent Alexander an insightful report about popular devotion in Germany, anticipating the upcoming Jubilee.[201] But he was hostile to France following a very difficult mission there in 1488–91,[202] and he adhered rigidly to Alexander's line that a crusade could only be set in motion once the French had been expelled from Italy and Maximilian crowned as emperor. He was also a dogmatic supporter of papal absolutism and clearly had a higher tolerance threshold for the corruption of Alexander's court than his rival Perault. In January 1496 Chiericati called on Maximilian to counter French ambitions in Italy in a speech at Augsburg, the violent Francophobia and heady imperial nostalgia of which were calculated to appeal to the emperor-elect.[203] Thereafter he missed no chance to condemn the French and encourage Franco-imperial belligerence.[204] It is hardly surprising that in 1497–8 Chiericati's reports to Rome included a stream of *ad hominem* abuse in reaction to Perault's attempted peace-making, which he construed as outrageous partisanship for the French cause.[205] The embattled Perault responded by linking crusade with reform of the Church.[206] A 'peace, then reform, then crusade' programme was a vote winner in

---

[196] *AR*, no 2023.   [197] Pellegrini, 'Turning-Point'.
[198] Somaini, 'La curia romana', 258–62; Felice Fossati, 'Milano e una fallita alleanza contro i Turchi', *Archivio storico lombardo*, 3rd ser. 16 (1901), 49–95, at 55.
[199] See in particular Heinz Angermeier, 'Der Wormser Reichstag 1495—ein europäisches Ereignis', *Historische Zeitschrift*, 261 (1995), 739–68, for Perault's efforts at the Worms diet of 1495.
[200] *DBI*, 24.682–9.   [201] *AR*, no 5881.
[202] e.g. his dismissal of French crusading proposals as mere camouflage in *AR*, no 6422.
[203] Ibid. no 3705.   [204] e.g. ibid. no 6422.
[205] e.g. ibid. nos 5014, 5109, 5158, 5415, 5600, 8558.
[206] e.g. ibid. no 6300.

Germany but it was no more conducive to speedy action than Chiericati's agenda of '(French) expulsion, then (imperial) coronation, then crusade'. In fact Perault's approach was counter-productive because the more Rome's shortcomings were condemned in Germany the less chance there was of a crusade materializing: Alexander's uncle Calixtus and his successors had been too successful in reaffirming papal direction of the crusade's major instruments.

Paradoxically, Perault's cause received more assistance from Constantinople than Rome, to the extent that renewed Turkish pressure on Hungary and Poland, and the lobbying that this generated, compelled Alexander and Maximilian alike to develop a more proactive approach. In June 1497 Chiericati reported that envoys from Maximilian's Austrian lands had been asking for assistance, though at this stage Maximilian calculated that he could use such pleas as pressure on Charles VII to climb down on his Italian demands.[207] At the Freiburg diet of June/July 1498 Chiericati functioned as the papal-imperial mouthpiece, denouncing the French as the 'Turks of the west', while Perault placed his hopes in reconciliation, to be effected through dynastic marriage.[208] Over the course of 1498–9 Chiericati was increasingly driven by external pressures to give more attention to the crusade project, though he could rely on the substantial differences between Maximilian and the French court to prevent these efforts bearing fruit.[209] Then Chiericati fell victim to Alexander's unexpected *rapprochement* with France and in October 1500 Perault replaced him, but as a cardinal-legate charged with the preaching of the Jubilee and the promotion of a crusade. The prediction made by the archbishop of Cologne five years earlier proved to be accurate: Perault continued to exert himself for peace between Louis XI and Maximilian, but only in order to advance his crusade project. From the start, Perault harboured no illusions about his position and prospects.[210] He had good grounds for assuming that the Pope had sent him largely as a public relations exercise, because he was well regarded at both the French and imperial courts. Alexander was at best duplicitous and at worst opposed to the very programme that he had set out, the realization of which would disturb the fragile balance of power that the Pope was intent on preserving while he advanced his family's interests.[211] The legate had given up talking about deposition, but in his discussions with the Venetian envoy, Contarini, he did not conceal his disgust with the moral behaviour of the Borgia court. He was also aware that as soon as he had started collecting money for the crusade he would have to watch out not just for Maximilian's attempts to secure it for other ends, but Alexander's too.

But however strong his feelings about the reigning Pope, Perault remained faithful to the papal office and its control over the crusade. Nothing, he wrote in 1503, could be initiated 'without the express consent of the High Pontiff, to whom alone it falls to make the final decision on the crusade'.[212] The very idea of excluding the

---

[207] Ibid. no 5014.   [208] Ibid. no 6287.
[209] e.g. ibid. nos 6583–4, 6606, 6684, 13519a.   [210] e.g. ibid. no 12528.
[211] e.g. ibid. no 12754, Alexander working behind Perault's back to maintain Franco-imperial friction, Dec. 1501.
[212] Mehring, 'Peraudi', 401–6, at 402.

Pope was nonsensical: 'No prince may take the cross or have the crusade preached against the Turks without papal authority, because that would be regarded as ridiculous, impeding the crusade rather than promoting it.'[213] So his criticism remained internal, like that of his fellow enthusiast, Stefano Taleazzi, who a few years later criticized Julius II for his failure to prioritize the crusade.[214]

It is likely that the papal *curia* regarded even Perault's activities in 1495–8 as mere irritation compared with external challenges, above all those that emanated from rulers. It makes sense to begin with the one that might appear to have posed the greatest danger, since it posited a thoroughgoing alternative to papal control over the crusade. This was George Podiebrad's proposal for a European assembly (*congregacio*) meeting in permanent session with the twofold aim of maintaining international peace and managing the military response to the Ottomans.[215] The idea arose from the king's eclectic and far-reaching ambitions, most of which dovetailed with the crusade against the Turks. In 1461, when Podiebrad had designs on the Holy Roman Empire, he was still working within an orthodox crusading framework: his adviser, Martin Mair, advanced a programme of peace and crusade that envisaged Podiebrad taking the cross.[216] But on 31 March 1462 Pius II abrogated the Compacts of Basel, the 1436 compromise that had brought the Hussite wars to an end. Conflict between Rome and Prague was now inevitable and, in his search for allies, Podiebrad switched to an anti-papal strategy.

Its first stage was a *memorandum... ad procedendum magnanime contra Turcum* that was presented to the kings of Bohemia and Poland at Głogów (Glogau) in May 1462. This was the creation of Antoine Marini of Grenoble, an inventor, economist, entrepreneur, and publicist in Podiebrad's service. Marini's memorandum was a clever attempt to subvert papal authority in the field of activity that lay closest to Pius II's heart, the crusade against the Turks. The text is rambling and repetitive, a curious synthesis of scholastic exposition and practical detail. The threat posed by Sultan Mehmed, Marini asserted, could be resolved in one of three ways: Turkish triumph, the restoration of papal and imperial power, or cooperation amongst Christendom's princes. The first was unacceptable and the second impracticable, so he intended to show how the third could be brought about. The answer was not a general council, which would take too long and was too cumbersome. Instead he advocated a league or fraternity to be formed by Bohemia, Poland,

---

[213] 'Non liceat alicui principi accipere crucem neque facere publicari cruciatam contra thurcos sine auctoritate pontificis cum aliter facere ridiculosum videatur esse: cum hoc potius sit ad impediendum dictae cruciatae quam ad prosequendum': Biblioteca Apostolica Vaticana, Palat IV. 1229 (5), printed open letter (n.d.), at 13. In both of these statements Perault was fending off an imperial initiative, but this does not detract from his essential stance on the issue.

[214] Bernardino Feliciangeli, 'Le proposte per la guerra contro i Turchi presentate da Stefano Taleazzi vescovo di Torcello a papa Alessandro VI', *Archivio della R. Società Romana di storia patria*, 40 (1917), 5–63, at 25 note 1.

[215] For the context see Frederick G. Heymann, *George of Bohemia: King of Heretics* (Princeton, 1965).

[216] Hermann Markgraf, 'Ueber Georgs von Podiebrad Project eines christlichen Fürstenbundes zur Vertreibung der Türken aus Europa und Herstellung des allgemeinen Friedens innerhalb der Christenheit', *Historische Zeitschrift*, 21 (1869), 245–304, at 262–3.

France, Burgundy, and Venice, building on a recent French offer to provide 40,000 foot and 30,000 horse; Hungary would of course also be involved. The army would be funded by a clerical tenth and a lay subsidy of one day's income, and Pope and emperor were assigned a number of auxiliary roles in the enterprise. The next step was to convene a meeting at Venice of the various allies, and Marini was handed the difficult task of selling this idea to the Venetians. Unsurprisingly, they adopted a 'wait and see' attitude.[217]

In the summer of 1463 there appeared the anonymous and better-known *Tractatus pacis toti christianitati fiendae* ('A tract for making peace throughout Christendom'); its principal author was again Marini, though he may have incorporated the views or editorial advice of others. The *Tractatus pacis* achieved wider diffusion than the 1462 text and it is a more coherent and integrated document. Marini's proposed league of princes was superseded by a *convencionem, caritatem et fraternitatem*, the institutional format of which would be an assembly (*congregacio*) made up of envoys representing the constitutive states. Voting rights within this assembly would be divided between France, Germany, Italy, and Iberia. The assembly's powers and influence made up the proposal's most iconoclastic political features, because states would in effect surrender their sovereignty to it. The assembly would have its own coat of arms, seal, treasury, archives, and administrative cadres. Funding for both peace-enforcement and campaigning against the Turks would come from a clerical tenth and a lay subsidy, a full tenth of the incoming money being set aside for the assembly's running costs. It would initially gather at Basel early in 1464, and would then be itinerant on a five-year cycle. The emperor no longer had any part to play and the Pope's role was reduced to enforcing the tenth, compelling belligerent bishops to make peace, and coordinating an Italian contribution towards the campaign's naval operations.[218] The proposal thus advocated the most fundamental reorganization of European government since the fall of Rome. As an approach to the Turkish threat it was no less radical, because the crusade was almost entirely expunged: it was the assembly that would settle all the practical issues thrown up by a campaign against the Turks, and there was no reference to the preaching of the cross, indulgences or other specified spiritual benefits. The only residue of traditional crusading was a reference to scripture testifying that those who assisted the faith would be rewarded after their death, while those who refused to do so would be aligning themselves with the 'enemies of the cross of Christ'. This was a military response that sprang from Hussite religious thinking rather than from traditional Catholicism, though the reference to refusal to cooperate carrying a spiritual price echoed similar assertions that we have seen the papal *curia* making, while the funding mechanisms proposed are distinctly resonant of those adopted at Mantua four years previously. As for the package of governmental ideas,

---

[217] Šmahel, 'Antoine Marini', 205–31.
[218] 'Tractatus pacis toti Christianitati fiendae', ed. Jiří Kejř in *The Universal Peace Organization of King George of Bohemia: A Fifteenth Century Plan for World Peace 1462/1464* (London, 1964), 71–80, English tr. 83–92; Jiří Kejř, 'Manuscrits, éditions et traductions du projet', in Václav Vaněček, ed., *Cultus pacis* (Prague, 1966), 75–82.

they are redolent of the endless and largely unproductive discussions that took place in Germany over the reform of imperial affairs.[219]

The programme set out in the *Tractatus pacis* commanded too little support to gain much traction. Venice and Hungary were not prepared to exchange a Pope who was wholeheartedly committed to a crusade for the distant and dubious prospects held out by this proposal. Neither was Burgundy, which in any case was locked in dispute with Podiebrad over Luxembourg. In fact the most substantial outcome was the impetus that Podiebrad's scheming gave to the network of military alliances that formed between these three powers in the second half of 1463, though as usual the major motor behind this was Ottoman successes and plans. The *Tractatus pacis* did assist in giving concrete form to the creation of a Franco-Bohemian axis, in the alliance between Podiebrad and Louis XI, the terms of which were agreed at Dieppe in June 1464. This alliance may have been the Czech king's main goal from the start, though he was unable to resist the siren call of much grander projects, including Constantinople. Certainly the Podiebradian proposal enjoyed its warmest welcome at Louis XI's court, where discontent with Pius II was riding high thanks to his unwavering support for the Aragonese at Naples. But even for the French, Podiebrad's idea was in essence a useful bogeyman to wave before Pius to try to make him yield on Naples. They were equally attracted by the more conservative idea of a general council that would meet, preferably at Lyons, and would impeach Pius for his failure to advance the crusade.[220] Podiebrad's scheming was dealt with by a citation to appear before the *curia*, appropriately issued on the eve of Pius's departure for Ancona in 1464. But the French threats pursued the Pope across Italy.[221]

Twentieth-century historians were fascinated by Podiebrad's proposal on the grounds of its apparent modernity, and it continues to attract attention, partly due to the human interest of a diary kept by a squire called Jaroslav who accompanied the Bohemian embassy to Louis's court in 1464. In Jaroslav's diary, Marini's animosity towards Pius, which he largely managed to conceal in the two texts that he wrote or helped to write, becomes apparent.[222] In the realm of ideas the assembly proposal is certainly intriguing, but it posed much less of a threat to the *curia* than more modest proposals to revive a general council. It was inconceivable that rulers would agree to pool sovereignty in the manner advocated in the *Tractatus pacis* and, in any case, the taint of heretical association hung over anything that emanated from Prague. That much is clear from what Jaroslav overheard of the discussions between Louis's councillors and Podiebrad's envoys.[223] Conciliarism, on the

---

[219] Thomas A. Brady, *German Histories in the Age of Reformations, 1400–1650* (Cambridge, 2009), pt 2.

[220] *Ungedruckte Akten*, 282–6, no 188, at 285.

[221] *Ungedruckte Akten*, 296–303, no 193, at 300. Despite its age, the key study remains Markgraf, 'Ueber Georgs von Podiebrad Project'.

[222] *Diary of an Embassy from King George of Bohemia to King Louis XI. of France in 1464*, ed. and tr. A. H. Wratislaw (London, 1871); Nejedlý, 'Promouvoir une alliance', 163–84.

[223] Nejedlý, 'Promouvoir une alliance', 172–3; Markgraf, 'Ueber Georgs von Podiebrad Project', 299–300.

other hand, presented a prospect that was less radical in its implications for secular government while bringing with it the popular appeal of reform in head and members.[224] The threat of a general council was a recurrent theme during Pius II's reign; as Baldi pointed out, even the congress of Mantua, on the face of it a clear expression of papal authority ('an anti-council'), could have mutated into a general council if the Pope's opponents, given this opportunity to assemble, had succeeded in presenting a common front; hence Pius's anxiety throughout the congress to drive its business forward in order to maintain control.[225] The Pope's anti-conciliar decree, *Execrabilis*, should be considered as part of the crusading package proclaimed at the congress's close, just as his citation of Podiebrad should be aligned with the group of measures that consolidated the revised crusade programme of 1463–4.[226] The danger always lay in a coalition of enemies, and the Franco-Bohemian one that formed in 1463–4 was not the first aimed against Pius: in 1460–1 his robust support for Ferrante infuriated France at a point when there were perilous currents of animosity in the empire focused on the archbishop-elector of Mainz, Dieter von Isenburg, and Sigismund, duke of Tyrol, assisted by the vociferous polemicist Gregor Heimburg.[227] In March 1462, in a famous *tour d'horizon* of the European political scene delivered during a meeting with Sforza's envoy, Ottone del Carretto, the Pope bleakly predicted a schism caused by a French alliance with dissident cardinals.[228]

After Pius's death the next major occasion on which the French threatened a general council in conjunction with a crusade was in 1494, when the idea was embedded in Charles VIII's November manifesto. Just as thirty years earlier, the suggestion got nowhere due to its obvious association with French claims on Naples, but it became more credible when events in the late 1490s made the need for a crusade imperative. By that point, however, Alexander VI had carried out his diplomatic volte-face, which enabled him to accept France as a crusading ally and, even, in June 1500, to concede Louis XII the dominant role that he sought.[229]

Maximilian worked more closely and harmoniously with Alexander on the crusade than Louis XII did, but in the *societas sancti Georgii* he created a chivalric vehicle that acted as an ongoing reference point for his crusading aspirations. Unlike Podiebrad's European assembly, or the recurrent French threat of a general council of the Church, the *societas sancti Georgii* did not represent a formal challenge to the papal position. But its hybrid and shifting character, which reflected its sponsor's notoriously fickle mindset, did show how crusading could be customized to different environments, and this makes it a revealing topic with which to close this discussion of centrifugal tendencies. The *societas* was an offshoot of Frederick III's Order of St George. He founded this in 1466/8 on the model of the Teutonic

---

[224] Generally see Aldo Landi, *Concilio e papato nel Rinascimento (1449–1516): Un problema irrisolto* (Turin, 1997).
[225] Baldi, *Pio II*, 162. [226] Ibid. 170, 252.
[227] Ibid. 189–91. [228] Ibid. 204–10, and see 214–15 for further French threats in 1462.
[229] Sanuto, *I diarii*, 3.435–8 (= *AR*, no 14160).

Knights, but it failed to make much headway.[230] The knightly order or fraternity of St George that Maximilian first created in 1493–4 made more impact, though not as much as he hoped. The privileges bestowed on its members by Alexander VI in April 1494 included indulgences that culminated with a plenary remission of sins as the reward for a year's service against the Turks.[231] At Antwerp in October 1494, consciously imitating the famed Burgundian Order of the Golden Fleece, Maximilian established a hierarchy of *milites coronati* ('crowned knights') and participant commoners. All stood to benefit from provisions that were clearly modelled on long-established crusading privileges, in particular substitution and a debt moratorium.[232] So this was a crusading fraternity. Indeed some of the language used by contemporaries about it implies that its members took the cross: thus in January 1495 Maximilian was described as having received (*suscepit*) the *insignia cruciate et ordinem* in connection with his interest in accompanying Charles VIII on his crusade.[233] The phrase is a cryptic one. Probably the best interpretation to put on it is that Maximilian donned the confraternity's tunic, emblazoned with the cross, as a sign of a personal but unspecified commitment to crusade: his intention of setting out in the company of his political archrival was questionable to say the least.

It is probable that in his more visionary moments Maximilian hoped that the *societas sancti Georgii* could become a genuine fighting force that would serve his purposes in Italy and the Balkans, thereby making up for the empire's notorious military shortcomings.[234] At Antwerp in the autumn of 1494 processions and printing were deployed to make an impact that was at once local and international. Maximilian's aspiration was that volunteers from the empire and abroad would flock to enjoy the papal and royal privileges showered on his fraternity, and to bask in the renown of fighting alongside Christendom's greatest knight against the enemies of the faith.[235] But the fraternity seems also to have served a purpose in terms of public relations, demonstrating to domestic and international opinion alike that Maximilian was serious about the crusade.[236] We shall see that this was certainly the case at the diet of Worms in 1495 and in his clash with Perault about the fate of indulgence proceeds in 1503. The point is that securing the papal concessions of 1494 for his fraternity enabled Maximilian to flag up his crusading intentions

---

[230] Heinrich Koller, 'Der St. Georgs-Ritterorden Kaiser Friedrichs III.', in Josef Fleckenstein and Manfred Hellmann, eds, *Die geistlichen Ritterorden Europas* (Sigmaringen, 1980), 417–29; Josef Plösch, 'Der St. Georgsritterorden und Maximilians I. Türkenpläne von 1493/94', in Helmut J. Mezler-Andelberg, ed., *Festschrift Karl Eder zum siebzigsten Geburtstag* (Innsbruck, 1959), 33–56, at 40; Holger Kruse, Werner Paravicini and Andreas Ranft, eds, *Ritterorden und Adelsgesellschaften im spätmittelalterlichen Deutschland. Ein systematisches Verzeichnis* (Frankfurt a.-M., 1991), 407–16.
[231] Plösch, 'Der St. Georgsritterorden', 46.   [232] Ibid. 51–2.
[233] AR, no 3230 and see no 1273 for the proposal to work with Charles VIII.
[234] It is striking that Maximilian chose St George's feast day (23 April) as the muster date both for an international crusade in 1493 and for regional defensive measures two years later: *Deutsche Reichstagsakten unter Maximilian I. Fünfter Band. Reichstag zu Worms 1495*, ed. Heinz Angermeier, 3 vols in 2 pts, Deutsche Reichstagsakten, mittlere Reihe, 5 (Göttingen, 1981), 89–99 at 94, 315–16.
[235] Plösch, 'Der St. Georgsritterorden', 52–3.
[236] Inge Wiesflecker-Friedhuber, 'Maximilian I. und der St. Georgs-Ritterorden. Zur Frage seiner Ordenszugehörigkeit', *Forschungen zur Landes- und Kirchengeschichte. Festschrift Helmut J. Mezler-Andelberg zum 65. Geburtstag* (Graz, 1988), 543–54, traces the later history of the fraternity.

when it was politically useful to do so, without needing constantly to defer to the Pope. Rome was thus cut out of the circuit, but this was a minor excision compared with the savage surgery proposed by Podiebrad in his scheme of 1463–4 for a European crusading *congregacio*. For Maximilian, as for his father's great enemy Matthias and even (had their crusade plans advanced thus far) for the kings of France, a major challenge to papal control over the crusade would have been counterproductive, in addition to generating a good deal of collateral damage. The point was not to dismantle the system but to subject it to enough pressure to make it operate as fully as possible to their advantage. In future chapters we shall encounter many examples of how they tried to do this, together with a papal response that varied considerably in effectiveness.

3
Strategy, mobilization, and control

In this chapter we move from ideological constructs to practical issues. The policies pursued by the papal *curia* will be crucial but, as we would expect from the challenges presented to those policies, they were subject to a constant process of accommodation and compromise necessitated by the political realities of the day.

3.1 STRATEGIC PERCEPTIONS AND PLANNING

In 1502, in a *Libellus de modo belli Turcis ingerendi* that is notable for its detail, the Croatian humanist, Felix Pentancius (Feliks Petančić, c. 1455–post 1517) advised King Wladislas II on the routes that an army operating from Hungary could take to strike at Ottoman power.[1] Pentancius referred to three. The first was the route that had been followed since Roman times: from Belgrade through Nish, Sofia, and Philippopolis to Adrianople (Edirne). What made this renowned route so attractive was its avoidance of mountain ranges and the fact that for much of its length it followed rivers: the South or Južna Morava from Smederevo to Nish, and the Maritsa from south of Sofia to Adrianople. This facilitated movement and guaranteed fresh water. Pentancius's second route favoured attacking the Turkish bases in the western Balkans, running southwards to Kosovo, and from there via Priština to Skopje. And his third route took the army eastwards via Transylvania to Varna on the Black Sea coast. Two features of Pentancius's *Libellus* are striking. The first is his awareness of the place that these routes and locations occupied in crusading history. The first, classic route had been followed by Godfrey of Bouillon four hundred years earlier on the First Crusade. The plain of Kosovo was the scene of many battles, including 'that ill-omened, accursed, and never to be forgotten massacre' in 1448 when Janos Hunyadi suffered his worst defeat. The third route brought to mind the conflicts waged by Vlad Dracul and Stephen of Moldavia, and the disastrous battle of Varna in 1444. The second feature is Pentancius's insistence on a coordinated and sustained offensive. If the Turks were to be expelled from Europe and the prospect secured of lasting peace, there was no point in fighting them on the frontiers. Rather than waiting for the Turks to invade their

---

[1] Much of the text in this and the following four paragraphs is drawn from my paper 'Crusading and the Danube', in Alexandru Simon, ed., *The Danube in the Middle Ages* (New York, 2012), 117–39, which explores in greater detail the range of strategic considerations thrown up by the religious confrontation in the Balkans.

homeland, the Italians should launch an attack on Epiros or Macedonia at the same time that the Hungarians struck south. Pentancius urged his readers to remember the examples of antiquity: Alexander the Great had overcome Darius in Asia, Xerxes had taken the war to the Athenians, Hannibal had invaded Italy, and Julius Caesar was famed for the speed and violence of his offensives. But they should look too at the career of Hunyadi. Constantly he had taken the war to the enemy rather than waiting for them to attack.[2]

Pentancius's formula of waging a defensive war through a series of powerful and coordinated attacks carried out in accordance with an agreed strategic plan was far from original: by the time he wrote, it had effectively become a commonplace in crusade planning.[3] The importance of *antemurale* thinking in juridical and political terms, and the key role allotted to the network of fortresses that protected Hungary's southern flank,[4] should not lead us to infer the prevalence of a Maginot Line mentality. That thinking was aimed at persuading states located in Christendom's interior to contribute; what was planned once they *had* agreed to take action was largely aggressive. Pentancius was correct to point to Hunyadi as a leading exponent of offensive warfare. We shall see that Hunyadi's response to Mehmed's threat to Hungary in 1455 was to advocate an offensive that would probably have taken Pentancius's first route, much of which the *vaivode* had already followed on his devastating Long March of 1443.[5] Giovanni da Capistrano called for such an offensive after his defensive victory at Belgrade a year later, when an army of crusaders was available (and, given plague and food shortages, was calling out for deployment) while the Turks were in disarray.[6] Hunyadi's belief in the value of the offensive was inherited by his son Matthias. In March 1462 he informed the Venetians that while 60,000 soldiers would be needed to fight the Turks, they would only require pay for six months; after that the war would pay for itself ('the soldiers would supply themselves from the war').[7] There is no doubting Matthias's skill in depicting his long periods of inactivity as a fabian strategy of containment. But his longest and most exultant reports to the *curia* gloried in the terrain covered by offensive campaigns, the sacrifices involved, and the cumulative damage that his troops had inflicted on the Turks.[8]

This last point was crucial. A major logistical selling point for offensive warfare was that the plunder acquired would relieve some of the burdensome financial costs of crusading; this argument gained strength from the fact that (so at least cardinals lobbying for the crusade argued in 1464) Hungarian combatants expected better rates of pay if they were serving at a distance from the kingdom, for

---

[2] *Annales regum Hungariae*, ed. Georg Pray, 5 vols (Vienna, 1764–70), 4.299–303. For Pentancius see Michael B. Petrovich, 'The Croatian Humanists and the Ottoman Peril', *Balkan Studies*, 20 (1979), 257–73, at 262–3.

[3] e.g. the Venetian approach at Mantua, which rested on hitting the Turks in Serbia, Albania, and the Straits: Picotti, *La dieta*, 446–9, no 23.

[4] Ferenc Szakály, 'The Hungarian-Croatian Border Defense System and its Collapse', in *FHR*, 141–58.

[5] *AM*, 12.292–4.   [6] *AS Oct*, 383–4.   [7] *MDE*, 1.125–8, no 80, at 125–6.

[8] *MKL*, 354–8, no 245, 449–51, no 303, are excellent examples.

example in Greece or Bulgaria.[9] Hunyadi was particularly bullish about self-funding campaigns: when attempting to woo Alfonso of Aragon for the Hungarian crown in 1447 he even claimed that the entirety of the costs incurred in campaigning against the Turks could be recouped from conquests made.[10] It was also widely believed that the Turks could not sustain their forces for long without the fuel of Christian plunder. In the last chapter we witnessed John Bessarion arguing that keeping a campaign going for a whole year would cripple the sultan's finances, because he did not possess sufficient revenues to pay his cavalry. These men were equipped and paid from income that had been assigned to them in the provinces where they resided, and that funding only covered four months' military service.[11] So as time passed the Christians would inexorably grow stronger and the Turks weaker.

There was therefore a broad consensus on what needed to be done and it led commentators in the direction of planning on a large scale. It is tempting to think that in the early 1530s François Rabelais was satirizing some of the more eccentric products of this planning in the first book of *Gargantua*, when he has King Picrochole's advisers outline a programme of ever more extensive military conquests that eventually come to comprise almost all of Europe and the Middle East. 'Shan't we kill all these dogs of Turks and Mohammedans?' asks Picrochole. ' "What the devil else shall we do with them?" they asked. "And we'll give their goods and lands to those who have served you faithfully." ' Their bubble is burst by a veteran captain who comments that it is nothing but day-dreaming.[12] What is certain is that the grand plans couched by Philip of Mézières in the late fourteenth century resurfaced with a vengeance a century later.[13] They were spawned in large numbers by the excitable and volatile diplomatic atmosphere of the 1490s and early 1500s, and the crusading proposals of Maximilian in particular have a Picrocholesque air about them. In January 1494, for example, Maximilian outlined his hopes to the Venetian envoys at Vienna. He proposed combining his substantial field army with Dalmatian irregulars (*uskoks*) to seize an unnamed but important Turkish fortress in the Adriatic; while this was happening, the Venetians would stop the Turkish fleet from intervening. To the horror of the envoys, for whom confidentiality was second nature, the emperor-elect called for a map and, with ten or more of his advisers present, outlined his ideas. Tactfully, the Venetians reported home that the whole proposal was less thoroughly thought-out than it needed to be.[14] A few days

---

[9] Mureşan, 'La croisade', forthcoming, annexe. See János M. Bak, 'The Price of War and Peace in Late Medieval Hungary', in Brian Patrick McGuire, ed., *War and Peace in the Middle Ages* (Copenhagen, 1987), 161–78, at 168–9, for restrictions on compulsory military service for the defence of the realm.

[10] Ryder, *Alfonso*, 300.

[11] *PG*, 161.667.

[12] François Rabelais, *Gargantua and Pantagruel*, bk 1, ch. 33, tr. J.M. Cohen (London 1955), 112. See Petrovich, 'Croatian Humanists', 268–9, for a real project dated 1545 for carving up the Ottoman empire that closely resembles the one suggested to Picrochole.

[13] See most recently Philippe de Mézières, *Une Epistre lamentable et consolatoire*, ed. Philippe Contamine and Jacques Paviot (Paris, 2008).

[14] *AR*, no 318.

later Maximilian again received the envoys. With a map before him on the table, he returned to the subject of the Turks and, this time, he was in more expansive mode. There was urgent need to support Hungary, he proclaimed, because the Turks had an army ready to march on Belgrade and another in reserve in Wallachia. If Portugal, Spain, Naples, and Venice would agree to provide naval support, Maximilian proposed besieging the lynchpin Bosnian stronghold of Jajce, which he evidently thought had fallen following the Croatian disasters of 1493. He would then march southwards through Albania, seize Durazzo and Valona, raid as far as Adrianople, and return to Thessalonica, where he would pick up supplies from the fleet. Needless to say, the Venetians saw numerous problems with the plan.[15]

In January 1502 Zaccaria Contarini, one of the envoys in 1494, again became the recipient of Maximilian's opinions on the best way to fight the Turks. Venice was now at war with the sultan and therefore more receptive to Maximilian's ideas, though probably not much more confident that anything would actually happen. Again maps were spread out. They showed Greece, the Danube basin, Europe from Germany to Constantinople, Anatolia, and the Mediterranean ports; clearly there was no shortfall in the geographical information that lay behind these discussions. Maximilian criticized the decision made by the Venetians and their French and Spanish allies to attack Lesbos. The island was too close to Constantinople for the Turks to allow it to be occupied by their enemies. Strategically, it would have been wiser to recapture one of the Peloponnesian ports, perhaps Modon. No doubt these negative comments from a bystander grated on the ears of the envoys, and Contarini tried to bring the discussion around to the pressing problem of the Turkish army that was massing at Valona, and the threat posed to Venetian strongholds in the Adriatic, such as Zadar. Maximilian was more concerned about threats to Hungary; he regarded his own lands as protected from a large Turkish army by the mountainous terrain, which posed insuperable logistical problems. This was misguided complacency, but when Contarini reminded Maximilian of recent Turkish attacks on Venetian Friuli, which enjoyed the same advantage, Maximilian dismissed the success of that raid as the result of Venetian incompetence.[16] Like their predecessors eight years earlier, the 1502 discussions showed that Maximilian was both interested in and well informed about the strategic scenario in the southern Balkans and eastern Mediterranean. In 1494 he was bursting with ideas for intervention, but in 1502, sidelined and irritated by Venetian cooperation with France and Spain, he was content to watch and carp; though his plans for getting his hands on Raymond Perault's indulgence money, and Venice's desperate hopes for an alliance with him, would shortly generate a call to arms issued with the ostensible intention of fighting the Turks.[17]

---

[15] *AR*, no 359, and cf no 369 for the political background to these ideas. For context see Hermann Wiesflecker, *Kaiser Maximilian I. Das Reich, Österreich und Europa an der Wende zur Neuzeit*, 5 vols (Munich and Vienna, 1971–86), 1.355–62, and for Maximilian's fondness for maps id., *Maximilian I. Die Fundamente des habsburgischen Weltreiches* (Vienna and Munich, 1991), 322.
[16] *AR*, no 15862.   [17] *AR*, no 15961.

From Calixtus III's reign onwards the papal *curia* adhered to the general strategic approach of maximizing and diversifying the offensive thrust against the Turks, at least in those periods when its overall policy was prioritizing the Ottoman threat. We shall later observe how this fed through into the process of mobilization, but in the meantime two examples, from 1464 and 1500, will serve to illustrate the permutations that could result from the same strategic template. The 1464 plan was generated in the aftermath of Pius II's death by the group of cardinals who wanted to carry forward the dead Pope's policy. The major thrust would come from the Hungarians who would make use of their own troops supplemented by 20,000 paid fighters from Germany, Poland, and Bohemia. There would be auxiliary operations in Albania and the Peloponnese, plus action by the sultan's principal enemies in the east, Uzun Hasan and the 'Grand Karaman' in Anatolia.[18] Thirty-six years later a programme set out by Pope Alexander VI envisaged three armies. As in 1464, the most important force, 'the pre-eminent and indispensable foundation for the whole expedition', would be Hungarian: others could only be expected to follow once the Hungarians had taken the lead, assisted by the Poles and Wallachians. The second army would be commanded by Maximilian, while a third would proceed east by sea on ships provided by Spain and Venice.[19] The relatively straightforward character of Alexander's 1500 programme, which, as Kenneth Setton observed, looks like the recycling of a 1490 project, reflected the deterioration of the Christian position since 1464: nothing could be expected now in Greece or Albania, both of which were under Ottoman control, while the hopes that had been held of Moldavia in Sixtus IV's reign had proved fruitless. Tacitly, it was agreed to keep the armies widely separated, to facilitate supply and avoid bickering over spoils.[20]

As the 1500 plan shows, it was axiomatic that the attacks on the sultanate should take place by sea as well as by land.[21] This would inject an element of surprise, make it more difficult for the Turks to manage their overall predicament, and bring to bear the might of Christian powers which could not easily reach the land frontier with the Turks; in this case, France and Spain. The problems of coordination that this created were enormous, but before they could be considered there was the question of where the fleet would originate. We saw in the last chapter that the deployment of Venetian naval power was the greatest advantage that resulted from Venice being dragged into war with the Turks. The other considerable Mediterranean naval power that was threatened by Ottoman ambitions was the kingdom of Naples, but, as Alan Ryder showed, when it was at its height under Alfonso the Magnanimous, royal policy was only marginally interested in engaging with the Turks. Alfonso's main interests lay elsewhere and his failure to keep any of his crusading promises proved to be one of the greatest disappointments in the years that

---

[18] Mureşan, 'La croisade', annexe.
[19] *VMP,* 2.269–76, no 297, a detailed brief given to Pietro Isvalies, November 1500.
[20] Setton, *Papacy,* 2.414–16, 531–2.
[21] e.g. *Monumenta historica Boemiae,* ed. Gelasius Dobner, 6 vols (Prague, 1764–85), 2.415–17; Picotti, *La dieta,* 446–9, no 23.

immediately followed the fall of Constantinople.[22] Paradoxically, his much weaker successor, Ferrante, contributed more, sending seventeen galleys eastwards in 1472.[23]

What has not been fully appreciated, although it has been described by historians including Ludwig Pastor and Setton, is the extent and significance of the papal *curia*'s investment in naval warfare. Arguably, this was the most important contribution that the Renaissance Popes made towards the anti-Turkish war; it was certainly the most practical one. Unable to rely on the assistance of the Genoese or Venetians, Calixtus III made an intense financial and administrative effort to raise war galleys in 1455–7. It included the creation of an arsenal (*fabrica galearum*) on the banks of the Tiber in Rome whose activities are richly documented.[24] The galleys constructed in Rome, together with others that the Pope hired, and a couple grudgingly supplied by Alfonso of Naples, enabled Cardinal Lodovico Trevisan to carry out desultory operations in the eastern Mediterranean in 1457. Writing to Juan Carvajal in November, Calixtus implicitly compared Trevisan's victory at Mytilene in August with Capistrano's success at Belgrade the previous year, possibly in an attempt to justify his financial outlay.[25] Alarmed perhaps by the costs of Calixtus's investment, or because he was unimpressed by what Trevisan had achieved, or simply because he regarded continental campaigning as more worthwhile, Pius II allowed the *fabrica galearum* to rot and instead relied on ships hired from or contributed by others.[26] It was ironic that chivvying the Italians into providing naval support was one of the few jobs that were allocated to the Pope in Marini's *Tractatus* of 1463.[27] But a more active contribution towards naval warfare was revived by Sixtus IV and Alexander VI. For all their failings, they did sink large sums of money into the conduct of war at sea (144,000 ducats in Sixtus's case), making the best use of Venice's belligerent status.[28]

No less axiomatic was the idea of making use of the services of third parties in association with crusading efforts. Some of these proposals lacked realism. A suggestion that the Tatars of the Golden Horde could be hired to fight the Turks, a variation on the 'let dog fight dog' *topos* that went back to the early 1200s, was voiced by the Poles in 1454: unsurprisingly they suggested that the money required

---

[22] See Alan Ryder, 'The Eastern Policy of Alfonso the Magnanimous', *Atti della Accademia Pontaniana* (1979), 7–25; id., *Alfonso*, 290–305.

[23] Imber, *Ottoman Empire*, 209.

[24] Ivana Ait, 'Un aspetto del salariato a Roma nel XV secolo: La *fabrica galearum* sulle rive del Tevere (1457–58)', in *Cultura e società nell'Italia medievale: Studi per Paolo Brezzi*, Istituto storico italiano per il Medio Evo, studi storici, fasc. 184–7, vol. 1 (Roma, 1988), 7–25; Weber, *Lutter*, 2.1.1; Setton, *Papacy*, 2.170–1.

[25] *DS*, 421–3, no 1272, at 422, where the language used is reminiscent of Belgrade: '...pauci et hi inermes et terrore hostium consternati innumerabilis multitudinis non modo impetum sustinuerunt sed victores cum summa gloria hostem...repulerunt'. See also Setton, *Papacy*, 2.188–9.

[26] Weber, *Lutter*, 2.1.1.   [27] 'Tractatus pacis', 79, clause 21.

[28] Setton, *Papacy*, 2.316–18, 533. Alexander's contribution towards the 1502 campaign was immortalized by Titian in his *Madonna di Ca' Pesaro*, commissioned by the papal commander Jacopo Pesaro.

should come from Rome.[29] Two years later Calixtus III, whose strategic vision was nothing if not broad, revived an even more venerable dream, that of Ethiopian assistance; the stick was the danger of a Mamluk-Ottoman alliance, the carrot the possibility of recovering Jerusalem.[30] The traffic in such proposals could be two-way: in 1496 Alexander VI had to field an overture from the king of the Georgians, whose envoy had visited Rome with the offer of an alliance 'to be prepared on all sides against those who have rebelled against the faith of Jesus Christ'; tactfully, the Pope replied that warfare within Christendom had to be dealt with first.[31] The most promising alliance, if it could have been engineered, would have been with the Mamluk sultanate. By 1490 the Mamluks were becoming concerned about the encroachments of Ottoman conquests and they welcomed overtures from the Christian West. In April 1494 Maximilian was eager to pursue an alliance with Cairo and set out detailed plans for its negotiation.[32] But as disappointing papal negotiations with Muscovy had already shown, the more distant the power involved was, the more difficult it usually proved to make concrete progress with these approaches. Added to which, the behaviour and trustworthiness of those charged with developing far-flung contacts were sometimes questionable. Above all, this applies to Lodovico Severi 'da Bologna', a Franciscan who wove in and out of papal policy from the mid-1450s through to the late 1470s. It was Severi who acted as Calixtus III's messenger to Ethiopia in 1456, and subsequent journeys took him as far as the Crimea in the north and Tabriz to the east. Almost certainly, Severi was to some degree a trickster, albeit one acting with good intentions rather than for personal gain. Weber has argued that assiduous travellers like Severi enabled the *curia* to give its crusading strategy a more solid geographical underpinning, but it came at the cost of much mis- and disinformation.[33] As Pius II—who came to regard Severi as a fraud—put it, the problem was that little of the data reported by such men could be verified.[34]

For obvious reasons, immediate neighbours of the Turks held out more realistic prospects for joint action than distant powers like Ethiopia or Georgia. Securing the support of Karaman, the biggest rival to the Ottomans in Anatolia, was an ongoing hope until that state was finally extinguished in 1472. But it was Uzun Hasan, the ruler of the White Sheep (Ak Koyonlu) Turcoman tribes of northern Iraq, whose lands stretched from Georgia to the Indian Ocean, who offered the best hopes of a Muslim who might combine with the Christians to launch an attack from two directions on the Ottoman state.[35] The Venetians actively pursued

---

[29] *AM*, 12.230–4, at 234. In 1238 the bishop of Winchester proposed that the Christians should remain neutral during the conflict between the Muslims and Tatars in the Holy Land: Matthew Paris, *Chronica maiora*, ed. H. R. Luard, 7 vols, Rolls Series, 57 (London, 1890), 3.489.

[30] *BF*, NS2.120–2, no 225.   [31] *VMP*, 2.258–9, no 287.

[32] *Vetera monumenta Slavorum meridionalium historiam illustrantia*, ed. Augustin Theiner, vol. 1 (Rome, 1863), 535–7, no 722 (= *Hungary as 'Propugnaculum'*, no 121; *AR*, no 571).

[33] The most recent treatment is Weber, *Lutter*, 1.2.2, who is better disposed towards Severi than Anthony Bryer, 'Ludovico da Bologna and the Georgian and Anatolian Embassy of 1460–1461', *Bedi Kartlisa*, 19–20 (1965), 178–98. See also Paviot, *Les ducs*, 265–70.

[34] *Pii II Commentarii*, bk 5, ch. 11, 321–4 (comment at 324).

[35] For context see H.R. Roemer, 'The Türkmen Dynasties', in *The Cambridge History of Iran, vol. 6: The Timurid and Safavid Periods*, ed. Peter Jackson and Laurence Lockhart (Cambridge, 1986), 147–88.

cooperation with Uzun Hasan during the first decade of their war of 1463–79: they had mutual interests, but, unlike the Hungarians, Uzun Hasan harboured no rival territorial claims. The republic built up strong diplomatic links with Uzun Hasan and attempted to supply him with war material including guns and munitions. Margaret Meserve has shown that for some years Uzun Hasan enjoyed something close to celebrity status in Italy; he was depicted as a 'good Muslim', ethnically Persian rather than Turkish, a virtuous and cultured ruler.[36] Whether for this reason or out of pragmatism, Sixtus IV raised no objections to an Islamic power being equipped with weaponry. But as an ally, Uzun Hasan proved to be a disappointment. The crisis came in 1472, when the fleet laboriously assembled in response to the fall of Negroponte operated in the East at the same time that an army commanded by Uzun Hasan's nephew invaded Anatolia from the east. Mehmed II feared for Constantinople itself. But the allied forces failed to coordinate effectively. As in 1457, the papal *curia* enjoyed a lacklustre return for its substantial investment in naval force, and in autumn 1472 Uzun Hasan inexplicably chose to attack the Mamluks in Syria. In August 1473 Mehmed defeated Uzun Hasan at Otlukbeli near Erzerum. The two Islamic powers made peace and, although Uzun Hasan maintained contacts with the West up to his death in 1478,[37] nothing came of them. For Venice, this set the seal on their loss of Euboea and effectively ended their hopes of winning the war.[38] In the case of both Karaman and Uzun Hasan, the mechanics of cooperation usually derived from the rulers of Venice, due to their realization that defeating the sultanate was impossible without the help of allies (whether Turcoman, Hungarian, or Moldavian) who could engage and destroy Mehmed's forces on land. But they were in full agreement with crusading theorists and enthusiasts like Pius II and the cardinals responsible for the 1464 proposal, who emphasized the advantages to be gained from mobilizing the sultanate's enemies in the East.[39]

An acceptable alternative to such external enemies was one who would undermine the sultanate's strength from within. Hopes for uprisings by subject Christian populations gradually faded in the face of experience: as Matthias Corvinus sceptically noted in December 1481, there was no sign of them at all.[40] But not long after Matthias wrote, an extraordinary opportunity of a different kind arose in the shape of the man to whom (notionally perhaps, given that he was only 12) Mehmed had entrusted the defence of Constantinople in 1472 when he took the field against Uzun Hasan. This was Djem Sultan, Mehmed's youngest son, who took refuge with the Knights of St John after being decisively defeated by his older brother in

---

[36] Meserve, *Empires*, 223–31.

[37] For differing views of Uzun Hasan in 1474 see Jacopo Ammannati Piccolomini, *Lettere (1444– 1479)*, ed. Paolo Cherubini, 3 vols, Pubblicazioni degli Archivi di Stato, Fonti XXV (Rome, 1997), 3.1858–9, no 745, at 1859; *MKL*, 1.300–1, no 213.

[38] For Uzun Hasan generally see Setton, *Papacy*, 2.315–21; Babinger, *Mehmed*, 302–27; Imber, *Ottoman Empire*, 192–217.

[39] e.g. *Pii II Commentarii*, bk 7, ch. 16, 460–3 (Karaman).

[40] *MKL*, 2.191–5, no 103, at 195. For no apparent reason, in 1500 Stefano Taleazzi still counted on the assistance of 40,000 inhabitants of Albania and Epiros, attracted 'solis armis et pane et benedictione': Feliciangeli, 'Le proposte', 52.

the struggle for succession in 1482. The grand master sent him to France and in 1489 he was handed over to Innocent VIII at Rome. The strategic thinking behind what Nicolas Vatin dubbed *la politique djemienne* of the succession of Christian powers who either held him in custody or hoped to do so varied considerably. Louis XI of France and Venice were wholly hands off; the first through lack of interest in crusading and the second (which just a few years earlier would have greeted Djem as a godsend) from fear of alienating Bayezid II. The Knights of St John were successful in using the threat that Djem posed to his brother's rule to extract lucrative payments and concessions from the sultan. For those who expressed aspirations towards the organization of a crusade, Djem came to form an important element in their strategy, the hope being that if he reappeared in Ottoman lands his supporters would flock to his banner, or at least that Bayezid would have to make provision for such a contingency. This was the case with Innocent VIII in 1490, Charles VIII in 1494, and Matthias on a number of occasions. Their optimism seemed to be corroborated by Bayezid's willingness to pay handsomely to keep his brother in safe custody, by a stream of attempts to get him assassinated, and, perhaps most tellingly, by the fact that the identification of Djem's corpse on arrival at Constantinople in 1499 (four years after his death) was quickly followed by Bayezid's war with Venice.[41]

Djem had predecessors, above all the *turchetto* ('little Turk') who was believed to be the brother of Mehmed II and was maintained in the West for four decades following his arrival at Rome in the company of Cardinal Isidore of Kiev in June 1456. In 1464 Pius II took him with him to Ancona to accompany his planned crusade, which implies hopes that he would prove useful in the Balkans. Paul II handed him over to Matthias in 1465 and the man thought it worthwhile staking his claim to the Ottoman throne when Mehmed died in 1481. But his prospects, already dubious, were overshadowed by Djem.[42] On the face of it, the strategy of incorporating Djem into an expedition was sound because his faction had been powerful. His father had appointed him governor of Karaman and he enjoyed the support of the Türkmen tribes of eastern Anatolia, which remained a notoriously unstable region even after Uzun Hasan's death. But Vatin has put forward arguments that weaken the thesis that Bayezid was terrified of his brother reappearing. Djem was only one factor behind Bayezid's relatively unaggressive approach towards the West in the 1480s, and he was still alive when Bayezid began pursuing a more hostile policy towards Hungary following Matthias's death in 1490. Djem acknowledged that his potential for seriously disturbing his brother's rule steadily waned as the 1480s proceeded. Nor would the fact that Djem's power base had been in Anatolia rather than Rumelia help in the case of a crusade launched from the West: the reverse applied to the ability of the Knights of St John to capitalize on Djem.

---

[41] See Nicolas Vatin, *Sultan Djem. Un prince ottoman dans l'Europe du XVe siècle* (Ankara, 1997), usefully summarized in his 'L'Affaire Djem (1481–1495)', in *Le Banquet du faisan*, ed. Marie-Therèse Caron and Denis Clauzel (Arras, 1997), 85–96. Setton, *Papacy*, 2.381–511 traces Djem's various interactions with crusading plans.

[42] See Weber, *Lutter*, 1.2.4.

The argument should not be taken too far in the reverse direction. It is plausible that Bayezid II was concerned when Djem was moved from France to Rome in 1489, given the historic association of the papal court with the promotion of crusades; this was something that Muslim rulers had never underrated. We need to distinguish between three things: the threat that Djem actually posed, genuine as opposed to rhetorical assessments of that threat at the western courts, and its effect on policy at Constantinople. In the case of all three, there is no way of avoiding a certain amount of hindsight and guesswork. One thing is certain: Djem's death emptied the stage of individuals who might, operating either externally or internally, assist the work of a crusade. The resulting situation was brutally summarized by Perault in the *tour d'horizon* that he laid out before the *Reichsregiment* in July 1501. The Turks had no enemies in the East. The Tatars of the Golden Horde provided them with paid troops; Karaman had been extinguished; nothing more was heard of the progeny of Uzun Hasan; the Mamluks were too terrified to be pulled into war with the Ottomans. Even if there was a potential ally east of Greece, communicating with them would be difficult now that the Turks controlled the sea ways of the eastern Mediterranean. Christian Europe would have to attend to its own defence.[43]

3.2 THE PAPAL *CURIA*: MEMORY AND METHODS

For initiatives, contemporaries looked towards Rome, some altruistically, others for the sake of appearances, in a spirit of criticism, or with malicious intent. As it had done since Innocent III's reign, the *curia* eagerly gathered information about the Turks and how best to combat them. It was Nicholas V or his commission of crusade cardinals who commissioned Lampo Birago to compile his comprehensive *Strategicon* in 1454,[44] and Croatian humanists like Felix Pentancius found the Roman *curia* among the most receptive audiences for the information that they brought westwards.[45] How the *curia* then proceeded was subject to myriad political contingencies, just like every other policy that it formulated. For that reason, any generalization about its promotion of crusading is inherently flawed, whether it is one that accepts at face value the programmatic couching of papal statements,[46] or one that takes for granted an unstated ambition to regain political ground that had been lost during the Great Schism and conciliar period.[47] If external pressures

---

[43] Kraus, *Reichsregiment*, 226–35, at 229.
[44] Damian is preparing an edition of the full text in which the vexed issue of its origins will be addressed.
[45] Petrovich, 'Croatian Humanists', *passim*.
[46] As can often be said of Setton, not because he naively accepted what the texts contained, but because of his technique of quoting or paraphrasing those texts at length without an accompanying critique.
[47] Robertson, 'Pietro Barbo-Paul II', 157, may be taken as typical: 'The crusade was also an attempt to reclaim for the papacy in a concrete way the leadership of Christendom.' Cf. Baldi, *Pio II*, 150, agreeing with Franco Cardini that papal pursuit of crusade was bound to be 'neo-hierarchical' for all the show of humility involved.

were important in shaping Rome's response, a role was also played by what can best be described as the *curia*'s 'memory' (*memoria*). Colin Morris described Christ's Sepulchre in Jerusalem holding the *memoria* of the Christian faith,[48] and consciousness of the past naturally helped fashion identity and purpose alike. In its approach towards crusading the fifteenth-century *curia* had its own *memoria*: a mosaic of reasoning and intuition that was formed from the holiness of Rome and its shrines (which as we have seen were perceived as threatened by the Turks), the nature of the papal office, but more specifically from an awareness of what had been done and could be tried to promote a crusade. It is self-evident that the Popes of the later fifteenth century realized how much had changed since the heyday of the medieval papacy. When Pius II declared in 1459 that he followed in the footsteps of Urban II, Eugenius III, Innocent III, Alexander III, and others, it was a particularly far-fetched rhetorical assertion.[49] The gap between what the *curia* was called on to do and what it could actually achieve was omnipresent; just as it was, even more glaringly, in the case of the Holy Roman Emperor. 'Like characters in fiction, figures in a painting, so do we look upon the Pope and the emperor', as Aeneas Sylvius Piccolomini put it in 1454 in one of his bleakest summaries of the contemporary political world.[50]

As a result, the *curia*'s crusading activities were characterized by constant oscillation between aspiration and realism. Revising Nicholas V's bull *Etsi ecclesia Christi* in May 1455, Calixtus III referred to the crusade as a crushing weight; it would be unmanageable without the assistance of God, who ensured that the 'vessel of Christendom' would never sink however fierce the storms that beset it.[51] If it was dispiriting to look back to what Urban II had managed to achieve, it was scarcely less discouraging to adopt a more short-term perspective. Nonetheless, reviewing recent attempts to promote the crusade often proved irresistible. In 1472 Sixtus IV looked back as far as Eugenius IV;[52] so did Innocent VIII in summoning his Rome congress in May 1489.[53] Most strikingly, in 1499 Alexander VI wrote in some detail to Grand Prince Alexander of Lithuania about the policies of his uncle Calixtus III, Pius II, Paul II, Sixtus IV, Innocent VIII, and himself. With fairness and some insight the Pope sketched the contours of each of his predecessor's crusading input. Most of it Alexander had helped shape, and none of it had worked. But the Pope was persevering and, like Pius and Innocent before him, he called for a congress of princes' envoys to organize resistance.[54] We can assume that there was an intended message behind these pessimistic retrospectives, though it was not necessarily the same one: most likely it varied between justification, disavowal, and

---

[48] Colin Morris, *The Sepulchre of Christ and the Medieval West: From the Beginning to 1600* (Oxford, 2005), p. xxii and *passim*.
[49] *Pii II orationes*, 2.7–30, no 2, also in Piccolomini, *Opera omnia*, 905–14; *Sacrorum conciliorum*, 32.207–21 (*Cum bellum hodie*).
[50] Piccolomini, *Opera omnia*, 654–7, *epistolae*, no 127, tr. Setton, *Papacy*, 2.153. Nonetheless, the idea of universal authority continued to hold great appeal for Piccolomini, as shown by John B. Toews, 'The View of Empire in Aeneas Sylvius Piccolomini (Pope Pius II)', *Traditio*, 24 (1968), 471–87.
[51] *DS*, 394–8, no 1251, at 394.   [52] Ibid. 545–8, no 1408, at 545.
[53] *Notes et extraits*, 5th ser., 165–6.   [54] *VMP*, 2.266–7, no 295.

implied rebuke. No Pope could hope to escape criticism. It is not surprising that Paul II was taken to task for the fall of Negroponte, given his decision to focus on Bohemia and his poor relations with Venice.[55] But even Calixtus III, who more or less devoted his short reign to the crusading cause, was criticized by Italian humanists, in Germany, and by Florence and Alfonso of Naples.[56]

The question of what methods should be pursued was raised very soon after the fall of Constantinople. It was bad luck for Nicholas V's reputation that his response to the disaster was judged inadequate by two contemporaries as influential and incisive as Capistrano and Piccolomini. Their written critiques make instructive reading. In a letter to the Pope from the diet of Frankfurt in October 1454, Capistrano complained about the fact that he had not received sealed crusading bulls, and had therefore had to work with copies; but the really biting comment comes at the end, when Capistrano seemed to set aside the standard courtesies. Passionately, he asked how others could be expected to offer up their children's bread for the cause of the crusade when Nicholas spent the Church's income on his building projects. It was wrong to put stone before Christian lives.[57] Piccolomini's critique of Nicholas was more detailed and clinical, and, in the light of his later policy as Pope, highly revealing.[58] Writing to his fellow enthusiast Carvajal at the start of 1454, the year that would prove decisive for his own reputation as an orator, he too took Nicholas to task for his inactivity.[59] He listed the Pope's deeds, which on the face of it were impressive: subsidies to George Kastriote and the Knights of St John, 40,000 ducats spent on shipping, liaison with Karaman and others who were threatened by the Turks. But the sum total was inadequate to the task in hand. Issuing bulls like *Etsi ecclesia Christi*, which proclaimed the crusade and set out various measures in its support, was a waste of time when there was no follow-through. Nicholas must take the initiative in such a way as to mobilize Christendom: 'We must copy our great men, Charlemagne, Godfrey, Conrad, Louis, and Frederick.'

How was this mobilization to be achieved? Piccolomini's answer was clear: there must be a *conventio generalis*, summoned with the goal of winning a *nationum consensus*. This congress or *generalis congregatio* would be summoned and presided over by the Pope, who would steer it towards commitments that in conjunction with measures of preaching and taxation would result in action. To this there were two potential objections, coming from opposite directions. One was that the Pope did not need to secure *nationum consensus* to proclaim a crusade because in matters

---

[55] Meserve, 'News', 462.

[56] *DS*, 421–3, no 1272, at 422; Piccolomini, *Opera omnia*, 822, 840; Ryder, *Alfonso*, 412; Baldi, *Pio II*, 176 (Florence).

[57] *AM*, 12.235–7, and cf. Petrovich, 'Croatian Humanists', 266, for a 1516 Croatian critique along the same lines.

[58] *Aeneae Silvii Piccolomini Senensis opera inedita*, ed. Josephus Cugnoni (Rome, 1883; facs. edn, Farnborough, 1968), 99–102, no 39.

[59] Criticism was prefigured in Pius's immediate epistolary responses to the fall of Constantinople, 12 and 21 July 1453: Aeneas Sylvius Piccolomini, *Der Briefwechsel. III. Abteilung: Briefe als Bischof von Siena, vol. 1 (1450–1454)*, ed. Rudolf Wolkan (Vienna, 1918), 189–202, no 109, 204–15, no 112; Baldi, 'Il problema turco', 62ff.

of faith he possessed a plenitude of power. True, but he needed to do it if he was to get results. The other objection was that such a gathering could mutate into a general council, or stimulate irresistible demands for one. Piccolomini's reply to this was frankly unconvincing: the *curia* should mend its ways so that it did not need to fear such a development. He was not yet a cardinal, so it was an easy answer to make. But in his defence, it remained his approach once he himself was carrying through his programme as Pope. It seems likely that Piccolomini/Pius decided that the danger of a conciliar revival simply had to be faced down. This was presumably also the attitude of Calixtus III, who adopted the congress policy late in 1457 and would have pursued it had he lived. It is hard to believe that Piccolomini could have guessed, when writing to Carvajal in 1454, that his suggestion would become mainstream crusading policy. But while there are other aspects of the idea that we need to address, this short letter remains the most incisive exposition both of the reasons why such a meeting of envoys was needed, and of the problems that accompanied it.

3.3 THE SEARCH FOR UNITY: CRUSADING CONGRESSES AND DIETS

There are various candidates for the originator of the idea of a crusading congress. When Philip the Good of Burgundy sent envoys to the leading courts in 1451 to promote a crusade, he suggested convening a congress; in his response Alfonso of Aragon volunteered to chair the meeting.[60] Piccolomini too referred to Alfonso in his letter to Carvajal, while Calixtus III mentioned that the preacher, Jacopo delle Marche, had promoted it.[61] What these names have in common is a familiarity with representative assemblies of one kind or another: diplomatic gatherings, meetings of estates, parliaments, and assemblies of religious orders. Just as there is no shortage of originators, so there were numerous prototypes: the imperial diets which Piccolomini, for one, got to know all too well in 1454–5, the ecumenical councils that had considered crusading plans between the twelfth and early-fourteenth centuries, and of course the series of general councils convened to end the Great Schism. The Italian leagues that the Peace of Lodi (1454) envisaged as the answer to resolving peninsular conflict certainly informed the strategic thinking of Calixtus and Pius. But origins and templates are less important than defining features, and these are clear from the letters and orations of Pius II. In the first place, the congress should be fully representative of the powers of Christendom. The Ottomans presented a common threat that must be met by a common response. In the second place, envoys must be mandated not just to discuss but also to commit, so that through *nationum consensus* a set of proposals could be agreed which could be followed through after the envoys had dispersed. Above all, the latter meant enforceable military and financial contributions.

---

[60] Paviot, *Les ducs*, 123–4, noting that Philip had attended the congress of Arras in 1435.
[61] *AM*, 13.6–7, at 7 (= *BF*, NS2.198–9, no 390).

Thanks to excellent analyses of the congress of Mantua by Giovanni Battista Picotti, Jocelyne Russell, and most recently Barbara Baldi, we have a clear view of how Pius's great project suffered shipwreck.[62] It is too easy to attribute failure exclusively to the vested interests and calculated sabotage of rulers who never intended any other outcome. Those factors were undoubtedly at work, but the congress was inherently unworkable. Juridically it had no foundations or indeed status, as Pius implicitly admitted when he made the bizarre announcement at its close that the congress was not ending at all, rather it was being absorbed into the papal *curia*.[63] The *Instrumentum in causa defensionis fidei* issued on 1 October 1459, setting out obligations agreed to date, opens with highly charged, emotional rhetoric relating to the cross, which looks rather like an attempt to disguise legal vacuity.[64] States sent envoys out of self-interest, a concern not to lose face, or in the hope of pursuing agendas unrelated to the crusade. And the diplomatic powers of these envoys were less clearly defined than Pius hoped for: as Riccardo Fubini has indicated, Renaissance diplomatic practice was less clear-cut than contemporary jurists liked to make out, being shaped as much by opportunism and *force majeure* as by commonly agreed procedures.[65] The alliances that Venice, Hungary, Burgundy, and the Pope formed in 1463 in relation to anti-Turkish action show that contemporaries could create mechanisms for common action speedily and effectively when they were propelled by outside forces and common need, in this instance Mehmed's conquest of Bosnia. One of Mantua's problems was that Capistrano had done his job too well in 1456, not just reinforcing complacency but persuading Mehmed to redirect his strategic thrust southwards. The threat to the Peloponnese caused concern, not least at Venice: but the republic saw nothing but danger in directing the attention of other Christian powers towards an area which it had ambitions to secure for itself. As a result, Mantua lacked the urgency of the meetings convened after the fall of Negroponte and Otranto, when alarm bells were sounding. It also suffered from the unavoidable logistical problems of such big gatherings, though five years later Lodovico Gonzaga's envoy at Ancona was to boast of how well things had been managed by comparison with the shocking conditions prevailing at the port.[66]

But such factors were incidental; the central problem was a juridical vacuum that hamstrung collective progress on a crusade, thereby releasing the congress to become instead the stage for acting out the political rivalries of the day. Pius effectively acknowledged this when he abandoned multi-lateral discussions in favour of bi-lateral negotiations. This allowed Pius to operate, in Russell's phrase, 'both by

---

[62] In addition to these names, see Arnold Esch, 'Pio II e il congresso di Mantova', in *SP*, 1–14; Sondra Dall'Oco, '"Mantuam ivimus...non audiverunt Christiani vocem pastoris". Fede, politica e retorica nelle "orazioni" e nelle "reazioni" mantovane', ibid. 503–15.

[63] *Pii II orationes*, 2.78–88, no 4, also in *Sacrorum conciliorum*, 35.113–120 (*Septimo iam exacto mense*).

[64] Picotti, *La dieta*, 436–44, no 21.

[65] Riccardo Fubini, 'Diplomacy and Government in the Italian City-States of the Fifteenth Century (Florence and Venice)', in Daniela Frigo, ed., *Politics and Diplomacy in Early Modern Italy: The Structure of Diplomatic Practice, 1450–1800* (Cambridge, 2000), 25–48, esp. 31–2.

[66] *Ungedruckte Akten*, 311–12, no 198.

cajolery and bargaining, and by majestic pastoral pleading'.[67] It also addressed the Pope's political quandary, enabling him to stave off the creation of alliances of anti-papal interests which might lobby for a general council.[68] The greatest danger lay in the convergence of France and Venice, which was hard to avoid given Angevin claims on Naples and Pius's embrace of the Naples–Rome–Milan axis. For that reason it is the Pope's relations with the French and Venetians that are most revealing. In June 1459 the Pope learned of a French ploy to move the congress to Germany, which would have been extremely dangerous for him given the surge of anti-papal feeling among the German clergy; and in September he was expecting news of an Angevin invasion of the *Regno*.[69] Baldi has argued that Pius's confrontation with the French was bound to become 'the central theme' of the congress, for which reason his containment of their hostility, confirmed at the end of the congress by the issue of the anti-conciliar decree *Execrabilis*, was a signal success.[70] Recorded exchanges with the French envoys were brusque: the Pope reminded them of France's glorious past, to which they replied that this time he could expect nothing from their kingdom aside from the Burgundian contribution. To their reference to French help in the past on the *Regno*, Pius made the telling riposte that the French had not done so badly out of it. The Pope entertained no hopes of assistance from this quarter: an appeal for René of Anjou to put on hold his plans to invade the *Regno* for the duration of the crusade, 'for the common good', was clearly made as a political gesture, showing that Pius could play to the gallery just as well as his opponents could.[71]

Papal relations with the Venetians were bound to be more complex, because Pius needed their fleet. It is worth setting out the main themes of their engagement with the congress, not only because, as Pius reminded them at the end of August when their envoys had still not appeared, they were more at risk of Ottoman aggression than most,[72] but also because they would soon play a key role in promoting and sustaining crusading leagues, which we shall be examining later. Over a century ago Picotti used the ample Venetian documentation to counter the claims by Pastor and others, relying heavily on the picture painted by Pius himself in his *Commentarii*, that Venice was duplicitous in its response to the congress.[73] It is important to bear in mind that, as Benjamin Weber has pointed out, the Venetians claimed they were still owed 29,500 florins for the naval assistance they had provided to Eugenius IV in 1443.[74] Their nightmare scenario was to be pulled into a war against the sultan in which their trade would suffer heavy damage; they would be abandoned by the other powers, including Italian rivals who would use the republic's preoccupation with the Turks to seize their mainland possessions.

---

[67] Jocelyne G. Russell, 'The Humanists Converge: The Congress of Mantua (1459)', in her *Diplomats at Work: Three Renaissance Studies* (Stroud and Wolfeboro Falls NH, 1992), 51–93, at 79.

[68] Baldi, 'Il problema turco', 60, notes that this was also the approach favoured by Calixtus III for his planned congress.

[69] Russell, 'Humanists', 65–6.   [70] Baldi, *Pio II*, 162–70.

[71] *Sacrorum conciliorum*, 32.225–30, 240–58.   [72] Picotti, *La dieta*, 414–17, no 12.

[73] Ibid., esp. 387–94; Pastor, *History*, 3.84–5.

[74] Weber, *Lutter*, 2.1.1, and see too Imber, *Ottoman Empire*, 32–3.

As Picotti put it, why should the republic lay its head on the block? Wait and see (*aspettazione prudente*) was a much saner approach. That said, there was a 'hawk' party at Venice, at least one of whose members, Lodovico Foscarini, was impressed by the Pope's ability and commitment.[75] Both the strategic arguments and the figures that the republic's envoys set out at Mantua in the autumn of 1459 commanded respect at the time, while the latter retain value, despite their polemical origins, as costings of military activity.[76] The republic's position rested on a vigorous exposition of its own vulnerability. Its trade and far-flung possessions alike exposed it to the full weight of Turkish fury. Hence it could only take action once it was convinced that the *apparatus sancte expeditionis* was in place: in practice, this meant that provision of the fleet would have to wait until the German and Hungarian land forces had assembled. Strategically of course this was deeply problematic. But, in a clever riposte to the accusation of Venetian self-interest, it was argued that since the republic was an *antemurale,* such prudence was in the long-term interests of the whole of Christendom. Hence too there must be no preliminary trade ban, which was the clearest indication of a forthcoming crusade and would be the signal for Turkish attacks.[77]

It was in respect of the Turkish threat to Venetian trade that the envoys made their single most bullish demand at Mantua: this was that the Pope should consent to pay an indemnity of 8,000 ducats each month should Mehmed attack before the Hungarians had their army ready. This was incorporated into terms worked out in January 1460, which in a number of respects surely went further than the Pope would have liked. There should be no crusade preaching or collection in Venetian territory until the land army was ready; similarly, no trade ban should be imposed until fighting commenced; Venetian conquests would be retained by the city (admittedly, as fiefs of the Church); and Pius should ensure that the Hungarians campaigned from the start of spring right through to the onset of winter (much longer than their customary practice of taking up arms in September, after the harvest was in).[78] Negotiations dragged on into the spring of 1460, though on 10 February the Milanese envoy smugly informed Francesco Sforza that Pius's patience was close to exhaustion. He thought the Pope would turn instead to Alfonso of Aragon for naval support, not least because he feared that the Venetians were intent only on securing the Peloponnese, which would yield them 300,000 ducats a year and make them totally insufferable.[79] Two months later the talks finally fizzled out.[80] Undoubtedly, the Venetians had played a tough hand, for instance pressing for all contributed galleys to take orders from their commanders.[81] But all of Venice's demands made political and military sense when we compare their situation with

---

[75] Picotti, *La dieta*, 389.
[76] See in particular ibid. 446–57, nos 23–4, 467–70, no 30.
[77] Ibid. 401–7, no 4, 421–3, no 16, 450–7, no 24, 472–4, no 33, 482–5, no 39.
[78] Ibid. 503–6, no 52. The campaigns of 1443 and 1444 had both started in the autumn, probably in the expectation that the Turkish heavy cavalry (*sipahis*) would have dispersed to collect their salaries, which derived from taxes paid after the sale of the harvest.
[79] Ibid. 517–18, no 60.   [80] Ibid. 526, no 66, 529–30, no 69.   [81] Ibid. 477–9, no 36.

that of the most prominent would-be crusaders. Aside from Pius himself, they were Burgundy and Hungary. Philip the Good had nothing to fear from Mehmed while King Matthias was already at war with the sultan. In such circumstances it was understandable that the Venetians, by contrast, should lay such stress on timing, guarantees, and indemnities. The price tag to *nationum consensus* was that each nation would defend and advance its own position: although in that respect Venice's *antemurale* status enabled it to seize the moral high ground, asserting that even the infrastructure costs of its fleets and fortresses should be ascribed to the crusading cause.[82]

Through hard work and a measure of self-deception, Pius II was able to salvage his congress from becoming a wholesale failure. His speech of 14 January 1460 ending the proceedings, *Septimo iam exacto mense,* was one of his cleverest performances as an orator. Notwithstanding the carping of the critics, he judged his congress to be a partial success. In the first place, the desired unanimity had materialized: 'With one heart and one voice, all those who assembled counselled declaring war on the Turks.' And in the second place, there were guaranteed ('promised') and hoped-for (*sperata*) contributions that would provide the means for such a war to be fought. The former comprised a total of 70,000 troops, 42,000 of them to be recruited in Germany, plus taxes to be levied on the clergy, laity, and Jews in Italy. The *sperata* contributions were wishful in the extreme, for example, Pius said that Henry VI of England would surely help once the civil war had been resolved.[83] On the same day that he delivered *Septimo iam exacto mense* Pius issued the bull *Ecclesiam Christi*, containing a package of indulgences and other measures in support of the projected expedition. The bull set a start date of 1 April 1460 for the crusade, which was wholly impracticable in terms of the 70,000-strong army, and perhaps implies hopes to despatch an advance party to Bosnia or Greece. *Ecclesiam Christi* makes reference to Mantua, but it also looks to the past for its authority,

> following the custom of our predecessors, who proclaimed general expeditions either to liberate the Holy Land, or against other unbelievers, we declare a general war and expedition against the very perfidious Turks, the most vicious of our God's enemies, a war that is to be taken up and fought by all Christ's faithful over a period of three years, and to which each and every Christian alike is summoned to contribute according to their ability.[84]

These two texts therefore complement one another, epitomizing the clumsy synergy of old and new in Pius's view of crusade at the start of 1460.

Alongside the tortuous negotiations with Venice, the future of the Mantua programme hinged on Bessarion's ability to persuade the Germans to keep the terms of the congress's *provisio Germaniae* by providing their 42,000 combatants. This task took him across the Alps in 1460 and into the snake-pit world of the imperial

---

[82] Ibid. 450–7, no 24.
[83] *Pii II orationes*, 2.78–88, no 4, also in *Sacrorum conciliorum*, 35.113–20.
[84] *VMH*, 2.366–9, no 551, also in *Sacrorum conciliorum*, 35.261–5 (some major passages paraphrased).

diets.[85] He received little assistance from Frederick III, whose appointment as captain-general of the crusade in January 1460 did nothing to alter his unwillingness to promote it.[86] Bessarion's experiences in Germany make for an instructive comparison with what had happened just months earlier at the congress. There was a major difference between the two assemblies: nobody doubted that the diets possessed a decision-making authority, though there were numerous uncertainties about how and when decisions were made, and to whom they applied. The problem was that envoys knew that their lords rarely wanted binding decisions to be made and they had learned to match the skills of the Mantua envoys in prevarication. Their two cleverest tricks were, first, to seize on changes in the political landscape as excuses to evade and backtrack and, secondly, to ensure that any major issue was referred to a future diet. Pius himself had encountered both tactical devices in 1454–5 at the sequence of assemblies (Regensburg, Frankfurt, and Wiener Neustadt) that discussed the crusade in the immediate wake of the fall of Constantinople. By the time of the Wiener Neustadt diet every angle of the project had been investigated, but death came to the rescue of Frederick III and the envoys: when news arrived of Nicholas V's demise on 24 March, the emperor eagerly seized on it to put crusade planning on hold. Against such a background, Pius's choice of Bessarion as his legate in 1460 is puzzling, since the cardinal was unfamiliar with Germany and there is evidence that the procedural maze at the diets irritated him. All we can say is that the Pope must have judged him to be the best person for the task, largely on the grounds of his unwavering commitment to the cause and insider knowledge of the military situation in the East. Four decades later Perault would handle the situation with less knowledge but greater finesse; though, it must be added, with no greater success.[87]

The first diet convened at Nürnberg in the spring of 1460[88] and the second at Vienna in September. The precise reconstruction of events remains difficult because the diets have not been included in the published *Deutsche Reichstagsakten*, but the ebb and flow of discussion is clear enough.[89] Bessarion encountered three major problems. The first two were the same ones with which Pius had wrestled in 1454–5 and, when the legate wrote to the Pope in March 1461 defending his actions, none of it can have come as a surprise. The biggest political issue that

---

[85] Generally on the diets see Gabriele Annas, *Hoftag—Gemeiner Tag—Reichstag. Studien zur strukturellen Entwicklung deutscher Reichsversammlungen des späten Mittelalters (1349–1471)*, 2 vols (Göttingen, 2004).

[86] *AE*, 10.226, ad ann. 1460, no 20.

[87] See my '*Robur imperii*' for a comparison of the experiences at the diets of Piccolomini, Bessarion, and Perault.

[88] Günther Schuhmann, 'Kardinal Bessarion in Nürnberg', *Jahrbuch für Fränkische Landesforschung*, 34/35 (1975), 447–65.

[89] Events have to be reconstructed from older sources such as *Des Heiligen römischen Reichs Teutscher Nation Reichs Tags Theatrum... 1440 bis 1493*, ed. Johann Joachim Müller (Jena, 1713), 780–9; *Selecta iuris et historiarum*, ed. H.C. Senckenberg, 6 vols (Frankfurt, 1734–43), 4.326–81; *Sammlung der Reichs-Abschiede*, ed. Johann Jacob Schmauss, vol. 1 (Frankfurt a. M., 1747), 190–8; also the documents that Mohler published in *Bessarion*, vol. 3. The main attempts at reconstruction are ibid. 1.294–302; Pastor, *History*, 3.159–75; Russell, 'Humanists', 72–3; Setton, *Papacy*, 2.217–18.

served to stall discussions relating to a crusade was the turbulence in Hungary following the death of Ladislas V. This was unquestionably a genuine problem for anybody who was contemplating the despatch of an army 42,000-strong through Hungarian territory, but Bessarion's reply also made sense: to insist that every such political and organizational issue was settled before an army assembled was a recipe for inactivity. Of course this was the unspoken point of the exercise, and the parallel with Venice's argument about the provision of naval assistance is unavoidable: the republic wanted to wait for the Germans and the Germans for the Hungarians. In the meantime, Bessarion might well have said (and in effect did) that Mehmed would once again be at the gates of Belgrade with no-one to stop him. If Bessarion was impatient with such feet-dragging, he showed even less sympathy for the tactic of holding irresolvable issues over for yet another diet. His response to this suggestion was robust: 'The time has come to set aside words and come to deeds. Distinguished listeners: our agenda is weapons; I repeat weapons, not words. A well-organized army, not ornate and polished oratory. Strong soldiery, not verbal display.'[90] Surely five diets and one congress were enough? One reason for his short temper may have been genuine anguish caused by the news that was reaching him about the whirlwind of killing and enslavement (15,000 and 30,000 people respectively) that the Turks had recently inflicted on the Peloponnese.[91] So when it was apparent that nothing further would come of the Vienna diet, Bessarion refused to join in the envoys' habitual game of deferral, and instead simply brought the curtain down on proceedings. He described the princely envoys as 'inconsistent and evasive people', and the fur flew in a polemical exchange of accusation and injured innocence.[92]

What seems to have caused most indignation at Vienna was Bessarion's handling of his third major problem. This was the envoys' outright denial that their lords were under any obligation to provide the 42,000 troops. For Bessarion this was intolerable: it meant that the undertakings successively made at Frankfurt, Wiener Neustadt, and Mantua were without any substance and that he had nothing on which to build. On the contrary, the legate said in his address *Multa quidem*, the agreements constituted a treaty (*foedus*) with God, to whom the imperial princes would have to answer if they did not honour their word.[93] When the envoys presented their reply to this address, they claimed that they were astonished to be confronted with an obligation (*debitum*), unanimously denying 'that their princes had ever promised an army or anything specific'. In what must have been an impressive piece of theatre, Bessarion proceeded to have the Mantua decrees publicly read out. He argued that the decrees only confirmed what had already been settled at Frankfurt, which was that while no *individual* commitments had been made, there was a collective one. To this the envoys made no reply.[94] They were not about to engage with an issue that went to the heart of the ineffectiveness of the imperial diets as decision-making assemblies. It was a state of affairs that for the most part

---

[90] Mohler, *Bessarion*, 3.384.　[91] Ibid. 3.393.　[92] Ibid. 3.403.
[93] Ibid. 3.388.　[94] Ibid. 3.399.

suited Germany's regional powers. In much the same way that Venice was content to manage its own defence against the Turks through a system of alliances with neighbouring states, often fuelled by subsidies, any German regional power that found itself threatened by the Turks knew that it could best defend its people in association with its immediate neighbours. The alternative was to consent to centralizing innovations that would have the effect of making the emperor stronger. This applied, above all, to measures of taxation. Eberhard Isenmann has reflected on the paradox that Germany's fiscal mechanisms were some of the most sophisticated in Europe at the level of city and prince, but were archaic in terms of the empire.[95]

Any crusading enthusiast who chose to look back in 1461 over the series of assemblies that represented the collective response of Christendom to the Turkish capture of Constantinople would have had to agree with the *topos* that the Christians answered unity with disunity. Nonetheless, diets and congresses continued to function as one of the major platforms for crusading efforts throughout the remainder of the century. It is not hard to see why this applied in the case of the imperial diets. Once most of Bosnia had been conquered, Turkish raiders began seeping through into the southern Austrian lands, whose estates started clamouring for assistance. For these territories, a growth in the power of the emperor held no terrors: given that the Habsburg dynasty exercised direct lordship, the mobilization of imperial resources to make that lordship more effective could only be a good thing. But while the plight and appeals of the Austrian *Erbländer* gave urgency and emotional impact to the debates at the diets, Turkish gains further south also played a role. The idea persisted that the diets had pan-European significance, because the emperor held *ex officio* responsibility for the defence of Christendom. Meeting in the aftermath of the fall of Negroponte, Frederick III's *Große Christentag* of 1471 was an event that carried substantial meaning for the crusade, not least because Frederick attended in person. There were impressive displays of oratorical skill, including three speeches by the legate, Francesco Todeschini-Piccolomini, though it seems that the finest oration, which had been prepared by Giannantonio Campano, was not actually delivered.[96]

When the nettle of imperial taxation was finally grasped, at Worms in 1495, the connection between the 'Common Penny' and the Turkish threat was theoretically tight. In July 1497 the canny Leonello Chiericati warned Maximilian that any peace negotiations with the Ottoman court could imperil the collection of the tax.[97] The Turkish menace was woven into the fabric of the period's diets, though anti-papal sentiment and ambivalence about indulgences meant that it was increasingly perceived as *Türkenkrieg* rather than crusade. Papal legates attended a high proportion of these assemblies, but the days had gone when a tax for fighting

---

[95] Eberhard Isenmann, 'The Holy Roman Empire in the Middle Ages', in Richard Bonney, ed., *The Rise of the Fiscal State in Europe, c. 1200–1815* (Oxford, 1999), 243–80.

[96] See Blusch, 'Enea Silvio Piccolomini', *passim*: Campano's speech was much admired when it was first printed *c.* 1487.

[97] *AR*, no 5109.

the Hussites could be pushed through largely by the connections and force of personality of a Henry Beaufort.[98] And the biggest problem for most of the 1470s and 1480s was that Matthias's ambitions in the west ruled out the sort of German-Hungarian collaboration that Bessarion had pursued in 1460.[99] Only after Matthias's death in 1490 could such joint action make its way back onto the agenda.

It is harder to explain the papal *curia*'s continuing fondness for congresses. Why persist with an approach that not only raised hopes, but was bound to prove time-consuming, expensive, and logistically taxing?[100] The most credible answer could be that they were handy shields. When faced with Maximilian's campaign to seize his crusade chests, Perault found it useful to shelter behind the memory of Mantua.[101] Again and again in the 1470s and early 1480s Sixtus IV used the idea of a papal congress to fend off French demands for a council and imperial suggestions for a congress of princes.[102] When Maximilian suggested holding a meeting of Christian powers at Cologne in 1494 to discuss ways of countering the Turkish threat, Perault commented that Basel would be a better location. Either he failed to see that Alexander VI would not willingly go to a meeting at the city that had hosted the last general council, or he made the suggestion with the intention of exerting pressure on the Pope to be more cooperative about the crusade.[103] There was no further attempt to hold a congress at a city like Basel, or Mantua, which would be convenient for transalpine delegates. The meetings convened at Rome in 1470, 1480–1 and 1490 were more clearly the expressions of a hierarchical and centralized apparatus of power than a congress that had required the Pope to undertake an arduous and disruptive journey northwards.[104] The three meetings were also limited in attendance: the 1470 and 1480–1 assemblies were effectively Italian occasions; and we shall see that the brief of the French envoys in 1480 was as empty of any genuine military intent as that of their predecessors at Mantua had been.[105]

---

[98] Helmut Wolff, 'Päpstliche Legaten auf Reichstagen des 15. Jahrhunderts', in *RK*, 25–40, esp. 30, 36; see also Studt, *Martin V.*, for the powerful legates of the Hussite crusades.

[99] *Deutsche Reichstagsakten unter Maximilian I. Erster Band. Reichstag zu Frankfurt 1486*, ed. Heinz Angermeier, Deutsche Reichstagsakten, mittlere Reihe, 1 (Göttingen, 1989) has numerous instances of Turks and Hungarians both considered as threats, e.g. 149–54, 186–91, 317–18, 705–7, 721, 889, 929, 979–80.

[100] In November 1480 Matthias Corvinus complained that the process by which he had been notified of Sixtus IV's summons to a meeting at Rome gave him just 24 hours to get an envoy there: *MKL*, 2.70–2, no 44.

[101] 'Quia ordinatio de dicta conservatione dictarum pecuniarum non potest fieri nisi papa vocet universos principes christianitatis et potentatus prout vocavit Pius II Mantue antequam aggrederetur cruciatam et qui aliter consulunt Cesari longe aberrant et parcant nobis sue dilecti': Biblioteca Apostolica Vaticana, Palat IV. 1229 (5), printed open letter (n.d.), at 13.

[102] e.g. Schlecht, *Zamometić*, 20–41 (1478), 104–5 (1476); Landi, *Concilio*, 93–157.

[103] *AR*, no 332.

[104] Pastor, *History*, 4.217–18, documents short-lived discussions following Sixtus IV's election in late 1471 to hold a congress outside Rome (with 7 alternatives being mooted).

[105] Though Sixtus IV claimed to be planning a more general meeting in his peace negotiations with Florence in 1479: 'Sua Sanctitas, quae nihil unquam magis desideravit, neque desiderat, decernet in Lateriano Dietam, ad quam omnes Principes convenient praesertim Imperialis Maiestas, et Christianissimus Francorum Rex personaliter si commode possunt, sin minus per solemnes Oratores plena, et sufficienta mandata habentes; hoc idem de reliquis Principibus Christianis intelligant'. Sigismondo de' Conti, *Le storie*, 1.387–92, *appendice*, no 3, at 391.

Innocent VIII's 1490 congress has left reasonable documentation, though much less than Mantua. It was underpinned by the presence of Djem, waning asset though he was. And in the oration that Bishop Pietro Mansi gave on 25 March 1490 there are both reminiscences of the grand themes that had been enunciated in 1459, and more contemporary references to alleged Ottoman setbacks at the hands of the Mamluks and Spanish victories in Granada.[106] The discussion that occurred was undoubtedly thorough. It covered such issues as the number of armies needed, their recruitment and funding, supply, command structure, the duration of hostilities, and the disposition of conquests. But it became apparent that the transalpine delegates were playing the same game that the Germans had used in the time of Piccolomini and Bessarion: they denied being mandated to make binding agreements and suggested that the Pope convene another congress. Innocent's response echoed Bessarion's riposte at Vienna. There was no time for another meeting; it was essential to move on to specifics.[107] It remains difficult even to pin down when the 1490 congress ended, and it is certainly hard to believe that when Alexander VI summoned another Rome congress in response to Croatian disasters in 1493,[108] and Venetian ones in 1499,[109] he was engaging in anything other than a face-saving exercise. The history of all the meetings held or planned at Rome confirms Christine Shaw's argument that the city was not the peninsula's diplomatic centre.[110]

3.4 SYNERGIZING SELF-INTEREST: CRUSADING LEAGUES AND SUBSIDIES

In a famous private meeting held with six chosen cardinals in March 1462 to review his crusading programme, Pius II ruefully admitted that contemporaries must be asking why the resolutions agreed at Mantua had not been carried forward. Effectively, Pius revisited the issue of mechanisms that he had written about in his letter to Carvajal eight years previously. At that point, his answer to the intractable problem of how to mobilize Christendom was achieving *nationum consensus* through a congress. But this had failed, and it therefore joined the list of unsuccessful approaches that Piccolomini had set out in 1454 and Pius reviewed in 1462.[111] One of those measures, the despatch of legates, continued to be employed but Pius's pithy verdict on it, 'if we send legates to ask for the support of kings, they are laughed at',[112] was for the most part painfully accurate. As representatives of the papal office, legates brought with them all the suspicions held about that office without the respect that was still shown towards the person of the Pope himself. This was above all the case when they faced the task of winning over audiences who were uninterested in the crusade, or overtly hostile towards it.

---

[106] Ibid. 2.413–23, *appendice*, no 13.   [107] Ibid. 2.424–36, *appendice*, nos 14–16.
[108] *AR*, nos 2764, 2777.   [109] *VMP*, 2.266–7, no 295.
[110] Shaw, 'The Papal Court', esp. 630.   [111] *Pii II Commentarii*, bk 7, ch. 16, 460–3.
[112] Ibid. 461.

Bessarion discovered this to his cost. In addition to his frustrating German legation in 1460, he was commissioned by Sixtus IV to carry out a legation to the French court in 1472, to make peace between France and Burgundy in the interests of a crusade. The mission proved so bruising that six years later Sixtus recalled his legate's 'expulsion' from France 'creating confusion for him and the apostolic see'.[113] Germany was arguably the most challenging of all legatine briefs because of the intractability of its political affairs and its numerous internal disputes; for most Italians its climate and mores were alike uncongenial.[114] Bessarion had to endure an Alpine crossing by sledge in the winter of 1460,[115] and in August 1498 Leonello Chiericati begged Alexander VI to recall him from what he described as his German exile (*relegatio*). He had endured two diets which surely was enough to do penance for his sins.[116]

Yet some legations did turn out to be successful and, arguably, none more so than that of Juan Carvajal, the recipient of Piccolomini's 1454 letter and legate in Hungary from 1455 to 1461. In his *Commentarii* Jacopo Ammannati Piccolomini wrote a passage praising in glowing terms what Carvajal had achieved in Hungary: he laboured there for six years at the cost of his health and in particular his teeth, which had been ruined (as was obvious to all) by the extreme cold of the Hungarian winter. Deserted by members of his household, he patiently bore all for Christ, leading to the frontline the many volunteers to whom he had given the cross with his own hands.[117] In the next chapter we shall see that this last plaudit was no exaggeration and, overall, Carvajal's Hungarian service did prove fruitful, not least his energetic lobbying for the election of Matthias as king in 1458.[118] It was not that Carvajal was more gifted or hard-working than Bessarion: in the autumn of 1463 Bessarion enjoyed an equally productive legation in his beloved Venice, writing in ecstatic terms to Pius II about the crusading zeal that he was encountering there, now that the republic was at war with Mehmed II.[119] The reason why Hungary in the 1450s and Venice in late 1463 proved more profitable fields of operations than Germany in 1460 or France in 1472 was simply that it was in their interests to work with the crusading cause. Bluntly, self-interest opened doors to crusading legates and facilitated their work. But in addition to the activity of able and committed legates, something of a more specific character was needed to reconcile the often diverse interests of receptive powers like Hungary and Venice, making it possible for them to pool and coordinate their efforts, and generating military collaboration over a sustained period of time. This was the formation of leagues sponsored by the *curia* and incorporating agreed subsidies.

---

[113] Mohler, *Bessarion*, 3.410–12; Schlecht, *Zamometić*, 26–7 (for quote).

[114] Though not for all: Erich Meuthen, 'Ein "deutscher" Freundeskreis an der römischen Kurie in der Mitte des 15. Jahrhunderts. Von Cesarini bis zu den Piccolomini', *Annuarium Historiae Conciliorum*, 27/28 (1995/96), 487–542.

[115] Mohler, *Bessarion*, 1.294.   [116] *AR*, no 6606.

[117] Iacopo Ammannati Piccolomini, *Commentarii*, in Frankfurt 1614 edn of Pope Pius II's *Commentarii*, 355.

[118] Pál Engel, *The Realm of St Stephen: A History of Medieval Hungary, 895–1526*, tr. Tamás Pálosfalvi (London, 2001), 298.

[119] Mohler, *Bessarion*, 3.525–8, no 56.

Crusading leagues in the broadest sense of the term were far from new: they originated in the early fourteenth century when they comprised the initial *modus operandi* for directing the mechanism of crusade against the Anatolian Turks.[120] The leagues of the later fifteenth century, however, were shaped by two fresh developments. The first was the Italian league (*lega italica*) that was established following the Peace of Lodi in 1454 and brought a measure of stability to peninsular affairs. Michael Mallett showed that this stability was far from being the golden age fondly recalled in the turbulent years that followed the French invasion of 1494, but Lodi did inculcate among the regional states a habit of approaching shared problems through alliances that were both detailed and robust. States got used to negotiating specific military quotas that two key players, Venice and Milan, were normally able to raise fairly easily thanks to their advanced techniques for retaining and paying troops (Florence faced greater difficulties).[121] Baldi has emphasized the respect that Pius II held for the Italian league,[122] and it is unsurprising that at Mantua Sigismondo Malatesta was praised when he advocated raising troops for the crusade in Italy, with the transalpine nations providing the payment: 'let others find the money and let Italians fight the war'.[123] One advantage of this would be that it would frustrate transalpine attempts to lay hold on coveted Italian wealth,[124] but it also made sense militarily. With the frontline rapidly approaching the Adriatic, mobilizing the peninsula's sophisticated military machinery had a *prima facie* rationale, so long as one ignored the fact that the main reason why first Venice and then Milan were such innovators in the waging of war was their implacable rivalry in Lombardy: late in 1463 Sforza's envoys at Rome had to calm his anxiety that the Pope's alliance with Venice and others was indeed anti-Turkish rather than (covertly) anti-Milanese. Hence there was no reason why he should bother joining it![125] No less telling was the Pope's warning to Florence that unless it joined the crusade, Venice would get all the gains, thereby increasing its power in Italy.[126] Notwithstanding the difficulty of squaring these various circles, the practice of forming leagues that would work together had become so ingrained and the benefits so palpable that the papal *curia* constantly resorted to it as a means of trying to bring about military action that would represent the entire peninsula. To this extent, its

---

[120] Norman Housley, *The Avignon Papacy and the Crusades, 1305–1378* (Oxford, 1986), 117–22.

[121] Michael Mallett, 'Diplomacy and War in Later Fifteenth-Century Italy', *Proceedings of the British Academy*, 67 (1981), 267–88; id., 'Preparations for War in Florence and Venice in the Second Half of the Fifteenth Century', in *Florence and Venice: Comparisons and Relations, vol. 1: Quattrocento* (Florence, 1979), 149–64; Michael E. Mallett and John R. Hale, *The Military Organization of a Renaissance State: Venice, c. 1400–1617* (Cambridge, 1984); Maria Nadia Covini, *L'esercito del duca. Organizzazione militare e istituzioni al tempo degli Sforza (1450–1480)* (Rome, 1998).

[122] Baldi, 'Enea Silvio Piccolomini', 659–60, 664–5.

[123] *Pii II Commentarii*, bk 3, ch. 34, 221.

[124] As Pius commented in reply to Malatesta, this was precisely why the northerners would refuse to pay, ibid. 221.

[125] Baldi, *Pio II*, 241: as she remarks, in winning Venice for his crusade Pius was bound to lose Milan. See also Marcello Simonetta, 'Pius II and Francesco Sforza. The History of Two Allies', in *Pius II*, 147–70.

[126] Baldi, *Pio II*, 235.

crusading policy became an extension of its Italian policy; the one shaping the other in a two-way traffic of ideas and methods.

The other new development was the impact of *antemurale* thinking on interstate cash flows. In essence this was straightforward. Since frontline states were defending their fellow Christians from the Turks, they deserved their support. In moral, religious, and pragmatic terms their claim was absolute, and we have seen that nobody advanced it more stridently than the rulers of those states. The king of Hungary pointed out how inconvenient it would be if he were to reconfigure his rampart into an open door for the Turks, while the Venetians claimed that their infrastructure of fortresses, garrisons, and galley fleets was, in practice, dedicated to the crusading cause and should therefore be credited to them in any assessment of contributions. So in the cases of Hungary, Albania, and Bosnia, it was usually impracticable for the *curia* to refuse to grant subsidies that as far as possible were sourced in the wider Catholic community. But this was far from constituting a blank cheque for the rulers of the *antemurale* states. It was not just that the transfer of money should be subject to accountability; the ultimate responsibility for funding the war had to lie with the frontline powers. It was possible to turn the core *antemurale* argument on its head. In a frank set of instructions to his legate Cardinal Pietro Isvalies in November 1500 Alexander VI told him to inform the Hungarians that

> Certainly it would be appropriate if, in an emergency as pressing as this one, His Majesty, together with his prelates and barons, were to contribute some of their own money. The army will need it, and the common cause of the faith, which is entitled to the support of everybody, is at one with the security of their position and dominions, for thanks to their proximity these are subjected to constant devastation, harassment, and danger from the Turks.[127]

In other words, a power that stood to gain from Turkish defeats, in the sense of its territories becoming more secure and taxable, should be prepared to spend its own money (*propria*) as well as money coming from the Pope and Church (*publica*).[128] The Pope told his legate to be no less muscular in his handling of Venice, which would be his first port of call. Alexander knew that the Hungarians would demand subsidies and he was prepared to provide 40,000 ducats a year; Venice should provide 100,000 (though Isvalies could settle for 80,000). The Pope listed and demolished the various excuses that the doge could be expected to offer: they simply could not afford it (if the Pope could, so could Venice, especially given the clerical tenths they had been allowed to collect); they faced numerous other outgoings for the war (so did the Pope); other powers should contribute (ideally yes, but the situation was too pressing for that). Then came the same argument that Isvalies was to use at Buda: 'This may look like a common war for the cause of God and the

---

[127] *VMP*, 2.269–76, no 297, at 273.
[128] For this distinction between private and public see also *VMH*, 2.530–4, no 719. 'Public' presumably meant relating to the needs of the *respublica Christiana* rather than those of individual states.

Christian religion, but the fact remains that it is the particular concern of those who are suffering the brunt of Turkish aggression, if greater disaster is not to befall first them and later their fellow-Christians.' For good measure, Alexander added that it was pointless for the doge to threaten to appeal to his main ally, the king of France: the subsidy issue was a matter for the frontline powers to resolve among themselves.[129]

The abrasive approach that Alexander espoused in 1500 sprang from his own experience of a subsidy system that had been functioning since the 1460s and had given rise to unending problems. It is clear that he could predict all the arguments and ruses that would be brought into play. From the start the *curia*, Venice, and Hungary had been its key participants, their mutual stances being essentially those that were anticipated by Alexander.[130] Ample surviving documentation affords us a good picture of the system at work, in particular during the years immediately following the cornerstone agreements that were concluded at Petrovaradin and Rome in 1463. The Venetians were correct when they observed in 1465 that their 1463 alliance with Hungary carried no commitment to paying Matthias subsidies: the obligations were couched in fairly general terms of large-scale offensive actions, accompanied by an undertaking to persist until a mutual agreement was reached to negotiate peace terms.[131] But the republic's elite was convinced that without the Hungarian alliance their city's war against Mehmed was unwinnable: 'Every well-informed person agrees that it is impossible to destroy the Turk without the help of the king and a powerful army based on land.' They were particularly keen to encourage Matthias's strategy of recovering Bosnia, 'which beyond doubt is the shield for our standing and dominions in Dalmatia'.[132] And possessing a fair idea of both military costs in Hungary and the constraints on royal finances,[133] the Venetians knew that, notwithstanding the Corvinian rhetoric about self-sustaining operations, Matthias could not attack the enemy as fiercely and tenaciously as the situation required unless he received assistance. So even before the 1463 alliance was sealed Venice and the Pope had begun subsidizing the king, though neither harboured illusions about the hazards involved: the republic suggested to Pius II in

---

[129] *VMP*, 2.269–76, no 297, at 270.
[130] Generally see Magda Jászay, 'Venezia e Mattia Corvino', in Sante Graciotti and Cesare Vasoli, eds, *Italia e Ungheria all'epoca dell'umanesimo corviniano* (Florence, 1994), 3–17; Gyula Rázsó, 'Una strana alleanza. Alcuni pensieri sulla storia militare e politica dell'alleanza contro i Turchi (1440–1464)', in Vittore Branca, ed., *Venezia e Ungheria nel Rinascimento* (Florence, 1973), 79–100; Szuzsanna Teke, 'Rapporti diplomatici tra Mattia Corvino e gli stati italiani', in Graciotti and Vasoli, eds, *Italia e Ungheria*, 19–36.
[131] *MDE*, 1.335–6, no 207, and cf. *VMH*, 2.380–2, no 566; Jászay, 'Venezia', 7. The terms agreed in 1463 were more specific for Venice (40 war galleys plus operations in Dalmatia and the Peloponnese) than for Hungary (attacks 'a parte terre omni suo conatu'), probably reflecting each contracting party's bargaining position.
[132] *MDE*, 1.262–3, no 160. Cf. *Ungedruckte Akten*, 217–23, no 159, at 221–2: 'Il principale fundamento de tutta l'impresa si è la potentia de Ungari.'
[133] *MDE*, 1.125–8, no 80, citing at 127 the going rate of 3 ducats per month for the lightly-armed Hungarian horsemen; see also ibid.1.380–5, no 231, at 381, an estimate by Girolamo Lando that the king needed 300,000 ducats a year from external sources to fight effectively. For more on pay rates see ch. 4.

May 1462 that a legate should manage the money, to ensure its expenditure *utiliter* on paid troops.[134] In January 1464 Venice undertook to pay Matthias a total of 60,000 ducats for the coming season's campaign, to release munitions from its Dalmatian fortresses, and to lobby for additional sums from the Pope and other rulers. As in 1462 the republic was cautious, requiring its envoy not just to find out details about the precise numbers and types of soldiers whom the king proposed paying for service, but also to investigate whether more could be hired for the same outlay if they were foreign mercenaries.[135] In the summer of 1464 it faced the task of coordinating its own troop movements in the Peloponnese with the contributions expected from both Pius and Matthias, not to speak of finding an outlet for the crusading volunteers who were arriving. Logistically and financially, the republic was pushed to the limit, but it was rescued by the 40,314 ducats from crusade funds that the cardinals channelled through Venice to Matthias following Pius II's death in August.[136]

In 1465 Venice undertook to pay Matthias 50,000 ducats, despite expenses for its own land and sea operations that were so great 'that in truth they challenge not just belief but even description'.[137] This was not hyperbole: Venice's estimate in October 1463 that the war would cost 600,000 ducats a year had proved to be just 50 per cent of its outgoings.[138] So the mobilization of Italian help beyond the limited holdings of the *depositeria della crociata* was a *sine qua non* for keeping the Veneto-Hungarian alliance in being. An Italian-Hungarian axis was the obvious way forward now that Burgundy was out of the equation. Late in 1464 Paul II and his powerful new crusade commission (comprising Bessarion, Guillaume d'Estouteville, and Carvajal) attempted to establish a quota system for Hungary's support, with 100,000 ducats apiece due from the Pope and Venice, and a further 258,000 in total to be paid by the other powers.[139] The predictable response from all the envoys including Venice's was that they would have to refer it to their masters.[140] The answers that came back were considered by Paul and the members of the commission, and at the end of March 1465 the Pope reviewed the situation in a consistory that was attended by the envoys. Some states had not yet replied; others offered less or wanted to commute all or part of their contribution into troops; Venice, Florence, and Milan made their offers conditional on grants of taxes that they could collect in their lands, while Ferrante wanted his accumulated census debts to the Pope cancelled. Predictably, the scenario was a rerun of Mantua

---

[134] Ibid. 1.125–8, no 80, 133–4, no 84, 153–6, no 96, 164–5, no 102.
[135] Ibid. 1.262–6, nos 160–1.
[136] Ibid. 1.276–88, nos 167–73, 291–3, no 176, 300–1, no 181; Damian, 'La *Depositeria*', 143–4, 150.
[137] *MDE*, 1.112–13, no190, 320–7, nos 197–200, 332–3, no 205, 335–6, no 207, 339–40, no 210, 344–9, no 213, with quote at 332.
[138] Ibid.1.242–3, no 150, at 243. Mallett and Hale, *Military Organization*, 130, reach 1,200,000 a year.
[139] This sum would have funded 30,000 Hungarian mounted troops for a 6 month campaign.
[140] Ammannati Piccolomini, *Lettere*, 1.572–8, no 88. The proposed quotas (in ducats) were: Ferrara 20,000; Florence 50,000; Lucca 8,000; Mantua 10,000; Milan70,000; Montferrat 5,000; Naples 80,000; Paul II 100,000; Siena 15,000; Venice 100,000.

as well as the discussions that Pius II had held with the Italians in the autumn of 1463. The alleged preference for sending troops rather than money was a remarkable reversal of the usual trend to commute service into cash payments, but it was probably no more than a delaying tactic. Even if the soldiers offered by Milan, Naples, and Florence were sent, the proposal was to ship them to Epiros, so the logistical nightmare of 1464 would recur; besides, there would be fewer combatants because Italians were paid more, while Matthias's wage bills would go unpaid. The Pope was indignant; the envoys were making him choose between impracticability and failure. They should go away and reflect, because in a matter of weeks the Turks would be on the march.[141]

Much of Paul's indignation was feigned: as a Venetian he knew better than most that assembling a peninsular league in order to support a Venetian war was never going to be straightforward; quite apart from the general dislike felt for the republic there was the legal consideration that its overseas dominions had in the past been excluded from the league. The fallback position was soldiering on with the tripartite alliance and, for operations in 1465, the Pope supplemented Venice's 50,000 ducats.[142] On 26 May he wrote to Matthias apologizing for his inability to provide more money, but granting full crusade indulgences to his soldiers and promising prayers; he also sent the king the *turchetto*, whom Matthias should use as well as he might.[143] Separately, on the same day he wrote in relation to a courteous exchange of gifts: Matthias had sent the Pope a horse and sword captured from the Turks and, in exchange, Paul sent a gold cross enclosing relics, which the king could use in war for their talismanic powers.[144] Already, however, Matthias was encouraging peace overtures with the Turks, establishing the terms on which he and his principal ally could free themselves from a war that both were finding cripplingly expensive and for which assistance from their fellow Christians was nugatory.[145] In Paul II's furious response to this news, dated November 1465, we encounter a full and eloquent statement of how the league formed two years previously was perceived at Rome. This was no ordinary war.

> This war was indeed proclaimed and initiated not by one individual or another, but by the prince of the faith, the high pontiff, Christ's vicar, by the decree and with the advice of the Church's sacred senate [sc. the College of Cardinals]. And not just one but many past Popes have sanctioned the conduct of such a war when the faith urgently needed it, in defence of Christ's Gospel, calling on every orthodox prince and all of the faithful, in the name of their common faith and shared peril.

To quit such a conflict was an act of desertion, 'than which the founders of civil law judged nothing to be more serious, for they condemned deserters in the harshest possible terms as traitors to the public's safety'. Matthias was reminded of Pius II's solemn statement that the cause was so crucial that its support by each and every

---

[141] Ammannati Piccolomini, *Lettere*, 1.683–8, no 132. See also Setton, *Papacy*, 2.275–6.
[142] The sources are opaque: *MDE*, 1.330, no 203 (57,500), 345, no 213 (62,000); *MCH*, 45–8, no 35 (just 7,550, but making a total to date of 100,000); Damian, 'La *Depositeria*', 146–7.
[143] *MCH*, 45–8, no 35.   [144] Ibid. 48–9, no 36.   [145] *MDE*, 1.341–9, nos 211–13.

Christian believer was *de necessitate salutis*. 'Pius established this by decree, taught it by example, and confirmed it by his own death...[and] who will dare to claim that one king or several can make peace or forge an alliance which flouts a general decree of the Church?' As for the peace negotiations,

> to such an extent did our holy fathers, and Popes long past, abominate every agreement made with the infidels once the Church had proclaimed war against them, that they banned and condemned not just trade with the infidels in prohibited articles, but commerce of any kind, subjecting the guilty to perpetual anathema, loss of status, and confiscation of property.

These lofty pronouncements, worthy of a thirteenth-century Pope, were buttressed not just by allusions to scripture and Roman history, but also by a juridical point: it was alleged that Matthias was in alliance with the Pope[146] and, having accepted subsidies, he was legally bound to persevere with the war.[147]

The Pope wrote with dignity, but no real hope of turning the situation around. It was telling that the letter's theological, juridical, scriptural, and classical content was supplemented by a more practical argument to the effect that the Turks broke their promises, as their relations with Bosnia had shown. Matthias's nonchalant reply was that Paul should not believe everything he heard. He would always be the enemy of the Turks, provided he was afforded the wherewithal to fight them. 'To conclude: if your holiness really wants to stop me making peace with the enemies of the faith, he has to give me the means to keep the war going.'[148] It was a theme that he never tired of repeating. As if to emphasize his point, he wrote shortly afterwards to Louis XI thanking the French king for a recent assurance of his zeal 'towards myself and the matter of defending the faith against the Turks'. Coolly, Matthias informed Louis that he was pleased to hear it; his brevity probably summed up his feelings on the subject.[149] By the end of 1465 Matthias had lost interest in pursuing the war against Mehmed, and a Milanese despatch reported that the Venetians, unhappy with the king's contribution, were intending to focus their efforts in 1466 on the Peloponnese.[150] Unwilling to lose the subsidies, Matthias responded to his allies' disappointment with his customary finesse. In a letter to Paul on 2 October he took issue with the Pope's claim that he had taken no action to resist vigorous Turkish offensives in Bosnia and Illyria (that is, Dalmatia and Albania). There were no fresh Turks in Bosnia, he argued, and the only ones further south were captives. There was no point in embarking on major offensives every year: it was much wiser to build up his forces for a really big campaign. In the meantime, he could account for every penny that had been sent him.[151] Shortly afterwards he expanded on this point in another letter to Paul:

---

[146] '...preter generale decretum speciali Romane ecclesie in exequendis omnibus, que ad hoc bellum pertinent, iunctus es federe': *MCH*, 64–7, no 45, at 66. It is unclear how Matthias was formally allied with the Pope, given that the king was not a party to the October 1463 Rome treaty.

[147] Ibid. 64–7, for the arguments including the quotations. See also *MKL*, 1.124–6, no 88, at 124–5.

[148] Ibid. 1.124–6, no 88, at 126.   [149] Ibid. 1.130–1, no 95.

[150] *MDE*, 1.380–5, no 231.   [151] *MKL*, 1.105–12, no 77.

It has always been my considered view and strategic goal to avoid campaigning on a limited scale (*particularibus expeditionibus*), which wears us down more than the enemy. In due course, once sufficient strength is assembled, I shall stage an attack with God's help on the heartlands (*viscera*) of our common foe. A single encounter with combined manpower will free both me and other Christians from this incessant harassment (*quotidiana molestia*).[152]

There was a military logic to this, but it did nothing to help the Venetians and it was hardly the 'maximum effort' that the Hungarians had agreed to provide in 1463.[153] As for the Pope, for all the lofty indignation that he directed at Matthias, his attention was already turning towards a show-down with George Podiebrad; a policy shift that Matthias proved happy to support.[154]

The alliance established in 1463 did not expire in 1465; it endured a long drawn-out demise in the years that followed. Matthias continued to cooperate with Venice when it suited him. In April 1467, for example, having heard about substantial Turkish preparations, he urged the republic to focus on organizing forces on land so that Hungary did not have to bear the brunt of the onslaught. 'We know from experience that the enemy can neither be damaged, nor damage us much, by way of the sea.'[155] As so often, strategic wisdom about the desirability of fighting both by land and by sea was tacitly set aside when self-interest was at stake. There were more than enough reasons for the allies to fall out, such as Matthias's ambitions on Herzegovina and Trieste, and Venice's on Segna, even before the king's three-year truce with the Turks in October 1467. Hungary's relations with Venice were dealt a severe blow by the diplomatic volte-face that Matthias executed at the end of 1476 when he married Beatrice of Aragon, thereby aligning himself with Naples.[156] In the 1480s the Djem issue became another destabilizing factor, with Venice fearing that Hungarian possession of the prince would be used not to attack Bayezid II but to channel Turkish aggression against them. The fact that the two powers never came to blows was due not to the Turks but to their mutual anxiety about Frederick III.[157]

Rome's relationship with Matthias also changed considerably. In 1473 Sixtus IV complained to the king about news that he was not just seeking terms with Mehmed but, shockingly, hoped to negotiate a Turco-Hungarian alliance directed against Uzun Hasan. The Pope's arguments contrast strikingly with the ones that his predecessor had deployed eight years earlier. Gone was the high-flying rhetoric about Matthias's religious and juridical obligations. Certainly, Matthias could expect to suffer God's wrath, but most of Sixtus's points were pragmatic: the notorious duplicity of the Turks; domestic discontent; loss of face abroad (where his

---

[152] Ibid. 1.122–3, no 86.   [153] *VMH*, 2.380–2, no 566.
[154] *MKL*, 1.112–14, no 78. *VMH*, 2.421, no 600, shows that even in the months following the fall of Negroponte, Paul II was unwilling to encourage Matthias to be diverted from Bohemia to put pressure on Mehmed.
[155] *MKL*, 1.194–6, no 133, at 195, and cf. ibid. 1.196–200, nos 134–5.
[156] Jászay, 'Venezia', 10–11.
[157] See Teke, 'Rapporti', 30 and *passim*. Jászay, 'Venezia', 16 points out that in 1488 Venice turned down a Croatian offer to assassinate Matthias.

Bohemian intervention would be construed as cynical adventurism); the Pope's hostility; and the forfeiting of all the personal fame accumulated in years of fighting against Turks and heretics.[158] Clearly, a Christian king who was prepared to help Mehmed fight the Muslim ruler in whom Venice and Sixtus alike had invested so heavily had forfeited (at least for the time being) any legal or moral claim to subsidies from either. That said, in the following years occasions continued to arise when either Matthias or his client Stephen of Moldavia engaged with the Turks, dressing their activities in the appropriate *antemurale* language, so money went on making its way eastwards, though never in quantities large enough to satisfy Matthias.[159]

Notwithstanding Paul II's failure in 1465, hopes persisted that an effective league of the Italian powers might be created. As early as February 1468 Paul issued the bull *Ut liberius iustissimum bellum*, which renewed the post-Lodi *confoederationem, unionem, intelligentiam et ligam*. Its major members were Naples, Venice, Milan, and Florence, and the condottiere Bartolomeo Colleoni of Bergamo was appointed to act as commander of an expedition against the Turks, working with quota payments from the contracting powers that totalled 100,000 florins.[160] The Pope appears to have been genuinely pursuing the twin cause of peace and crusade, and his proposed payments were significantly more modest than those of 1465, but, if Paul hoped that these factors would advance his cause, he was disappointed.[161] On the face of it, the league that was formed in late December 1470 had more traction, thanks to the fall of Negroponte in the previous summer. This disaster generated much anxiety and foreboding, inspiring Bessarion to make his last big effort to promote a crusade. The members of the league formed in July between Naples, Milan, and Florence had agreed that none of the provisions of their 'particular league' would be allowed to stand in the way of the Pope's general one.[162] This appeared to be a useful acknowledgement of peninsular common interests, but in reality it highlighted the complexity of the political entanglements involved. Even Venice had resorted to playing a dangerous double game, trying to balance its need for Italian assistance in Greece against its anxiety about Paul's ambitions in Romagna.[163] The result was that it proved no easier than in the past to secure agreement on the quotas that were to be applied. In a letter to his father in January 1471 Cardinal Francesco Gonzaga reported Venice's ungracious response to an offer by Paul to contribute 50,000 ducats a year in addition to the dedicated alum revenue. Although this was a full quarter of his revenue, it was

---

[158] *MCH*, 89–93, no 69.
[159] e.g. ibid. 95–6, no 71, 120–1, no 91. Generally see Weber, 'La croisade impossible', 309–21.
[160] *AE*, 10.454–7, ad ann. 1468, nos 15–20. The proposed quotas (in florins) were: Florence 15,000; Lucca, Modena, and Siena 9,000; Milan 19,000; Naples 19,000; Paul II and the *camera apostolica* 19,000; Venice 19,000. See also Pastor, *History*, 4.156–8.
[161] See *DBI*, 27.9–19, at 15. It may be significant that in 1475 Colleoni bequeathed 100,000 ducats to the crusade, jointly with an equestrian statue (eventually designed by Andrea del Verrocchio).
[162] *AE*, 10.492–3, ad ann. 1470, no 42.
[163] Pastor, *History*, 4.172–3; Robertson, 'Pietro Barbo-Paul II, 168–71. Setton, *Papacy*, 2.299 and note 104 does not capture the political manoeuvring behind the 1470 leagues.

only half of what he had been prepared to offer in 1465.[164] Venice argued that, given the critical situation facing Italy, the Pope should sell his jewels and the cardinals pay half of their revenue.[165]

It was in Sixtus IV's response to Gedük Ahmed Pasha's capture of Otranto in August 1480 that the complexities of Italian politics impinged most conspicuously on the prospects of organizing an Italian league.[166] Ferrante was Sixtus's enemy, but the Ottoman threat was not something that the Pope could ignore, because 'this enemy of the Christian name, seeking to subvert religion and all things sacred, had set foot in Italy, and unless he was rapidly dealt with, he would entirely destroy the papacy and the Roman name'.[167] According to one contemporary report, Sixtus gave serious thought to abandoning Rome.[168] His immediate assistance to Naples was therefore generous: he issued crusade indulgences, rerouted money that had been raised for Rhodes, sent southwards troops who were in his pay, and appointed Gabriele Rangoni as his legate to manage the various contributions.[169] His bull *Super securitate Italiae*, issued on 16 September, attempted to restore peace to Italy, and the Pope summoned a meeting of the powers at Rome for 1 November.[170] Although this was couched as a general invitation, Sixtus's thoughts were clearly focused on his fellow Italians.[171] But French envoys also attended the Rome meeting and what was formulated in April 1481 was, on the face of it, an impressive programme intended to last for three years. It comprised naval power accompanied by relatively handsome subsidies intended for the use of Matthias. The Pope would provide twenty-five galleys and 50,000 florins *de camera*, while Ferrante would equip forty galleys and send his Hungarian son-in-law 100,000 ducats. Other galleys and subsidies were allocated between the various contracting powers, with the total reaching eighty-two galleys and 200,000 gold pieces.[172] Venice, which had only recently concluded peace with Mehmed after its long war and adamantly refused to play any role, reacted to Sixtus's summons with astonishing candour: 'Many noble and impressive things will be said and proposed, but they will resemble the fantasies of the past rather than anything substantial and appropriate.'[173] A contribution was, however, expected from Louis XI. It was to assume the form of either ships or money; and the king was allowed to decide which and how

---

[164] It is not clear whether the 1465 papal quota was intended to include money from the alum account.

[165] Pastor, *History*, 4.497–8. See too Setton, *Papacy*, 2.312.

[166] For the campaign see Imber, *Ottoman Empire*, 249–51; Setton, *Papacy*, 343–5, 364–73.

[167] Sigismondo de' Conti, *Le storie*, bk 3, ch. 5, 1.109.

[168] Somaini, 'La curia romana', 213: Somaini provides an exhaustive analysis of the crisis. See also Fossati, 'Milano'.

[169] Somaini, 'La curia romana', 232–3, 235–6, summarized in Sigismondo de' Conti, *Le storie*, bk 3, ch. 5, 1.109–10.

[170] Somaini, 'La curia romana', 233–4.   [171] Fossati, 'Milano', 55, 58.

[172] *AE*, ad ann. 1481, nos 4–13, 11.2–4. The full breakdown was: Bologna 2 galleys; Ferrara 4 galleys; Florence 20,000 ducats; Genoa 5 galleys; Lucca 1 galley; Mantua and Montferrat 1 galley; Milan 30,000 ducats; Naples 40 galleys and 100,000 ducats; Siena 4 galleys; Sixtus IV 50,000 florins *de camera* and 25 galleys.

[173] Cit. Setton, *Papacy*, 2.367, note 13. The bruising effect of the war of 1463–79 was still in evidence 13 years later: *AR*, no 237.

much. By contrast, any Italian power that defaulted on its quota would be fined 1,000 marks. This was anomalous, but it was only the tip of an iceberg of incongruity generated by the deeply politicized character of Sixtus's crusade policy.

There were two levels of complexity in the Pope's proposed league. The first derived from Louis XI's involvement. Felice Fossati and Francesco Somaini showed that the French intervention was driven largely by the prospect of securing concessions from Sixtus (above all on the Burgundian succession), and that once Louis's envoys had got what they wanted, this broader background fell away.[174] This mattered because the inclusion of France would have established what Sixtus was doing as a European rather than an Italian engagement. Given their real objectives, Louis's envoys were not going to enter a legally binding league, and this approach was deemed acceptable on the specious grounds that the framework had to be kept as loose as possible to encourage other European powers to join later. Sixtus described what was proposed as *fraternità et non lega*, implying less juristic formalism.[175] The draft resolution was therefore hybrid in character. In part, it followed the pattern of Pius II's approach at Mantua and, in part, that of the Italian leagues that Paul II had repeatedly tried to form. Of course, Louis XI also had Italian interests. In 1479 he had intervened in the Pope's dispute with Florence, taking his cue from Sixtus's crusading language and the disheartening news of the Veneto-Turkish peace to lobby for the Pope to be less severe in his dealings with Lorenzo de' Medici, 'so that Christian arms may be redirected against the most savage Turk'.[176] The background to Sixtus's handling of events at Otranto was thus a diplomatic discourse that was thoroughly marinated in crusading rhetoric, but a rhetoric lacking the urgency that was bestowed by the presence of a Turkish army 10,000 strong in Apulia. Given that the Turkish threat had been constantly deployed both for Lorenzo (by Louis) and against him (by Sixtus), it is unsurprising to find a degree of detached *Schadenfreude* in the Medicean commentary on the 1480–1 crisis.[177]

The second level of complexity arose from the fact that on 25 July 1480, just three days previous to the Turkish landing, Naples had entered a league with Milan, Florence, and Ferrara in response to Sixtus's recent alliance with Venice. With the Turks on his soil, this entitled Ferrante to demand assistance from the other three contracting powers and, since he was not a member of the league, Sixtus could have remained aloof from the whole business. But with the French watching his every move this would have been a disastrous course of action. More to the point, the Otranto crisis gave Sixtus the opportunity to frustrate the 1480 league by creating an anti-Turkish one. It stood to reason that a peninsular league, formed to confront an external and common threat, overrode the provisions of any specific

---

[174] Fossati, 'Milano', 68, and cf. Somaini, 'La curia romana', 236–8, note 50.
[175] Ibid. 254–6, with quote at note 104; Fossati,'Milano', 68–9.
[176] Sigismondo de' Conti, *Le storie*, 1.396–404, *appendice*, no 5, with quote at 399, and cf. 1.387–92, no 3.
[177] Lorenzo de' Medici, *Lettere, V (1480–1481)*, ed. Michael Mallett (Florence, 1989), esp. 40–61, no 468, 63–74, no 470, 104–7, no 477, 122–48, nos 482–3, 151–9, no 485, 192–9, no 487, 180–93, no 491, 219–30, no 497, 260–72, no 504.

league, though it proved impossible for him to persuade Venice to assist in driving the Turks from Otranto.[178] In political terms, Otranto therefore presented Sixtus with both a threat and an opportunity.[179] It added a further degree of unpredictability to a scenario that was already volatile, not least thanks to the behaviour of Sixtus's nephew, Girolamo Riario; and it provided the French with dangerous ammunition. But more importantly, like *Super securitate Italiae,* it offered the prospect of Sixtus deploying his spiritual authority in a crisis situation, like the sword of Damocles, to cut through the unresolved issues of the day.[180] In April 1481 the bull *Cogimur iubente altissimo* decreed a truce to last for three years starting on 1 June.[181] This did not stop the Pope covertly persisting with his own machinations on behalf of Riario.[182] While leaving the most unscrupulous activities to his nephew, the Pope himself played a double game, running a stop-go policy on the provision of help to Ferrante and failing to follow through on his own measures of pacification.[183] Sixtus's procedure of negotiating bilaterally with the envoys who assembled at Rome usefully sowed suspicion among the members of the 1480 league.[184] Lorenzo was driven to toying with the idea of subverting Sixtus's position by promoting a 'general or universal league' under the aegis of Federico da Montefeltro, who enjoyed the respect of all.[185] But for the moment Sixtus had the upper hand and he made the most of it. For instance, when granting the Florentines their long-delayed absolution on 3 December, the Pope made it conditional on a previously undiscussed demand for fifteen fully equipped galleys for the crusade.[186] The Florentine and Milanese envoys at Rome had to battle to secure acceptable terms for their masters, and the eventual split into naval and financial quotas was the outcome of some hard bargaining that spring.[187]

In practice the league came to nothing. In part, this was due to Mehmed II's death in May 1481, though as with the similar cases of Nicholas V's demise during the Wiener Neustadt diet of 1455, and Matthias's during the Rome congress of 1490, we have to distinguish between cause, catalyst, and excuse. Such were the political conundrums bedevilling the Rome talks in the spring of 1481 that it is impossible to gauge what would have happened had the Turks at Otranto been reinforced.[188] Lorenzo de' Medici's most telling commentary on the whole sequence

---

[178] Sixtus had asserted in 1479 that a 'generalis confederatio' formed to fight the Turks took priority over 'ligarum particularium conditiones': Sigismondo de' Conti, *Le storie,* 1.387–92, appendice, no 3, at 390.

[179] Somaini, 'La curia romana', 220.

[180] Lorenzo de' Medici, *Lettere,* V, 40–61, no 468, at 53–4, 63–74, no 470, at 66–7; Shaw, 'Papal Court', 626.

[181] *AE,* ad ann. 1481, nos 20–3, 11.5–7.

[182] Lorenzo de' Medici, *Lettere,* V, 122–36, no 482.

[183] Somaini, 'La curia romana', 244–5, and more broadly 248–9.

[184] Lorenzo de' Medici, *Lettere,* V, documento II, 118–21. [185] Ibid. 122–36, no 482.

[186] Ibid. 81–92, no 473, at 83–4, noting that d'Estouteville, one of the cardinals charged with managing the crusade, told the Florentine envoys not to take the demand seriously.

[187] Ibid. 137–48, no 483, 151–9, no 485, 162–9, no 487, 180–93, no 491.

[188] Somaini's verdict ('La curia romana', 257) is forthright: neither 'una grande mobilizatione della Cristianità' nor 'una piena ed autentica collaborazione tra i vari Stati italiani' was realizable under Sixtus IV.

of events came in a letter of instruction to Niccolò Michelozzi on 3 July. Lorenzo asked what stood in the way of 'this most holy proposal' for a general league. His reply was two-fold: the antagonism between Sixtus and Ferrante, and Venice's peace with the Turks. The only solution to the first issue was to bring the Pope into the 1480 league. This would have the beneficial effect of isolating Venice, though it would make the league itself unstable. As for Venice and the anti-Turkish league, the republic was so averse to breaking its peace with the Turks that the only way to induce it to join would be to suppress any open statement of the league's intention.[189] It was ironic that whereas leagues that actually had peninsular objectives had started to broadcast their crusading credentials,[190] a league that actually *was* directed against the Turks would have to be camouflaged. Lorenzo's musings confirm that a reliance on leagues had no more chance of bringing war to the Turks than it had of restoring peace in the peninsula. But as so often, it was the frontline powers that passed the most incisive comments on events. Venice, as we have seen, dismissed the whole business as play-acting and fantasy. Matthias was more interventionist. He sent troops to his father-in-law and gave him useful advice on retaking Otranto;[191] he told the Pope that while he was pleased to hear about the money supposedly coming his way, he placed little hope in it;[192] and, when Cardinal Gabriele Rangoni complained about his losses in the Otranto campaign, he told him that to experience *real* war with the Turks he would have to come to Hungary.[193]

3.5 *UNUM TANDEM REMEDIUM*: LEADING FROM THE FRONT

When he delivered his overview of his crusading plans to a select group of his cardinals in spring 1462, Pius concluded that there was 'one last remedy' to get his stalled programme moving again. This final resort was to offer personal participation in the expedition. Such a proposal would exert moral pressure on Philip of Burgundy to keep the vow that he had sworn, and in turn this would lever others, above all, France, Venice, and Hungary, into providing the troops and ships required. Scepticism would give way to zeal when people saw that the Pope was prepared to offer 'not just his money but his body itself for Christ's name'.[194] All of the techniques of mobilization that we have examined so far were attempted by Pius II, but this last one is uniquely associated with that Pope. It became the hallmark of his programme, finding eloquent expression in such texts as *Ezechielis prophetae*, his last substantial crusade statement of October 1463, and *Suscepturi*

---

[189] Lorenzo de' Medici, *Lettere*, V, 260–72, no 504.   [190] e.g. ibid. 294.
[191] *MKL*, 2.104–10, no 61, at 107–9.
[192] *MCH*, 165–9, no 127, at 166, and cf. 139–40, no 111 (22 May 1481, misdated 1480); *MKL*, 2.104–10, no 61, at 106, 125–6, no 71.
[193] Ibid. 191–5, no 103.   [194] *Pii II Commentarii*, bk 7, ch. 16, 460–3, with quote at 463.

hodie, the sermon he gave on 18 June 1464 at St Peter's when he took the cross.[195] Rodrigo Sánchez de Arévalo prepared an oration for delivery to the army once it had assembled at Ancona, and he planned to open it with a rhetorical flourish by quoting Isaiah 49.18 and 60.4: 'Lift up your eyes round about, and behold: all these have gathered themselves together, and come to you.'[196] By that stage, the Pope's personal commitment needed support from Sánchez and others because it had become highly controversial, but it seems that the criticism and polemics that it generated were successfully countered by Pius's apologists. For with hindsight, his death while waiting for the Venetian ships became both praiseworthy and symbolic, sealing his reputation as the greatest crusading Pope of the age and providing a valuable seam of kudos for his successors to mine.[197]

There is no reason to doubt the essential veracity of Pius's own recording of his decision in the *Commentarii*. In *Cum bellum hodie*, his crusade oration of 26 September 1459 at Mantua, he had already stated that he would go in person if that was the wish of his audience. As in 1462, the context for the offer was his perception that one of the most important reasons why the call to crusade was received with scepticism was that people no longer believed what the Pope said. In coming to Mantua, Pius had already prioritized the defence of the faith over the interests of his health and the patrimony of St Peter.[198] Going on crusade would be an extension of that, and the reason why he pursued it in 1462 and not in 1459 was the failure in the mean time of his *nationum consensus* approach, and the potential for action that still appeared to reside with Burgundy, Hungary, and Venice (the hopes that he expressed about France were surely there for effect). The absence of precedent in terms of previous Popes is irrelevant, given the radical westwards shift of the location for campaigning. Aside from Calixtus, no Pope before Pius would have had the option of presiding over a crusade by simply crossing the Adriatic. No other explanation than the practical one stands up well to scrutiny. It is probable, though improvable, that Pius was influenced by the inspirational effect of Capistrano's leadership at Belgrade in 1456. As for the difficult political situation facing the Pope, who had suffered the failure of his Mantua programme and felt threatened by the accumulation of hostile forces in France, Bohemia, and Germany, pursuing the idea of personal participation was a high risk strategy, carrying the danger of worsening Pius's predicament. Naturally a successful crusade, or one that could be depicted as such, would rescue Pius from criticism, but the history of recent crusading offered little hope of that, and nobody was better acquainted with that history than Pius.

---

[195] *Vetera monumenta Slavorum*, 474–81, no 660, also in Piccolomini, *Opera omnia*, 914–23; *Anecdota litteraria ex MSS codicibus eruta*, ed. J.C. Amaduteus and G.L. Bianconius, 4 vols (Rome, 1773–83), 3.287–96.
[196] Benziger, *Zur Theorie*, 154–8, esp. 155.
[197] For a full consideration of this subject in terms of Pius's crusade programme and policies see my 'Pius II'.
[198] *Pii II orationes*, 2.7–30, no 2, also in Piccolomini, *Opera omnia*, 905–14; *Sacrorum conciliorum*, 32.207–21.

Pius's personal commitment did break down scepticism, but arguably not in the way he hoped. We shall see that voluntary service was encouraged by the prospect of the Pope accompanying his crusaders on campaign. There was an uncontrollable surge of recruitment, which the ramshackle military framework of the Pope's enterprise proved incapable of accommodating. Other gains were minimal. No princes leapt to arms; in fact Pius suffered the crippling blow of Philip the Good's withdrawal from the crusade under French pressure. The *rex christianissimus* was not shamed into offering support for the crusade by the Pope's example, nor was he deterred from hindering it by the severe sanctions threatened in *Ezechielis prophetae*.[199] Neither clerics nor lay folk paid their taxes for the crusade more willingly because of papal participation. His actions assisted with few if any of the expedition's military prerequisites. In fact, they may even have contributed towards its mismanagement, and the Pope's apologists had to defend his reputation against the charge that the administration of the Roman church and the government of its lands had suffered as a result of his absence. Jacopo Ammannati Piccolomini in particular shouldered the burden of defending the dead Pope. In January 1465 he wrote to another of Pius's intimates, Goro Lolli, citing the backbiting that came from Pius's critics in relation to both Mantua and Ancona: 'such was the fruitlessness of the congress at Mantua, such the empty and pointless hope of setting out against the Turks'.[200] At the beginning of autumn 1465 he wrote again to Lolli commending Campano's *Vita* as a fitting apologia for the maligned Pope.[201] And in 1466 Ammannati wrote to Cardinal Francesco Todeschini Piccolomini overtly defending Francesco's uncle against the charge of excessive absence from Rome. He argued that convening the Mantua congress had been essential to secure any progress on the crusade, while the journey to Ancona was undertaken to pressurize Philip of Burgundy into keeping his promise.[202]

But while personal participation turned out to be unprofitable in military terms, it does seem to have restored at least some of the *curia*'s seriously diminished moral credit. Or to put it more pragmatically, it came to be viewed as a significant feature of a Pope's crusading profile. In Rodrigo Sánchez's history of Spain, published at Rome in 1470, the *topos* of Pius's weak body and strong spirit was already in place, together with the claim that the Pope was betrayed by the cowardice and quarrelling of others.[203] As Ammannati put it in a letter to Francesco da Toledo in July 1475, in a wicked world it was better to say 'come' than 'go'.[204] Of course, not all such claims can be taken at face value. An assertion by Sixtus IV in 1476 that he would do all in his power to resist the Turks, even shedding his own blood if necessary, may safely be regarded as rhetorical.[205] Following the Turkish capture of Otranto the Milanese envoys at Rome reported that Sixtus IV was so fired up by

---

[199] Piccolomini, *Opera omnia*, 923.
[200] Ammannati Piccolomini, *Lettere*, 2.614–22, no 104, at 616.
[201] Ibid. 2.835–41, no 192, at 836–7.   [202] Ibid. 2.885–92, no 212, at pp. 887–91.
[203] Rodrigo Sánchez de Arévalo, 'Historiae Hispanicae partes quatuor', in *Hispaniae illustratae seu rerum urbiumque Hispaniae...scriptores varii*, ed. Andreas Schott, 4 vols (Frankfurt, 1603–8), 1.121–246, at 244–5.
[204] Ammannati Piccolomini, *Lettere*, 3.1976–8, no 819, at 1977.   [205] *MCH*, 120–1, no 94.

events 'that maybe one day, sick as he was, he would climb on a horse with the cross before him, to campaign against the wicked Turk'.[206] We detect here the distancing irony that tended to characterize the despatches of the envoys, but in the calmer circumstances of the Rome congress in the summer of 1490 Innocent VIII declared that he would accompany the crusade that was being discussed, if he thought it would help.[207] Alexander VI made the offer on several occasions. In April 1494 he countered the crusade call that Charles VIII had issued at Lyon by declaring that he would accompany a crusade provided Charles, Maximilian, and Ferdinand of Spain all took part.[208] He returned to the offer several times in 1500,[209] and in February 1502.[210] The Venetian report that described the last of these offers began by recounting the Pope's desperate manoeuvring to stop Maximilian and Louis XII reaching the agreement that brought even the possibility of a joint crusade back onto the diplomatic agenda. If that was going to happen, the Pope was concerned to keep his control over the sources of funding, especially tenths and indulgences.[211] Alexander seems to have judged that making the offer of personal participation played a part in that bargaining process, presumably because it checked the offers of leadership that were being advanced by the secular rulers with whom he was dealing.

The resulting divorce between claims and substance was colourfully demonstrated by Leonello Chiericati in the sermon that he delivered in St Peter's on Palm Sunday 1495, celebrating the anti-French alliance that had been concluded between Alexander, Maximilian, Ferdinand, Venice, and Milan. Ostensibly, this was a crusading coalition and Chiericati built his sermon around that fiction. 'With incomparable piety', he declared, 'the world's leading princes have offered and dedicated themselves and all that they possess, for the holy Roman church and the protection and extension of the *respublica Christiana*.'[212] Echoes of 1464 were inescapable. Many in the audience must have known that thirty-one years previously Pius II had taken the cross on this very spot, and Chiericati pressed into service the same passage from Isaiah that Sánchez had proposed using at Ancona. The preacher declared that Alexander, like Pius before him, would accompany the crusaders; a second Moses, he would raise his hands in prayer for Christian victory. Charles VIII, who had expressed his yearning to fight against the Turks, would surely not hold back when he saw the Pope offering his old age to Christ's service. Chiericati's eloquent exercise in camouflage powerfully illustrates the central paradox of contemporary diplomacy, which was that it was altogether easier to mobilize states to get the French out of Italy than to stop the Ottomans getting in.[213]

---

[206] Somaini, 'La curia romana', 234.
[207] Sigismondo de' Conti, *Le storie*, 2.429–36, *appendice*, no 16, at 429.
[208] *AR*, no 2974.
[209] *VMP*, 2.269–76, no 297, at 269; Burchard, *Liber*, 2.220–4 at 222 (= *AR*, no 14158); Sanuto, *I diarii*, 3.1256 (= *AR*, no 14790).
[210] Ibid. no 16034.   [211] e.g. ibid. no 16035.
[212] Sigismondo de' Conti, *Le storie*, 2.439–44, *appendice*, no 18, with quote at 443.
[213] For details on the 1495 Holy League see Pastor, *History*, 5.465–7; Setton, *Papacy*, 2.487–9 incl. note 25 on Chiericati's Palm Sunday sermon.

4

Recruitment and finance

In this chapter we shall focus on the two elements that contemporaries agreed to be the key to successfully waging war: recruitment and finance. We shall ask whether crusading, as it was reformulated and managed in the second half of the fifteenth century, was able to deliver these human and material resources in a way that offered the prospect of defeating the Turks. And we shall do so largely in terms of a tension between the voluntary and the obligatory that was of long standing in crusading ideology. Given the way war-making developed in medieval Europe, it is not surprising that this tension dominates our enquiry, just as it shaped the debates of contemporaries. In the central Middle Ages the successful conduct of war by any state came to hinge on the ability of its rulers to compel their subjects to sustain hostilities through taxation. And in the late Middle Ages and early modern period the process went a stage further: success depended on the capacity to maintain standing armies.[1] How should we locate the attempt to deploy the crusade against the Turks in relation to these general developmental trends?

4.1 *CRUCESIGNATI* AND FIFTEENTH-CENTURY CRUSADING

On 20 May 1459, just before the scheduled opening of the congress of Mantua, Cardinal John Bessarion wrote to his close associate, the Franciscan Observant, Jacopo delle Marche, about 'a truly weighty matter, excellent and beneficial for the Christian people'. He sought Jacopo's assistance in assembling an expeditionary force to go to the aid of Thomas Palaeologos in the Peloponnese. Following the Turkish conquest of the region in 1458, in the early months of 1459 the despot had succeeded in recovering the lost lands, but now he faced a counter-attack. There could be no question of waiting for decisions to be made at Mantua. Thomas had desperate need of military reinforcement by mid-July and Pius II had agreed that it should be provided 'by way of crusaders (*crucesignati*)'. Between 300 and 500 soldiers would be needed, and the men whom Jacopo succeeded in persuading to go should be well armed and provided with enough money for a full year, fifty or sixty ducats 'either from their own goods or from the charity of others'.

---

[1] See the essays in Tallett and Trim, eds, *European Warfare*; Steven Gunn, David Grummitt, and Hans Cools, 'War and the State in Early Modern State: Widening the Debate', *War in History*, 15 (2008), 371–88.

Combatants and sponsors alike would receive the full indulgence. The Pope would provide a sailing ship to transport them from Ancona. Jacopo was therefore asked to preach the cross in the March of Ancona and to ensure that the condition about financial support was met in full; he should also brief Pope and cardinal on progress so that Pius could get the ship ready. To help Jacopo carry out this commission, Bessarion opened the letter with a detailed preamble about the economic and strategic significance of the Peloponnese, and the threat posed there by the Turks, 'to inform you of all the specifics needed to exhort and encourage the Christians to undertake this matter in a spirited way'.[2]

As long ago as 1878 Bessarion's biographer Henri Vast recognized the interest of this remarkable letter and the project that it was intended to make possible.[3] First and foremost, it is testimony to Bessarion's advocacy of Palaeologan interests and to his skill as a lobbyist on behalf of the Greek lands that were threatened by Mehmed.[4] But it is revealing also on the place that taking the cross to fight could still occupy in this period in the thinking of crusading enthusiasts like Bessarion and Pius. Vast characterized the task force as 'une sorte de croisade particulière', and it is striking that its participants should be *crucesignati*, financially supported either by themselves or by others. Working with a timetable of less than two months to embarkation, why would Bessarion aim to recruit crusaders rather than hiring mercenaries? The answer may lie precisely in the difficulty of raising such numbers on the mercenary market at short notice and during the campaigning season. Timing was of the essence, and Bessarion appears to have considered it a viable proposition that in about fifty days up to 500 crusaders could be assembled at Ancona. It is possible that he was encouraged to believe this by his encounter a few weeks earlier with Gerard Déschamps. In January 1459 this ebullient crusading enthusiast and entrepreneur had persuaded Bessarion to use his influence with Pius to agree to sanction a *societas Iesu* of up to 10,000 *crucesignati* whom he would recruit in the Burgundian lands, Lorraine, Savoy, and in his home town of Liège. Like the projected Peloponnese contingent, they would be sponsored by others in exchange for the full indulgence. Although Déschamps's scheme looks highly dubious, Pius gave him a warm reception at Mantua in September 1459 and there is some evidence that he did raise recruits, who took part in the Hungarian siege of Jajce in the autumn of 1463.[5] Bessarion's project certainly yielded results. Three hundred well-equipped young men (the lowest figure deemed viable by Bessarion) were despatched in July, co-funded by the Pope and Bianca Maria Sforza, duchess of Milan.[6] The idea of sponsorship was thus promoted on two separate occasions

---

[2] Mohler, *Bessarion*, 3.490–3, no 39, also in *AM*, 13.119–20.
[3] Henri Vast, *Le cardinal Bessarion (1403–1472). Étude sur la Chrétienté et la Renaissance vers le milieu du XVe siècle* (Paris, 1878), 236: 'une letter extrêmement curieuse... une sorte de croisade particulière. Sa lettre est celle d'un homme d'affaires qui expose avec une netteté parfaite tout ce qu'il veut dire.'
[4] Ronchey, 'Malatesta/Paleologhi', *passim*.
[5] Paviot, *Les ducs*, 173–4; Weber, *Lutter*, 2.1.3.
[6] *Pii II Commentarii*, bk 3, ch. 3, 176–7 ('egregie armata et robusta iuventus'); Setton, *Papacy*, 2.210–12.

in 1459, and it may have rendered assistance to both of Christendom's leading pressure points. But this was not exceptional. More than four decades later, in May 1502, Cardinal Raymond Perault wrote confidently that well-off people in Cologne, both men and women, could be persuaded to sponsor crusaders to fight against the Turks.[7] And a year later the emperor-elect, Maximilian, outlined a scheme whereby the quasi-crusading members of his Society of St George would receive half of their support from sponsors and the other half from Perault's indulgence money.[8] The *societas sancti Georgii* raises the same suspicions as Déschamps's *societas Iesu*, and it is a telling reflection on Maximilian's track record as a crusader that even the elusive Déschamps has more credibility.

We must infer that in 1459 the prospect of a campaign whose combatants would be *crucesignati* was located in the real world, while even in 1502–3 such an idea could be floated with a degree of plausibility during the polemical exchanges over what should be done with Perault's collected money. This is surprising for two reasons. In the first place, the period witnessed substantial advances in military professionalism. Such pace-setters as republican Venice and Sforza Milan were moving in the direction of armed forces that were contracted, controlled, and rewarded in accordance with centralized and accountable bureaucratic systems.[9] And in the second place, it was apparent that confronting the Ottoman threat with any hope of success called for a similar approach to be applied to crusading. Dividing the operation of crusade between financial support and military action had been advocated by crusade lobbyists since the late thirteenth century, notably by the Venetian theorist, Marino Sanudo Torsello, in his *Liber secretorum fidelium crucis* (*c*. 1306–21).[10] One would expect this trend to be given fresh impetus by the developments of the mid- to late fifteenth century. Contemporaries were acutely aware of the need to avoid further disasters like the defeat at Varna in 1444.[11] In the detailed treatise that he offered to the papal *curia* during Nicholas V's reign, the Milanese humanist Lampo Birago argued that this could best be done not solely by studying the way the Turks organized their armies but also by learning from past mistakes; though his insight was vitiated by his focus on the Genoese defeat at Solgat in the Crimea in 1434, where they had fought not the Turks but the Tatars.[12] Commentators like Birago were aware of how innovative European war-making had become, and the resulting optimism is summed up by the words that Giovanni da Tagliacozzo placed in Mehmed II's mouth following the rout of the

---

[7] Mehring, 'Peraudi', 398–401, no 6, at 400.

[8] *Volumen*, 214–17. See also Eugen von Frauenholz, *Das Heerwesen in der Zeit des freien Soldnertums, zweiter Teil: Das Heerwesen des Reiches in der Landsknechtszeit* (Munich, 1937), 173–7.

[9] Mallett and Hale, *Military Organization*; Covini, *L'esercito*; Michael Mallett, 'Condottieri and Captains in Renaissance Italy', in D.J.B. Trim, ed., *The Chivalric Ethos and the Development of Military Professionalism* (Leiden and Boston, 2003), 67–88.

[10] The 1611 edition by Jacques Bongars is still the only one for Sanudo's text; but we have a full English tr. by Peter Lock, *Marino Sanudo Torsello, The Book of the Secrets of the Faithful of the Cross* (Farnham, 2011), incl. commentary on Bongars's edn at 16–19.

[11] *The Crusade of Varna, 1443–45*, tr. Colin Imber (Aldershot, 2006).

[12] Iulian Damian, 'La disfatta di Solgat (Crimea) e i suoi echi nei trattati d'arte militare rinascimentale', *Ephemeris* (forthcoming).

sultan's troops at Belgrade in 1456. Mehmed laments in alarm that his janissaries have been crushed by mere peasants. 'If these villeins can chase me away, what will proper soldiers be able to do?'[13] This set the tone for most retrospective commentary on the events of 1456: Capistrano's army, which all agreed was rag-tag, unprofessional, and poorly armed, was seen as a model for future crusaders in terms not of their military profile but of their faith. They had been 'country folk, equipped not with weapons but with faith and devotion', as Calixtus expressed it in November 1456.[14] In his lengthy 1460 description of the Turkish army at Belgrade, Tagliacozzo drew a comparison between Mehmed's elite janissaries and the *provisionati* hired by states like Milan and Venice.[15] And the debates that had been conducted some months earlier at Mantua had centred on military professionalism, which would derive from state commitments to invest in Pius's venture.[16]

Yet the Peloponnese proposal of 1459, which originated with one of the most original crusade lobbyists of the day and was sanctioned by another,[17] indicates that the place of volunteering within the crusade that they aspired to was more important than this trend might lead us to suppose. There are, of course, a range of possible explanations for this, including the continuing pull of the pilgrimage element within crusading, the constraints imposed by circumstances, and the possibility that recruitment through crusade preaching might be reconciled with military prerequisites. The holy grail of crusading enthusiasts was an army whose combatants would synergize the training and skills needed to defeat their formidable opponents with the devotion which had carried the day at Belgrade. Most of the analysis that follows will relate to people who took the cross or were otherwise recruited to fight in field armies planned to execute agreed plans of action, as exemplified by the Mantua model. But a point that must be made beforehand is that the papal *curia* was willing to respond to petitions by granting indulgences directly to the inhabitants of frontier areas that were under military threat from the Muslims. This did not only apply to the Turks. In 1449 Nicholas V allowed the archbishop of Seville to raise a force of crusading volunteers in the city to combat Moorish aggression; as in 1459, both combatants and their sponsors were brought within the remit of the indulgence.[18]

The frontier in the Balkans benefited in a similar way on a number of occasions. In June 1463 Pius II made a grant, valid for eight months, of the full indulgence to all Hungarians who, 'with or without assuming the sign of the life-giving cross', helped to defend the river crossings of the Danube and Sava at their own or others' expense. Volunteers were to join 'the Catholic army' and to stop the Turks from

---

[13] Giovanni Battista Festa, ed., 'Cinque lettere intorno alla vita e alla morte di S. Giovanni da Capestrano', *Bullettino della R. Deputazione Abruzzese di storia patria*, serie 3, 2 (1911), 7–58, at 55. The *topos* of elite Muslim troops being defeated by devout Christian pilgrims went back at least as far as the First Crusade, e.g. Robert the Monk, *Historia Iherosolimitana*, bk 9, ch. 21.
[14] *BF*, NS2.118–19, no 214, at 118.
[15] 'Relatio', 757: 'quos italice *Provisionati* vocamus'.
[16] *Pii II Commentarii*, bk 3, chs 34–5, 219–25.
[17] Though in his *Commentarii* (bk 3, ch.3, 176) Pius claimed that he had only done so to humour Bessarion: 'Bessarioni noluit denegare, cui ea res cordi erat.'
[18] José Goñi Gaztambide, *Historia de la Bula de la cruzada en España* (Vitoria, 1958), 647–9.

getting across the rivers, thus breaking into Hungary's interior.[19] The specificity in the text leads us to suspect lobbying and it is probable that the grant was indeed made in response to a request from Matthias Corvinus's envoy, Bishop Albert of Veszprém, because Pius made other concessions on the same day; one granted indulgences for donations towards building work at Veszprém, and a second empowered commissioners to investigate the illicit occupation of Albert's lands.[20] So it is likely that Matthias had judged it worthwhile to secure the indulgence to help mobilize local volunteers to hold the all-important river crossings against the Turks. In 1469 Paul II acceded to a request from Frederick III that the inhabitants of the county of Möttling and their neighbours in Carniola (Krain, now Slovenia) could win a plenary indulgence for fighting for three months against Turkish raiders; the grant was necessary because these communities had enjoyed peace for so long that their way of life had become thoroughly demilitarized, so they needed encouragement to build up their military skills again.[21] Similar 'home guard' style measures featured amid the endless discussions about the best way to deploy imperial resources against the Turks in the last quarter of the century. The author of one undated proposal in Nürnberg's archives entered into intricate detail on the subject, outlining a system of coloured crosses (red, white, and yellow) corresponding to the severity of the threat.[22]

Militarizing frontier communities like Möttling was one way of securing border defence; another was to give that responsibility to groups of devout combatants who had dedicated themselves to it. It was this time-honoured practice that gave birth to that remarkable chameleon of Habsburg crusading endeavours, the Order/fraternity of St George. Frederick III founded the Order of St George in 1468/9 on the model of the Teutonic Order, with its base at Millstatt in Carinthia (Kärnten, now southern Austria). Its faltering progress is apparent from a papal grant of 1487 that allowed serving brethren from the Order of St John and the Teutonic Order to transfer to the Order of St George, to improve its devotional life. The Order staggered on to its dissolution in 1598.[23] More successful, or at least more in evidence, was the associated fraternity or society of St George that Maximilian established in 1493 and which remained close to his heart throughout his reign. We have already seen it functioning as the showcase for his crusading aspirations, but it is important also to consider the military role that Maximilian intended it to play. These are most to the fore in the fraternity's statutes, which were ratified in September 1493. Maximilian became aware of the problems faced by his father's Order when he recovered Wiener Neustadt from the Hungarians in 1490 and on Christmas Day 1490 he received the insignia of the English Order of the Garter before hearing mass in the Church of St George in Wiener Neustadt. This provided the chivalric context for the 1493 statutes: the military background was the catastrophic defeats suffered by the Croatians in the summer of 1493.

[19] *VMH*, 2.378, no 563. [20] Ibid. 2.378–80, nos 564–5.
[21] Ibid. 2.408–9, no 583. [22] *Notes et extraits*, 3rd ser., 88–103, at 89–90.
[23] Koller, 'Der St. Georgs-Ritterorden', *passim*.

Josef Plösch argued that Maximilian's plan was to use the fraternity to keep the situation in the east stable while he dealt with the French. This is plausible and is certainly reflected in the content of the statutes. They announced that the master and brethren of the Order had informed Maximilian that they desperately needed assistance. What was proposed was a fortress on the frontier (Brežice/Rann, in Carniola, not far from Möttling) holding between 2,000 and 3,000 armed men, and reinforced by volunteers who would serve for short spells. There would be a register of members, who received a variety of secular privileges from Maximilian and religious ones from Alexander VI. As Plösch put it, the fraternity's job was the well-defined one of providing frontier defence ('eine Art bewaffneten Grenzschutzes'). But this programme made no more progress than the Order of St George had done. In mid-November 1494, with characteristic volatility and perhaps under the spell of Burgundy's chivalric traditions, Maximilian steered his fraternity in a wholly different direction. He now associated its members—who he hoped would flock to his standards from the whole of Christendom—with plans for an offensive campaign against the Turks (*publicum et apertum bellum*). It would be commanded by himself, would begin in March 1495 and last for two years. In one sense nothing had changed: in 1494 as in 1493 Maximilian's first and main target was the French, and it was no coincidence that his printed manifesto of 15 November was followed exactly a week later by Charles VIII's own crusade manifesto, issued at Florence on his march to Naples. These were opening salvoes in a long war of propaganda. There is no evidence that potential did exist for mobilizing chivalric energies for a cost-effective defence of the Austrian frontier, but if there was, it was never tapped.[24]

It is Philip the Good's crusading programme that best demonstrates how aspirations for a more professionalized crusade co-existed with diverse and sometimes discordant methods of delivery. Documents issued by Philip's court reveal that the duke expected to play a central role in bringing the Burgundian contingent into being: texts written in 1457 and 1463–4 spelled out the numbers of 'lances' (i.e. combat teams) to be recruited and how their personnel would be split between the two Burgundies and the Low Countries. Their costs, embarkation, provisioning, and equipment were similarly addressed in detail, and the crucial issue of assembling Philip's artillery was entrusted in 1463 to the Lord of Moreuil.[25] The force envisaged in the ducal texts, around 2,000 horse and 4,000 foot, was the same as that promised at Mantua in 1459.[26] But the extent and character of Philip's contribution to the crusade was shaped by a range of other expectations and forces, some

---

[24] See Plösch, 'Der St. Georgsritterorden', *passim*. More broadly, see Wiesflecker-Friedhuber, 'Maximilian I.', 544–7. Key documents are *AR*, nos 42, 215, 1155–6, 2772, 2982, 2984–5; *Deutsche Reichstagsakten… 1495*, 101–6, 108, 112, 114–16.

[25] Norman Housley, 'Crusading and State-Building in the Middle Ages', in Peter Hoppenbrouwers and others, eds, *Power and Persuasion: Essays on the Art of State Building in Honour of W.P. Blockmans* (Turnhout, 2010), 291–308, at 301–2.

[26] Henri Stein, 'Un diplomate bourguignon du XVe siècle: Antoine Haneron', *Bibliothèque de l'École des chartes*, 98 (1937), 282–348, at 315. In a despatch sent in February 1455 a Milanese envoy referred to up to 10,000 combatants, including 6,000 archers: *Carteggi diplomatici*, 1.23–6, no 2.

external and some internal. We shall see later that Philip's famed enthusiasm for the crusade caused him to be pulled into Hunyadi's fantasy plans of 1455 to the extent of providing 20,000 soldiers.[27] Rather more pressing were obligations that were agreed with Pope and empire. As noted above, Philip reached agreement with the Pope on what he would provide at Mantua, though his envoy argued that he had consented to only one year's service, not three.[28] And, as an imperial prince, Philip was party to the rather eccentric proposal (*scedula*) passed at Regensburg in 1454 that recruitment for the crusade should be based on groups of hearths, each of which would provide combatants.[29] The duke went through the motions of applying the *scedula* to his lands, sending Simon of Lalaing to Charles VII at the end of November 1454 to get Charles's permission to enforce it in territories that lay within the kingdom of France.[30]

A more important impact on recruitment was exerted by social forces that were internal to Philip's lands. At the Feast of the Pheasant in April 1454 Philip had deployed chivalric theatre to corral some of his leading nobles into supporting his crusade, and their assistance in the process of recruitment was expected and welcomed: various texts written in December 1463 expected a high percentage of the combatants to accompany those who had sworn to help in 1454, 'through devotion, that is to say by those who made vows and who will want to go on the said expedition as volunteers (*voluntairement*)'.[31] Then there was the urban culture of Philip's Flemish lands, which helped to shape their collective response to crusade preaching, just as it furnished the milieu for the preaching itself and the elaborate civic processions that often accompanied it. Ghent provided a contingent of eighty *crucesignati* under the command of Hector Hughes. Their names and equipment were carefully noted in the town's journal. The men who set out from the little town of Axel went through an elaborate ceremony of blessing before their departure. The fact that they sported the cross of St Andrew shows their pride in their political allegiance, but it is questionable whether they made up an overtly 'ducal' body of recruits. Ghent and Axel were perhaps atypical in their careful organization: Jacques du Clerc commented disparagingly on the groups of ten, twenty, or forty individuals who set off from Burgundian lands in 1464 'without captains, some of them with little money or military equipment, and on foot'.[32] The result of these aristocratic and urban contributions was that the impressively streamlined force assembled through and by ducal authority, which we witness in documents issued by Philip's bureaucrats, was in various respects different from what came about in 1464. This in turn surely differed from the force that would have set out under ducal command, had Philip not yielded to French pressure to remain at home.

---

[27] *AM*, 12.293.   [28] Stein, 'Un diplomate', 315.
[29] See *Codex diplomaticus*, 2.193–5, no 260, for one contemporary's perception of Philip's twofold contribution, as imperial vassal and enthusiast.
[30] Paviot, *Les ducs*, p. 139, specifying one man-at-arms for each sixty hearths and one archer for each thirty, lighter terms than those decreed at Regensburg. The plan may have been to commute service to cash: *Carteggi diplomatici*, 1.23–6, no 2.
[31] Paviot, *Les ducs*, 328–34, with quote at 331.   [32] Ibid. 171–2.

4.2 VOLUNTEERISM AND MILITARY SERVICE IN HUNGARY

Both the eclectic character of the Burgundian dominions and Philip's failure to carry through his programme act as constraints on what these sources can teach us. A more revealing terrain for analysis is the kingdom of Hungary and its satellite lands.[33] Given their frontier status, it was inevitable that these territories would provide more evidence for military activity, even though the crusading contribution made by Matthias fell short of the hopes vested in him. It is impossible to avoid giving a good deal of attention to the most substantial army of *crucesignati* raised in this period, the one recruited and led by Giovanni da Capistrano. But it makes sense to set the sensational events of 1456 in a broader context, above all to ask how it was envisaged that the services of such *crucesignati*, whether Hungarians or foreigners, would mesh with plans to defend the kingdom by more established and familiar processes.[34] The best starting point for such an enquiry is the imperial diets that convened in 1454–5 at Regensburg, Frankfurt, and Wiener Neustadt. The three assemblies won fame for the splendour of the oratory that was deployed by Aeneas Sylvius Piccolomini and others trying to secure assent for an imperial army that would assist the Hungarians in defending Christendom's acknowledged *antemurale*. By the time of the Wiener Neustadt diet (February–April 1455) that project was patently foundering, and, while the major impediments were the lack of commitment of Germany's princes and the ramshackle imperial constitution, the turmoil of Hungary's domestic politics did not help: Hungary's envoys pleaded with good reason for German military might, though they were well aware of the fears of their kingdom's baronial elite that this could assist Ladislas V to assert royal authority more vigorously.[35] But this ultimately sterile oratory was accompanied by crusade preaching carried out by Capistrano. Capitalizing on the fame that he had accumulated since arriving north of the Alps in 1451, Capistrano suspended his conversion work in the Bohemian crown lands to preach the crusade in a number of German towns. He was urged by Piccolomini to attend the Frankfurt diet and preached there to good effect.[36] Other religious assisted, for example the Franciscan, Bernhardin of Ingolstadt, at Legnica (Liegnitz, Silesia) in June 1454,[37] and the Dominican, Heinrich Kalteisen, in the Rhineland.[38] But Capistrano was the star.

---

[33] See Gyula Rázsó, 'Military Reforms in the Fifteenth Century', in László Veszprémy and Béla K. Király, eds, *A Millennium of Hungarian Military History* (New York, 2002), 54–82; László Veszprémy, 'The State and Military Affairs in East-Central Europe, 1380– c. 1520s', in Tallett and Trim, eds, *European Warfare*, 96–109.

[34] Generally see Bak, 'Price', 161–78.

[35] *Notes et extraits*, 4th ser., 106–10.

[36] *AM*, 12.234–7; *Opera inedita*, 105–8, no 43, 110–13, no 46 (to be treated with care given that Piccolomini had urged Capistrano to come to Frankfurt); Hofer, *Kapistran*, 2.307–11.

[37] Ibid. 2.299, note 3.

[38] Thomas Vogtherr, '"Wenn hinten, weit, in der Turkei…". Die Türken in der spätmittelalterlichen Stadtchronistik Norddeutschlands', in Franz-Reiner Erkens, ed., *Europa und die osmanische Expansion im ausgehenden Mittelalter*, Zeitschrift für historische Forschung, Beiheft 20 (Berlin, 1997), 103–25, at 117.

It is likely that the hundreds of *crucesignati* who eventually marched out of Nürnberg and Vienna had taken the cross in response to his preaching there in the autumn and winter of 1454–5.[39] The result was that over the course of 1455 large numbers of German and Austrian *crucesignati* were preparing for action. They may well have asked themselves how they would discharge their vows if no imperial expedition took shape; and their dilemma would be resolved not by the strategic programmes that were debated at the diets, but by the progress of events in Hungary.

At Nürnberg in November 1454 Capistrano was undecided whether to return to his work of conversion in central Europe, which was dear to his heart, or carry on with his preaching in the empire, proceeding onwards to Hungary to promote resistance to the imminent Turkish invasion. Responding to divine guidance, he chose the latter option and, following the frustrations of the Wiener Neustadt diet, attended the Hungarian assembly at Raab (Győr) in June 1455. Two letters that he wrote from Raab to Pope Calixtus III take us to the heart of his thinking in the aftermath of imperial failure. In the first, he urged the new Pope in excited but generalized terms to be more proactive than his predecessor in driving the crusade forward, and promised his own services to that end.[40] In the other, he reported the extravagant undertakings made by the celebrated *vaivode* (governor) of Transylvania, Janos Hunyadi, to expel Mehmed II from all of his European provinces, and even to recover Jerusalem, if he were provided with an army 100,000 strong. This force would consist of 20,000 horsemen supplied by Calixtus, 10,000 by the king of Aragon, 10,000 by the rest of Italy, and 20,000 troops (half horse, half foot) by Philip the Good. The remaining 40,000 troops would derive from the despot of Serbia, George Brankovics (10,000), Hunyadi himself (10,000) and the rest of Hungary (20,000). Alfonso of Aragon would also be expected to provide the indispensable naval support. The whole force must be professional, 'warriors...not youths (*pueri*), but vigorous men, experienced in the use of arms'. They would only require wages for three months, and Calixtus should send a cardinal 'as it were, to preside over' the army with sufficient money for this purpose; for the remainder of the campaign, which was expected to last 'for one or more years, as the work demands', they could live off goods and lands seized from the Turks. Indeed, beside recovering the lost lands of the southern Balkans and Palestine, and spreading the faith, the army would come into the possession of the 'riches of the infidels'.[41]

It is tempting to dismiss Hunyadi's offer, made on 21 June 'here, in the presence of all these lords and barons', as a grandstanding attempt to steal a march on his rival, Ulrich of Cilli, and on the absentee king Ladislas.[42] The hero of Varna and the 'long campaign' of 1443 not only offered to defend the kingdom, but claimed

---

[39] Hofer, *Kapistran*, 2.321–2, 324–5, 330–4, 415. Especially noteworthy are the several hundred students at the University of Vienna who took the cross (ibid. 2.331 and note 79) and the 800 *crucesignati* who eventually set out from Nürnberg (ibid. 2.415). Lodrisio Crivelli enthused about the 600 students, whom he compared with Leonidas's Spartans: *De expeditione Pii papae II*, ed. G.C. Zimolo, RISNS 33, pt 5, 58–9.
[40] *AM*, 12.285–7.   [41] *AM*, 12.292–4.
[42] For the Hungarian domestic context see Engel, *Realm*, 288–95.

that he could achieve every possible item on the wish list of crusading enthusiasts like Capistrano and Calixtus, and without the need for more than three months' financial backing. In its way it was as cynical an exercise of showmanship as much of the debating at the recent imperial debates had been. But it would be unwise simply to ignore Hunyadi's proposal, because complacency was not an option for Hungary as it was for the empire. In 1455 Hungary was threatened, Serbia already under attack, and Hunyadi had spent much of his adult life fighting the Turks. Most importantly, while most of the *vaivode*'s dream evaporated, over the course of the years that followed parts of it were realized in campaigns or resurfaced in plans that were led and hatched by Hunyadi and his son, Matthias. In its combination of altruistic aspiration, political game-playing, and strategic good sense, the proposal is one of the period's most interesting and emblematic texts. In the immediate context of recruitment, two points should be made. The first is that for all the proposal's high-flying rhetoric, on military practicalities it was sound: at its core there lay Hunyadi's own 'following' (*banderium*) of approximately 10,000 experienced fighters, a clear emphasis on the need for trained combatants (*non pueri*), and a readiness to address—albeit in a rather sketchy fashion—the need adequately to fund such an army. The second point is that when it became apparent that Hungary's chronic political divisions were hindering the mobilization of the kingdom's resources by its governing elites, Capistrano reverted to preaching the crusade in the same inclusive manner that he had practised hitherto. In his strenuous tour of Hungary's western counties in the summer of 1455 and of Transylvania during the winter of 1455–6, he seems to have ignored the practicalities highlighted by Hunyadi at Raab. The outcome was that he brought to besieged Belgrade, in the crisis summer of 1456, an army of *crucesignati* that Hunyadi, in despair, judged wholly unfit for purpose.[43]

To assess how far this paradox was appreciated by leading contemporaries, it is important to examine their response to events as they unfolded in 1456. Calixtus's appointment of Cardinal Juan Carvajal as his legate to Hungary in the summer of 1455 meant that papal policy was mediated within the kingdom and the dangers that flowed from Capistrano's exuberance might be contained.[44] The hierarchy that was established found visible expression at Buda on 14 February 1456 when Capistrano received from the legate's hand the cross that Calixtus had sent, together with the authority to preach 'both by papal brief and by the commission of the said lord cardinal'.[45] In a letter to Capistrano written from Ladislas's court at Vienna, Carvajal had already made clear his aspiration to send on campaign an army that would integrate sizable contingents contributed by the various individuals identified by Hunyadi at Raab, with groups of volunteers who came 'some out of devotion and others for honour'. The danger was likely to be not insufficient recruits

---

[43] See the definitive study by Johannes Hofer, 'Der Sieger von Belgrad 1456', *Historisches Jahrbuch*, 51 (1931), 163–212.
[44] Setton, *Papacy*, 2.165–6.
[45] 'Relatio', 752, and for Capistrano's commentary *AM*, 12.374. Naturally the cross became a treasured memento: Stanko Andrić, *The Miracles of St John Capistran* (Budapest, 2000), 66.

but a shortfall in the supplies needed to sustain them: a wise comment given the poor yield of the 1455 harvest.[46]

Carvajal must have realized already that given the discord within the kingdom's ruling elite, he would need the services of the volunteers. If he retained any illusions, they were dispelled by events at the Buda diet of February–March 1456. Both the king and Hunyadi attended, but the *vaivode* arrived late and with a strong escort. The decree that was passed, levying a specified number of fighting men on groups of households,[47] resembled the proposal adopted at the Regensburg diet in 1454 and stood no more chance of success. On the other hand, Capistrano's daily crusade preaching in the capital drew crowds of admirers and added to the reservoir of *crucesignati*. The new recruits were a mixed bunch, 'very many prelates and barons… [and] a multitude of lesser folk', as Capistrano informed the Pope.[48] They were sent home with orders to await a summons to the front;[49] the plan was for an army to march southwards once supplies could be relied upon, at the start of August.[50] Then came the news of Mehmed's advance on Belgrade. Hunyadi was the obvious candidate to take charge of the kingdom's defences. Capistrano travelled south and preached in the densely populated region around Pécs (*Quinqueecclesiae*), from where recruits could most rapidly reach the combat zone. Carvajal remained for the most part at Buda, to organize the crusaders gathering there; in the light of the crisis, the earlier plan to wait for the 1456 harvest was set aside.[51]

We have a number of letters written by Carvajal and Hunyadi from April through to June and they show the two men doing their best to work together and with Capistrano, to spur on the assembling of Hungary's resources. The lassitude of the royal court was frustrating, and writing to Francesco Sforza on 17 April, Carvajal allowed his irritation to show; behind his deployment of *antemurale* themes ('this is not just a matter for this great kingdom') lay the harsh fact that Hungary's own defence mechanism was proving dysfunctional.[52] Inexorably the volunteers moved from holding auxiliary status to comprising the main force. On 14 May Carvajal told Capistrano that Hunyadi was so dismayed by the calibre of the crusaders that he witnessed when he met with the legate at Petrovaradin, that he told Carvajal to proceed no further lest it demoralize the defenders and encourage the enemy. Delay and confusion in Hungary might persuade capable foreign volunteers to redirect their energies to Albania. The legate reported a sighting of a French crusader at Venice making his way with fifty others to fight with Iskanderbeg, and this could set a trend.[53] On 25 May he wrote from Buda to Capistrano about Hunyadi's hopes that the preacher would stir up the southern counties, and

[46] *AM*, 12.371.
[47] Festa, ed., 'Cinque lettere', 50: each 100 households were to supply 10 men at arms and 2 foot soldiers.
[48] *AM*, 12.373–4.   [49] Festa, ed., 'Relatio', 752–3.
[50] *Codex diplomaticus*, 462–4, no 529.
[51] *Monumenta historica Boemiae*, ed. Gelasius Dobner, 6 vols (Prague, 1764–85), 2.415–17. Doubts remained about the prospect of mobilizing a large force before August: *Codex diplomaticus*, 203, no 269 (18 June report from Venice to Sforza).
[52] Ibid. 462–4, no 529.   [53] *AM*, 12.385–6.

then join Carvajal in soliciting help from Ladislas and Frederick. He was pessimistic: 'I have said and suggested a lot of things here, but got nowhere.'[54] His gloom was not misplaced. Shortly afterwards Ladislas fled to Vienna, under cover of going hunting, and lingering hopes of a general mobilization perished. Johannes Hofer believed that those prelates and barons who had taken the cross, notably at Buda in the spring, regarded the king's flight as constituting release from their vows.[55] Canonically this made no sense, but he was right to say that they took their cue from the king to retreat to their fortified places. Tagliacozzo's comments were insightful as well as judiciously balanced: 'Many of the nobles and their retainers were signed with the cross, but none, or to be more accurate, very few turned up; the reason being the Hungarian custom that they set out on campaign in their lords' company, and the lords did not come.'[56] It is a revealing passage, more so than János Thuróczy's comment that they had fallen into a deep sleep.[57] What doomed Capistrano's hopes of recruiting fighting men was not lethargy, or a lack of devotion or patriotic feeling on their part (a point to which we shall return), but the breakdown of the hierarchical structure of obligation, starting at the top. So paralyzing was the kingdom's factional division that the archbishop of Kalocsa, who was a bitter enemy of Hunyadi, refused to respond even when Capistrano went to see him.[58] Hence the defence of Belgrade was left to 'the three Johns', of whom one vociferously espoused a crusading approach, the second was throughout sceptical about its viability,[59] while the third, Carvajal, carried the burden of making the volatile scenario work.[60]

By the time Mehmed's advance troops reached Belgrade on 3 July, it was only the garrison under Michael Szilágyi (Hunyadi's brother-in-law), Capistrano's crusaders, and the troops available to Hunyadi that counted for anything.[61] Even Capistrano, who was normally discrete about Hungary's internal affairs, allowed his anger to surface in a letter written that day to his close colleague the bishop of Assisi, Francesco Oddi: if the king, princes, barons, and prelates did not stir themselves and come south, or at least send troops, the Turks would soon be paying them a visit.[62] Capistrano's recruits arrived in two phases: the first, comprising those who had assembled at Petrovaradin over the course of June under the care of Oddi, marched or sailed down the Danube, their advance guard

---

[54] Ibid. 12.386–7.
[55] Hofer, *Kapistran*, 2.369: 'Die Prälaten und Barone hielten sich demnach nicht mehr an ihr Kreuzzugsgelübde gebunden.'
[56] 'Relatio', 767.
[57] Johannes de Thurocz, *Chronica Hungarorum*, ed. Elisabeth Galántai and Julius Kristó, 2 vols, Bibliotheca scriptorum medii recentisque aevorum, series nova, 7, 9, (Budapest, 1985–8), tr. Frank Martello as János Thuróczy, *Chronicle of the Hungarians*, Indiana University Uralic and Altaic Series,155 (Bloomington IN, 1991), ch. 250.
[58] 'Relatio', 758–9; Hofer, *Kapistran*, 2.377.
[59] Though Hunyadi himself had taken the cross, perhaps to encourage his fellow-barons to do so: *Codex diplomaticus*, 199–200, no 265.
[60] e.g. ibid.467–9, no 532.
[61] For attempts to estimate the numbers commanded by Hunyadi, see Hofer, *Kapistran*, 2.384; Joseph Held, *Hunyadi: Legend and Reality* (New York, 1985), 166–7.
[62] *Codex diplomaticus*, 465–7, no 531, reflected in 'Relatio', 753.

arriving one day ahead of the Turkish scouts. In response to Capistrano's urgent summonses to his brethren, the barons, and prelates,[63] other groups later joined them in the crusade encampment that was set up a few kilometres south-east of Zemun (Semlin), where the River Sava joined the Danube.[64] Eventually reaching around 60,000,[65] their numbers exceeded several times over the professionals commanded by Hunyadi and Szilágyi. The Turkish blockade of the Danube meant that Carvajal's earlier concerns about shortages of food were more than justified, at least until the blockade was broken on 14 July; and even after that there was plague to contend with.[66] It was a crusade of the poor, but more importantly one of the ill-equipped and untrained,[67] a point on which the sources agree even when due allowance is made for exaggeration. Tagliacozzo in particular is admirably precise:[68]

> All those who assembled were commoners, country folk, poor people, priests, secular clerics, students, monks, friars of various orders, mendicants, members of the third order of St Francis, and hermits. Among them you saw few weapons, except for their retainers; we saw no horses, except those carrying provisions, and no lances. Those who wore armour resembled David, armed by Saul against Goliath. There were lots of swords, cudgels, slings, staffs of the type that shepherds carry, and everybody had a shield.

Naturally the crusaders possessed no artillery, though this turned out to be less problematic than their lack of horses; this meant that they could not engage in the pursuit of the fleeing Turks after their victory on 22 July.[69] Hunyadi remained the leading sceptic. The doubt about their military capability, which Carvajal reported the *vaivode* expressing in mid-May, was frequently reiterated,[70] to the extent of his counselling on 21 July that the defence of Belgrade should be abandoned, and then withdrawing to his ship on the Sava.[71] Although this led the crusaders to despise him,[72] it was a thoroughly rational move. What he was working with at Belgrade did not deserve the name of an army; these were the very *pueri* against whom he had counselled at Raab a year earlier.[73]

Thanks to Hofer's painstaking reconstruction of events at Belgrade, it is clear that victory was achieved primarily by Capistrano's crusaders, notwithstanding

---

[63] Ibid. 758–9: '…sicque fama per totum regnum diffunditur'.
[64] For map see Hofer, *Kapistran*, 2.379.
[65] 'Relatio', 765, 766. Hofer, *Kapistran*, 2.391, note 176 comments fully.
[66] 'Relatio', 760, 765–6 (severe punishment of profiteers).
[67] Some may have been trained under the *militia portalis* defence system introduced by Sigismund, but this is looking increasingly limited in its impact; for the theory, as outlined in January 1459, see *The Laws of the Medieval Kingdom of Hungary, Volume 3, 1458–1490*, ed. and tr. János M. Bak and others (Los Angeles CA, 1996), 9–14; for practice, see András Borosy, 'The *Militia Portalis* in Hungary before 1526', in *FHR*, 63–80; Bak, 'Price', pp. 171–2.
[68] 'Relatio', 767, and cf. the equally detailed passage on 782.
[69] Festa, ed., 'Cinque lettere', 55; *Codex diplomaticus*, 210–11.
[70] 'Relatio', 758, reviewing the situation at the start of the siege.
[71] Ibid. 771.
[72] e.g. *Notes et extraits*, 4th ser., 130–2, a German report stating (at 132) that the crusaders would have killed Hunyadi if they could have caught him.
[73] Hofer, 'Der Sieger', 193, is balanced on this issue.

Hunyadi's immediate campaign to marginalize them.[74] Their success was extraordinary and severe problems on the Turkish side must have contributed a good deal.[75] But the relief of Belgrade was only one episode in the defence of Hungary, and Capistrano's crusade preaching had repercussions that lasted well beyond July 1456. Tagliacozzo relates that the crusaders who fought at Belgrade were mainly Hungarians: there were some (*nonnulli*) Germans, Poles, Slavonians (i.e. northern Croatians), and Bosnians, but it is evident that the majority of those who had taken the cross outside Hungary did not have time to reach Belgrade.[76] On 23 July Capistrano dismissed the victorious crusaders, partly because of the build-up of resentment against Hunyadi, but also because of continuing supply problems and, perhaps, concerns that the unburied corpses would spread infection. Tagliacozzo's brusque comment on the event, 'in this way the crusade was dissolved', is misleading. Behind it lies his irritation at the veto that had been imposed the previous day on pursuit, with the result that a precious opportunity was lost. But while he was surely mistaken in his view of what the victors might have gone on to achieve, he was not alone in his disappointment. On 29 July Carvajal appeared with fresh and better-equipped crusaders, including cavalry. It was the vanguard of the large force that was taking shape at Buda and, in the letter that he wrote to Sforza on the same day, the legate could not contain his chagrin that, if the Turks had delayed their attack for just a few more days, this powerful Christian army would not just have defeated them but followed up its success with a determined pursuit.[77] What could they be given to do now, to get them away from Zemun's inadequate and insanitary facilities and food shortages?[78] In a letter to the Pope written on 17 August, Capistrano revived Hunyadi's 1455 project for an advance into Turkish-held territory that would press onwards to the recovery of Jerusalem. For this, Calixtus was asked to send 12,000, or at the very least 10,000, cavalry 'paid wages by you following Italian practice'. These professionals would join forces with the crusaders and the Hungarians. The Italian mercenaries would only require pay for six months; thereafter they would be rewarded with plunder.[79] In his reply on 16 September Calixtus embraced the idea with enthusiasm.[80] Such a project would of course take months to assemble; it was no solution for the crusaders who were kicking their heels at Zemun. But by this point the plague was already intervening: Hunyadi fell victim on 11 August, and Capistrano followed on 23 October.

The onus of responsibility for organizing the contribution of the crusaders now fell largely to Carvajal. It was a thankless task. Hofer commented that 'Carvajal war weder ein Hunyadi noch ein Kapistran',[81] but well-informed contemporaries

---

[74] *Monumenta historica*, 2.417–18; *AS Oct*, 382–3; *Codex diplomaticus*, 208–9, no 276.
[75] Reports testified to severe food shortages in the Turkish camp, causing heavy losses of men and horses, demoralization, and desertion: ibid. 204–6, no 273, 469–71, no 533. Cf. Hofer, 'Der Sieger', 205.
[76] 'Relatio', 765. The French crusaders whom Carvajal mentioned in his 14 May letter seem to have been unusual in making their way to the front via Venice.
[77] *Codex diplomaticus*, 209–10, no 279.
[78] Ibid. 217–18, no 294 (report dated 12 September); see also ibid. 469–71, no 533.
[79] *AS Oct*, 383–4.   [80] Ibid. 384–5.   [81] Hofer, *Kapistran*, 2.421.

admired the way he handled the Hungarian legation,[82] and in the absence of a Turkish invasion to provide a focal point, coping with unpredictable numbers of German volunteers would have taxed the most brilliant of strategists. A returning crusader wrote home to Salzburg from Vienna on 26 August 1456 that there were still many crusaders both there and at Buda, but they were not being given any instructions.[83] This really was a missed opportunity, because these arrivals were numerous, well equipped, and enthusiastic. Castiglione, writing from Vienna three days later, wrote of no fewer than 6,000 'well-armed men' taking ship to Buda within three days.[84] An authoritative report compiled at Buda a month earlier confirms this impression: even the 700 students from the University of Vienna were 'well equipped'.[85] A worsening of the kingdom's factional divisions soon made the situation yet more problematic for the volunteers, who got caught up in the strife. When King Ladislas finally made the journey southwards to Belgrade in early November, he brought many of the German crusaders with him. The king and Ulrich of Cilli exerted pressure on Ladislaus, Hunyadi's elder son, to surrender fortresses and revenues that his father had succeeded in holding onto when he surrendered the regency four years previously. In the citadel at Belgrade, which a few weeks previously had nearly been lost to the Turks thanks to internal disputes, the same disputes took a violent turn and Ladislaus had Cilli murdered. The king and the legate had to allow the Germans to leave for home and, according to a report sent to Sforza from Venice in December, the message they took with them was none too good: not only had they seen no action against the Turks, but they had been robbed and in some cases murdered by their hosts. Hence 'they went home in the worst frame of mind, determined never to return, thanks to the awful way that they had been treated by the Hungarians'.[86]

In assassinating Cilli, Ladislaus had overstepped the mark; the king succeeded in getting both him and his younger brother, Matthias, arrested and Ladislaus was executed at Buda in March 1457. The fortunes of the house of Hunyadi seemed extinct, but in fact they soon enjoyed a phoenix-like revival. For in November 1457 the king died prematurely and without an heir, and in January 1458 Matthias's succession was engineered by a party that included Michael Szilágyi and Cardinal Carvajal.[87] Given such turbulence we would expect the crusade to have stalled. But reality was more complex; in particular, there are grounds for believing that in 1458 the presence of crusaders on the southern frontier was fully as marked as it had been in 1456. The main reason why the momentum, built up in 1454–6, did not simply tail off was Calixtus III's resolve to continue bringing Hungary into the heart of his *amprisia cruciate*.[88] The threat to Belgrade remained serious and one kingdom's problems could not be allowed to derail the mighty effort that Calixtus was planning. In April 1457 he wrote to Carvajal to say that, notwithstanding the turbulent

---

[82] Ammannati Piccolomini, *Commentarii*, 355.   [83] Hofer, *Kapistran*, 2.412.
[84] *Codex diplomaticus*, 216, no 291.   [85] Ibid. 469–71, no 533.
[86] Ibid. 220–1, no 300. Cf. Thomas Ebendorfer, *Chronica regum Romanorum*, ed. Harald Zimmermann, pt 2, MGH SRG nova series, XVIII (Hannover, 2003). 851; Hofer, *Kapistran*, 2.421–2.
[87] Engel, *Realm*, 296–9.   [88] *VMH*, 2.204–5, no 460, for the phrase.

situation, the legate was to persevere in promoting the crusade: 'Work for unity, preach the cross, sign with the cross, because God is with us, provided that with your assistance the king and his people oppose the enemy of the cross manfully.'[89] The Pope was willing to countenance crusade subsidies going even to such a questionable destination as Stephen Thomas, the king of Bosnia, and in the spring of 1457 he sent Jacopo delle Marche to succeed Capistrano in preaching the crusade in Hungary.[90] Crusade preaching was promoted as vigorously as circumstances allowed not just in Hungary but also in Bosnia, Serbia, and Dalmatia, and volunteers were actively sought.[91] Calixtus was a firm believer in a 'mixed economy' of volunteers and donations: some front could always be found for *crucesignati* to fight in person (such as on the Pope's own galleys).[92] They provided heroes and heroines: not just the victors of Belgrade but those of Mytilene were held up by the Pope as shining examples of Christian devotion.[93] By the autumn of 1457 Calixtus had hopes of activity in Hungary, Albania, and Bosnia: the sort of three-fold front that the *curia* constantly dreamed of, even though it meant splitting crusade subsidies (and possibly volunteers) three ways.[94] One month before Ladislas's death, Piccolomini wrote on Calixtus's behalf urging the king to maintain the momentum acquired a year earlier at Belgrade: 'When the enemy flees, pursue him; when he falters, assail him; when his spirits flag, attack him.'[95] Like his legate, Calixtus warmly backed Matthias's candidature and harboured great expectations of this son of Hunyadi.[96]

The Pope may have hoped for Jerusalem but in 1458, as in 1456, it was the threat to Belgrade that generated activity. A renewed attack on the fortress was expected in the spring, and in March Szilágyi wrote to Carvajal asking him to alert all those who still had vows to fulfil to await Szilágyi's summons to make their way southwards.[97] In April the Venetian envoy, Petrus de Thomasiis, wrote to the doge from Buda that Carvajal had to persuade the new king to set aside his suspicions of Germans so as to renew the flow of crusaders from the empire; it was hard enough persuading them to come after the reception they had received in 1456.[98] Through the summer and autumn of 1458 de Thomasiis's despatches yield a revealing and, at times, colourful picture of crusaders numbering several thousand assembling at Buda, and of a range of issues relating to their southwards movement. It is clear that the Hungarian army that mobilized in 1458 included a high proportion of crusaders. Early in July some 200 were captured in a skirmish near Belgrade.[99] A despatch written on 1 October, and reporting a Hungarian victory, claimed that 'they say that more than 25,000 *crucesignati* have arrived in camp, with more joining them each day; every hour they come down the Danube by boat from the north, in a way that seems

---

[89] Ibid. 2.287–8, no 450, and see too 2.281–3, nos 445–6.
[90] Ibid. 2.291–2, nos 456–7, 294–6, nos 460–2.
[91] Ibid. 2.296–9, nos 464–8, and cf. 2.327, no 501 (Pius following same policy 1459).
[92] e.g. *AM*, 12.376–7 (preaching in the kingdom of Naples).
[93] *BF*, NS2.181–5, no 353; *DS*, 421–3, no 1272, at 422. For Mytilene see Setton, *Papacy*, 2.188–9. For women fighting at Belgrade see Festa, ed., 'Cinque lettere', 53; Tagliacozzo, 'Relatio', 774.
[94] *VMH*, 2.303–4, nos 472–3.
[95] *Aeneae Silvii Piccolomini Senensis opera inedita*, 130–3, no 60, at 133.
[96] *VMH*, 2.309–11, no 479. Cf. *MDE*, 1.19–21, no 14, at 21 (its arrival at Buda).
[97] Ibid. 1.15–16, no 11.   [98] Ibid. 1.19–21, no 14.   [99] *Codex diplomaticus*, 237, no 326.

miraculous'. The queen was personally overseeing the purchase of horses and supplies (above all, wine, which was in short supply, and 'these people do not make war without wine').[100] Eight days later de Thomasiis wrote that the Turks had retreated into Serbia. The excitement was remarkable: the whole realm seemed to be on the move and 'I do believe that there will be more than 80,000 people counting horse and foot, above all thanks to the large number of *crucesignati*, who as peasants (*vilani*) may not seem to count for much, but possess some value against the Turks who include a lot of the same sort'.[101] At the end of November the Milanese envoy at Venice reported to Sforza that the Turks had decided not to engage in combat against 'the king with so many people and *crucesignati* at Belgrade'.[102]

The 1458 campaign lacked a Capistrano, a Tagliacozzo, and, above all, a victory as exceptional as the relief of Belgrade. Because of this, it has rather more to tell us about how volunteer service meshed with standard processes of mobilization in Hungary, when factional disputes did not get in the way.[103] A despatch from de Thomasiis written on 25 August succinctly portrayed the system at work: at the king's command the fighting elite were mobilized, wages for an anticipated three-month campaign were set, and Carvajal was requested to organize the *crucesignati*.[104] The Italian envoys' despatches point towards the large army that assembled, 'si Barony come Zentilhomini et Cruci Segnati', as de Thomasiis put it in September,[105] comprising people who responded partly out of duty and partly for devotional reasons—'some from love and some from fear', to cite de Thomasiis again.[106] The fear may well have been as much of the king as of the Turks. Two years earlier the 'barons' and 'gentlemen' had sought refuge in their castles and country estates: it would have been ill-advised to do so again, with a young king on the throne who was mindful of the difficulties that his father had faced as a result. We might posit an overreaction from some, coupled to a sense of excitement, even the hope of another 1456, in the case of others. Either way, it made for an occasion that for different reasons turned out to be scarcely less atypical than the 1456 campaign. The army was too large for its limited purpose of driving the Turks away, its assembly was too slow and unpredictable, and it created major difficulties of supply; all problems traditionally associated with mobilization through crusade preaching. They were not likely to recur, because the contributory factors noted above would not; and in any case, although successful preaching by Jacopo and Carvajal cannot be ruled out, it is more likely that the *crucesignati* of 1458 had taken the cross during Capistrano's preaching in 1455–6. But it is not hard to imagine the effect on the young monarch. It was better to rely on summonses, hiring troops, creating a standing army,[107] or negotiating a truce with the Turks; all of which methods he used, and the last of which he was suspected by the Italians of doing as his way out of a troubling situation in the autumn of 1458.[108]

---

[100] *MDE*, 1.36–7, no 25.   [101] Ibid. 1.38–9, no 26.   [102] Ibid. 1.39–40, no 27.
[103] *Laws*, 1–3, 4–8, for the decrees of January and June 1458.
[104] *Codex diplomaticus*, 241, no 331.   [105] *MDE*, 1.35–6, no 24.   [106] Ibid. 1.38–9, no 26.
[107] Gyula Rázsó, 'The Mercenary Army of King Matthias Corvinus', in *FHR*, 125–40.
[108] *MDE*, 1.39–40, no 27.

Following the 1458 campaign Matthias had plenty of opportunity, over the course of his thirty-two-year reign, to ponder on crusading and what its principal benefits were. We have witnessed the king expounding his strongly held views about his realm's *antemurale* status and his entitlement to be supported by the Pope and the rest of Christendom. That support could usefully assume several forms: financial backing, diplomatic leverage, the promotion and sustaining of alliances. But Matthias did not want thousands of non-Hungarian crusaders. In particular, as debates at numerous imperial diets and at the Mantua congress demonstrated, for the remainder of the century the prospect of organized bands of German crusaders making their way through Hungary to fight the Turks raised problems more troubling than those posed by their ancestors making their way to the Holy Land crusades. It was more than just their need for guides, safe conducts, and fair prices.[109] Might they not constitute a Habsburg fifth column? The idea was nourished at Matthias's court that his brother, Ladislaus, had Cilli murdered at Belgrade in 1456 because his followers convinced him that the German crusaders in the royal entourage formed the advance guard of a plan to fill the kingdom's offices with Germans.[110] It is easy to see how the fear came about. After fleeing to Vienna King Ladislas had issued an appeal for volunteers in which he offered wages, one Hungarian florin a week for a horseman and thirteen *groschen* for a footman.[111] It is clear that many of those who responded (including no fewer than 800 at Breslau) were much better equipped than Capistrano's crusaders; and they took their orders from their paymaster, Ladislas.[112] And we have seen that Corvinian distrust of the Germans was reciprocated by the crusaders who had experienced Hungarian hospitality in 1456.

As for Hungarian *crucesignati*, there was at least one occasion after 1458 when Matthias made use of their services, which was his spirited attempt to recover Bosnia in 1464. In the desperate letter that he wrote to Pius II in July 1464 pleading for the campaign to get off the ground, he included the preaching of the crusade among his demands.[113] When the campaign did start, Hungarian operations included a strong volunteer element: a Venetian report written on 28 September referred to 7,000 *crucesignati* in a royal army 30,000-strong that crossed the Sava.[114] Given the excitement generated by *Ezechielis prophetae* and Pius's ambitious planning, such a resurgence of Hungarian volunteerism is not implausible, though Venetian hopes that non-Hungarian *crucesignati* too might be packed off to help Matthias do not appear to have been followed up on.[115] Thereafter, as combat with the Turks slipped down Matthias's agenda, it may be questioned whether he placed much value on volunteer service, with the exception of border fighting. It was useful to have 1456 to refer to, because it advanced and exemplified Hungary's

---

[109] *Monumenta historica Boemiae*, 2.413–15.   [110] Thurocz, *Chronica,* ch. 253.
[111] *Peter Eschenloer's… Geschichten der Stadt Breslau*, ed. J.G. Kunisch, 2 vols (Breslau, 1827–8), 1.28; *Codex diplomaticus*, 2.471, no 533 (Cilli's offer of wages). A florin a week, or 4 per month, for a mounted soldier from Germany may have been the standard rate (comparing favourably with the 3 fl. offered to the lighter-equipped Hungarians), since it was quoted by the cardinals who wrote a crusade programme in 1464: Muresan, 'La croisade en projets', annexe.
[112] Ebendorfer, *Chronica regum*, 850.   [113] *MKL*, 1.52–3, no 40.
[114] *Acta Bosnae*, 263: 17,000 horse, 6,000 foot, 7,000 *crucesignati*.
[115] *Ungedruckte Akten*, 280–1, no 185.

bulwark claims. Matthias made much of Capistrano and lobbied for his canonization;[116] and we have no reason to doubt that he felt genuine devotion towards the preacher. But the 1456 relief had been anomalous in a number of respects and it cast a shadow over his father's military record. It is striking that in the Olomouc fresco painted in 1468—which at 46 square metres is the largest surviving visual testimony to the battle of Belgrade—Capistrano is depicted more than life-size but the preacher's famous banner, a symbol of command, has migrated into the hands of an armoured figure that almost certainly represents Hunyadi. This divided but complementary leadership, with Capistrano providing spiritual inspiration and Hunyadi military command, probably represents the mature Corvinian interpretation of 1456. It is exemplified by János Thuróczy's account of the battle, in which Hunyadi gives a rousing speech to raise the spirits of the garrison.[117] And it was not radically out of step with Rome's view, in part because the *curia* wanted to nurture the crusading image of the *gens corviniana*.[118]

It would be wrong to conclude from this that the Hungarian nobility were left cold by the idea of personally crusading, or that the king himself was not susceptible to the image of the *athleta Christi*. There is evidence testifying to both. Recent Hungarian historians, such as Jeno Szűcs, have played down the appeal of patriotic sentiment, and it is true that the overall performance of Hungary's fighting elite from this point through to the catastrophe at Mohács in 1526 does not give much backing to the thesis of a 'national crusade'.[119] There was Hungarian enthusiasm for the crusade in 1443, as in 1458.[120] As usual in crusading history, devotion interwove with other factors, such as lineage and ambition. Tagliacozzo, an inquisitive and perceptive outsider, was under no illusions about the diversity of motivation that made Michael Szilágyi fight so tenaciously in 1456: 'on account of the Christian faith, the kingdom, Lord Janos the *vaivode*, to whom he was related...as well as by reason of his own honour and renown'.[121] Other Hungarian nobles may not have shared Szilágyi's illustrious marital connection and high office, but they would certainly have been influenced by the attractions of honour, fame, faith, and guaranteed wages. There seems to have been a special kudos attached to fighting the Turks. Admittedly, in provisions relating to military service in legislation passed in 1478 and 1486 they were listed alongside other likely enemies—Germans, Czechs, and Poles—with no attempt at differentiation.[122] But Andrić was surely correct in suggesting that the popularity of Capistrano's cult with the nobility derived in part from their retrospective honouring of what he had achieved in 1456.[123]

---

[116] e.g. *MKL*, 1.10–13, no 8, lobbying in 1460, allegedly as soon as domestic circumstances permitted.

[117] Thurocz, *Chronica*, ch. 250.

[118] e.g. *BF*, NS2.117, no 210, 118–19, no 214, 181–5, no 353 (institution of the Feast of the Transfiguration, August 1457).

[119] Jenő Szűcs, 'Die Nation in historischer Sicht und der nationale Aspekt der Geschichte', in his *Nation und Geschichte: Studien* (Budapest, 1981), 11–160, esp. 88–9.

[120] *Crusade of Varna*, 113. [121] 'Relatio', 772.

[122] *Laws*, 32–3, 41, 67. [123] Andrić, *The Miracles*, 332, reflecting Tagliacozzo, 'Relatio', 795.

Having said that, in this period's increasingly court-orientated culture what counted for most was military service to the prince and, even in a universally accredited *antemurale,* this did not normally entail taking the cross. Hungary does not appear to have had an equivalent to Philip the Good's Feast of the Pheasant or Maximilian's Society of St George. As for Matthias, the picture of the devout warrior that Andreas Pannonius drew of him in his *Libellus de virtutibus Mathiae* was more or less what he wanted to believe, with its eclectic conflation of dynastic, national, classical, and scriptural exemplars and references.[124] The crusade was something to which he subscribed and aspired, but as in the case of his arch-enemies, the Habsburgs, it had to compete for his attention with much else.

4.3 PIUS II, PERAULT, AND VOLUNTEER SERVICE

One of the contemporaries who was most impressed by Capistrano's achievement in 1456 was Piccolomini. When he became Pope two years later he pressed on with Calixtus III's crusading endeavours, moulding them in ways that sprang from his own, distinctive views about the nature of crusading.[125] On volunteerism, these views seem to have developed over time in parallel with changes to his overall programme. His approach at Mantua in 1459 was that while an effective crusading response to the Turks had to be a collective Christian enterprise, the organization of individual contingents could be left to states, each managing the contribution that it had agreed to make. To assist in funding these contingents, there would be a common levy of taxes and, writing to Philip of Burgundy in September 1459, the Pope made it clear that he anticipated the proceeds being used to pay troops, 'with the help of this measure the soldiers' wages can be paid'.[126] This did not rule out volunteers, and we have already observed duke and Pope alike making use of the services of *crucesignati* and responding positively to the approaches of Gerard Déschamps. It did, however, point towards state-managed systems of recruitment, muster, payment, movement, and discipline. The First Crusade might be pressed into service as an uplifting example but not as a military template, and Pius's reading of Capistrano's 1456 victory followed the *e fortiori* model: if such a victory could be won by an army of untrained and ill-equipped volunteers, how much more might be achieved by professionals, especially when they were supplemented by volunteers and inspired by their religious conviction? As the Pope put it in *Septimo iam exacto mense*, his closing address at Mantua on 14 January 1460, 'there will be enormous contingents of Christians, and they will be reinforced by bands (*cunei*) of *crucesignati*, whose virtue, proved three years ago [sc. in 1456] will guarantee a great and brilliant victory'.[127] *Ecclesiam Christi*, the congress's summative crusading statement, issued on the same day, was therefore traditional in its treatment of volunteers, addressing such essential issues as start date, length of service

---

[124] Pannonius, 'Libellus', *passim*.
[125] See Housley, 'Pius II'.
[126] Picotti, *La dieta*, 424, no 17.
[127] *Sacrorum conciliorum*, 35.113–20, at 116.

required, surrogacy, and sponsorship.[128] But what mattered more was the levy of taxes, and this was bound up with the Pope's ability to persuade Europe's rulers to honour their Mantua commitments. In this context (or indeed any other) the start date set in *Ecclesiam Christi*, 1 April 1460, was so unrealistic as to be perplexing.

The failure of Pius's Mantua programme forced the Pope to rethink his approach and, in *Existimatis*, his private address to six trusted cardinals in March 1462, he expounded a more selective crusading project. Its most radical innovation was Pius's own presence on the campaign, relying on self-interest (Hungary) and moral obligation (Burgundy) to provide him with a solid core of support. In addition to these and other contingents, there would be 'more than a few' (*non pauci*) volunteers from Germany, England, and Spain; in other words, Pius fell back on voluntary service as a means of bringing non-participatory *nationes* into the project.[129] At this stage, the papal plan lacked credibility, but Mehmed's conquest of Bosnia in 1463 and the outbreak of the Veneto-Ottoman war made it feasible. An alliance system was created: a robust bilateral alliance between Hungary and Venice on 12 September 1463 at Petrovaradin; a rather vaguer trilateral one between the Pope, Venice, and Philip of Burgundy on 19 October in Pius's palace at St Peter's. This was followed three days later by the release of *Ezechielis prophetae*, Pius's last important crusade bull. The text set out in full the revised approach towards the crusade that the failure of his congress had forced on him, with particular reference to the storm of criticism that his planned participation had unleashed. Volunteers were now actively sought. The able-bodied (*validus*) should come in person and serve for six months, while others could send surrogates, with up to ten sponsors permitted for each combatant. Departure would occur at Ancona on 5 June 1464, and the Pope undertook to ensure that those who answered the call to arms would be able to find shipping at a fair price at Venice.[130]

It is necessary to ask what lay behind *Ezechielis prophetae* because its widespread preaching in the autumn and winter of 1463–4 brought results that replicated the surge of enthusiasm that Capistrano had generated almost a decade earlier, but across a geographical span that included Castile, Poland, and Crete.[131] The personal charisma of a Capistrano was replaced by the seductive prospect of papal participation, but the result was similar: large numbers of groups of *crucesignati* setting out with the intention of fighting the Turks. One interpretation, which constantly recurs in the dispatches of the Italian envoys and has recently been forcefully stated by Barbara Baldi, lays emphasis on the alarming political situation facing Pius in 1463–4, as the failure of his attempt to seize leadership of the Christian world against the Turks coincided with a crescendo of French criticism, German anti-papalism, Podiebradian scheming, and discontent within the college of cardinals. Baldi comes close to saying that if Pius had not embraced the role of

---

[128] *VMH*, 2.366–9, no 551, also in *Sacrorum conciliorum*, 35.261–5 (some major passages paraphrased).
[129] *Pii II Commentarii*, bk 7, ch. 16, 460–3.
[130] *Vetera monumenta Slavorum*, 474–81; also in Piccolomini, *Opera omnia*, 914–23.
[131] For details on the response see Housley, 'Pius II'; id., 'Indulgences', 303–5; Pastor, *History*, 3.352–61.

papa crociato then he would not have been Pope at all for much longer. He was boxed in by his many enemies to such an extent that the crusade was his only escape route.[132] In terms of the volunteers' role, such an argument implies a beleaguered Pope appealing to the Christian faithful to shelter him against his encroaching enemies. In the summer of 1464 Louis XI's animosity towards the Pope was certainly keen-edged. In July it caused him to ignore his counsellors' advice and enter into an alliance with Podiebrad that formally embraced the main features of the Czech king's eccentric approach towards the Turkish war.[133] But to infer that this was the principal driver behind Pius's actions is to overplay the role of politics. The diplomatic scenario within Europe constantly informed Pius's crusade policy, but it did not create it. The Turkish threat had been a preoccupation of Pius since the 1440s.[134] He was determined to address it, and in 1463 the critical situation in the western Balkans both made an effective response imperative and seemed to offer a viable framework for collective action. But it also called for personal commitment, notwithstanding the daunting political and administrative challenges that this brought with it. The problem was that this personal commitment sparked off so many thousands of others. Almost certainly there were many more than Pius—who in 1462 had spoken cautiously of 'more than a few' volunteers—had anticipated.[135]

The debacle that resulted from Pius's encouragement of volunteer service in 1464 was one corner of a broader picture of mismanagement. Making the alliance system that was created in September–October 1463 operationally effective was a demanding enough task. Virtually nothing went right. The date set for departure from Ancona (5 June) passed before the Pope had even left Rome. Throughout June and July Matthias clamoured for news of action so that he could launch his land campaign. Doge Cristoforo Moro's delay in arriving at Ancona with the Venetian galleys until 12 August has never been fully explained, though it is likely that the reason was habitual Venetian caution rather than duplicity or incompetence.[136] The troops whom Philip of Burgundy sent under his bastard son, Anthony, engaged in a diversion to Portuguese Ceuta en route to Italy.[137] None of this is surprising in the light of what we know about warfare at the time, let alone the fraught diplomatic atmosphere, the distance separating the allies, the uncertainty created by Duke Philip's withdrawal, and the underlying absence of clear strategic planning. The odds were always heavily

---

[132] Baldi, *Pio II*, 231–60.

[133] *Mémoires de messire Philippe de Comines*, ed. Abbé Lenglet de Fresnoy, vol. 2 (London and Paris, 1747), 424–34; Lassalmonie, 'Louis XI', 189.

[134] As his letters clearly show: Barbara Baldi, 'La corrispondenza di Enea Silvio Piccolomini dal 1431 al 1454. La maturazione di un'esperienza fra politica e cultura', in Isabella Lazzarini, ed., *I confini della lettera. Pratiche epistolari e reti di communicazione nell'Italia tardomedievale* (Florence, 2009), = *Reti Medievali Rivista*, 10, 1–22.

[135] As late as June 1464 he was hedging his bets on the response: 'Addite fidelis populi per Italiam, Germaniam, et alias Transalpinas provincias excitationem, quam nostra profectio factura est': *Anecdota litteraria*, 3.287–96 (*Suscepturi hodie*), at 290.

[136] Setton, *Papacy*, 2.269; Pastor, *History*, 3.262–7 (highly critical of Venice).

[137] Paviot, *Les ducs*, 175.

stacked against the successful coordination of forces. Large but unpredictable numbers of *crucesignati* who had to travel hundreds of miles even to reach the peninsula could only aggravate a problematic situation. Pius made some attempt to assist their passage. On 11 April, for example, he asked Moro to give Swiss crusaders, 'with people, horses, possessions, arms, and everything needed for the holy war', safe passage through Venetian lands.[138] A similar but more detailed request went to Sforza at Milan. Arriving crusaders were to be treated well, in particular their currency should be accepted at fair rates of exchange and prices for staples that they needed should not be raised; nor should they be subject to tolls.[139] But Pius had also created the potential for confusion by leaving it unclear whether these volunteers should make their way to Venice or Ancona. In the event, many made for Rome, including some Hungarians (who were clearly going the wrong way).[140]

Mutatis mutandis, events in 1464 bear a strong resemblance to what we have already observed happening to the German volunteers in Hungary in 1456; indeed, Thomas Vogtherr has suggested that the north Germans experienced exactly what the south Germans had gone through in 1456.[141] Ancona was Zemun revisited. Crusaders arriving at the port had to contend with stifling midsummer heat; a shortfall in accommodation, food, and water; the outbreak of plague; and a lack of clear direction. On 23 May the senate of Ragusa set in motion elaborate preparations for the anticipated arrival of Pope, doge, and crusaders, addressing precisely the types of issue that would shortly become so problematic at Ancona.[142] No record has survived of similar preparations being undertaken at the Adriatic port, but if they were, they proved to be inadequate. The crusaders met with hostility from the Italians, particularly the Romans. Most of the volunteers were eventually dismissed without seeing action, and they returned home bitter and disillusioned. Some declared that they would never believe Pope or preachers again.[143] Carvajal in particular must have found the whole sequence of events distressingly familiar because, alongside Girolamo Lando, Cardinal d'Estouteville, and Rodrigo Sánchez, he played a leading role in assessing the military capability of the volunteers who assembled at Ancona. Twice in fewer than ten years he had to make the decision whether *crucesignati* who had travelled long distances were fit for service. Lando's varied role raises particularly interesting questions. He had preached the crusade during Lent at Lübeck, where a local source states that he managed to recruit

---

[138] *Ungedruckte Akten*, 281, no 186, with a rare reference to vicarious service: '...ac gentes mittere et personaliter proficisci'.

[139] Piccolomini, *Opera omnia*, 864, ep. 389 (undated but sent *anno sexto* from Petriolo, where Pius was taking the waters in April 1464).

[140] According to Niccolò della Tuccia the pope tried to disperse them homewards, 'dicendo voleva far denari per portare in quel paese, e non genti': 'Cronaca di Viterbo', in *Cronache e statuti della città di Viterbo*, ed. Ignazio Ciampi, Documenti di storia italiana, 5 (Florence, 1872), 1–272, at 269.

[141] Vogtherr, '"Wenn hinten"', 120.

[142] Lopud Vicko Lisičar, 'Program Dubrovačkoga senata za doček Pape Pija II (1464)', *Croatia sacra*, 5 (1933), 97–109, at 99–104.

[143] Guido Levi, ed., 'Diario Nepesino di Antonio Lotieri de Pisano (1459–1468)', *Archivio della R. Società romana di storia patria*, 7 (1884), 115–82, at 140 and compare 117.

2,000 volunteers.[144] Just a few weeks later he was at Ancona handling the difficult situation that developed there ahead of Pius's arrival.[145] Worried that enforced idleness would aggravate desertion or disorder, he suggested to the Pope that some of the crusaders be transported by sea to the Peloponnese.[146] As always, the Venetians preferred to use their own paid troops and they were sceptical about the military worth of the volunteers. In April they claimed that their shipping was tied up in ferrying paid troops to the Peloponnese and Albania, and suggested that the *crucesignati* (whom they presumably anticipated arriving soon in Venice, as directed in *Ezechielis prophetae*) should proceed overland to help the Hungarians.[147] It was only reluctantly that they agreed on 21 June to use two available *naves* to transport 2,000 Saxon crusaders gathered at Ancona for service in the Peloponnese, after filtering out the 'useless and unarmed'.[148] A force several thousand strong assisted Sigismondo Malatesta in his unsuccessful siege of Mistra; they were the only crusaders recruited by Pius who saw action.[149] This raises the question whether the 'Saxons', notwithstanding their name, were the same people whom Lando had recruited in Germany, or whether the figure is just a coincidence. Either way, we have an echo of Capistrano's continuity from preaching through to later management of recruits, a suggestion of what might have been done to make the process laid down in *Ezechielis prophetae* operate more effectively.

The question of responsibility naturally arises. Unsurprisingly, sources representing Pius's inner circle, notably Jacopo Ammannati Piccolomini and the early biographers, Giovanni Antonio Campano and Bartolomeo Platina, emphasized the efforts that the ailing and anxious Pope made to assist people who had responded to his call, and blamed the volunteers for making inadequate preparations in terms of money and equipment.[150] The latter point seems unfair: the requirement that a volunteer be 'able-bodied' was not much of a direction for either preachers or their audiences to work with. Nor were clarifications, to the effect that volunteers should be able to fight and have sufficient support for a year, much help

---

[144] *Die Chroniken der niedersächsichen Städte. Lübeck, vol. 4*, ed. Historische Commission bei der königl. Academie der Wissenschaften, Die Chroniken der deutschen Städte vom 14. bis ins 16. Jahrhundert, 30 (Leipzig, 1910), 351–5; Vogtherr, '"Wenn hinten"', 118–19. German town chronicles offer much information for 1464: see in particular *Die Chroniken der niederrheinischen Städte. Cöln, vol. 3*, ed. Historische Commission bei der königl. Academie der Wissenschaften, Die Chroniken der deutschen Städte vom 14. bis ins 16. Jahrhundert, 14 (Leipzig, 1877); *Die Chroniken der niedersächsichen Städte. Magdeburg, vol. 1*, ed. Historische Commission bei der königl. Academie der Wissenschaften, Die Chroniken der deutschen Städte vom 14. bis ins 16. Jahrhundert, 7 (Leipzig, 1869); *Hamburgische Chroniken in niedersächsicher Sprache*, ed. J.M. Lappenberg (Hamburg, 1861), 257.

[145] Mureşan, 'Girolamo Lando', 166–7.

[146] Ammannati Piccolomini, *Lettere*, 2.501–26, no 74, at 504.

[147] *Ungedruckte Akten*, 280–1, no 185 (= *MDE*, 1.274–5, no 165).

[148] *Ungedruckte Akten*, 305–6, no 195, and cf. 310, no 198, on the two *naves*, which were still on offer for use by the Ancona *crucesignati* on 16 July. These Saxons were presumably the crusaders referred to by Lando in his letter to Pius.

[149] Soranzo, 'Sigismondo', 228–9.

[150] *Le Vite di Pio II di Giovanni Antonio Campano e Bartolomeo Platina*, ed. Giulio C. Zimolo, RISNS 3, pt 3, 83 (Campano), 110 (Platina). Ammannati concurs with both (*Lettere*, 2.514, no 74), and may have been their source of information. See too Johannes Simoneta, *Rerum gestarum Francisci Sfortiae Commentarii*, ed. G. Soranzo, RISNS 21, pt 2, 477–8.

in practice.[151] There are a number of sources that point towards the volunteers possessing equipment and, if they became destitute, the high prices and long wait at Ancona were more than enough to explain it. There are also sources that indicate organization and leadership, usually deriving from an urban milieu as at Bologna, Lübeck, and (as we have seen) Ghent.[152] Designated leaders, uniforms, musical instruments, ceremonially bestowed banners, and civic receptions are not normal features of crusades featuring 'the lower classes', 'the poorest class', or 'mere vagrants'.[153] Rather, they testify to planning, a respectable social origin, and reasonable military capability. Of course the scattered sources and geographical breadth of response in 1463–4 make any generalization hazardous; but for every Castilian *crucesignatus* begging door to door,[154] there could have been a well-equipped Gantois fighting in the company of his peers and well able to hold his own against the Turks.[155] The absence of a command structure did not help; Alberto Guglielmotti, the historian of the papal navy, long ago stressed that there were no '*condottieri*, princes, and captains of reputation who could have controlled and managed groups of such a diverse character'.[156] But it is hard to see why the volunteers' military potential should have been inferior to that of the German contingents in 1456, particularly once they had been thoroughly reviewed at Venice or Ancona. Common to both was the fact that they were not given the chance to prove their worth. This confirms the wisdom of Pius's Mantua approach: bands of *crucesignati* acting essentially as inspiring auxiliaries to professionals who had been assembled under an agreed quota system. Of course there would still have been substantial issues of strategy and deployment to be settled, but at least there were grounds for expecting that the mobilization process would run more smoothly.

The homewards trudge from Ancona of Pius's disappointed volunteers brought to a conclusion the trajectory of preaching and recruitment that had been initiated by Capistrano a decade earlier. Although it was fragmented in character, this was at root a collective response to Constantinople's fall and to Mehmed II's subsequent gains. Its scale and significance alike have rarely been given their due: for this was a massive venture, one which demands comparison with the Holy Land crusades of the twelfth and thirteenth centuries. Adding together those who fought alongside Capistrano in 1456, the volunteers who returned to Germany without fighting, the people from Hungary and its satellite lands who took the cross in 1458 and 1464, and those who volunteered to accompany Pius in 1463–4, there can be little doubt that we are considering tens of thousands of volunteers, to whom of course must be added their sponsors. Taking into account also their families, the lives of numerous Europeans were profoundly altered by crusading in a way that was not dissimilar to the experience of their ancestors. It is worth

---

[151] Weber, *Lutter*, 2.3.2.
[152] *Corpus chronicorum bononensium*, RISNS 18, pt 1, 4.326–9; *Cronica gestorum ac factorum memorabilium civitatis Bononie*, ed. A. Sorbelli, RISNS 23, pt 2, 97; *Della historia di Bologna parte terza del R.P.M. Cherubino Ghirardacci*, ed. A. Sorbelli, RISNS 33, pt 1, 185–6; Vogtherr, '"Wenn hinten"', 119; Paviot, *Les ducs*, 172.
[153] Pastor, *History*, 3.352, 358.   [154] Housley, 'Indulgences', 304.   [155] Paviot, *Les ducs*, 172.
[156] Alberto Guglielmotti, *Storia della marina pontificia*, vol. 2 (Rome, 1886), 335.

asking why this has made so little impact on the written history of the period. The answer is probably two-fold. In the first place, the scale of events is to a large extent concealed by the extended period of time over which they happened and the diffused geography involved. And in the second place, impressive as this response was when considered in the round, contemporaries perceived it to be inadequate to the task that faced Christendom. Hence it was overshadowed by the dominant *topoi* of apathy, disappointment, and failure. And yet the response seems to reveal that a large proportion of Catholic Europe's inhabitants were still willing to respond to the call of personal service, the problem being that their authorities were no longer able to furnish them with the wherewithal to make that service operate effectively.

There was one further proposal in this period to assemble an army that would be made up of volunteers who had taken the cross, and it was advanced by Perault in the spring of 1502. Even more so than in 1456 and 1463–4, Perault's scheme was a *faute de mieux*. Capistrano and Pius II would have preferred their crusade preaching to function as an auxiliary measure within the context of imperial and Hungarian mobilization on the one hand, and that of the entire *respublica christiana* on the other. To date, Perault had placed his hope in Maximilian at last living up to his obligations and promises, under the watchful eye of Berthold von Henneberg and the *Reichsregiment*. It was on that basis that his preaching of indulgences had already achieved financial results that impressed him, but unfortunately also came to the attention of Maximilian. By May 1502 he had come under heavy pressure from Maximilian to authorize payments ahead of anything military being organized. In January 1502 Maximilian issued a call to arms against the Turks without any reference to a *Reichstag*. The army was to assemble for 1 June, a timescale that for lack of realism came close to that set out in *Ecclesiam Christi* in 1460. The point was that it enabled him further to ratchet up the pressure on Perault. Boxed in and panicky, the legate came up with a plan of action in which he himself would create a crusading army of volunteers. He wrote from Cologne, a city which seems genuinely to have impressed him with its response to his preaching and lobbying. He declared that he would be the new Capistrano. 'The said legate will be able to create an army in Germany of 40,000 or 50,000 fighting men, just as fr. John of Capistrano did', and he would do this without needing to use any of the indulgence proceeds. The city authorities of Cologne had already promised that if Maximilian made peace with France, and proceeded against the Turks in alliance with Venice and Hungary, they would provide 500 armed men for a year. There were individual promises too, both noble and common, undertaken by the city's matrons, merchants, and churchmen; one widow had promised six fighters, others three or two, the total reaching about 1,000.[157] So Cologne alone would send 1,500 men off to war, and provided there was genuine hope of action ('if a crusade really happens'), this pattern would be repeated elsewhere. Perault himself would preach 'to sign with the cross' throughout Germany.[158]

[157] *Crucesignati* had been sponsored by women in 1456: *Codex diplomaticus*, 471, no 333.
[158] Mehring, 'Peraudi', 398–401, no 6.

In a fascinating assessment of Perault's character written in December 1493, the Venetian envoys commented that Perault's good will regarding the crusade was not in question but 'in other respects he is not suited to such a great undertaking'.[159] In other words, he lacked the diplomatic qualities needed to bring a crusade into being.[160] Does his 1502 proposal bear this out? Yes and no. Perault's optimism about German devotion was certainly naive, springing from his overwhelming commitment to his mission. It is important to remember that in common with everybody else he shaped his message to his audience. Writing to the *Reichsregiment* in July 1501, he claimed that the common people were eager to help, and needed only the leadership of the elite.[161] On the other hand a letter to the Swiss, probably written at the same point as this one, asserted that Maximilian and the princes were on fire to fight the Turks.[162] Overall, it is probably true to say that he did credit the Germans with the potential to mount a crusade; indulging in the customary flattery, he wrote that if only Germany were united, it could subdue the Turks single-handedly.[163] That said, it remains hard to attribute this extraordinary plan to anything but desperation, driven by the fact that the alternative, which was handing over any of the collected money to Maximilian, was anathema to him. So the 1502 proposal was his escape plan and, in this respect, its advantage lay in the timescale that Perault proposed. Given that an army of this unaccustomed type could not be put together half way through the year, the expedition would have to wait until 1503. By that time everything would be in place for it, including an agreement between Maximilian and the *Reichsregiment*. What motivated Perault was the need to kill Maximilian's plan for a June assembly, which he suspected derived solely from the emperor-elect's desire to exert additional leverage regarding the handover of the money. In presenting Maximilian with a plan of action that guaranteed him his crusade in 1503, without the need to draw on the indulgence money for its first year's service, Perault hoped to check Maximilian as cleverly as Maximilian had tried to check him with his January call to arms.

Hence Perault's 1502 appeal to German voluntary service has the look of a tactical move, and by no means a bad one, in his protracted game of cat and mouse with Maximilian. This is not to say that voluntary service did not form one feature of 'the way to make a good crusade', to borrow the engaging title of one of his polemical tracts of 1504.[164] His plan to stop fraudulent use of the indulgence money seems to have revolved around its distribution on a decentralized basis to local or regional recruits who agreed to take part in a crusade in exchange for a 'decent and appropriate wage'.[165] In December 1502, for example, Perault wrote to the canons of Utrecht that they should conserve money collected by preaching the

---

[159] '...la reverendissima Signoria Sua, la qual per dispositione et bona volonta, credemo sij ben dotata. Ma dubitemo, ché le altre parte non siano per corrisponder ben a tanta imprexa': *AR*, no 236.
[160] cf. ibid. no 332, accusing Perault of speaking his mind too readily.
[161] Kraus, *Reichsregiment*, 226–35, at 231 (= *AR*, no 15504). The text is close to being a manifesto, including (at 234) a reference to the legate's resolve to accompany the army.
[162] *AR*, no 15505.   [163] Mehring, 'Peraudi', 385.
[164] *De modo fiende bone cruciate*: ibid. 382.   [165] Ibid. 385.

Jubilee 'until such a time as an expedition against the ferocious enemy of Christ is genuinely (*realiter*) set in motion'; they would then, the cardinal hoped, distribute it 'with their own hands to those soldiers of Christ...setting out to fight'.[166] There was more substance in this idea than in Maximilian's equivalent: his proposal in 1503 to harness voluntary service to his Society of St George. As we have seen in the case of Philip the Good's Burgundy, voluntary service in exchange for the crusader's indulgence, organized and rewarded at a local level, could still function as one feature of a diverse programme of recruitment, especially in an urban milieu. What Perault anticipated being done at Utrecht would not be dissimilar to what we have seen happening at Ghent in 1464. But it was impracticable to expect it to be the core or backbone of that programme, which Perault seemed to do in 1502. There needed to be an overarching structure of *some* kind, even if it was federalist or decentralized in character. Perault's fellow enthusiast, Stefano Taleazzi, recognized this: *crucesignati* were welcome, he observed in 1500, but the army's critical mass (its *robur*) had to be composed of professional combatants and this called for sustained organization.[167] The conundrum faced by Perault in 1502 was in essence the same as that confronted by the man whose exploits he claimed that he could emulate: like Hungary under Ladislas V, the Holy Roman Empire was a dysfunctional polity.[168]

4.4 CRUSADE TAXATION AND THE FUNDING SHORTFALL

This continuing tendency to look towards volunteer service as a means of locating at least a proportion of combatants, including specialists such as naval personnel,[169] was accompanied by a trend to advocate universal taxation as a way of funding the venture. At first glance, this trend seems contradictory to voluntarism, but in practice it complemented it, in so far as the papal *curia* was willing to accept either a personal or a financial contribution. In the immediate aftermath of Mantua Pius II's approach was that lay donors had to pay a sum in addition to their taxable contribution in order to get the full indulgence.[170] But under the pressure of events this stance softened and, at the height of his preparations in 1464, the Pope decreed that a one-off payment by the secular power secured a full indulgence for all of its citizens, even if they had paid nothing individually towards the crusade.[171] The thinking underpinning such obligatory contribution hinged on Nicholas V's statement in his bull *Etsi ecclesia Christi* (September 1453) that since the crusade

---

[166] *Codex documentorum*, 425, no 293.
[167] Feliciangeli, 'Le proposte', 55 and see also 51–2.
[168] In Hungary the pattern recurred in 1514, but with more tragic consequences than in 1456: Housley, 'Crusading as Social Revolt', *passim*.
[169] *Ungedruckte Akten*, 241, no 170 (Siena). Ibid. 279, no 184, has similar suggestions for Florence.
[170] *Sacrorum conciliorum*, 32.265 (*Adversus impiam*).
[171] Piccolomini, *Opera omnia*, 864–5, ep. 391, also in *BF*, NS2.631–2, no 1220.

affected all Christians, their salvation depended on their supporting it. We shall see that in practice it was viewed as an obligation on Jews as well, which raises the intriguing question of what the Church's response would have been towards a Jewish request to fight in person or send surrogates, instead of paying the twentieth that was stipulated in their case. What drove the *curia* to embrace obligatory payment was of course the financial burden of crusading, which Calixtus characterized well when he reissued *Etsi ecclesia Christi* with additions and changes in May 1455: so crushing was this burden, the Pope wrote, that it was virtually impossible to support it. Ideologically, the idea derived from the papacy's *magisterium*, its responsibility to save souls. This made taxation for crusading close kin to the parcel of measures that were annually reiterated in *In coena domini*, the Holy Thursday bull that reminded Christians of the claims of Christ's vicars to intervene in their economic and legal lives.[172] Its normative ban on trade in military-related merchandise with non-Christians prepared Christians for the full commercial ban that was associated with a projected expedition.[173] In common with liturgical programmes, *In coena domini* served as a reminder that the crusading message was an all-inclusive one.

The taxation scheme that the papal *curia* adopted had the virtue of simplicity: a clerical tenth, Jewish twentieth, and lay thirtieth, to be collected in all cases within the boundaries of individual states, the rulers of which would then use the cash to pay stipendiary soldiers and meet their various needs.[174] We have already noted that the haggling involved can be viewed in the greatest detail in the evidence bequeathed by the Mantua congress. At Mantua the relationship between these funds and the expenses they would have to address was pinpointed, notably by the Venetians, who did not mince words about the shortfall involved: at one point they asserted that their own annual outgoings in warfare against the Turks reached 810,000 ducats, as against anticipated income from the three taxes of 22,000 (tenth), 5,000 (twentieth), and 60,000 (thirtieth). This discrepancy of close on 1:10 pointed towards cross-subsidy, with powers that did not face military outgoings allowing their money to be channelled towards those that did. In particular, the Venetians argued at Mantua, the non-Italians must help out with Italian expenses.[175] Neither Pius nor his successors were in principle opposed to such cross-subsidy, but in practice the problems involved rendered it impracticable outside the legal framework of a coalition. If such a framework was unattainable, universal obligation accompanied by decentralized financial management was clearly the only way to avoid suspicion of favouritism and fraud, as well as recognizing the realities of political life in Europe. In 1463 George Podiebrad and Antoine Marini paid indirect tribute to Pius II's approach by grafting it onto their secularized crusading programme; in some ways the federalism that it implied lay

---

[172] *DS*, 385–7, no 1243, 394–8, no 1252.
[173] See Norman Housley, 'Crusading and Interreligious Contacts in the Eastern Mediterranean: The Religious, Diplomatic and Juridical Frameworks', in conference proceedings, *Slavery and the Slave Trade in the Eastern Mediterranean 11th to 15th Centuries*, forthcoming.
[174] Picotti, *La dieta*, 424, no 17, expresses Pius II's essential thinking clearly.
[175] Ibid. 467–70, no 390, at 468–9.

at the heart of that programme.[176] In 1490 the idea of nation-based contributions was axiomatic in the discussions at Innocent VIII's Rome congress.[177] Ten years later Taleazzi cut to the heart of the issue when he observed that the mechanism for gathering in money (taxes, donations, indulgences, dispensations etc.) mattered much less than the underlying principles of fairness and accountability; if people saw that these were being respected, they would contribute in whichever way best suited them.[178]

In collection terms, each of the three tax bases presented its own problems. In certain respects, the most straightforward was the clerical tenth, which had over two centuries of history behind it and rested on the solid premise that the crusade was the primary concern of the Church.[179] Around 1500 the Venetians reckoned that, if collected across Christendom, the tenth would yield between 500,000 and 600,000 ducats a year, which was enough to raise and maintain a powerful field army to defend the Hungarian *antemurale*. But as they observed, there was no question of the richest territories, England, France, and Germany, permitting such a transfer of specie.[180] When such large-scale transfers were mooted, the context usually involved a high degree of wishful thinking. In 1500 Taleazzi managed to conjure up an impressive crusade treasure of over a million gold pieces, to be raised from quotas levied on the Italian states, but it comprised individual sums far higher than most states had agreed to pay in the past (and in practice they had paid nothing).[181] Diplomatic game-play surely lay behind the suggestion made by King Wladislas of Hungary in 1493 that Maximilian and he should split on a 50:50 basis all crusade funds sourced from outside their own dynastic territories (meaning, for example, that they would split the bulk of the empire's contribution).[182] Hardly less brazen was Maximilian's own proposal seven years later that Louis XII could retain Milan as an imperial fief in exchange for a massive annual subsidy towards the war against the Turks plus all the profits of crusade preaching in France.[183] The reality with which the *curia* lived was stated clearly by Calixtus III in a letter to Roberto Caracciolo in April 1457 *a propos* collection of the tenth and crusade preaching in the duchy of Milan. Sforza was unhappy with the tenth being raised because he feared its export. Carracciolo was to reassure him:

> The crusade must be preached and the tenth must be collected; as for what happens to the proceeds, we shall make provision in such a way that the duke will have no cause to complain. God forbid that we should appropriate any of the proceeds of the crusade, but it is fitting that we control their distribution, as is everywhere the case. In that way

---

[176] 'Tractatus pacis', para. 15, 77, Engl. tr. 89; and see *Mémoires*, 428, for the model adopted in 1464.
[177] Sigismondo de' Conti, *Le storie*, 2.424–36, *appendice*, nos 14–16.
[178] Feliciangeli, 'Le proposte', 47.
[179] Weber, *Lutter*, 3.2.1.
[180] Girolamo Priuli, *I diarii*, ed. A. Segre, RISNS 24/3, vol. 1, 317 (= *AR*, no 14161). These figures look hypothetical.
[181] Feliciangeli, 'Le proposte', 62.
[182] *AR*, no 141: Wladislas claimed that he could expect 'paucas vel potius nullas pecunias' from his own lands.
[183] Ibid. no 11250.

the duke's prestige will be preserved in this matter, the preaching of which takes precedence over anything else.[184]

Calixtus and his successors lived in a political world in which crusading activity had to be fashioned piecemeal from a mosaic of such compromises and face-saving formulae. The clergy were well aware of this and sheltered behind the indifference or active hostility of their rulers; even legates avoided tackling such an intractable problem. All the Popes could do was reissue the decrees of their predecessors and threaten the princes with God's wrath.[185] In Germany during Pius II's reign the higher clergy went onto the offensive. With Gregor Heimburg (Pius's *bête noire*) as their spirited mouthpiece, they not only rejected the tenth but worked their rejection into a broader strategy of resistance to Roman demands, one that assumed an overtly conciliarist form.[186] Because conciliarism retained its potential to mobilize clerical resistance to papal demands, it presented a serious threat to crusading's tax base; this was one reason why anti-conciliarist decrees went hand in hand with crusading ones.

The result was that the clerical tenth, once the backbone of crusading finance, shrank to an essentially auxiliary role. It recurred in any major crusade programme that was attempted, such as Alexander VI's in 1500, in which a three-year tenth was decreed across the whole of Christendom, 'due to the urgent need of the *respublica Christiana* and the orthodox faith'.[187] By that point, however, rulers and Popes alike were taking the tenth for granted and looking beyond it. In 1498–1500 the papal *curia* had to contend with a German attempt to seize annates (an established papal revenue source) for the benefit of the crusade.[188] Religious houses were looked on as untapped sources of wealth. Most crusading bulls included provision for communities to benefit from the indulgence by sending troops: typically, *Ezechielis prophetae* specified that a group of ten religious could send a soldier. This accorded with the *curia*'s policy that all Christians ('every age and sex, of whatever calling') should have the chance to reap the rewards of crusading.[189] Characteristically, suggestions began to be advanced that this opportunity should be transformed into an obligation. An eccentric plan of monastic mobilization was concocted in the early 1470s,[190] and at the Freiburg diet in 1498 it was proposed that all religious houses send troops, for whom the monks would pray.[191] As always with diets, the danger was that consideration of crusade would unleash anti-clerical feelings as well as anti-papal ones.

---

[184] *BF*, NS2.151, no 288.   [185] *Opera inedita*, 141–2, no 69, at 144.

[186] For Heimburg see *LdM*, 4.1682–3.

[187] Burchard, *Liber*, 2.220–4 (= *AR*, nos 13934, 14158), and see also Burchard, *Liber*, 2.226–30, the taxable income of the *curia* itself, from cardinals to domestic staff.

[188] L. Péllisier, ed., 'Documents sur la première année du règne de Louis XII tirés des Archives de Milan', *Bulletin historique et philologique du Comité des trauvaux historiques et scientifiques*, (1890), 47–124, no 53, at 98–9 (= *AR*, no 8962); ibid. nos 6584, 14407, 14727.

[189] *Vetera monumenta Slavorum,* 474–81, also in Piccolomini, *Opera omnia*, 914–23, at 921. It was not specified how this would operate in practice.

[190] *Notes et extraits*, 5th ser., 58–62, but for dating see Setton, *Papacy*, 3.188–9, note 68.

[191] *AR*, no 6583.

As for the proposed Jewish twentieth, information on collection is scanty and its chief interest resides in its rationale. The supporting argument was that of benefit: as Alexander VI put it in 1500, the Jews practised their trades and enjoyed other privileges under the protection of Christians, so they should contribute towards Christendom's defence.[192] It is tempting to deduce that this indicates a move towards crusade being reconfigured as a civic obligation rather than a religious one, but the *curia*'s deployments of the *de necessitate salutis* argument undercut this. The logic was inconsistent: believers should contribute because of their faith, Jews because it was only fair for them to do so. Nor was the justification entirely consistent. In 1473 Sixtus IV deployed the argument of general protection against the Turks but also narrowed it to the specific protection afforded to the Jews by the papacy: assisting with the Holy See's crusade expenses would therefore be a more focused way to express gratitude.[193] The disproportionate burden proposed is explicable only in pragmatic terms: Calixtus III, no friend to the Jews, had pitched his tax at a full tenth, while Alexander VI threatened not just to double his twentieth should there be any fraud or tax evasion, but to add a 4 per cent fine, payable to the person who disclosed the misdemeanour.[194] There was probably some satisfaction in hitting this unpopular outgroup harder than Christians. As Calixtus III put it in 1456, there could be no better destination for money earned through usurious practices than its collection 'for conversion into this holy undertaking'.[195]

The key tax was naturally the lay thirtieth, which the Venetians at Mantua estimated to be worth close on three times the value of the clerical tenth. On this, precedent was not promising. Attempts at taxing the laity for the Holy Land crusade in the thirteenth century had fallen flat. Nothing similar had been attempted since, and Philip the Good's envoys at Mantua described the tax as 'something very new', doubting whether it could be levied in Burgundy.[196] After securing the agreements of most of the Italian states Pius pushed ahead with collection in 1460,[197] and the spring of 1464 witnessed frantic attempts to get the tax collected in some Italian cities, by one means or another, in order to meet pressing papal expenses.[198] It was far from easy: Pius resorted to threatening the Perugians with confiscation of their property in a desperate attempt to squeeze 15,000 ducats out of the city.[199] Outside Italy, as the Pope admitted to the Sienese in March 1464, the lay contribution was tacitly dropped.[200] The reasons for the overall failure of the project are easily identified. In addition to novelty there was of course suspicion about the prospect of a crusade materializing, but more significant was the failure of advocates for crusade to convince contemporaries of the universal character of their programme. Putting it bluntly, the inhabitants of any state that was directly threatened by the Turks would look to their rulers to set in train the taxation measures required to deal with it. The result was that the most interesting echoes of the papal

---

[192] Burchard, *Liber*, 2.224–6 (= *AR*, no 14159).   [193] Weber, *Lutter*, 3.2.3, including text.
[194] Ibid.; Burchard, *Liber*, 2.226.   [195] *BF*, NS1.63–5, no 116.
[196] Stein, 'Un diplomate', 315.   [197] Baldi, *Pio II*, 176.
[198] For details see Housley, 'Pius II', forthcoming.
[199] Piccolomini, *Opera omnia*, 864–5, no 391.
[200] *Aeneae Silvii Piccolomini Senensis opera inedita*, 142–4, no 69.

thirtieth are to be found in the borrowing of crusade ideas by those same rulers. Early in 1481 the Milanese, perhaps aware of similar measures adopted *in extremis* by Pius II in 1464, proposed to raise their allotted 30,000 ducats for Otranto's relief by levying a 2 per cent income tax, payment of which would be rewarded with a plenary indulgence. Sixtus IV was unwilling to agree, probably because it would damage the market for indulgences.[201] But by far the most fertile territory for such interactions of Church and state was the Holy Roman Empire.[202] Here a synthesis of crusading and imperial motifs had characterized taxation levied in the 1420s for the Hussite crusades.[203] Following 1453 one of the most revealing examples was the ambitious attempt to establish an imperial tax, the Common Penny (*Gemeine Pfennig*) at the Worms diet in 1495. The need for action against the Turks was much discussed at the diet. Arguments based on the Ottoman threat and referencing Turkish atrocities played important roles in the attempts made to 'sell' the tax to the public following the diet. But the diet's debates were shaped as much if not more by the conflict with France.[204] When the preamble to the tax referred to the need to take action 'to resist Christ's enemy the Turks, and other foes of the holy empire', everybody knew who the other foes were. The same applied to the threat of expulsion coupled with confiscation of property against anybody who assisted the Turks 'or others', 'against Christendom, the empire, or the nation'.[205]

When Maximilian and the German political elite returned to the theme of anti-Turkish taxation at Augsburg in 1500, European diplomatic issues again exercised a major impact on their approach.[206] Provoked by Alexander VI's recent call to crusade, issued in association with the Pope's *rapprochement* with France, Maximilian announced a comprehensive package of anti-Turkish measures, integrating them structurally with the new imperial administration (*Reichsregiment*) that had been agreed by the diet. Detailed provision was made for troops and money to be raised against the Turks and those who were indirectly assisting them (i.e. the French). One provision, that every 400 parishioners should contribute one soldier,[207] calls to mind the proposal made at Regensburg in 1454 that units of thirty hearths should provide either a horseman or two foot-soldiers.[208] But the Regensburg proposals were simplicity itself compared with the highly complex scheme proposed in 1500 at Augsburg. Nobody was to be exempt from contributing:

---

[201] Lorenzo de' Medici, *Lettere*, V, 165–6, note 5.
[202] See Isenmann, 'The Holy Roman Empire', esp. 264–6.
[203] This is best approached via *The Crusades against Heretics in Bohemia, 1418–1437*, tr. Thomas Fudge (Aldershot, 2002).
[204] *Deutsche Reichstagsakten…1495, passim*, esp. 315–16, 903, 1209–11, 1241–51, 1302–13, 1504–91.
[205] *Kaiser und Reich: Verfassungsgeschichte des Heiligen Römischen Reiches Deutscher Nation vom Beginn des 12. Jahrhunderts bis zur Jahre 1806 in Dokumenten*, ed. Arno Buschmann, vol. 1, 2nd edn (Baden-Baden, 1994), 206, no 9, para. 24.
[206] Generally see Heinz Angermeier, 'Der Wormser Reichstag 1495—ein europäisches Ereignis', *Historische Zeitschrift*, 261 (1995), 739–68.
[207] *Kaiser und Reich*, 188–94, no 9, at 189, 193.
[208] *Deutsche Reichstagsakten unter Kaiser Friedrich III., fünfte Abteilung, erste Hälfte 1453–1454*, ed. Helmut Weigel and Henny Grüneisen, Deutsche Reichstagsakten, 19.1 (Göttingen, 1969), 278, para. 3.

religious houses should pay a tax of 2.5 per cent on their income and Jews one florin a year each, with the richer Jews assisting the less well off. This was followed by a remarkable appeal to the empire's nobles

> to do whatever lies within their power in this praiseworthy Christian work and enterprise, as pious Christian folk and from their noble disposition, for the safety and deliverance of themselves, their country, their honour, their persons and property, to resist the unbelievers and the other assailants of Christendom and the empire.

Most extraordinary was the decree that priests should be commissioned to exhort the people to provide additional donations 'for this praiseworthy and Christian undertaking'. To that end chests should be placed in churches 'to hold the money that pious and devout Christian people contribute of their free will', which would be forwarded in accordance with the decrees of future diets.[209] A recent editor of the text called these proposals a 'crusade to rescue the country and resist the enemies of the empire and Christendom'.[210] It was only a slight exaggeration. To a greater degree than the *societas sancti Georgii*, the Augsburg proposals constituted Maximilian's most brazen raid into ideological territory that for centuries had been dominated by the papal *curia*. The decrees only added to the tense situation a year later when a papal legate turned up to preach a real crusade using chests for collection purposes. In practice of course, Maximilian's elaborate proposals for raising funds were no more realistic than Alexander's attempt a month earlier to renew the clerical tenth and Jewish twentieth. Both papal and imperial proposals were largely shadows of programmes that four decades previously had constituted genuinely aspirational though impracticable endeavours.

The fact that taxation could not meet the financial needs of crusade forced its advocates to resort to an eclectic range of alternative sources of revenue. From Nicholas V onwards the bureaucracy of the *curia* and the entire Papal State found themselves being taxed regularly for a tenth of their salaries.[211] Calixtus III reacted forcefully against what he construed as Nicholas V's mistaken priorities by engaging in domestic economies in a dramatic manner that was surely intended in part to impress.[212] Most spectacularly, in April 1461 there was the discovery of alum, a mineral used for colour fastening, at Tolfa in the Papal State and the decision to dedicate the proceeds of its sale to the crusade. This made possible a pleasing synergy: in 1463 Pius II added the import of alum from Muslim lands to the activities that were vetoed by the *curia*, boosting the sales of Tolfa alum that advanced the crusading cause. Paul II's pre-election vow included the dedication of alum proceeds to the crusade,[213] this measure forming part of a bigger package including the creation of a *depositeria della crociata* under the supervision of a group of cardinals

---

[209] *Kaiser und Reich*, 195–214, no 10, at 206–11.
[210] 'Kreuzzug zur Rettung des Vaterlandes und zum Widerstand gegen die Feinde des Reiches und der Christenheit': *AR*, no 10445.
[211] *DS*, 385–7, no 1243 (*Etsi ecclesia Christi*).
[212] *AM*, 12.336, tr. by Setton, *Papacy*, 2.164. Weber, *Lutter*, 3.2.3, notes that Calixtus's actions were less theatrical than they appear, since tableware made of gold and silver was commonly regarded as a form of capital reserve.
[213] Ammannati Piccolimini, *Commentarii*, 371.

who were enthusiastic supporters of warfare against the Turks.[214] Ironically, this consolidation of the *curia*'s funding mechanism for a large-scale crusade occurred just at the point when the pontificates most dedicated to embarking on such a war ended. So the opportunity created by the alum discovery, the medieval equivalent of finding a substantial oil deposit today, was lost. Importing alum from Muslim sources was dropped from the annual publication of *In coena domini*; it is questionable whether it could have been enforced in any case. Proceeds from alum sales reached a ceiling of 57,000 ducats in 1465 and thereafter declined dramatically.[215] Following Bessarion's death in 1472 Sixtus IV wound down the operations of the *depositeria della crociata*, bringing crusading activity back into the remit of the *camera apostolica*.[216] No more than economies or sale of offices, or for that matter monastic armies, was the providential discovery of alum capable of bridging the funding shortfall that was arguably the most acute problem facing enthusiasts for a crusade. There was a remorseless logic to the situation. Given that volunteer forces were, for a variety of reasons, proving impracticable, crusading had to have access to substantial revenues. They could not be generated through taxation. That left only one real possibility: raising money by preaching indulgences.

---

[214] Weber, *Lutter*, 4.2. is now the definitive study of the *depositeria* from Pius to Sixtus IV. See also Damian, 'La *Depositeria*'. Still valuable despite its age is Adolf Gottlob, Aus *der Camera apostolica des 15. Jahrhunderts. Ein Beitrag zur Geschichte des päpstlichen Finanzwesens und des endenden Mittelalters* (Innsbruck, 1889).

[215] Géraud Poumarède, *Pour en finir avec la croisade: Mythes et réalités de la lutte contre les Turcs aux XVIe et XVIIe siècles* (Paris, 2004), 341, and see 323–41 for the fullest discussion of the alum issue, supplemented by Weber, *Lutter*, 3.2.4. More generally see Jean Delumeau, *L'Alun de Rome XVe–XIXe siècle* (Paris, 1962).

[216] Weber, *Lutter*, 4.2.4.

5

Communication

The interaction of old and new is a theme that stands at the heart of this book and in no respect was this truer than in the spectrum of means by which the call to contribute towards the crusade was communicated to the faithful. Persuading people to take the cross had always been a diverse process. For generations, the preaching of crusade by resident clergy and agents despatched for the purpose had been reinforced by pressure from neighbours, family, and lords. This foreground of insistent urging was set against a broader background of cultural approbation made up of the memorialization of past crusades in verse, image, and the recollections of family and community, as well as the scriptural and liturgical references to the holy places, which no contemporary attending church services could escape. A good deal of this accumulated repertoire of persuasion was still fit for purpose in the fifteenth century: lobbying of princes, for example, relied heavily on the call to imitate distinguished ancestors, and liturgical reminders relating to Palestine were corroborated by more sharply tuned references to the perils posed by the Turks. As in the past, the Church did not overlook the importance of one-to-one exhortation in the case of influential individuals.[1] But such traditional levers were complemented by novel methods of winning hearts and minds for the cause. The first was the systematic deployment of oratory before an audience composed of elites, and gathered at courts, assemblies, and diets. This was subject to tactical management that took into account occasion, listeners, and goals; it was carefully modulated and, subject to caveats, can be expected to reflect with reasonable accuracy the themes, arguments, and images that orators hoped would achieve their objectives. The second new method, the promotion of crusading and the Turkish threat in printed literature, was more heterogeneous in character. In certain printed formats, intentionality to persuade was as conspicuous as it was in orations, but, in commercial output, aim and impact alike were often more opaque. Nonetheless, the volume of material reaching the eyes and ears of contemporaries in relation to the Turks and crusading was enormous. Adapting F. M. Powicke's famous observation about thirteenth-century Europeans and the recovery of the Holy Land, we can state with confidence that for their descendants in the later fifteenth century, the call to crusade remained 'inseparable from the air they breathed. However indifferent or sceptical they might be, they could not escape its influence'.[2]

---

[1] *AM*, 13.9; *DS*, 400, no 1252.
[2] Maurice Powicke, *The Thirteenth Century 1216–1307*, The Oxford History of England, 4, 2nd edn (Oxford, 1962), 80.

5.1 THE FRANCISCAN OBSERVANTS AND PREACHING: THE PATTERN OF INVOLVEMENT

Papal reliance on the Franciscans, and above all the Observants, to preach the crusade is well established and not hard to explain.[3] It predated 1453, as for example in Eugenius IV's commissioning of San Bernardino da Siena in 1443 to collect various revenues associated with the crusade for the benefit of the *curia*'s naval expenses.[4] According to a complaint that Giovanni da Capistrano voiced to Bernardino in 1440, it was part of a broader trend: 'Whenever there is anything hard or dangerous to be done the Curia thinks at once of the Friars Minor...Ah well, we are only Lesser Brothers (*fratres minores*), sheep fit for the slaughter-house'.[5] The other mendicants may have disputed this claim (the Dominicans for one boasted some significant crusade preachers), but it contained some truth. Pius II, whose appointment of John Bessarion as the Order's cardinal-protector in September 1458 sprang at least in part from their shared commitment towards the crusade, noted in his letter of commission to Jacopo delle Marche in November 1463 that Jacopo and his fellow Observants were 'prepared and suited' for the task'.[6] For a more detailed exposition of what this meant in practice, we have to turn to a letter that Capistrano wrote to Calixtus III on 29 June 1455: Capistrano's specifications for good crusade preachers were enthusiasm, respectable ways, sound beliefs, the proven ability to preach well, and a disdain for worldly vices, including greed; they should seek only God's honour and glory, and the salvation of souls; and they should be willing to die defending Catholic truth and belief.[7] The subtext here is that Capistrano's own brethren of the Observance best fitted the bill and, in a letter written two years later, Calixtus agreed that nobody sowed the seed of God's word more effectively than the members of the mendicant orders.[8] Even if individual friars were not as dedicated to the crusading cause as Capistrano was, they could normally be relied upon to preach out of obedience or the threat of censure,[9] and the Order as a whole enjoyed a buoyant popularity that gave them a head start on other clerics, whether religious or secular. We shall see that preaching caused problems for the Observance, and Marco da Bologna complained to Capistrano that even finding sufficient preachers was taxing;[10] but its leaders probably judged it

---

[3] For a useful summary with names, see Alberto Ghinato, 'La predicazione francescana nella vita religiosa e sociale del Quattrocento', *Picenum seraphicum*, 10 (1973), 24–98, at 78–9.

[4] Benvenuto Bughetti, ed., 'Documenta inedita de S. Bernardino Senensi O.F.M. (1430–1445)', *Archivum Franciscanum historicum*, 29 (1936), 478–500, at 493–7. Generally see P. De Guasconibus, 'S. Bernardino predicatore delle indulgenze per la crociata', *Bolletino senese di storia patria*, 2 (1895), 130–6.

[5] John Moorman, *A History of the Franciscan Order from its Origins to the Year 1517* (Oxford, 1968), 469, citing Hofer, *Kapistran*, 2.226–7.

[6] *AM*, 13.308.   [7] Ibid. 12.285–7.

[8] *Bullarium Franciscanum, Supplementum*, ed. Caesar Cenci, vol. 1, (Rome, 2002), 622–3, no 1307.

[9] For the threat of censure see Ludwig Mohler, ed., 'Bessarions Instruktion für die Kreuzzugspredigt in Venedig (1463)', *Römische Quartalschrift*, 35 (1927), 337-49, at 338.

[10] Hofer, *Kapistran*, 2.318, note 46.

unwise to shun the commissions because refusal might make the *curia* more sympathetic towards the Conventuals. It was a collective version of the strong hint made by Jacopo Amannati Piccolomini to Jacopo delle Marche in November 1463 to the effect that while the investigation of the friar's orthodoxy on the sanctity of Christ's blood had been suspended, it was in his interest to make a success of preaching the crusade at Perugia.[11] It is noteworthy that all of the men characterized by Mariano da Firenze as the 'four pillars of the Observance' preached the crusade against the Turks.[12]

This mixture of pastoral strengths and intra-Order politics converged in a letter that Matthias Corvinus wrote to Sixtus IV in the early 1480s. The king was concerned by rumours that at a forthcoming general chapter of the Order, the Observants would come under attack from the Conventuals. This would prove highly unpopular in Hungary, where the Observants enjoyed enviable and socially broad-based veneration. An assault on the Observants, the king argued, would generate scandal and uproar in his lands. It is possible that Matthias wrote at the behest of his confessor, Gabriel de Paly, the Order's vicar-general in Hungary, whom he sent to Sixtus as envoy to argue the case.[13] But the ties that he described to Sixtus were real enough; they facilitated Capistrano's success in 1456 and, in turn, were bolstered by it.[14] A concession granted by Pius II in September 1461 shows the Pope's acceptance that Hungary's Observants were preaching, suffering, and even fighting alongside the laity there: around two dozen of their churches and houses had been destroyed by the Turks and a number of their brethren needed to be absolved of excommunication incurred by killing or wounding the enemy.[15] Their sufferings in neighbouring Bosnia were of course even worse.[16] Other documents testify to the interweaving of the Observance with Hungary's fighting elite. In September 1466, for instance, Pope Paul II absolved a nobleman from a variety of misdeeds committed while fighting against the Turks in his youth and during service as Janos Hunyadi's captain. He had entered the order and maintained twelve soldiers for three months against the enemy.[17] Such frontline engagement was by no means confined to Hungary.[18] In August 1456, when enthusiasm was riding high, Baptista de Levante, the vicar-general of the Observants in Italy, appointed a commissioner to vet the suitability of brethren 'who have taken the cross or take it later'.[19] In March 1457 the collector Lorenzo da Palermo was (briefly) given permission to use collected crusade money to fit out a galley or its equivalent in smaller sailing vessels,

---

[11] AM, 13.310. The dispute related to blood lost during the crucifixion, which Jacopo considered to have forfeited some of its divinity after its separation from Christ's body.

[12] Cit. Moorman, *History*, 377: they were Bernardino da Siena, Alberto da Sarteano, Jacopo delle Marche and Giovanni da Capistrano.

[13] *MCH*, 2.260–1, no 209, also in *MKL*, 2.1–2, no 1.

[14] Andrić, *Miracles*, 18–22.   [15] *BF*, NS2.497–8, no 955.

[16] Ibid. 720–1, no 1437.

[17] Ibid. 689–90, no 1375, and see also 447, no 860, p. 447, 810–11, no 1628.

[18] *BF*, NS4.881–2, no 2429 (Granada, 1492) and cf. the interesting case addressed ibid. 878–9, no 2421.

[19] *AM*, 12.380–1.

which he would accompany to the East to fight the Turks with Calixtus's other warships.[20] Business relating to a number of Observants who went on campaign against the Turks was left for Calixtus's successor to deal with.[21] And in 1464, when enthusiasm again reached a peak on the eve of Pius's own departure for Ancona (16 June), Baptista de Levante's successor, Marco da Bologna, had to attend to the same issue of suitability that had arisen in 1456.[22]

Hence it was probably never in doubt that in the decades following the fall of Constantinople Nicholas V and his successors would turn to the Observants as their principal preachers, publicists, and collectors. Typically, Nicholas despatched Matteo da Reggio OFM in October 1453 to urge the faithful in the kingdom of Sicily to assist the crusade 'in person or with their belongings'.[23] The two most instructive networks are those created by Calixtus III and Sixtus IV, in part because of the chance survival of many of their briefs, where the working of the managerial levers is usually most visible. Calixtus began creating his network in July 1455, just a few weeks into his reign. A more proactive approach was certainly called for: in October 1454 Capistrano had complained to Nicholas V that he had been compelled to preach using copies of the Pope's crusade bull, having no sealed original or clear idea of what the Pope wanted done.[24] On 20 July 1455 Calixtus renewed the Hungarian commission of his old friend and ally, Capistrano, and a week later he appointed Jacopo delle Marche to work in the March of Ancona, significantly, the Papal State's Adriatic province.[25] Between then and January 1456 other appointments were made: Angelo da Bolsena in the patrimony of St Peter in Tuscany; Antonio de Montefalcone in Perugia (in practice, probably Umbria); Bartolomeo da Colle in Sabina; Roberto Caracciolo at Rome; Lorenzo da Palermo in the kingdom of Naples; Ludovico da Vicenza in Romagna; and Francesco de Carbonibus.[26] Not all were Franciscan: the Dominican Giovanni da Napoli, for example, was entrusted with preaching and collection at Florence.[27] Calixtus did his utmost to prepare the ground for their preaching. In June 1456 he released *Cum hiis superioribus*, which was probably the most ambitious attempt for 150 years to weave the crusading cause into normative liturgical practice throughout Christendom.[28] The following November, as Calixtus geared

---

[20] *BF*, NS2.144, no 274; revoked 5 days later, ibid. 145, no 278, on the grounds that the existing squadron was large enough and needed financial support rather than additional fighting power.
[21] Ibid. 251, no 503.
[22] *AM*, 13.398. See also *Regestum*, 49, 51, 73; *B. Bernardini Aquilani Chronica fratrum minorum Observantiae*, ed. L. Lemmens (Rome, 1902), 72–5, 78–82, 96–7.
[23] *AM*, 12.204–5.   [24] Ibid. 235–7.
[25] *BF*, NS2.28, nos 59–60.
[26] *AM*, 12.375 (Wadding's summary of the 1455 appointments); 376–7 (Lorenzo da Palermo, kingdom of Naples, January 1456, and see too ibid. 377–9); *BF*, NS2.34, no 70 (Angelo da Bolsena, patrimony, September 1455); ibid. 45, no 86 (Antonio da Montefalcone, Perugia etc., September 1455); ibid. 45, no 87 (Bartolomeo da Colle, Sabina etc., September 1455); ibid. 48, no 91, also in S.E. Bastanzio, *Fra Roberto Caracciolo. Predicatore del secolo XV, vescovo di Aquino e Lecce (†1495)* (Isola del Liri, 1947), 265–6, doc. no 21 (Roberto Caracciolo, Rome, October 1455), and see too *BF*, NS2.56, no 105, also in Bastanzio, *Fra Roberto*, 266–7, doc. no 22; *BF*, NS2.58–9, no 109 (Francesco de Carbonibus, 1455); ibid. 65, no 117 (Ludovico da Vicenza, Romagna, January 1456).
[27] Black, *Accolti*, 244–6.
[28] Linder, *Raising Arms*, 118–19, 237–41.

up to capitalize on success at Belgrade, directing the war 'not just against the most wicked Turk but also against every other sort of unbeliever', he made a series of fresh appointments and extensions in the Papal State's provinces.[29] In January 1457 he despatched Mariano de Senis on what proved to be a protracted and fraught mission of preaching and collection in Dalmatia (above all Ragusa), Hungary, Bosnia, and Serbia.[30] Further renewals followed in March 1457[31] and in May Jacopo delle Marche was sent to Hungary and Bohemia to replace Capistrano.[32] To store proceeds, Calixtus resorted to the time-honoured practice of setting up collection chests presided over by multiple key holders, while for transfer he used an eclectic mix of bankers and (within the Papal State) the standing provincial administration.[33]

Just before engaging on this second wave of commissions the Pope demanded reports on who held the collected money and called in reports and receipts alike.[34] This paper-driven system may have originated in this Pope's penchant for micromanagement, but it was facilitated by the relative proximity of most of his preachers/collectors to the *curia*. Naturally it was hard to combine accountability with speed, and the Pope sometimes had to sanction short cuts. In a letter to Francesco de Carbonibus in June 1457 he complained that, although Francesco was doing well, things were moving too slowly; so the preacher was given permission to set aside such time-consuming procedures as consulting with diocesans on suitable preachers, and setting up a collection chest in each town. Instead, he should use his own initiative; as long as Calixtus received full reports on what was done, he would be happy.[35] A letter to Francesco some weeks later shows that this tireless Pope also read letters sent to others at his *curia*, in this instance the papal datary and secretary.[36] Notwithstanding the message of the June 1457 letter, there were occasions when Calixtus intervened on matters that even in normal times we would expect him to have left to his collectors or even their sub-collectors, as when he handled the negotiations with the clergy of Castello on their contribution to the crusade in October 1457: the sum involved was a mere 200 florins.[37]

Surviving papal briefs, some of which have been edited more than once, take us into the heart of the Calixtine system and they disclose both successes and failures. In a number of briefs Calixtus lavished praise on his commissioned preachers: if we can believe such texts then men such as the Minister General Jacopo de Mozzanica,[38] Francesco de Carbonibus,[39] Angelo da Bolsena,[40] and Cherubino da Spoleto,[41]

---

[29] *BF*, NS2.119–20, nos 217–21.
[30] *AM*, 13.9–10 (also in many other editions); *AM*, 13.138–40 (commission renewed by Pius II, June 1459).
[31] *BF*, NS2.136, nos 262–4. [32] *VMH*, 2.294–6, nos 460–2.
[33] *BF*, NS2.162–3, no 323, 180–1, no 351, 223, no 442 (proceeds to go to the treasurer of the March of Ancona); *AM*, 13.15–16, *BF*, NS2.154, no. 296 (proceeds to go to representatives of the Pazzi bank). For papal use of bankers see Michele Cassandro, 'I banchieri pontifici nel XV secolo', in Sergio Gensini, ed., *Roma capitale (1447–1527)* (Pisa, 1994), 207–34.
[34] *BF*, NS2.119, no 215.   [35] Ibid. 162–3, no 323.   [36] Ibid. 189, no 365.
[37] Ibid. 198, no 389.   [38] *AM*, 13.32–3; *BF*, NS2.172, no 330.
[39] Ibid. 144, no 275 (Francesco is commended above all for his efficient transportation of timber to the galleys being fitted out at Ancona), 180–1, no 351, 235–6, no 472.
[40] Ibid. 176–7, no 343, 187, no 358, 237–8, no 475.   [41] Ibid. 190, no 367.

served Calixtus well. One of the Pope's appointees, Lorenzo da Palermo, was suspected of fraud but succeeded in clearing his name.[42] The Pope knew that they faced an uphill and solitary struggle in carrying out their commissions. At times they were crushed by their workload[43] and, while the Pope sympathized with their plight, he was also impatient for results.[44] Knowingly or otherwise, their commission involved them in transgressions of their Rule, which led Calixtus in June 1458 to ask Baptista de Levante to work out how best to reconcile the Rule with papal needs.[45] They also encountered challenging suspicion among the populace about the destination of *cruciata* proceeds. In September 1457 Calixtus sympathized with Francesco de Carbonibus about the rumours that were flying because he had assigned his proceeds to the provincial treasurer: surely by now the whole world was aware of how much Calixtus was spending on the crusade?[46] Though apathy or hostility towards the crusade rarely make an overt appearance in the surviving texts, occasional excited references to enthusiasm, such as that reported by Jacopo de Mozzanica at Alessandria and Cremona, may indicate that it was unusual.[47] In this as in later periods there were undoubtedly the usual human errors: fraud, theft, and misunderstandings.[48] There was predictable competition from other indulgence preachers, both official and fake. In September 1457 it was the brethren of St Anthony of Padua,[49] but a year earlier Francesco's predecessor in the March of Ancona, the Dominican, Johannes de Curte, had had to contend with a freelance crusade preacher who claimed to be an Observant.[50] But it was the tax collecting aspect of the brethren's commission, and the opposition that this engendered among both clergy and civic or provincial administration, that registered most frequently in the briefs. Calixtus was determined that no cleric should enjoy exemption from paying the clerical tenth,[51] and he wanted to tax the salaries of his officials.[52] These policies created a serious tension in the system: the advice of the clergy and the support of papal officials, which were essential if the *cruciata* was to be communicated effectively, were prejudiced by the preacher doubling up as tax collector.

Were the proceeds worth the effort? Individual receipts issued to Calixtus's collectors between 1456 and 1458 never reached four figures,[53] but it is arguable that there were gains other than the purely financial. For example, it was advantageous

---

[42] Ibid. 200–1, no 394, 219–20, nos 435–6, 225, no 451, 228, no 455.
[43] Ibid. 155–6, no 305.   [44] Ibid. 174, no 337.   [45] *AM*, 13.62–3.
[46] *BF*, NS2.194–5, no 380.
[47] *Bullarium Franciscanum, Supplementum*, 1.605, no 1258 and see also note 76 for Cremona.
[48] e.g. ibid. 613, no 1280 (Trevisan to investigate abuses practised at Rome).
[49] Cf. *BF*, NS2.206–7, no 412 (money that they collected to be channelled into crusade).
[50] Ibid. 114–15, no 200.
[51] Ibid. 156, no 306, 174, no 337 (hospitals to pay); *Bullarium Franciscanum, Supplementum*, 602, no 1250.
[52] *BF*, NS2.189, no 363.
[53] Caesar Cenci, ed., 'Documenta Vaticana ad Franciscales spectantia, ann. 1447–1458', *Archivum Franciscanum historicum*, 93 (2000), 217–59, at 245–59, though there is no guarantee that these are complete figures. *BF*, NS2.224, no 448 refers to the impressive sum of 2,000 ducats collected by Jacopo de Asculo in addition to various goods that he had yet to convert into specie.

that money and foodstuffs donated in Italy and Sicily could be rapidly brought into play for the benefit of the papal galleys and their crews.[54] Francesco de Carbonibus, whose commission in the March of Ancona placed him in the ideal location for matching incoming money with naval expenditure, was instructed to channel the former directly into the latter.[55] In April 1458 the papal familiar who was acting as accounts clerk to the Ancona squadron, one Ch. Vila, was expected to liaise with the collector on the issue.[56] Additionally, the Pope may have valued the raised consciousness that his commissions achieved: at the end of his September 1457 brief to Francesco he tried to encourage his demoralized agent by reminding him of the importance of what he was doing. Francesco should not allow resistance and cavillers to grind him down. As for methods, he and his sub-collectors would achieve more through 'humanity and ingenuity' than through coercion.[57] But irrespective of technique, the Pope appears to have realized by then that there were limits to what could be done by this hands-on procedure and within a rather circumscribed geographical zone. A month after this revealing brief he announced to Jacopo delle Marche that he was following his advice 'about summoning the Italians and others against the Turk and the unbelievers', soliciting Jacopo's help in persuading various rulers to attend and in countering anti-papal slanders in the empire.[58]

In the wake of Mantua Pius II followed in his predecessor's footsteps by pressing men like Matteo da Reggio and Angelo da Bolsena into service again.[59] Their task now was gargantuan, since they were supposed to levy the Jewish twentieth and lay thirtieth, as well as preaching the crusade and collecting the clerical tenth. They were granted sweeping powers, but evidence is not strong on how, and even if, they tried to carry out such a challenging agenda. This stage of Pius's programme was soon shipwrecked on the rocks of Italian politics,[60] but the network of preaching and collection that he established in the winter and spring of 1463–4 looks like a rerun of Calixtus's campaign in 1455–8.[61] During these most dramatic months of Pius's reign the Observants were in the eye of the storm and there seems no reason to deny them some of the credit for the success of the preaching, even if that success generated more trouble than it was worth. Pius's death was followed by a redirection of crusading efforts and it was not until Sixtus IV's reign that the Observants found themselves once again being drafted into the papal *curia*'s preaching against the Turks to a degree that can be compared with 1455–64.[62] In September 1480 the Pope asked the vicar-general of the Observants to appoint brethren to preach indulgences for Rhodes, and three months later Sixtus chose Angelo Carletti da Chivasso as his nuncio and commissioner to preach the crusade for the relief of

---

[54] Ibid. 145, no 277, 148–9, no 283, 216, nos 427–9, 223, no 442.
[55] Ibid. 123, no 230.   [56] Ibid. 225, no 449.   [57] Ibid. 194–5, no 380.
[58] *AM*, 13.6–7.
[59] E.g. *BF*, NS2.381, no 739, 456–8, no 876.
[60] It continued in the Scandinavian lands under the vigorous management of Marinus de Fregeno: Jensen, *Denmark*, 93–6.
[61] Summarized in *AM*, 13.308–12.
[62] For a comparison between the two periods see Celestino Piana, 'Nunzi apostolici nella regione Emiliana per le crociate del 1455 e 1481', *Archivum Franciscanum historicum*, 50 (1957), 195–211.

Otranto.[63] Carletti was allowed to appoint preachers who would themselves set up teams; we have the names of the five Observants whom one of Carletti's preachers, Antonio de Mugnano, the provincial vicar of Rome, chose in March 1481 shortly after his own appointment.[64] This pyramidal approach towards preaching in Italy may be an organizational advance on Calixtus's methods, though he had implemented something similar in the far north.[65] North of the Alps Sixtus entrusted the preaching to Emerich von Kemel OFM, and here, as in Italy, it was the Observants who were expected to bear the burden of preaching.[66] The uterine brothers, Pietro and Bartolomeo da Camerino, did excellent work as nuncios in Poland and Denmark.[67]

By chance, we possess most of the papal briefs for the period August 1481 to August 1482 and they are indispensable for comparing the Calixtine and Sixtine networks. Of course there are recurring themes, above all, the need to insist on the suspension of other indulgences, which had mushroomed since Calixtus's days.[68] Competition between preachers for Rhodes and Otranto was bound to generate problems. The former continued to promote their cause even after their right to do so had been revoked,[69] and in October 1481 the Pope reacted against particularly belligerent behaviour by the Knights of St John, who had laid hands on money donated in Poland to Otranto.[70] There were instances of fraud, abuse, and disobedience,[71] and at least one case of a critic who criticized the bull of crusade so vehemently that he was censured for it.[72] Like Calixtus before him, Sixtus had no option but to make deals with the secular authorities as a means of securing permission to export specie from their lands. Gian Galeazzo Sforza, for one, proved as tough a negotiator as his grandfather Francesco had been: in September 1481 Carletti was told to do his utmost to recover crusade money that the duke had sequestrated in the duchy of Milan, if necessary settling for a half of it and leaving the rest with Sforza. The duke's promise to use it only for crusading purposes was, as always, a handy fig leaf.[73] But there were changes too in Sixtus's approach, above all, the proliferating details about contributors and benefits, which formed one of the Pope's major preoccupations,[74] and the complexity of which caused Carletti to write a 'declaration or interpretation' for the guidance of his team.[75] Although a Franciscan himself, it is possible that Sixtus behaved less sensitively in his management of his

---

[63] *BF*, NS3.660, no 1322, 684, no 1367. For Carletti see *DBI*, 20:136–8; Mario Viora, 'Angelo Carletti da Chivasso e la crociata contro i Turchi del 1480–81', *Studi Francescani*, ns. 22 (1925), 319–40.
[64] *BF*, NS3.704–6, no 1409, with the names of Carletti's team at note 3.
[65] *DS*, 409, no 1259.   [66] *BF*, NS3.710, no 1415.
[67] Jensen, *Denmark*, 148–9; Weber, *Lutter*, 4.1.2. Ties of kinship or affinity existed between most of the preachers sent to the north, but they are frustratingly opaque.
[68] *BF*, NS3.704–6, nos 1409–10; Schlecht, *Zamometić*, 2.112–13, no 99.
[69] Ibid. 2.113, no 100 (September 1481).
[70] *BF*, NS3.756, no 1493, and see also 959, no 1502.
[71] e.g. ibid. 756, no 1493, 764, no 1514, 827, no 1625, 852, no 1684.
[72] Ibid. 764, no 1514.
[73] Ibid. 744, no 1466 and see also 745–6, no 1470, 749, no 1479; *Regestum*, 347–9, no 54.
[74] e.g. *BF*, NS3, 739, no 1455, also in *AM*, 14.325–6.
[75] Ed. Viora in 'Angelo Carletti', 326–9.

Observant brethren than Calixtus had. He was, after all, a Conventual and his decision to canonize Bonaventure rather than Capistrano in 1482 indicates, at the very least, that he did not go out of his way to grant favours to the Observants.[76] He wanted collected proceeds to be stored at the Church of the Aracoeli on the Capitol and, if necessary, the friars should transport both money and goods themselves (via Venice if they were working north of the Alps):[77] he insisted that this was not a breach of their Rule since it was done for the common good.[78]

The most intriguing feature of the Sixtine preaching for Otranto and Rhodes is a series of events in 1482, which remain obscure, but were probably connected to the political tempest that for a brief period threatened to engulf the Pope's reign. The sequence began in December 1481, when in a letter to Carletti, Sixtus announced that, notwithstanding the recovery of Otranto, he intended to capitalize on Mehmed II's death by taking the war to the Turks in the form of an attack on Valona. Hence Carletti's original three-year commission remained valid.[79] Then in early May 1482 came a volte-face: on 4 May Emerich von Kemel was ordered to call off all crusade preaching immediately. He should assure all recipients of the Rhodes indulgences, which had already been suspended, that they retained their validity and forward proceeds to the Aracoeli chest as soon as possible. He himself should come to Rome without detours to France or Spain, and 'when you get here, you will find out the reason that has moved us to act thus'.[80] A circular issued nine days later explained the move in terms of Turkish quiescence.[81] So much for the 'time of salvation, time of glory, time of victory, which if ignored will never come again', which the Pope had excitedly hailed when news of Otranto's recovery reached him the previous autumn.[82] Other letters sent in the weeks that followed reiterate Sixtus's concern to gather in the collected money without clarifying the change in his approach. In one letter to Emerich he added only that he was 'moved by sound considerations and reasons', referring in an aside to scandal generated by the preaching of the crusade.[83] A letter to the archbishop of Gniezno on 13 June sought refuge in obscurity,[84] while another to various German civic authorities on 23 May claimed that the reason for ordering that preaching should continue after the Christian victories was news that the Turks were preparing a mighty fleet. Having spent 133,000 ducats on the recovery of Otranto and other large sums on relieving Rhodes, 'we were forced to declare a holy crusade' to meet these fresh expenses. But the news turned out to be false, hence the revocation.[85] Just to add to the confusion, on 25 July Sixtus denied in writing to Emerich that he had ever revoked his commission to preach, adding however that he should only preach in locations where collection chests already existed, and until he emptied them.[86]

---

[76] Andrić, *Miracles*, 158–9.
[77] e.g. Schlecht, *Zamometić*, 2.104–5, no 87.
[78] *BF*, NS3.735–6, no 1453, also in *AM*, 14.312–13.
[79] *BF*, NS3.766–8, no 1516.   [80] Ibid. 806–7, no 1574.
[81] Ibid. 810, no 1582.   [82] *MCH*, 186–7, no 139, quote at 186.
[83] *BF*, NS3.810–11, no 1583.   [84] Ibid. 816, no 1594.
[85] Ibid. 813, no 1588, also in Schlecht, *Zamometić*, 2.114, no 101.
[86] *BF*, NS3.827, no 1624.

What was going on? Writing to one of Emerich's collectors in September 1482, the Pope claimed that he had revoked the preaching when reports reached him that the indulgences had been preached for venal reasons, in a deceptive way, and that secular princes were laying hands on the proceeds.[87] All valid points, but a more pressing reason was the convergence in the spring of 1482 of military and political threats in Italy with the danger of unrest exploding in Germany, stimulated by Andrija Jamometić's audacious conciliar initiative at Basel.[88] Jamometić was the catalyst: the papal u-turn was actioned a matter of days after news of his initiative reached Rome, and on the same day that Emerich was ordered to stop preaching he was also instructed to join in the manhunt to arrest the Croatian.[89] It was no alarmist measure. Following his complicity in the Pazzi conspiracy, Sixtus's reputation was so shabby that it was all too easy for his numerous enemies and critics to construe his decision to continue the preaching as deriving from the hope of finding funds to pursue his own controversial policies.[90] At the very least, such arguments would be deployed as camouflage by the secular authorities to seize the money, so that Sixtus would gain no money from the exercise but plenty of obloquy.[91] If even Calixtus III had to defend himself against similar charges of deception, how much the more so a Pope with Sixtus IV's track record? The crisis passed, but the experience seems to have been a bruising one for the Observants who served Sixtus. In the wake of the confusion that his stop-go policy created in 1482, the Pope had constantly to reiterate that indulgences granted to date retained their validity.[92]

Members of the preaching network that the *curia* created in 1480 became demoralized, some for political reasons, others because of a broader-based disenchantment with the way indulgences were being preached. As Bishop Georg of Chiemsee balefully informed Cardinal Francesco Piccolomini in 1481, 'a big deception (*magnus error*) is being perpetrated on the people'.[93] The Observant chronicler Nicholas Glassberger testified to his brethren's distaste: 'Because of this they did not want to get involved with indulgences in future.'[94] It seems likely that, as one of the Order's finest historians commented, popular disenchantment meshed with waning enthusiasm on the part of the friars, forming a vicious circle of disengagement.[95] But withdrawal from the system was impracticable, because however problematic the work had become, they remained the best people for it. Doris Carl has argued that Benedetto da Maiano's pulpit in Santa Croce (Florence), which dates from the

---

[87] Ibid. 830–1, no 1632.
[88] Schlecht, *Zamometić*, 1.132–3; Nikolaus Paulus, *Geschichte des Ablasses am Ausgange des Mittelalters* (Paderborn, 1923) = *Geschichte des Ablasses im Mittelalter*, vol. 3, 207; Pastor, *History*, 4.357–66.
[89] Schlecht, *Zamometić*, 1.83–4, 2.50–1, no 34, also in *BF*, NS3.807, no 1575.
[90] e.g. Schlecht, *Zamometić*, 2.55–60, no 39, at 59; Attila Györkös, 'La guerre des Pazzi et les relations franco-hongroises (1478–1481)', in *ML*, 393–404.
[91] e.g. Schlecht, *Zamometić*, 2.123–4, no 113 (Nürnberg lobbying for retention of half of its chest's contents to alleviate poverty, 20 July 1482).
[92] e.g. *BF*, NS3.830–1, no 1632, 844, no 1669, 887, no 1768, 913, no 1810, NS4.188, no 353.
[93] Schlecht, *Zamometić*, 2.98–9, no 78. Georg focused on the sharp practices of the *commissarii Rhodanorum*, but the reception given to crusade preachers was obviously affected.
[94] Nicholas Glassberger, *Chronica*, Analecta Franciscana, 2 (Quaracchi, 1887), 488.
[95] Moorman, *History*, 519.

early 1480s and has a relief showing the five Franciscan proto-martyrs of Marrakesh (1220), was part of an attempt on Sixtus's part to associate the preaching for Otranto's relief with heroic episodes in his Order's past. The argument is robust, because the Pope verbally sanctioned the cult of the 'Marrakesh five' in November 1480, just when he was setting his preaching in motion, and issued a written recognition of their status in August 1481, fixing 16 January as their feast-day. Hopefully, the pulpit would encourage Florence's friars in their preaching efforts, both for Otranto and in the future; Angelo Carletti was one of those who lobbied for their written recognition and Francesco Sansone, a papal confidant, general of the Order for twenty years and crusading enthusiast, died at S. Croce. The choice of subject was important: we shall see that hopes for martyrdom and its rewards, for preachers and crusaders alike, were interwoven with Capistrano's preaching and probably with that of Franciscan preachers generally. So the relief would be a sermon in stone for S. Croce's friars and worshippers.[96] In addition, the pulpit was a high-profile but discrete way of criticizing Lorenzo de' Medici's policy of distancing himself from the Pope's crusading agenda; for contemporaries Marrakesh would be Otranto.[97] Whether all or any of these objectives were attained it is impossible to say.[98] In November 1482, when crusade preaching was set in motion again in the Austrian frontline provinces, it was suggested that Observants be drafted in 'if they can be had in sufficient numbers'.[99] Meanwhile the laborious process of gathering in the remaining proceeds from the Otranto preaching continued,[100] with some of it being hived off for the building projects of Pope, princes, and Observants.[101]

5.2 THE FRANCISCAN OBSERVANTS AND PREACHING: INDIVIDUALS, TECHNIQUES, AND THEMES

There are limits to what we can learn from tracing the overall pattern of Observant involvement in crusade preaching. In assembling a picture of the skills that they

---

[96] A similar argument has been made for Donatello's *Judith and Holofernes*: Claudia Märtl, 'Donatellos Judith—Ein Denkmal der Türkenkriegspropaganda des 15. Jahrhunderts?', in *OEEH*, 53–95.

[97] Doris Carl, 'Franziskanischer Märtyrerkult als Kreuzzugspropaganda an der Kanzel von Benedetto da Maiano in Santa Croce in Florenz', *Mitteilungen des kunsthistorischen Institutes in Florenz*, 39 (1995), 69–91, with fig. 7 at 78. Lorenzo's policy went as far as welcoming Ottoman domination over southern Italy, on a medal that he had struck in the sultan's honour: James Hankins, 'Renaissance Crusaders: Humanist Crusade Literature in the Age of Mehmed II', *Dumbarton Oaks Papers*, 49 (1995), 111–207, at 125–6, esp. notes 36–8.

[98] Carl, 'Franziskanischer Märtyrerkult', 82–3, asserts that there was domestic discontent with Lorenzo's stance but does not substantiate it: it is noteworthy that Roberto Caracciolo appears not to have made reference to the crusade in his Lenten 1481 preaching in Florence's cathedral: Zelina Zafarana, ed., 'Per la storia religiosa di Firenze nel Quattrocento: una raccolta privata di prediche', *Studi medievali*, serie 3, 9 (1968), 1017–113, at 1037–9, 1047, 1088–9, 1095–7, nos 2, 7, 28, 32.

[99] *BF*, NS3.846, no 1672 (Bartolomeo da Camerino), and cf. 896, no 1784 (Bartolomeo again, this time in Sweden and Norway).

[100] Ibid. 874, no 1736, NS4.188, no 353.

[101] e.g. *BF*, NS3.874–5, no 1738 (Observant convent at Imola), 894, no 1779, 931, no 1849 (Sixtus's chapel of St Francis at Savona); Schlecht, *Zamometić*, 2.106, no 90 (deal with Duke George of Bavaria for the church of St Martin at Landshut, 'in quo soles residere').

brought to the task and the message that they conveyed, it is helpful to start by briefly outlining a few individual careers. Naturally, these were exceptional men, who were repeatedly brought into the service of crusade because they were committed to it and were good at it. If the individuals selected were all at their most active under Calixtus III and Pius II, this is not to denigrate the contributions made by later Observants, men such as Carletti and the Camerino affinity. But the strengths of the latter seem to have resided in the spheres of organization and administrative finesse rather than inspiration; while in documents bequeathed by the 1450s and early 1460s we detect that preachers were pursuing a common enterprise in the face of Mehmed's alarming successes, an ethos which recurred only intermittently after Pius II's death.

One of the most celebrated preachers was Jacopo delle Marche.[102] Jacopo was born in 1393 and his involvement with crusading began in the 1430s in conjunction with a challenging mission to Ragusa, Bosnia, and Hungary. In 1437 the emperor, Sigismund, invited Jacopo to join him on an expedition against the Turks. The Hungarians were inspired by his call to crusade, and his work on behalf of the Christian cause led Bartolomeo da Giano to describe him in 1438 as 'God's trumpet'.[103] In 1443 Eugenius IV commissioned him to preach alongside Alberto da Sarteano, and we have seen him being selected to preach by Calixtus in 1455 and 1457, and by Pius in 1463. It is clear that all three Popes rated Jacopo's ability and discretion highly: witness Calixtus's view that this 'servant of God and most ardent soldier of Christ' was the best person to carry forward Capistrano's mission in 1457,[104] and his selection by Bessarion and Pius in 1459 to raise their planned expeditionary corps of crusading volunteers to assist the Greeks in the Peloponnese.[105] Arguably, what made him ideal for missions to Greece, Hungary, and Bohemia was his wealth of experience in handling heresy and schism: in his 1457 commission Calixtus renewed all of Eugenius IV's bulls against heretics in favour of Jacopo.[106] Such issues called for sensitive handling in the decades that followed the *curia*'s reconciliation with the Hussites at Basel and the Orthodox at Florence, both of which processes Jacopo had observed at close quarters. It was not just a question of avoiding overreaction in liaising with the locals: just days after he appointed Jacopo in 1457 Calixtus had to take action against his nuncio in Albania and Serbia who had (allegedly) publicly preached the superiority of the Orthodox faith.[107] From 1467 sickness compelled the aged Jacopo to discontinue preaching, but his concern about the Ottoman advance did not abate: in 1473, called to the sickbed of Alfonso, duke of Calabria, he prophesied the duke's role in expelling the Turks from Otranto in 1481, and in 1474, two years before his death, he exhorted Matthias Corvinus to fight the sultan.[108]

---

[102] *DBI*, 54.214–20; Moorman, *History*, 473–8 has a brief biography in English.
[103] Bartolomeo da Giano, 'Epistola', 1064.
[104] *VMH*, 2.295–6, no 462.   [105] *AM*, 13.134–5.   [106] *VMH*, 2.204–5, no 460.
[107] *Vetera monumenta Slavorum*, 424–5, no 600: political issues may have lain behind this incident.
[108] G. Caselli, *Studi su S. Giacomo della Marca pubblicati in occasione del II. centenario della sua canonizzazione*, 2 vols (Ascoli Piceno, 1926), 2.239–53.

Born around 1425, Roberto Caracciolo (da Lecce) belonged to the generation that followed Jacopo's.[109] After early association with the Observants he left them for the Conventuals in 1452, but this move did not prevent him working closely with Observants in preaching the crusade, a point that should make us wary of exaggerating intra-Order difficulties in this context. It was Caracciolo who announced the fall of Constantinople at the *curia* in the course of a sermon in July 1453, and his oratorical skills made him a natural choice for Calixtus when assembling his team in 1455: the Pope described him as 'most committed and effective in preaching God's word'.[110] Initially given the Roman province, he was moved to Lombardy in February 1457.[111] Here his attempt to collect a second tenth for Calixtus sparked off a tax revolt by the clergy with popular backing, leading to Francesco Sforza appealing to Calixtus on behalf of his subjects, and the Pope having to climb down on the issue.[112] Caracciolo's relations with the civil regime must, however, have been better than this exchange implies because in July 1457 Sforza was prepared to lobby for the preacher's appointment as vicar general of the Franciscans.[113] Early in 1464 Caracciolo was a member of Bessarion's team preaching in the Venetian *terraferma*. As collector, he again resorted to coercive methods, this time applied directly to the Brescian laity who were taxed for the thirtieth. As at Milan he proved unsuccessful.[114] According to a Milanese envoy's report written in October 1480, Carcacciolo's last encounter with crusading was both incidental and anticlimactic; infected by the panic that swept Lecce following the Turkish capture of Otranto, the friar repeatedly tried to join the exodus from the town.[115] His involvement with crusade preaching thus lasted for only a decade, but it left a substantial legacy: a full generation after Caracciolo's death in 1495 Erasmus included an anecdote in his *Ecclesiasticae* about the preacher interrupting a sermon about the crusade to throw off his habit, revealing that underneath it he wore armour and a sword.[116] Such rather whimsical stories should not obscure Caracciolo's fame and skill as a preacher: in 1448, still in his early twenties, he could muster an audience of 1500 for a Lenten sermon at Perugia, at the close of which his listeners cried and shouted 'Jesus, have mercy' for about half an hour.[117]

It is no reflection on Jacopo and Caracciolo that their achievements were overshadowed by those of Capistrano. Very few medieval preachers could match Capistrano's charisma and vitality, and the strength of his personality establishes him as the most inspirational force in the fifteenth-century crusade against the Turks. What is striking about Capistrano's crusade preaching, however, is that it only

---

[109] *DBI*, 19:446–52.   [110] Bastanzio, *Fra Roberto*, 269, no 25.
[111] *BF*, NS2.48, no 91, 56, no 105, 131–2, no 249, 133, no 253.
[112] Bastanzio, *Fra Roberto*, 269–70, nos 25–6, 271–4, nos 28–31.
[113] Ibid. 274, no 32, and see also 274–7, nos 33–6.
[114] Cristoforo da Soldo, *La cronaca*, ed. G. Brizzolara, RISNS 21, pt 3, 143–4.
[115] C. Foucard, ed., 'Fonti di storia napoletana nell'Archivio di Stato in Modena. Otranto nel 1480 e nel 1481', *Archivio storico per le province napoletane*, 6 (1881), 74–176, at 167.
[116] *Ecclesiasticae*, bk 2, ref. Robert Schwoebel, *The Shadow of the Crescent: The Renaissance Image of the Turk (1453–1517)* (Nieuwkoop, 1967), 40.
[117] Norman, 'Social History', 158–9.

became the key theme of his activity in the final years of his life, when he was well into his sixties. Born in 1386, he entered the Franciscan Order in 1416 and embarked on a career that focused on preaching, the investigation of heresy, and deep engagement with his Order's internal politics: a similar agenda to Jacopo's, who also entered the Order that year. In 1430 he drafted a reform programme (dubbed 'Capistrano's shears') that looked set to restore Observant austerity to the whole Franciscan family, until Pope Martin V withdrew his support.[118] He first appears to have shown a concern for the Turkish threat in 1443–4,[119] but in the decade that followed his main responsibilities were establishing the Observance, preaching penitence, and taking action against heresy in Italy and the Czech lands. The fall of Constantinople appears to have persuaded him of the urgent need for action, and from 1453 until his death in 1456 he was one of the key individuals in the currents of debate, exhortation and planning that led, via the imperial diets of 1454–5 and the urgent activity of Calixtus's first months, to the relief of Belgrade in July 1456 and Capistrano's death from plague in October. Whatever question marks hang over the success of Observant crusade preaching at other times do not apply to Capistrano's preaching in the German and Hungarian lands in 1454–6.[120] According to Jan Długosz, having to use an interpreter did not dent his appeal: audiences happily sat through two hours of the preacher's Latin followed by two hours of the translator's vernacular.[121] Capistrano's companion and biographer, Giovanni da Tagliacozzo, has left a vivid portrayal of Capistrano's impact, and it is corroborated by the eagerness of Hunyadi and Cardinal Juan Carvajal to make use of his services.[122] This success was made possible by his stamina, the pursuit of an itinerary that, to use the 70-year-old man's own words, would have exhausted the very stones.[123]

In a letter to Calixtus, Capistrano described himself conventionally as an abject 'mongrel and worm',[124] but the same text and other surviving letters, in particular a detailed critique sent to Nicholas V in October 1454, reveal a man who had strong views and expressed them in a forthright fashion.[125] There is no reason to think that he was alone in this. The more prominent and successful preachers were well aware of the need to mould their brief and instructions to local circumstances, in so doing exercising a degree of initiative and even autonomy. We have

---

[118] Moorman, *History*, 447.
[119] Hofer, *Kapistran*, 1.291–2; Andrić, *Miracles*, 25.
[120] Hofer, *Kapistran*, 2.299–372 comprehensively covers events from spring 1454 to June 1456.
[121] Cited by Ottó Gecser, 'Itinerant Preaching in Late Medieval Central Europe: St John Capistran in Wrocław', *Medieval Sermon Studies*, 47 (2003), 5–20, at 8. Tagliacozzo, 'Relatio', 784, affirmed that the Hungarians listened to the translations of a man called Paul who acted as interpreter for all the friars.
[122] *AM*, 12.384.
[123] *AM*, 12.372–3. Andrić, *Miracles*, 26, calculates 600 km between 30 May 1455 and 2 July 1456.
[124] *AM* 12.287, and see too *AS Oct*, 382 ('inermis et inutilis servus'), *AM* 12.798 ('pusillus vermiculus').
[125] AM, 12.235–7.

seen that Calixtus III did not object to such plasticity provided that he was kept informed of it. From the *curia*'s perspective, what mattered were results, and as long as doctrinal abuses and fraud were not sanctioned, some working with the grain of each locale could be ignored and even anticipated. Naturally, this called for the cooperation of the civil authorities. When Pius II sent out his preachers into the provinces of the Papal State in the autumn of 1463 he laid down detailed instructions to try to maximize such assistance. In the first place, the papal officials should provide accommodation for the whole preaching team. Then the civic authorities should make sure that they attended the sermons; they should compel the whole population, including the enclosed orders and the Jews, to attend; and they should shut the taverns and apothecaries while the preaching was in progress.[126] A few weeks later Francesco Sforza wrote to Caracciolo in terms that are revealingly specific about the best places to preach in his eastern dominions. Caracciolo should start with the Cremonese, where reports indicated resistance. He should begin at Casalmaggiore Cremona; but Sforza advised him to include Cremona itself in his itinerary because its people were more responsive, and they deserved encouragement 'to confirm them in their good disposition and strengthen their resolve'. After that Sforza counselled pursuing a trajectory situated to the northwest of Cremona that began at Soncino and ended at Lodi, preaching twice at each place 'as you judge that the situation requires'. Or perhaps Caracciolo would prefer coming straight to Milan after Casalmaggiore Cremona? 'We leave it to your discretion, and you should do whatever seems appropriate.' The advice is detailed and helpful, but the tone restrained: the duke respected Caracciolo's judgement, and he relied on the proceeds of the tenth and twentieth to fund his contribution to Pius's expedition, so it was in his interests to steer the friar as well as he could. At the same time he had, at best, moderate expectations of the crusade, the success of which would in any case mainly serve the interests of his Venetian rivals.[127] It is probable that Caracciolo had enjoyed stronger backing from Venice when preaching in its lands: the republic's final acceptance in 1463 of the need to confront Mehmed had generated a surge of crusading fervour among the Venetian elite, which delighted Bessarion and surely facilitated the well-organized preaching that the legate set in motion throughout Venetian lands in 1463–4.[128] Though, as we have seen, this did not prove much help at Brescia, the inhabitants of which shared the scepticism of their neighbours in the Cremonese.

Without the support of the civic authorities, preaching was impossible; and even their assistance was far from guaranteeing success. What techniques were brought to the task by the Franciscans themselves? There is nothing to suggest that when they preached the crusade, the Observants employed practices that were

---

[126] Ibid. 310–12.
[127] Bastanzio, *Fra Roberto*, 281–2, no 45.
[128] Mohler, ed., 'Instruktion', *passim*; id., *Bessarion*, 3.519–28, nos 53–6.

radically different from those used on other occasions, and given the deep reverence felt by both Jacopo and Capistrano for Bernardino da Siena, it is likely that Bernardino's well-attested preaching style set the pattern for the way sermons were delivered in the 1450s and 1460s.[129] Preaching under Sixtus almost certainly differed in tone and content, as preachers had to spend more of their time explaining the details of the indulgence terms that were on offer: there was a shift from cause to reward. By 1480 the age of the indulgence commissioners (*Ablasskommissaren*) was dawning and with it a considered and tactical deployment of staging and ceremony to achieve the best effect. At the same time the commercial aspects of indulgences, chests, the issue of *confessionalia*, the visible handing over and counting of money, became more prominent, contributing to the distaste expressed by some Observants. But these were refinements rather than transformations. The collection of specie (alongside other types of contribution) was a constant in the preaching of the anti-Turkish crusade. And as scholars like Alberto Ghinato, John Moorman, and Cynthia Polecritti showed, theatricality was a hallmark of Observant technique: satirists and critics took issue with their resort to props, abrupt costume changes like that executed by Caracciolo, and the planting of stooges and fake hecklers in the audience.[130] Capistrano felt compelled to defend dramatic shifts in vocal register, hand gestures, and the use of signs on the basis that they had been approved by Cicero and Augustine.[131]

Bernardino da Siena was famous for such practices. In 1424–5 he spontaneously performed exorcisms at Prato and Siena. His most controversial innovation, the veneration of the Name of Jesus (YHS), served him well as both calling card and rallying point; and it is hard to imagine a more effective device than the bonfire of the vanities, which made people converge on one point, creating an exhilarated atmosphere and an audience primed to hear a stirring appeal. At the bonfire that Capistrano presided over at Augsburg in September 1454, three or four wagonloads of artefacts were incinerated, including 1,500 board games and seventy sledges.[132] But both the Name of Jesus and the bonfire of the vanities were grounded in serious intentions: on the one hand, the deployment of a unifying religious image, one that offered an alternative to factional livery badges and a healing response to the violence of the urban vendetta; on the other, a conspicuous crossing of the spiritual Rubicon, the signal for a *reformatio vitae*. In an analysis of Capistrano's Lenten sermons at Wrocław in 1453, Ottó Gecser demonstrated that the preacher could put as much theological and canonistic weight into his sermons as anyone, when occasion and audience called for it.[133] The success enjoyed by the Observants as preachers derived not just from their own austerity and holiness, but

---

[129] For context see Beverly Mayne Kienzle, 'Medieval Sermons and Their Performance: Theory and Record', in Carolyn Muessig, ed., *Preacher, Sermon and Audience in the Middle Ages* (Leiden, 2002), 89–124.
[130] E.g. the Saxon Conventual Matthias Düring, ref. Hofer, *Kapistran*, 2.441–2.
[131] Cited by Gecser, 'Itinerant Preaching', 10.
[132] Hofer, *Kapistran*, 2.307 and cf. note 21 for a similar event at Frankfurt.
[133] Gecser, 'Itinerant Preaching', 14 and *passim*.

also from their highly sensitive radar: their sensitivity to the spectrum of religious and social anxieties and expectations held by their contemporaries.[134]

Most of the elements of this approach could be channelled into crusade preaching, and while direct evidence for the sermons that were delivered is scanty,[135] indirect evidence of various kinds enables us to build up a relatively clear picture of the resulting tone and texture. This applies, above all, to Capistrano's preaching in 1454–6, which was described by Tagliacozzo in July 1460 in a memoir taking the form of a long letter to Jacopo delle Marche.[136] The *Relatio de victoria Belgradensi* is deservedly famous; in addition to being astonishingly vivid it has been judged to be solidly reliable evidence.[137] Many of its themes are already present in a much shorter account that Tagliacozzo wrote in Italian just days after the defeat of the Turks, and throughout the *Relatio* he was very cautious in his handling of issues that by 1460 were hotly contested. A more substantial caveat about using Tagliacozzo's writings as evidence for Observant preaching generally is the fact that in 1455–6 Capistrano was trying to raise recruits in response to an urgent military crisis. This was bound to make both his themes and delivery different from preaching that occurred far away from the frontline and was geared towards financial contributions; *a fortiori*, his exhortatory sermons to the crusaders at Belgrade in July were tuned to the needs of the hour. That said, two themes that constantly recur in Tagliacozzo's evidence are striking. Both are conspicuous in one passage in which Capistrano encouraged his crusaders 'to the defence of the Christian faith and the full remission of all their sins and to martyrdom, by invoking and acclaiming the Name of Jesus'.[138] The first theme, zeal for martyrdom, was common to both crusading and Franciscan ideology, and it would be surprising if it were not highlighted. It was described as one of the rewards that Capistrano offered to his crusaders, together with the hope of victory and 'fame throughout the world'.[139] For crusading friars and combatants alike, the crusade was a *tempus acceptabile*, a *dies salutis*, a *tempus coronae*, that is an unrivalled opportunity to win the martyr's crown.[140] 'Happy are those who perish in this fight for Christ', Capistrano was quoted as saying, 'because straightaway they will be crowned by the angels alongside the holy martyrs, who died for the faith.'[141]

---

[134] Generally see Cynthia Polecritti, *Preaching Peace in Renaissance Italy: Bernardino of Siena and his Audience* (Washington DC, 2000); Ghinato, 'La predicazione', *passim*; Moorman, *History*, esp. 517–32; Andrić, *Miracles*, 15–18. More broadly, Thomas Worcester, 'Catholic Sermons', in Larissa Taylor, ed., *Preachers and People in the Reformations and Early Modern Period* (Boston and Leiden, 2003), 3–33; Corrie E. Norman, 'The Social History of Preaching: Italy', ibid. 125–91, with bibliography at 187–91.
[135] See Hofer, *Kapistran*, 2.361, note 49, 365.
[136] *AM*, 12.750–96.
[137] Robert Lechat, 'Lettres de Jean de Tagliacozzo sur le siège de Belgrade et la mort de S. Jean de Capistran', *Analecta Bollandiana*, 39 (1921), 139–51.
[138] 'Relatio', 761.
[139] Ibid. 759.
[140] Ibid. 772, and cf. 787 on Capistrano's chagrin at being denied martyrdom. See also Festa, ed., 'Cinque lettere', 26.
[141] Cristoforo da Varese, 'Vita S. Joannis a Capistrano', in *AS Oct*, 491–541, at 532. Cf. Festa, ed., 'Cinque lettere', 51.

The emphasis on the Name of Jesus, on the other hand, is more distinctive and it calls for explanation. The *Nomen Iesu* occurs right at the start of the *Relatio* when Tagliacozzo expressed his intention of giving a full account of the victory won in 1456 'under the banner of the most holy cross with the acclamation of the Name of Jesus Christ, at the time of the crusade'. His positioning of the Name of Jesus alongside the cross was no more coincidental than the carefully managed hierarchy of credit for victory that followed it (first God, then Capistrano, then Hunyadi, and finally the fortress commander).[142] Thereafter the Name of Jesus occurs too frequently to list at length, as the target of Turkish aggressive aims,[143] a battle cry (in response to the Turks calling on Mohammed),[144] the focus of devotion, a consolatory mantra, and, crucially, one of the key sources of victory.[145] The apologetic intent is clear. Tagliacozzo's account of events is overtly a defence of Capistrano against his critics,[146] more discreetly a piece of early lobbying for the preacher's canonization, and in the broadest sense a showcasing of the virtues and influence of the Observants at a time when they were under Conventual pressure.[147] But Tagliacozzo's version should not be dismissed on these grounds: the YHS was an established favourite of Capistrano,[148] it was popular and there is no sign that contemporaries regarded Tagliacozzo's testimony as discredited polemics. It is true that the campaign to advance Capistrano's canonization stalled, but there were plenty of reasons for this. If the astonishing (and hence arguably miraculous) victory at Belgrade did not prove as useful as the lobbyists hoped, that was because it was so difficult to ascertain who was owed the credit: there was too much conflicting evidence.[149] So we can conclude that, while Tagliacozzo probably did gild the lily, the emphasis that he placed on the *Nomen Iesu* should not be discounted. We find Capistrano seamlessly weaving the *Nomen Iesu* into more familiar crusading motifs in his preaching.[150] Victory at Belgrade, which the Pope decreed should be associated with the Feast of the Transfiguration in the Christian calendar, was the vindication of a devotional practice that in 1427 had narrowly escaped condemnation as heresy.[151] The problem we face is that this rich evidence for the Name of Jesus being integrated into crusading preaching and devotion in 1454–6 does not have echoes in other preaching campaigns.

Expanding the frame of reference, the poles between which the Franciscan preachers moved may be summarized as penitence and peril. It is usually assumed that they were more at home with the first than the second.[152] But, for all the talk of obedience, the evidence indicates that both Capistrano and Jacopo delle Marche became convinced of the gravity of the Turkish threat. After years spent dealing with the insidious internal menace of heretical belief, whether in the Czech lands

---

[142] 'Relatio', 750–1.   [143] Ibid. 784.   [144] Ibid. 773–4.
[145] Ibid. 788–9.   [146] Ibid. 777, 790–1, 794–5.
[147] Hofer, *Kapistran*, 2.421–4, a succinct summary of the facts.
[148] Famously, at Aquila in 1426: Roberto Rusconi, 'Giovanni da Capestrano: Iconografia di un predicatore nell'Europa del '400', *Venezie Francescane*, 6 (1989), 31–60, at 40–1.
[149] Andrić, *Miracles*, 86–90, and see too 29, 'a troublesome and polyphonic tradition'.
[150] esp. 'Relatio', 783–4.   [151] Moorman, *History*, 464.   [152] e.g. ibid. 519.

or in the western Balkans, events persuaded them, albeit with great reluctance, to switch their energies to defeating this external one.[153] Tagliacozzo even portrayed Capistrano asserting that he would welcome the company of schismatics, Jews, heretics, and infidels of any persuasion if they would fight at his side: 'The battle now is against the Turks, against the Turks I say.'[154] As Capistrano himself wrote to Calixtus, the despot of Serbia may hold religious beliefs that were at odds with their own, but he stood side by side with them against the Turks.[155] It was a liberal approach, one unprecedented for Capistrano,[156] though, as noted in Chapter 2, it does not wholly agree with the evidence for the preacher's activities during his time in Hungary.[157] One of the first texts in which an indication of preaching themes springing from the Turkish threat may be seen is the informative letter about recent Turkish advances that Bartolomeo da Giano sent from Constantinople to Alberto da Sarteano, a significant preacher, in December 1438. Bartolomeo told Alberto that he should feel free to use the text—effectively an *exhortatoria*—as he saw fit, and this points to its possible use in preaching. Bartolomeo dwelt poignantly on the sufferings of the Greeks, Serbs, and Transylvanians, on casualties, enslavements, heavy losses of territory, the threat to Constantinople, and the urgency of combating the enemy. Faith, freedom, and renown would be the rewards of the Christian victor, plus booty in abundance.[158] In the post-1453 world we can assume that the emphasis on atrocities and compassion remained, while the sense of urgency escalated. The earliest *Missa contra Turcos*, composed by Bishop Bernard of Kotor in 1453/5 and confirmed by Pope Paul II in 1470, incorporated a *prosa* of thirty-nine stanzas dwelling on the horrors of the sack of Constantinople and emphasizing the threat to the West.[159] In October 1454 Capistrano expressed his belief that if the Hungarians were driven to make peace or a truce with the Turks, Italy and Rome would be their next targets.[160] His biographers, Tagliacozzo and Cristoforo da Varese, referred to Belgrade as the key to Hungary and to Hungary as the door to the rest of Christendom.[161]

The *causae predicationis* that Bessarion set out in the instructions that he gave to his crusade preachers in August 1463 were threefold: vengeance for injuries suffered at the hands of the Turks, help to fellow Christians, and defence of home and hearth.[162] Of course, there is no certainty that Bessarion's preachers followed his advice closely, but his suggestions were sound ones and it would have been against

---

[153] Hofer, *Kapistran*, 2.303, 322, 341–2, emphasizes the quandary facing Capistrano, not least due to pressure from his fellow Observants to help them resist Conventual pressure in Italy.
[154] 'Relatio', p. 766, and see too Festa, p. 55.
[155] *AS Oct*, 383.
[156] As Tagliacozzo and later Hofer acknowledged: 'Relatio', 766; Hofer, *Kapistran*, 2.394, referring to 'a general religious peace' in the crusader camp.
[157] See ibid. 2.357–60, for Capistrano's bullish conversion work in Transylvania in the winter of 1455–6.
[158] Bartolomeo da Giano, 'Epistola', *passim*, esp. 1065–7.
[159] Linder, *Raising Arms*, 186.
[160] *AM*, 12.235–7.
[161] Festa, ed., 'Cinque lettere', 55; Tagliacozzo, 'Relatio', 753, 789; Cristoforo da Varese, 'Vita', 532.
[162] Mohler, ed., 'Instruktion', 339–41.

their own interests to neglect them. Certainly Bessarion's themes had been used by Capistrano in the course of his preaching in 1454–6. Unsurprisingly, Bessarion's first *causa* retold familiar stories from the sack of 1453, and Cristoforo da Varese described Capistrano too dwelling on Turkish atrocities: churches destroyed, altars desecrated, virgins raped on altar surfaces, Christians slaughtered and hauled off into slavery. Cleverly, the preacher associated these contemporary horrors with the 'fierce torments' of the faith's martyrs and with the Passion itself, weeping like a child 'out of love for the crucified Jesus' and drawing responsive tears from his audience.[163] Bessarion's third *causa*, like the *antemurale* references used by Capistrano's biographers, flowed naturally from humanist crusading ideas: 'If love for religion and disaster do not stir us, then surely our country, our possessions, our children, our parents, our wives, will do so.'[164] It was a natural theme to use in areas directly threatened and, in his account of Capistrano's life, Niccolò da Fara described the preacher exhorting the Hungarians to fight 'for Christ, for your own benefit, and for the common good of all'.[165] In this situation, the books of Maccabees provided valuable material and Cristoforo testified that Capistrano drew heavily on them.[166] In his *Relatio*, written three years before Bessarion drew up his *causae*, Tagliacozzo described Capistrano quoting 1 Maccabees 3:21 ('they come against us...to destroy us, and our wives and children, and to despoil us') in 1456.[167]

Here lay a danger. The Maccabees text went on to refer to God's people fighting 'for our souls and for our laws', and of course it was the duty of rulers and their nobles to defend the *patria* and its laws. One theme reportedly deployed, by Jacopo delle Marche among others, was that Christendom's rulers had failed in their duty to hold back the Turks.[168] It is hardly unexpected since this was a recurrent *topos* in crusade bulls and other sources. The Austrian historian, Thomas Ebendorfer, for example, an eyewitness of events at Vienna, indulged himself in a list of the great and good who should have done the job that was instead left to Capistrano's 'unarmed farmers, blacksmiths, fullers, tailors and cobblers, artisans and students'.[169] Such dereliction of duty appeared in Mandeville's *Travels*, one of the most popular texts of the period.[170] The motif was a useful device in preaching because it explained why the Turks had been so successful ('our sins permitting it') and why the opportunity had therefore arisen for ordinary people to contribute, a concept that chimed with Franciscan ideals. When preachers were collecting money, no tensions

---

[163] Cristoforo da Varese, 'Vita', 531.
[164] Mohler, ed., 'Instruktion', 340.
[165] Niccolò da Fara, 'Vita clarissimi viri fratris Joannis de Capistrano', in *AS Oct*, 439–83, at 471.
[166] Cristoforo da Varese, 'Vita', 532.
[167] 'Relatio', 783. Though note Ferenc Szakály, 'Das Bauerntum und die Kämpfe gegen die Türken bzw. gegen Habsburg in Ungarn im 16.–17. Jahrhundert', in Gusztáv Heckenast, ed., *Aus der Geschichte der ostmitteleuropäischen Bauernbewegungen im 16.– 17. Jahrhundert* (Budapest, 1977), 251–66, at 251–2, arguing for peasant indifference towards patriotic appeals in 1456.
[168] Bartolomeo da Giano, 'Epistola', 1062, 1064.
[169] Thomas Ebendorfer, *Chronica Austriae*, ed. Alphons Lhotsky, MGH SRG nova series, XIII (Berlin/Zürich, 1967), 434.
[170] Mandeville, *Travels*, tr. C.W.R.D. Moseley (London, 1983), 44.

need result: it could be assumed that the proceeds would be used to pay for the war effort, to the benefit of all parties. But in Hungary in 1456 the *topos* acquired a subversive potential from the failure of most of the country's nobility, taking their cue from the king, to support Hunyadi's attempt to mobilize its resources. 'Now the poor are stirred into action while the rich and noble stay at home', as Tagliacozzo succinctly put it.[171] As I have noted elsewhere, in such a troubled context 1 Maccabees 3.17–22 was a controversial text to use because while verses 18–19 held the consolatory message that God would favour the blessed few against the wicked many, verses 21–2 would remind the poor crusaders of the absent nobility. They registered their feelings following their first victory over the Turks on 14 July, when they incinerated the captured plunder, 'without telling the holy father, so that it would not be carted off by the well to do, who had not been there'.[172] It is worth emphasizing that this was a social rather than a devotional gesture: while Capistrano shared the concern of all military leaders that his troops should not be diverted during combat by the search for plunder,[173] preacher and *crucesignati* alike regarded its assembly in the aftermath of victory as a legitimate reward for service;[174] in August 1456 the preacher proposed an offensive against the Turks that would be sustained for three years by captured goods.[175]

After their decisive victory some of the crusaders became more strident in their criticism, publicly taunting Hunyadi for not helping out more. They were angered by the veto that had been imposed on their pursuing the fleeing Turks, and they thought that it arose from the elite's greed rather than its military judgement. The popular disturbance (*commotio in populo*) that resulted caused Capistrano hastily to disband the crusaders to forestall further trouble.[176] Much worse would happen in 1514 when a broadly similar scenario span out of control and a crusade preached by the Observants mutated into an uprising that was viciously suppressed.[177] But the situation in Hungary in 1456 was exceptional: culpably absent lords, preaching to raise an army rather than money, the celebration of that army's being composed mainly of the lower orders, and an apparently miraculous victory, made up a highly volatile compound. Other sources do not point towards the social order being overtly challenged by preachers. Tagliacozzo, for instance, allowed himself a wry comment on the arrival of various barons after hearing news of the Turkish defeat, 'once the game was over'.[178] But his overall approach towards the absence of the nobility was detached curiosity about the reasons why they did not rally to the

---

[171] 'Relatio', 759.
[172] Ibid. 762; Hofer, *Kapistran*, 2.389: is there an echo in this of the bonfire of the vanities?
[173] Festa, ed., 'Cinque lettere', 25.
[174] 'Relatio', 766.
[175] *AS Oct*, 383–4, pursuing a suggestion of living off the land that had been made by Hunyadi at the Raab diet in June 1455: *AM* 12:292–4, at 294; Hofer, *Kapistran*, 2.351–2.
[176] 'Relatio', 793–4, and see the discussion in my *Religious Warfare in Europe, 1400–1536* (Oxford, 2002), 65–7.
[177] The pattern of thinking behind this was thoroughly analysed by Jenő Szűcs in 'Die Ideologie des Bauernkrieges', in his *Nation und Geschichte: Studien* (Budapest, 1981), 329–78.
[178] '...date erano le candele': 'Relatio', 794.

defence of the besieged fortress; to which the answer, voiced by his fellow Observant, Paul, was a providential one: it was so that the honour of victory could be shared by God, the Name of Jesus, the cross, and Capistrano.[179] On one occasion at least, 'internal foes' were identified and suffered a backlash from crusade preaching, but they were a much more traditional target: according to Długosz, at Easter 1464 the Jews of Cracow were attacked and over 300 killed by *crucesignati*.[180] We are not told the reasons for the attack or whether Franciscan preaching was to blame. Diane Owen Hughes established links between Observant preaching against the Jews and their condemnation of urban vices for which Jews were blamed;[181] but to date no direct association of this linkage with the call to crusade has been identified.[182]

In 1463 Bessarion told his preachers to instruct their audiences that the crusade was an occasion for all who had indulged in 'murder, theft, robbery, arson, and any other sort of wickedness' to escape the penalty for the sum total of their offences.[183] Even in a world that was saturated with salvation through works and above all with indulgences, the certainty of heaven that crusade offered retained its allure. Indeed, a generation earlier the preaching of the Hussite crusades in Germany had been closely associated with programmes of church reform and pastoral concern during the legations of Branda da Castiglione (1421), Giordano Orsini (1426), and Giuliano Cesarini (1431). Although the promotion of crusades took priority, all three men pursued what Birgit Studt has characterized as a 'double strategy', intended to counter the propaganda emanating from the Hussites as well as subjugating them militarily.[184] The Observants found much to attract them in the association of crusade with personal and collective renewal and it formed one of the key themes in their preaching. Caracciolo's response to the fall of Constantinople, in the Pentecost sermons that he delivered at Rome in 1453, focused on the need for penitence to turn aside God's wrath and avoid the fate of the Greeks: 'Change your ways, and God will change his sentence ... [for] there are times when God punishes a city and a people, not as a judge would, but as a father.'[185] But it is Capistrano who provides the best evidence of this: as Otto Gecser and Johannes Hofer have demonstrated, preaching the crusade against the Turks was not a diversion of effort from the programme of penitential preaching that he conducted north of the Alps from 1451 onwards, but an extension of it.[186] The devotion that it stimulated was remarkable

---

[179] Ibid. 795.
[180] Długosz, *Annals*, 548.
[181] Diane Owen Hughes, 'Distinguishing Signs: Ear-rings, Jews and Franciscan Rhetoric in the Italian Renaissance City', *Past and Present*, 112 (1986), 3–59, esp.17–38.
[182] Though see Daniela Rando, 'Antitürkendiskurs und antijüdische Stereotypen: Formen der Propaganda im 15. Jahrhundert am Beispeil Trient, in *OEEH*, 31–52.
[183] Mohler, ed., 'Instruktion', 341.
[184] Studt, *Martin V.*, esp. 713–22.
[185] *Testi inediti e poco noti sulla caduta di Costantinopoli*, ed. Agostino Pertusi (Bologna, 1983), 296.
[186] Hofer, *Kapistran*, 1.430–56, 2.9–38, provides detailed analysis of Capistrano's preaching techniques in 1451–4 and his well-documented preaching at Vienna in June–July 1451.

and once again it is in Tagliacozzo's *Relatio* that we encounter the richest evidence for it. The reason is that the crusaders whom Capistrano had recruited were assembled together and subjected to highly stressful conditions, which they dealt with by calling on their spiritual reserves. It is fair to assume that the devotional patterns that they manifested arose to a large degree from the preaching that had led them to take the cross, perhaps the clearest evidence for this being their adoption of banners, which displayed on one side the cross, on the other a leading Franciscan saint: Francis of Assisi, Antony of Padua, Louis of Toulouse, or Bernardino of Siena.[187]

The key point about the devotion of Capistrano's motley host is that it does not depart from the concerns of the Franciscans in their preaching in contemporary Italy and Germany. Most importantly, there was a concern with devout behaviour:

> There was no idleness, no weakness, no lax behaviour. Drunkenness, gluttony, dishonesty, and prostitution were absent. Idle gossip, gambling, theft, and pillaging were nobody to be seen. Nobody complained about people who had not come, there was no grumbling or plotting, no quarrelling. Instead there was devotion, prayer, and frequent masses.

Patience, peace, and harmony reigned, and crime was punished harshly and publicly, 'as an example to others'. A thief had his right ear cut off. One black marketeer had his overpriced loaves thrown into the Danube and would have followed them but for the intervention of Tagliacozzo and another friar. The atmosphere described in the camp of these *crucisignati povirelli* is that of an ideal Franciscan community.[188] Tellingly, Tagliacozzo compared the crusaders to novices in their veneration for Capistrano, for whom they would have gone through fire or water.[189] But it is also reminiscent of the campaigns waged by the Observants in their urban preaching against vices like sodomy and gambling, and corrosive social ills like usury, vanity, and envy, as well as their attempts to encourage charity, piety, and altruism. Hofer put it well: 'His camp at Semlin was less like a military encampment than a religious gathering, just as they had taken shape everywhere during his missionary travels.'[190] The continuation into the campaign of Capistrano's preaching themes hinged on his leadership and this meant that the circumstances of the crusaders' camp outside Belgrade could not be replicated: there is no evidence for anything similar, for example, at Ancona eight years later, where impatience, discontent, and quarrelling were uppermost among the *crucesignati* who were waiting for Pius II to arrive.

As evidence for the character of Capistrano's preaching in 1454–6, texts like those of Tagliacozzo and Capistrano's other biographers are complemented by surviving paintings from the iconographical tradition that rapidly took shape, and

---

[187] 'Relatio', 764.
[188] Festa, ed., 'Cinque lettere', 54: 'Crucisignati povirelli', 'poverelli Crucisignati'.
[189] 'Relatio', 765–6.
[190] Hofer, *Kapistran*, 2.392, reiterating his comment in 'Der Sieger', 205–6.

was analysed by Roberto Rusconi. Prominent Observants became associated with easily identified visual clues: YHS in the case of Bernardino da Siena, the Holy Blood in the case of Jacopo delle Marche, and a *Mons Pietatis* for Bernardino da Feltre. In Capistrano's case, the identifier was the preacher's banner, which Tagliacozzo described in 1457 as 'a fine and great banner depicting the cross on one side, and San Bernardino on the other'.[191] Initially, the banner depicted only Bernardino: Capistrano had the cross added following a vision he experienced at Petrovaradin on his way to Belgrade, after which he gave the cross more prominence in his preaching.[192] The banner was first depicted by Bartolomeo Vivarini in 1459 in a full-length portrait painted in association with the first attempt to secure the preacher's canonization. In his right hand, the gaunt Capistrano holds a banner topped with a cross, the banner shown precisely as Tagliacozzo had described it two years earlier. In his left hand, Capistrano holds a Bible. The portrait's associations are clear and positive: a crusade preached at the command of the Pope, whose predecessor had canonized Bernardino; and a glorious victory won through the leadership of the standard-bearer, whose plain sandals mark him out as an Observant.[193] By 1488, when Carlo Crivelli painted an altar-piece for the Observants' church of St Pietro di Camerino, the iconography was set: Capistrano can immediately be recognized on the left by his banner, Jacopo on the right by his ampoule. A number of similar polyptychs followed, painted for Observant churches in Abruzzo.[194] Most remarkable is the sole surviving portrait of Capistrano that includes flanking narratives from his life, one of which shows the final battle at Belgrade. Both in the portrait (which depicts an anachronistically youthful preacher) and in the battle scene the banner makes its appearance, though Bernardino has been replaced by the saint's familiar YHS monogram.[195]

Interestingly, north of the Alps representations of Capistrano did not include the Belgrade banner, focusing instead on his practice of holding a crucifix as a prompt for penitence, and on his robust preaching against social vices, including his use of bonfires of the vanities.[196] This bifurcation is not easy to explain; but both ways of depicting the preacher were rooted in his life, and the change of direction that he took in 1454 in response to Mehmed's victories did not involve a radical change of goals, techniques, and themes. Cristoforo da Varese claimed that many Germans took the cross and travelled to Hungary because they heard that Capistrano was preaching there, so that they could see again the preacher who a few years previously had performed miracles in their towns.[197] Indeed, in one sense the fresco of the siege of Belgrade that was painted in the Observant church at Olomouc in Moravia in 1468 synthesizes the northern and southern traditions.

---

[191] Festa, ed., 'Cinque lettere', 22, and see too 53: '...co lo confalone de Sancto Bernardino et de la croce.'
[192] Tagliacozzo, 'Relatio', 754.
[193] Rusconi, 'Capestrano', 34–6, 49 fig. 1.
[194] Ibid. 37–8, 50–1, figs 2–3. Capestrano's crusader habit ended up in the Franciscan convent in l'Aquila: Andrić, *Miracles*, 66. [195] Rusconi, 'Capestrano', 38–40, 52–5, figs 4–7.
[196] Ibid. 42–7, 56–60, figs 8–12.   [197] Cristoforo da Varese, 'Vita', 531–2.

True, the preacher is not shown holding his banner, which has been transferred to a captain standing further along the walls,[198] but he stands, larger than life, on the ramparts of the besieged town, defying the Turks and clutching in his left hand a painting of Christ as the Man of Sorrows. Given Olomouc's status as a Catholic stronghold on the border with Hussite Bohemia, the meaning of this *Bildpredigt* was more transparent than that of Benedetto da Maiano's pulpit at St Croce: the successful defence of the Hungarian *antemurale* should encourage Observants and citizens alike to stand firm in the face of the heretics, from whose wholesale conversion the great preacher had been diverted only by the more urgent needs of Hungary.[199] The depiction of Capistrano at Olomouc would carry forward his work there in much the same way that the veneration of the great man's physical remains at Ilok encouraged the people living along Hungary's southern frontier to resist the pressure from neighbouring Turks, schismatics, and heretics.[200]

5.3 ORATIONS

At the imperial diet held at Frankfurt in October 1454 Capistrano's charismatic crusade preaching coincided with a cutting-edge example of the new humanist oratory. The latter took the form of Aeneas Sylvius Piccolomini's speech on the fall of Constantinople, *Constantinopolitana clades*. Johannes Helmrath has described the significance and impact of Piccolomini's deliberative oration (*symbouleutikón*), which lasted two hours and was modelled on Cicero's *De imperio Cn. Pompei*. The fact that there are fifty extant manuscript copies demonstrates the unusually high regard in which *Constantinopolitana clades* was held for its structure, language, and style. Reading the text today, one admires the skill with which the author steered his audience through the three standard arguments in favour of waging war: the justice of the conflict, the benefits that will arise from fighting, and the chances of success. Piccolomini's handling of the situation confronting Christian Europe was comprehensive and elegant, with ample citation of precedent, example, and authority. Biblical, classical, and medieval themes were seamlessly interwoven. But the oration was also cleverly tailored to the circumstances of the Frankfurt diet. Speaking as Frederick III's envoy, Piccolomini proceeded steadily towards big questions of ways and means, dealing in a detailed way with challenging political issues, such as the conflict between Poland and the Teutonic Order, which threatened to divert attention from the Turks. The weaknesses of *Constantinopolitana clades* are its author's misguided assertions on certain central issues, above all, the enemy's alleged military deficiencies, and his historical misconceptions, for example on the

---

[198] This figure probably represents Hunyadi, in which case the iconographic change is likely to have sprung from deference to his son Matthias, who was using Olomouc as his military base when the fresco was being painted.
[199] Andrić, *Miracles*, 157–9, including a reproduction of the fresco at fig. 5.2. Tagliacozzo, 'Relatio', 751, claimed that Capistrano had converted about 16,000 Hussites before his energies were channelled against the Turkish threat. See also Hofer, *Kapistran*, 2.303.
[200] Andrić, *Miracles*, 60–1.

First Crusade. The last section, on the war's management, is the weakest: the author's military expertise did not match his learning and political insights, though, in his defence, it should be added that this was precisely the area that was up for discussion.[201]

Piccolomini himself distorted the reception of his Frankfurt oration. In letters written immediately or shortly afterwards his reporting of events was gloomy: excuses were plentiful, nobody could be trusted, and the political obstacles were insuperable.[202] But in the *Commentarii* a very different picture was painted. It looked like the resolutions carried forward from the Regensburg diet were doomed, but *Constantinopolitana clades* saved the day. Spitefully, Piccolomini even contrasted the reception of his oration with that given to Nicholas V's legate, Giovanni da Castiglione (who had died by the time the *Commentarii* were penned). According to Piccolomini, the legate's metaphor of the Church as a beautiful woman bewailing her misfortunes was misjudged, whereas during his own speech 'the audience was so utterly absorbed that no one even cleared his throat or took his eyes off the speaker's face'. The oration 'was praised by all and written down by many, and because of it the declaration of war passed at Regensburg was reaffirmed'.[203] Almost certainly Piccolomini confused reception with effect. *Constantinopolitana clades* was admired as an oratorical *tour de force*, in particular by individuals who hoped to learn from it to hone their own technique. But it was asking too much to expect one speech, however powerful and well received, to counterbalance deeply ingrained scepticism, a mass of political problems, and the empire's underlying structural shortcomings. The most that it could do was subtly to shift the dynamic at the diet, reinforcing the arguments of those who were positively inclined and giving fresh momentum to the pro-crusade lobby. This Piccolomini may have achieved at Frankfurt.

Piccolomini's vanity, together with his perennial tendency to oscillate between pessimism and hope, sometimes make it hard to gauge whether he fully grasped this. *Cum bellum hodie*, his keynote address at the Mantua congress on 26 September 1459, illustrates this well.[204] In the *Commentarii* this speech too received lavish self-praise: '[Pius] spoke for three hours amid such rapt attention that not a single word went unremarked.' On this occasion Bessarion played the role of foil to Piccolomini's greatness, though he was treated less brutally than Castiglione had been: 'His oration received compliments, though it did reveal the extent to which Latin

---

[201] *Deutsche Reichstagsakten*, 19.2 (forthcoming); *Pii II orationes*, 1.262–86, no 13; Piccolomini, *Opera omnia*, 678–89; Helmrath, '*Reichstage*', 60–1.

[202] *Aeneae Silvii Piccolomini Senensis opera inedita*, 105–8, no 43, 108–13, nos 45–6, 115–16, no 48.

[203] *Pii II Commentarii*, bk 1, ch. 27, 82–4. I have used the translation in Pius II, *Commentaries*, ed. and tr. Margaret Meserve and Marcello Simonetta, I Tatti Renaissance Library, 12 (Cambridge, Mass., 2003–), 1.135, 137. Castiglione's rhetorical shortcomings come under renewed criticism in bk 1, ch. 28.

[204] *Pii II orationes*, 2.7–30, no 2, also in Piccolomini, *Opera omnia*, 905–14; *Sacrorum conciliorum*, 32.207–21.

eloquence surpasses Greek.'[205] Its author's status conjoined with his reputation and the gravity of the subject matter to endow *Cum bellum hodie* with a renown that surpassed even that of *Constantinopolitana clades*. There exist 120 manuscript copies and at least sixteen printed versions, so that 'it could well be the most widely disseminated oration of European humanism'.[206] Of course, Piccolomini spoke now as Pope, and he was careful to point out that he followed in the footsteps of such illustrious forerunners as Urban II, Eugenius III, and Innocent III. In addition to the spoils of war and eternal fame, participants would earn salvation as crusaders: 'We shall sign with the cross all those Christians who are setting out on this expedition.' But for all that, structurally *Cum bellum hodie* had much more in common with *Constantinopolitana clades* than it varied from it: the same three-fold argument was deployed (though in a different order) and many of the same points were made, once due allowance is made for the changes in the political and military scenario between 1454 and 1459. As we would expect, it constituted an impressive display of learning, but the Pope's phrasing often seems shop-worn and faltering; it is almost as if the long and dispiriting wait for the delegates to arrive at Mantua had drained Pius of both energy and conviction.[207] And in one famous passage, when he reached the section on rewards, the Pope commented sadly that if the leaders of the First Crusade were present, they would by now be shouting 'Deus vult!' rather than awaiting the end of the oration.

It might seem from this that Pius regarded his oration as the equivalent of his great predecessor's sermon at Clermont, and was hoping for immediate commitment, a recruitment surge similar to what Capistrano had achieved, spectacularly, just a few years previously in Germany and Hungary. But this is misleading: the comment about Godfrey, Baldwin, Eustace, Hugh, Bohemund, Tancred, and the rest surely relates to what follows, which is Pius's declaration of his own physical commitment to the crusading cause. He reminded his audience that in travelling to Mantua he had prejudiced his own health as well as the best interests of the patrimony of St Peter, prioritizing the defence of the faith. If he were younger he would go on crusade in person, and he still would if that was what his audience wanted. They need only ask it. It was the first time that Pius had referred to personally setting out on crusade, as Capistrano had done, and it is surely in this context that his reference to a Clermont-like surge should be understood. It was a rhetorical device, a way of underscoring the radical nature of the offer that the Pope was about to make, as opposed to a genuine expectation. For all his own spin-doctoring, Pius did not really expect *Cum bellum hodie*, any more than he had *Constantinopolitana clades*, to turn the situation around. He knew that the purpose of the

---

[205] *Pii II Commentarii*, bk 3, ch. 32, tr. in Pius II, *Commentaries*, 2.137, 139; *Anecdota veneta nunc primum collecta ac notis illustrata*, ed. Joannes Baptista Maria Contareni OP, vol. 1 (Venice, 1757), 276–83 (Bessarion's oration). For Bessarion as latinist see John Monfasani, 'Bessarion latinus', *Rinascimento*, 2nd ser., 21 (1981), 165–209.
[206] Helmrath, '*Reichstage*', 63.
[207] As will be clear, I disagree with Russell's comment, 'Humanists', 75, praising '...the surge, the ebb and flow, of a very eloquent Latin', as well as Helmrath's view that *Cum bellum hodie* established 'a new apogee', '*Reichstage*', 63.

Mantua congress was to make possible a series of gruelling but indispensable bilateral negotiations. And it was these that enabled him, in his second major Mantua address, *Septimo iam exacto mense* given on 14 January 1460, to expound in detail the various promises that had been made as well as the hopes that he still entertained of the uncommitted.[208] Much as at the imperial diets in 1454–5, the function of deliberative oratory at the congress was to set out one's stall, providing information, arguments, and perspectives that furnished a backcloth to more detailed discussions.

Orations that were less grand than the ones so far considered could form part of the debating process at diets or congresses. Pius's exchanges with the French at Mantua are revealing on this. The heated cut and thrust on both sides is apparent, but it does not prevent the argumentation remaining relatively sophisticated.[209] A particularly interesting sequence is that between Cardinal Bessarion and the delegates at the imperial diets that convened in 1460 to work out the details of the German contribution to the crusade programme agreed at Mantua. In Chapter 3 we examined the legal and diplomatic context and implications of these exchanges; but interwoven with these issues of authority and commitment were the various arguments that Bessarion employed. *Cum salvator noster*, the oration that Bessarion gave at the Nürnberg diet, is a fairly straightforward and unexciting text. The legate eulogized peace; spoke of the need to resist the Turks before they reached the imperial lands ('if we don't go to them they will come to us'); recalled the various undertakings made at the 1454–5 diets and at Mantua; and expressed confidence that if the Christians acted in unity, the Turks would vanish like dust from the face of the earth. It was a mixture of platitude and *résumé*.[210] More impressive is Bessarion's oration *Multa quidem*, which he delivered at Vienna in the autumn of 1460. The legate was responding to a text in which objections to a German contribution were set out one after the other, at considerable length, the intention being to kill the whole idea. He dealt with the objections and reiterated the juridical obligation of the Germans, but he also set out two further arguments: on the one hand, the urgency of the military situation, on the other, the disastrous consequences of a German withdrawal from the project. *Multa quidem* was a powerful but controlled riposte to outrageous special pleading, factual and logical in approach but also driven by passionate conviction.[211] It could not succeed because the diet's delegates had closed ears, and the sequence of events thereafter shows both sides slipping inexorably into accusation and apologia.[212]

The major differences between orations and sermons sprang from both speaker and audience. Preachers and orators addressed common themes like the Ottoman threat to hearth and home, and the need for collective military action, but, when considering rewards, humanists could not resist turning to classical themes, such as fame. This applied whether they adopted the closely reasoned, classical approach epitomized by the orations of Piccolomini/Pius, or the less structured and more

---

[208] *Pii II orationes*, 2.78–88, no 4, also in *Sacrorum conciliorum*, 35.113–20.
[209] *Sacrorum conciliorum*, 32.225–30, 240–58.   [210] Mohler, *Bessarion*, 3.377–83.
[211] Ibid. 3.384–98.   [212] Ibid. 3.399–403.

mannerist style of orators like Giannantonio Campano, who were influenced by Quintilian's *Institutio oratoria*.[213] So when answering the question why soldiers should fight to save civilized values from the Turks, Piccolomini referenced the comment that Alexander supposedly made at the tomb of Achilles to the effect that the Greek hero had been lucky to have his deeds celebrated by Homer.[214] One of the most revealing sources on this topic is Benedetto Accolti's ambitious history of the First Crusade, written in the early 1460s with the goal of stimulating enthusiasm for the crusade at Florence.[215] Accolti inserted a number of orations into his account, and they constitute a fascinating insight into how one of the leading Renaissance humanists considered it appropriate for clerical promoters and military leaders of the First Crusade to persuade and inspire their listeners.[216] Repeatedly, the intrinsic value of fame and the desirability of avoiding its negative counterpart, shame, are given prominence alongside the religious character and rewards of the enterprise. Thus Pope Urban asks of his Clermont audience 'if any of you seek glory, or more lands to rule over, what greater opportunity could there be?' Even though Urban was preaching an expedition to recover Jerusalem, Accolti could not resist the temptation to allude to current events, having the Pope conclude by saying that if the Turks were not defeated in the east they would come to the west: hence 'I would wish you to set out against the foe with the same spirit, with which great men used to fight for their country, their household gods, their wives and children, and their own well-being'.[217] When Bohemund promotes the crusade to his soldiers, he assumes that his audience will be receptive to his message because they are used to combat and eager for glory. In a stream of rhetorical questions he imagines his own failure to respond being judged as shameful by his ancestors. Better death than such ignominy.[218] Before the battle of Antioch Bishop Adhemar of Le Puy refers to the praise of posterity, 'above all because it is not desire for conquest or greed for wealth that has brought you here, but piety, devotion, and a worthy love of true glory'.[219] And before the climactic assault on Jerusalem Patriarch Arnulf tells the crusaders that once the city has fallen they can return home covered in glory (*cum summa laude*), while Godfrey argues that an honest death is preferable to a shameful life.[220]

When devotional themes do feature in orations they are remarkably classicized. This is most striking, and incongruous, when the oration is voiced through a chosen saint who possesses advanced skills in Ciceronian rhetoric. The most famous example is the dialogue between Saints Andrew and Peter when the former's exiled relics arrived at St Peter's in Rome at Easter 1462. As Pius reported it in his

---

[213] See Blusch, 'Enea Silvio Piccolomini', *passim*.
[214] Piccolomini, *Opera omnia*, 678–89, at 682.
[215] Black, *Benedetto Accolti*, 224–85.
[216] Benedetto Accolti, *De bello a christianis contra barbaros gesto*, Recueil des historiens des croisades, Historiens occidentaux, 5 (Paris, 1895), 529–620, at 536–8 (Urban II, Clermont), 549–51 (Bohemund, Apulia), 557–9 (Suleyman, Nicaea), 569–71 (Godfrey, Antioch), 576–7 (Godfrey, Antioch), 584–6 (Adhemar, Antioch), 586–7 (Kerbogha, Antioch), 605 (Arnulf, Jerusalem), 606–6 (Godfrey, Jerusalem), 609–10 (Robert of Flanders, Jerusalem).
[217] Ibid. 537.   [218] Ibid. 550.   [219] Ibid. 585.   [220] Ibid. 605, 607.

Commentarii, Bessarion spoke as Andrew and the Pope as his brother, Peter. Bessarion/Andrew appealed to Peter's successor to raise an army to defend the embattled Peloponnese against the Turks, and Pius/Peter promised to do his utmost 'to recover your sheep and your home here on earth'. The scene is a reminder that the play acting for which the Observants were famous, and sometimes taken to task, had its appeal for those at the highest level in the Church: the previous day had witnessed a scarcely less theatrical scene when Pius venerated the relics at an altar set up in the fields beside the Via Flaminia, north of Rome.[221] There is no reason to doubt that for Bessarion and Pius, as well as the thousands who flocked to watch, the reception in Rome of Andrew's treasured relics was an occasion of much focused devotion: but the language in which their orations were recorded in the *Commentarii* is measured and reflective rather than emotionally charged. So the effect on the reader is to distance rather than engage. Much the same applies to the address that Bessarion's secretary, the humanist bishop of Siponto, Niccolò Perotti, gave at the congress of Mantua on the feast of the Assumption in 1459. It is not hard to imagine some of the themes that are elegantly enunciated by Perotti's Virgin being used by the Observants in their preaching. This includes her reference to Turkish atrocities and a passing reference to the Jews murdering Jesus. The latter was the sort of comment that in past crusade preaching had helped to inflame anti-Jewish feelings (and possibly would do so again at Cracow in 1464). But it is hard to imagine her detailed list of Turkish conquests forming part of the repertoire of the Observants.[222] As with similar lists in the orations of Piccolomini and Bessarion, this was directed at an elite audience, whose members would have the education to appreciate the significance of the losses sustained, and hopefully have some influence on the decision to mobilize a collective response.

Not that the audience being targeted is always obvious. We possess an *exortatoria oratio* by Rodrigo Sánchez de Arévalo that purports to be intended for delivery to Pius II in the presence of the crusaders assembled at Ancona: at the start the Pope is exhorted to look around at his army gathered before him, ready to set out for the war. This might lead us to expect a rousing sermon with a strongly devotional message. But in both content and style, what follows is closely argued, humanistic, and learned. Sánchez's survey of the nature of the imminent crusade followed the classical pattern that we have witnessed Pius himself adopting in *Constantinopolitana clades* and *Cum bellum hodie*. 'In the first place he proves the justice of the war, then the courage of the combatants, and finally the certainty of victory.' Moreover, Sánchez was intent on establishing the propriety of the Pope's accompanying the crusade, and the arguments he used closely resembled those that he also deployed in his commentary on *Ezechielis prophetae*. This thematic convergence points towards Sánchez's *exortatoria oratio* belonging to a coordinated response by Pius to the Franco-Bohemian diplomatic agitation against his

---

[221] *Pii II Commentarii*, bk 8, chs 1–3, 467–90. For the context see Bernard Hamilton, 'The Ottomans, the Humanists and the Holy House of Loreto', *Renaissance and Modern Studies*, 31 (1987), 1–19.

[222] Hankins, 'Renaissance Crusaders', 198–201.

programme. In appearance a sermon, in substance an oration, and in purpose (at least partly) a riposte to criticism, this intriguing text is a good example of the chameleon-like character of many humanistic crusade texts.[223] Among the finest surviving examples of the genre are Bessarion's two *Orationes ad principes christianos contra Turcos*, which he wrote in response to the fall of Negroponte and consciously modelled on Demosthenes. We have already noted their importance and originality, but their title is misleading, for as Margaret Meserve observed, 'it is extremely unlikely that he ever pronounced them orally in any sort of public assembly'.[224] As we shall shortly see, the format that Bessarion *did* favour for the dissemination of his texts is disputed, but in the autumn of 1470 there existed no public forum for him to speak at. Together with Sánchez's supposed Ancona sermon, Bessarion's so-called orations constitute a lesson not to take any humanist oration at face value in terms of either its targeted audience or the mode of its delivery.

That said, humanistic orations *contra Turcos* are normally distinguishable by the fact that their authors, whether lay or clerical, deployed classical language to construct arguments in the style advocated by Cicero, and addressed sophisticated audiences gathered at assemblies and courts. They were usually *pièces d'occasion*, the promotion of a crusade being either formally on the agenda or attached to a wedding, coronation, or other event of political significance. In different ways, these distinguishing features have all contributed to the bad press that the orations have often received. Part of the problem is the volume and quality of the material involved. Because the crusade against the Turks was so widely promoted at the diplomatic level, numerous humanists desperate for career advancement saw in the oration *contra Turcos* the easiest way to impress. The available repertoire of arguments and allusions was comparatively slender and staleness could easily result. The result is well summarized in the title that Michael Heath gave to his pioneering 1986 study of the subject: *Crusading Commonplaces*.[225] This does not apply to the orations we have so far considered, which emanated from gifted and committed men like Piccolomini, Bessarion, Sánchez, and Accolti. But all too often their fellow orators were not of the same calibre and they bequeathed a mass of mediocre texts. Of course, there is no reason to suppose that many of the crusade sermons given in the twelfth and thirteenth centuries were any more impressive, but they are lost to us. Moreover, knowing as we do that the crusading message failed to persuade contemporaries at diet, court, and congress, it is tempting to infer that

---

[223] See analysis of content in Benziger, *Zur Theorie*, 154–8. For the commentary see ibid. 141–9, and Thomas M. Izbicki, 'A New Copy of Rodrigo Sánchez de Arévalo's Commentary on the Bull "Ezechielis" of Pope Pius II', *Revista española de teologia*, 41 (1981), 465–7. The MS of the *exortatoria oratio*, Cambridge Corpus Christi College MS 166, fols 63r–74r, has not been edited.

[224] Meserve, 'Patronage', 524.

[225] Michael J. Heath, *Crusading Commonplaces: La Noue, Lucinge and Rhetoric against the Turks* (Geneva, 1986). Heath structured his study like an anti-Turkish oration, with chapters headed 'Justice and necessity', 'Ease', and 'Profit'.

the law of diminishing returns was at work and that the inherent weakness of repetitive *contra Turcos* oratory contributed to the indifference so frequently remarked on by contemporaries, and epitomized in Francesco Filelfo's comment that Christian rulers observed the Ottoman advance 'as if they were watching a play'.[226] The result was that the need for a crusade became the political correctness of its day, to which speaker and audience alike paid lip service before moving on to the issues that really preoccupied them.

It is hard to take issue with any of this, but it is important to reiterate the other side of the picture: that the Ottoman advance was genuine, that it induced anxiety and the search for a collective response, and that the crusading cause attracted the services of some of the finest humanists of the day. Individual speeches must be judged on their merits, based on reception and the context in which they were given. This is far from straightforward. We have already observed Piccolomini spin-doctoring his contemporaries' response to his orations. And contemporaries themselves could be two-faced: James Hankins observed the divergence between the formal discussion of the fall of Constantinople that took place at Cosimo de' Medici's house in 1453, in which all was sympathy and sorrow, and the comments that Matteo Palmieri made to Cosimo privately afterwards, to the effect that the Greeks had brought the disaster on themselves.[227] Nor does the quality of individual orations always help in sifting the grain from the chaff. Most humanists were pursuing careers as clerics, envoys, or courtiers and the best could deliver powerful and elegant speeches more or less on demand. For example, the speeches made by Leonello Chiericati on behalf of an anti-Turkish crusade are well-crafted constructions. His oration at the French court in January 1488, delivered with the main purpose of securing Djem for the Pope, displayed a familiarity (albeit not wholly accurate) with French contributions toward the crusading movement in the past.[228] Yet we have seen that in the early 1490s Chiericati went on to devote his talents to Alexander VI's policy of getting the French out of Italy, and this presupposed delaying the crusade.

As a means of communication, orations are best viewed not as an elite counterpart to sermons, but as a ritual reflecting the absorption of crusade into a framework of negotiation and decision-making that was more heavily politicized than it had been in the past.[229] The 'justice, ease, benefit' sequence on which it rested was not radically different from that used in papal bulls of the time: Pius II's *Ezechielis prophetae* of October 1463, for example, refined many themes that had earlier been developed in

---

[226] Cited by Meserve, 'News', 452. Filelfo had a picturesque turn of phrase: a few months later he wrote that trying to get Christian princes to take action against the Turks was 'as useful as washing a brick': ibid. 468.

[227] Hankins, 'Renaissance Crusaders', 131–2.

[228] Sigismondo de' Conti, *Le storie*, 2.428–35, *appendice*, no 12, misnaming Louis IX as Philip at 428; Setton, *Papacy*, 2.404; *DBI*, 24.685.

[229] See generally Dieter Mertens, '"Europa, id est patria, domus propria, sedes nostra…" Zu Funktionen und Überlieferung lateinischer Türkenreden im 15. Jahrhundert', in Franz-Reiner Erkens, ed., *Europa und die osmanische Expansion im ausgehenden Mittelalter*, Zeitschrift für historische Forschung, Beiheft 20 (Berlin, 1997), 39–57.

the Pope's orations. And orations could be written as, or closely resemble, sermons. But such affinities do not disguise a fundamental shift from an approach that was grounded in shared religious belief (even, as the papal *curia* continued to argue, obligation), to one that was built around collective needs and anticipated gains. Contemporaries would have recognized the modern tendency to couch alliances of enduring strength in terms of 'common interests and shared values'.[230] This association with embryonic diplomacy meant that just as the greatest threat to the work of crusading preachers in the thirteenth century had been the way that *Deus vult* was undercut by repeated defeat, so the greatest problem faced by the anti-Turkish orator was the perception that self-interest was insufficiently collectivized. This makes the analysis of orations a particularly useful way to grasp the thought processes that accompanied the gradual metamorphosis of crusade into the Holy Leagues of the sixteenth and seventeenth centuries. And while such processes owed a good deal to crusading, they also marked a radical departure from it.[231]

5.4 PRINTING

Printing with movable type was harnessed for the crusading cause from its origins.[232] Indulgences for Cyprus were printed in the 1450s and Pius II's bull *Ezechielis prophetae* was printed for circulation in late 1463: the availability of multiple copies may have contributed to its effect, though it is likely that the key factors behind this were an energetic preaching campaign and the promise of papal participation. But the most demonstrable impact came in the wake of Negroponte's fall to the Turks in the summer of 1470. As Meserve has shown, it was not just that the news of Mehmed's capture of Venice's mighty Euboean fortress set off in Italy 'a strident mix of panic, self-recrimination, and prurient interest in the gruesome details'; it also precisely coincided with the peninsula's embrace of the new technology. The loss of Negroponte, which for commentators and above all crusade enthusiasts was coupled with the imminent threat of an Ottoman invasion of Italy, thus immediately found expression in print. Significantly, it was not the initial newsletters that were printed but a variety of treatments written for different types of audience, ranging from ballads and epics to orations, letters, and devotional verse. There is a strong case for arguing that this diversified response forms our best window into the intersection of three worlds: humanism, diplomacy, and book-publishing. This in turn has implications for the way in which crusading, and more

---

[230] e.g. the affirmation of US/UK collaboration in foreign affairs in 2011: *The Guardian*, 24 May 2011, 1.
[231] The key study of this change is Poumarède, *Pour en finir*.
[232] Generally on the impact of print see Alexandra Walsham and Julia Crick, 'Introduction: Script, Print, and History', in their *The Uses of Script and Print, 1300–1700* (Cambridge, 2004), 1–26; David D'Avray, 'Printing, Mass Communication, and Religious Reformation: the Middle Ages and After', ibid. 50–70; Bernd Moeller, 'Die frühe Reformation als Kommunikationsprozeß', in Hartmut Boockmann, ed., *Kirche und Gesellschaft im Heiligen Römischen Reich des 15. und 16. Jahrhunderts* (Göttingen, 1994), 148–64.

broadly the 'Turkish question', operated in what early modernists have dubbed 'the public sphere': an emerging arena of open discussion and activity that interacted with the agencies of Church and state, but was also shaped by such social forces as urban and regional assemblies and diets, education, and print culture.[233]

Some of the issues noted above in relation to the crusade oratory that emanated from Italian humanists take on yet more complex form when we consider this published output about the fall of Negroponte, and its effect on the reading public. There is no doubt that both contemporaries and their descendants found much of the printed work appealing, with the result that it stayed in print decades after it had ceased to be newsworthy: the anonymous *Lamento di Negroponte*, printed at Milan in 1471/72, was reprinted nineteen times between 1500 and 1615.[234] Such enduring appeal proves that the interest of buyers and readers went beyond any considerations of responsive military action, though it is worth noting that a residual topicality remained because Venice's last outpost, Crete, was still resisting the Turks. It is likely that job-hunting rather than enthusiasm for a crusade explained the willingness of two authors, Antonio Cornazzano and Paolo Marsi, to write about the disaster.[235] And even when we are dealing with printed works by prominent figures who were undeniably promoters of crusading, we can make no assumptions about why they took them to the printer or even if they were responsible for that process. In this regard, Bessarion's two *Orationes ad principes christianos contra Turcos* are a salutary lesson. They were printed at Venice by Christophorus Valdarfer in 1471 in an Italian translation by Ludovico Carbone, who had somehow managed to get hold of a text of the original. Like Cornazzano and Marsi, Carbone was looking for employment, in his case with Borso d'Este, duke of Ferrara, to whom he addressed the preface. Bessarion seems to have had no say in this translation or its publication. More importantly, the spring of 1471 witnessed the printing of Bessarion's original Latin text at Paris through the initiative of the university professor Guillaume Fichet. Bessarion had sent Fichet a transcript of the orations, but he had not suggested the idea of printing it. There is a strong argument for both Carbone and Fichet taking the action that they did largely as a means of self-promotion, though in Fichet's case, as we shall see, one motivation was the same advocacy of crusade that had been Bessarion's own goal in composing the texts.[236]

Meserve's argument that Carbone and Fichet piggy-backed on Bessarion's reputation in 1471 helped contribute to her conclusion that 'men of letters, not governments, were the first to recognize the advantages that print could bring'.[237] Her view sees Bessarion in effect being used by others, though he twice expressed his warm thanks to Fichet,[238] and probably was not unhappy at the appearance of Carbone's translation. Dan Mureşan has taken issue with Meserve's views, setting out a case for Bessarion playing a key role in the editions of both Carbone and

---

[233] Meserve, 'News', *passim*. [234] Ibid. 458. [235] Ibid. 465–6.
[236] Ibid. 468–71. [237] Ibid. 471.
[238] *Cent-dix lettres grecques de François Filelfe*, ed. Émile Legrand (Paris, 1892), 236–7.

Fichet. For Mureșan, this constituted evidence that the aged cardinal recognized from the start the potential that printing possessed for disseminating the message to which he had dedicated so much of his life.[239] He factors in additional perspectives, first Frederick III's summoning of a diet in December 1470, to meet at Regensburg on St George's Day 1471 to address the Turkish threat, and secondly the death of Paul II on 26 July 1471. Mureșan argues that both Carbone and Fichet acted on Bessarion's assumption that they would steer the *Orationes* into print: located as they were at the leading cities outside Germany for the burgeoning technology, they did not need to be instructed, especially since both men were sent copies of Bessarion's printed response of 1469 to George of Trebizond, his virtuosic *In calumniatorem Platonis*. Bessarion's hope was that Fichet would have copies of the *Orationes* ready for the Regensburg diet, enabling his detailed arguments to shape the discussions of the envoys there in the same way that the circulation of manuscript copies in Italy had been intended to win over the peninsula's rulers. And Mureșan links the dating of Carbone's translation, for which the *proemion* was composed between 26 July and 19 August 1471, to the group of individuals who were lobbying for Bessarion's election as Pope. In the event, although Regensburg hosted a sizable cluster of Bessarion's supporters who naturally found the circumstances propitious for their advocacy, the brevity of the 1471 conclave (26 July to 9 August) meant that the pro-Bessarion campaign barely got off the ground before news reached the diet of Sixtus IV's election.

The flaw in Mureșan's interpretation of events in 1470–1 is the lack of direct evidence pointing to Bessarion's direction of what Carbone and Fichet did with his text. In any case, it must be asked, what could printing contribute at this point that was both new and helpful for the dissemination of the crusading message? Fichet's edition of the *Orationes* is the clearest indication of how closely printing for the elites clung to traditional manuscript formulae and techniques. The print run may not even have reached three figures and Fichet maintained individuality by varying rubrication and decoration from copy to copy. The most splendid surviving copies are those that Fichet presented to Edward IV of England, Emperor Frederick III, and Duke Ludwig of Bavaria. Edward's copy was printed entirely on vellum and richly decorated; the miniature on the first page shows Fichet handing the text to the seated monarch, encouraged by its aged author, who carries a cross in his right hand. The copies intended for emperor and duke were alike downgraded to paper, and while Frederick's prefatory letter is printed on vellum, Ludwig's, also on vellum, is in manuscript. The key marks of distinction were the use of vellum and the amount of decoration. By contrast, the decision to employ print or manuscript was largely down to convenience, hence Fichet's use of print for the prefatory letters in the copies presented to Edward and Frederick: since he was largely recycling the text of the manuscript letter written for Louis XI's copy, having it set up in type gained economies of scale (albeit marginal ones) over copying the same letter twice.

---

[239] '…absolument conscient de l'importance radicale apportée par la révolution de l'imprimerie': Mureșan, 'Les Oraisons', at note 11.

Arguably the main advantage of printing for Fichet was speed, and it carried a price in the shape of the mistakes that he and his 'assembly line of rubricators and illuminators' occasionally made in producing their various combinations of material, text, and decoration. Each one was different.[240]

The individuality of Fichet's output in 1470–1 is at its most striking in his prefatory letters. Here he faced the challenge of matching Bessarion's call to crusade with each recipient's background, viewpoint, and potential to assist. On the whole his knowledge and versatility are admirable. To Charles the Bold he wrote that crusading was in his blood. The key reference points were his grandfather John's heroism at Nicopolis, the aspirations of his father Philip the Good, and more broadly the heroes of past crusading; Charles had the resources and military experience to surpass them all.[241] Amedeo of Savoy and his brothers were reminded of their dynastic claims in Cyprus, Armenia, and Jerusalem, as well as their (mythical) Macedonian origins.[242] The church of Pamplona conjured up Roncevaux and Roland.[243] For the Cistercians, Fichet called to mind St Bernard's preaching of the Second Crusade at Vézelay,[244] while the Franciscans and Dominicans were reminded of their great preachers,[245] the Carmelites of the Muslim occupation of Mount Carmel,[246] and the Augustinians of the loss of North Africa and Louis IX's ill-fated Tunis crusade.[247] The Carthusians caused Fichet to reference Peter the Hermit, and the clergy of Lyons were reminded that two Church councils had convened in their city.[248] The prefaces are elegant and to the point, and there is no reason to cast doubt on Fichet's altruism as an enthusiast for the crusade. But Meserve has pointed to a number of other motivations lying behind his initiative and hard work: it was a chance to showcase his own ability, to bask in Bessarion's reflected prestige, and to pave the way for his own move to Rome, escaping a Paris that had become uncongenial for him.[249]

The lesson to be learnt from the reception of the news of Negroponte's fall in the emerging print culture of the early 1470s is that change was gradual and largely accommodated within familiar parameters; it was evolutionary rather than revolutionary. Within a generation Europe would experience the *Turcica*: the corpus of orations, treatises, alliances, newsletters, ballads, prophecies, doggerel, and woodcuts produced to feed the public's insatiable curiosity about the Turks and their rulers.[250] In his magisterial study of the topic, Carl Göllner showed how every conceivable response towards the Turks found its expression in this explosion of printed output.[251] Arguably, its greatest impact on the promotion of crusading lay

---

[240] Meserve, 'Patronage', pp. 537–70 for a full and admirable discussion of the subject: the illustration of Edward IV's copy is at 545.
[241] *Cent-dix lettres*, 260–2, no 17.   [242] Ibid. 262–8, no 18.
[243] Ibid. 272–4, no 22.   [244] Ibid. 274–6, no 23.
[245] Ibid. 276–9, nos 24–5, and see also Meserve, 'Patronage', 559, for Fichet's technique.
[246] *Cent-dix lettres*, 282–3, no 27.   [247] Ibid. 280–2.
[248] Ibid. 285–6, 288–9, nos 29, 31.
[249] Meserve, 'Patronage', 564–8.   [250] *Turcica, passim*.
[251] Carl Göllner, *Turcica, III. Band, Die Türkenfrage in der öffentlichen Meinung Europas im 16. Jahrhundert* (Bucharest and Baden-Baden, 1978).

in the way it facilitated the work of those who were charged with managing crusade preaching, especially collecting money in exchange for indulgences. Detailed guidelines for preachers (*avisamenta* or *summariae*) came to be printed as a matter of course. While such advice had existed since the time of Innocent III, the speed with which the operation could now be effected meant that preaching campaigns could proceed more rapidly and that those in charge could be confident that their agents were properly briefed. They had no excuse for inefficient or fraudulent behaviour, though we shall see that the solution was far from total. At the same time, large-scale print runs of confessional letters and indulgence receipts became part and parcel of the campaigns. Thus we find that Alexander VI's bull of June 1500 levying a crusade tenth was printed,[252] that the Pope authorized the printing of his key crusading bull of October 1500 by Raymond Perault at accredited presses for the purposes of his legation,[253] and that in December 1501 the *Reichsregiment* laid down the specifications to be applied in the confessional letters that Perault was authorized to have printed, including their number.[254] Like the *Reichsregiment*, Perault and Maximilian seem to have been alert to the opportunities offered by printing. Impressed by the oration given about the crusade by the Milanese envoy, Jason Maynus, in March 1494, Perault took steps to get it into print at Basel before the year was out.[255] A number of incunabula lists and collections testify to the heavy use that the cardinal made of printing in the course of his preaching campaigns.[256] His collectors carried thousands of confessional letters with them, which would have been impossible before printing.[257] As for Maximilian, Stephan Füssel has emphasized that printing held its place together with proclamation and pulpit in the emperor-elect's arsenal of techniques for disseminating and justifying his policy on the Turks, and the fiscal demands that it necessitated.[258] And Larry Silver has shown how woodcuts showing Maximilian as St George featured in the attention that he gave to visual imagery.[259] In a particularly striking, and somewhat rash, gesture, two printed works that appeared almost at the end of Maximilian's reign seem to have incorporated his continuing aspirations to lead Christendom in a crusade. The elaborate printed edition by Schönsperger of Maximilian's autobiographical verse romance, *Theuerdank*, included three blank pages for Chapter 117 that probably signified the as yet unrealized crusade.[260] And Albrecht Dürer's

---

[252] *AR*, no 14158 (noting Strasbourg copy); text in Burchard, *Liber*, 2.220–4.
[253] *AR*, no 14471. [254] Ibid. no 15834.
[255] Stephan Füssel, 'Die Funktionalisierung der "Türkenfurcht" in der Propaganda Kaiser Maximilians I.', in *OEEH*, 9–30, at 22.
[256] *Codex documentorum*, 288–9, no 215, 300–1, no 226, 304–6, nos 228–9, 312–14, nos 231–4, 421–3, no 291, 426–7, nos 295–7; *Notes et extraits*, 5th ser., 153, 172; *DS*, 640–8, no 1513, 653–62, no 1521; *Turcica*, 20–1, nos 3–6, 25–6, nos 14–16, 27–8, no 19, pp. 28–9, no 21, 29–30, no 24, 32, no 27.
[257] *DS*, 670–1, no 1529.
[258] Füssel, 'Funktionalisierung', *passim*.
[259] Larry Silver, *Marketing Maximilian: The Visual Ideology of a Holy Roman Emperor* (Princeton and Oxford, 2008), 109–45, and see too Stephan Füssel, *Emperor Maximilian and the Media of his Day: The Theuerdank of 1517, a Cultural-Historical Introduction* (Cologne, 2003); *Theuerdank*, facs. of 1517 edn (Cologne, 2003).
[260] Silver, *Marketing*, 118.

woodcut for Maximilian's Arch of Honour ended with an empty space that probably also represented the deferred but still hoped-for expedition.[261]

On crusading matters, as in everything else of public concern, the authorities tried to control printing's capacity for promoting subversion, whether overt or potential. Perault's mobilization of the presses to advertise his grievances against Maximilian in the early months of 1504 forms the clearest example of this. Following his clashes with the emperor-elect over the disposition of the money that he had collected for a crusade against the Turks, the exhausted legate spent thirteen weeks at Strasbourg. Here, comfortably lodging with the Knights of St John, he enjoyed the company of like-minded reformers and humanists, including Geiler von Kaysersberg and Sebastian Brant, celebrated author of *The Ship of Fools*. It is possible that they persuaded Perault to clear his name before leaving the empire, though it is likely that he needed little encouragement to publicize both his opinions and his indignation. Strasbourg abounded in presses and he was able to mount what can only be described as a sustained campaign of publication to establish his innocence and (by implication), the emperor-elect's double-dealing. Perault's polemical broadsheets (*Streit-* or *Flugschriften*) began in January and ended in March. By that point, Gebhard Mehring observed, he had stated his case in full and saw no reason to produce any more. He could focus on sending them with accompanying letters to people who might be won over.[262] Some of what Perault printed was effectively private correspondence with Maximilian, so he was engaging in a shocking breach of protocol. The emperor-elect took vigorous steps to muzzle the printers. On 18 March 1504 he wrote to the burgomaster and council at Strasbourg to complain about the output from their city. No doubt, he commented diplomatically, this was being done without their knowledge, but it must stop. The printers responsible were guilty of *lèse-majesté*, which was punishable by execution and the seizure of all their property. Maximilian ordered their arrest and the impounding of their goods, as well as the detention of anybody found disseminating the pamphlets.[263] Clearly, Maximilian was concerned about the consequences of Perault's *Flugschriften*: on the same day he requested Duke Albrecht of Bavaria to pay no attention to their content and to imprison anybody caught spreading them.[264] Strasbourg proved unresponsive to his complaint, and on 3 April he had to write again in much tougher language: they had three days to stop affording Perault protection so as to get him out of imperial territory.[265] Nonetheless, it was only in late April that Perault travelled southwards to Basel.

It is tempting to argue that Maximilian's enthusiasm for print and the visual media as ways of projecting a favourable image of himself and his activities made him overreact to the situation created by Perault in 1504. Could the circulation of a few broadsheets really inflict damage on imperial authority? The answer is that they could. Simply in terms of internal opinion, the cardinal's broadsheets could

---

[261] Füssel, 'Funktionalisierung', 26 and illus. at 27; Füssel, *Emperor Maximilian*, 19, 86. While this is improvable, and looks like a remarkable gift to Maximilian's critics, it was not out of character.
[262] Mehring, 'Peraudi', 381–90.   [263] *AR*, no 18415.
[264] Ibid. no 18416.   [265] Ibid. no 18500.

stimulate resistance towards the handing over of crusade funds deposited in chests; and it offered fresh arguments to groups that were already opposed to Maximilian's authority. In July Perault himself, addressing the Swiss confederates at Lucerne, commented bitterly if obliquely that certain princes whom he had once considered to be friends of Christendom had shown themselves more favourable to the Turks. His audience would have been highly receptive.[266] And there were specific reasons in the spring of 1504 for Maximilian to be anxious. In late March he started his own publicity campaign to crank up enthusiasm for the latest version of his *societas Sancti Georgii*.[267] It is safe to say that, given his low credit rating on crusading issues, this was already a rather fragile venture, so the simultaneous circulation of Peraultian *Flugschriften* was the last thing he wanted to see. In May, moreover, Pope Julius II's authorized the diversion of the assembled indulgence money for use against the Venetians. This appeared to confirm all that Perault had said in print, and it naturally added to Maximilian's sensitivity on the subject; on 18 May he wrote again to Duke Albrecht urging him to detain people spreading Perault's troublesome texts.[268] In his essay on Perault's Strasbourg *Flugschriften*, Francis Rapp concluded by citing Perault's warning to a papal consistory that there would be a disastrous breach unless papal relations with Germany were mended. Just a few months later, Rapp noted, Luther entered the Augustinian order at Erfurt.[269] The link that Rapp made between Perault and Luther in terms of the need for reforming measures could equally well be applied to the way both men grasped the potential of the press. Obviously Luther's embrace of print culture had far greater consequences, but Perault and his contemporaries had shown what could be done. Perault's preaching campaign in Germany had demonstrated that nothing, printing included, could save the crusade: but the press could disseminate Perault's views on what had gone wrong and why, thereby adding to the problems of the man whom he held chiefly responsible for his failure.

---

[266] Mehring, 'Peraudi', 390–1. [267] *AR*, no 18449. [268] Ibid. no 18775.
[269] Francis Rapp, 'La fin décevante d'une campagne d'indulgences: le cardinal Péraud à Strasbourg (1504)', in Jean Kerhervé and Albert Rigaudière, eds, *Finances, pouvoirs et mémoire: Mélanges offerts à Jean Favier* (Paris, 1999), 578–86, at 586.

6
Indulgences and the crusade against the Turks

In February 1492 bonfires were lit in Rome, and jousting and bull fighting staged, to celebrate a momentous Christian victory over an Islamic power.[1] The defeated enemy were not the Ottoman Turks but the Moors, the occasion the fall of Granada and the end of a ten-year war that itself brought to a close the protracted narrative of the Iberian *Reconquista*. As Miguel Ladero Quesada showed, the raising of specie through the systematic distribution of indulgences was integral to the financing of the Granada war.[2] It is hard to believe that advocates of crusading against the Ottomans did not observe with interest the way the crown of Castile was adapting the mechanisms of crusade to the novel requirements of warfare in the later fifteenth century, but it is difficult to know how far they accurately gauged its success. The principal historian of the Iberian *bula de la cruzada*, Jose Goñi Gaztambide, charted the series of largely unsuccessful attempts made by the papal *curia* under Sixtus IV and Innocent VIII to secure a fixed proportion of the proceeds of the Granada indulgences for their war against the Turks,[3] but we cannot infer from this that the Popes anticipated rich pickings: their policy could reflect the *curia*'s adherence to an inclusive view of the various theatres of warfare against Islam, the high costs of the anti-Turkish struggle, and (more crudely) the application of the *do ut des* principle in its management of financial negotiations with secular rulers. It is striking that in 1500 the French crown assessed the income from the Jubilee indulgence in Spain at only 80,000 ducats, which seems a remarkable underestimate, though there are various possible explanations for that.[4] But irrespective of what contemporaries made of developments in the Iberian peninsula, it is worth keeping in mind the successful deployment there of indulgences to fund warfare, as we analyse the concerted attempt that was made to do the same thing in the East. Our agenda in this chapter will be threefold.[5] First, we shall assemble a picture of what, in economic terms, would be defined as 'the product and its marketing'. One key aspect of this discussion will be Raymond Perault's role: was he as innovative and influential as he has commonly been depicted, or did he simply take to their logical conclusion developments that were already well under way? Secondly, an attempt

---

[1] Setton, *Papacy*, 2.422–4.
[2] Miguel Angel Ladero Quesada, *Castilla y la conquista del reino de Granada* (Valladolid, 1967), 201–13.
[3] Goñi Gaztambide, *Historia,* ch. 13 *passim*. See also Ladero Quesada, *Castilla*, 212.
[4] Sanuto, *I diarii*, 3.870–1 (= *AR*, no 14436).
[5] For the immediate context see my 'Indulgences', *passim*; and for the broader context the whole collection, which valuably updates the fundamental study by Paulus, *Geschichte*.

must be made to assess the financial returns, not just quantitatively but also qualitatively, in terms of their character and processing. Obviously, the popularity of indulgences and the criticism that they generated will form part of this analysis. The third area of discussion is best defined as 'control and retention', and the focus here will be on Perault's sustained attempt in 1501–3 to ensure that the money he had raised in the lands of the empire should be spent solely on the crusade against the Turks. He failed, but the reasons for that failure are complex and revealing.

6.1 *EA BULLA, QUAM CRUCIATAM DICIMUS*[6]: THE CHARACTER AND ADMINISTRATION OF CRUSADE INDULGENCES

The core spiritual benefit granted to the recipient of a crusade indulgence was the remission of penance due for all the sins that he or she had committed. The idea of a simple exchange or substitution can be misleading. In the first place, penitential practices were still sometimes followed. When crusade was formally associated with Jubilee, as was increasingly the case, the procedure was to transplant the Jubilee requirements (i.e. those set in lieu of personal visits to the Roman basilicas) as far as possible to the recipient's religious milieu. So when Sixtus IV granted the Jubilee indulgence to the port of Ragusa and its hinterland in 1476 for the dual purpose of repairing the city's walls and assisting the crusade, he set out in detail the churches to be visited, and the psalms and prayers to be recited.[7] The bishop of Marcana was given the job of appointing confessors who would allocate penance and dispense from various vows 'to be commuted for the work of the holy crusade'.[8] The grant was renewed three years later on the basis of Ragusa's ongoing vulnerability to Turkish attack, but it seems that the penitential framework modelled on the Jubilee was now considered superfluous.[9] Even when the crusade indulgence was not overtly associated with a Jubilee, creating a penitential ethos was deemed to be important, presumably in order to raise sensitivity to the message that was being conveyed. Normally, this ethos was a collective one, characterized by crowds attending sermons or taking part in processions. When the Dominican, Giovanni da Napoli, preached at Florence in October 1455 'great processions numbering as many as 6,000 people were formed in the four quarters of the city, with the people dressed in white bearing a red cross on their breasts'.[10] It was common practice to organize processions in response to disasters, as at Rome and

---

[6] Giovanni da Castiglione, bishop of Pavia and papal legate at the diet of Regensburg, May 1454: *Deutsche Reichstagsakten... 1453–1454*, 273.
[7] Seven penitential psalms 3 times 'cum letanis, aut sexagesies dominicam orationem cum angelica salutatione': *Vetera monumenta Slavorum*, 503–5, no 678.
[8] Ironically, the vows subject to dispensation by these confessors excluded the major pilgrimages, so believers who had made a vow to visit Rome would still have to do so, unless they secured dispensation through another channel.
[9] *Vetera monumenta Slavorum*, 515–16, no 686, valid for as long as the danger lasted.
[10] Black, *Accolti*, 245.

Venice in 1470 when news arrived of the fall of Negroponte.[11] And of course the 'buzz' generated by the imminent arrival of charismatic preachers created an atmosphere that powerfully facilitated their work: Cristoforo da Soldo painted a vivid picture of the excitement building up at Brescia in February 1451 as Giovanni da Capistrano approached, 'because he was such an excellent and holy preacher, who performed miracles in healing the sick'.[12]

Nor did this collective response necessarily end when the indulgence itself was conferred. In essence of course this was an individual act, covering the penance due for sins committed and confessed in full. As surviving receipts from Sweden for 1460–1 demonstrate, a chosen confessor was given the right to grant absolution twice: once at the time of delivery and again at the point of death. In theory, therefore, no further indulgence would ever be required, though this is to assume an overly arithmetical approach on the part of the recipient. The formula of absolution given in these receipts is commendably clear and merits reproduction in full:

> May our lord Jesus Christ absolve you through the merit of his most holy Passion; and by the authority of the same lord Jesus Christ and the blessed apostles Peter and Paul, and the apostolic see, entrusted to me in this matter, I absolve you from all sentence of excommunication, suspension, and interdict, as well as from any ecclesiastical penalties and censures imposed by law or by man. In addition I absolve you from all irregularity that you may have contracted, with the exception of bigamy or murder, and I restore you to the sacraments of the Church and to the union of the faithful, and readmit you to all the processes of the Church. Furthermore I absolve you of all your criminal sins and excesses, no matter how serious, provided that you are contrite and have confessed them, and those you have forgotten, including those cases which are specifically or generally reserved for the apostolic see. And I remit all punishments (*penas*) due in this life and in purgatory, and grant you on this occasion that full remission of sins which it is the Church's custom to bestow on those setting out to recover the Holy Land or going to Rome at the time of a Jubilee.[13]

Individual then, but as these Swedish receipts also reveal, groups too could benefit. Just as the inhabitants of religious houses all stood to gain if they combined their resources to send a soldier to fight,[14] so they could receive the indulgence *en masse* as part of a single transaction.[15] The same applied to kinship groups, with numerous examples surviving of families benefiting from the indulgence.[16] Gabriele Rangoni, whom Sixtus IV sent as nuncio to Hungary in August 1474 with full legatine powers, was allowed to negotiate on indulgences with 'urban communities and the populations of towns and [other] places'.[17] In 1502 Bianca Sforza,

---

[11] Meserve, 'News', 448–9.
[12] Festa, ed., 'Cinque lettere', 7–58, at 8, note 1. Generally on Capistrano's technique see Ottó Gecser, 'Preaching and Publicness: St John of Capestrano and the Making of his Charisma North of the Alps', in Katherine L. Jansen and Miri Rubin, eds, *Charisma and Religious Authority: Jewish, Christian, and Muslim Preaching, 1200–1500* (Turnhout, 2010), 145–59.
[13] *DS*, 459–60, no 1305.
[14] e.g. Mohler, ed., 'Instruktion', 343: 10 religious to provide 1 fighter.
[15] e.g. *Codex documentorum*, 421–3, no 291; *DS*, 464, no 1313, 473, no 1325, 478–9, no 1332. See also Jensen, *Denmark*, 124–7.
[16] e.g. *DS*, 460, no 1306, 467–8, no 1319.   [17] *BF*, NS2.261–3, no 619.

Maximilian's wife, secured concessions for no fewer than 500 individuals in her entourage.[18] Even the dead stood to gain, thanks to the extension of the indulgence to those suffering in purgatory, though we find surprisingly little resonance of this remarkable concession in the sources.[19]

Like the Jubilee, the *cruciata* was a 'special time' in the devotional lives of these individuals and communities. The spring of 1464, when the response to Pius II's preaching was excited and widespread, was described in one indulgence receipt as the 'time of the holy crusade'.[20] The normal pattern of devotional life was suspended and new opportunities arose. As some years earlier in Sweden, Rangoni in 1474 received among his *amplissimas facultates* the privilege of granting absolution for sins that were normally reserved for the Pope's own court: among them were homicide, apostasy, simony, and repeated trade in prohibited goods with non-Christians.[21] But if doors opened for some, they shut for others because, in common with the Jubilee, the crusade usually entailed the temporary suspension of other indulgences. In 1474 the only exception in Rangoni's theatre of operations was indulgences granted against the heretics of Bohemia (*rei Bohemicae*), the reason for this being that Bohemia also came within Rangoni's brief: he was even allowed to dispose of the property of heretics.[22] Naturally, this caused dissatisfaction among those charged with managing other good causes,[23] and bouts of confusion on the part of the *curia* did nothing to help. In April 1481 Sixtus IV had to clarify the situation regarding the hospital of St Anthony at Vienna and the indulgences that were being preached for the recovery of Otranto. He confirmed that the hospital's indulgences remained valid, not just because of the importance of its work for the poor and infirm, and because its indulgences were not plenary ones in any case, but also due to an oversight which had led to its inadvertent inclusion in the letters for Otranto.[24]

The management of these complex operations called for the creation of a middle management tier between Pope and preachers, and German scholars have dubbed its elite practitioners *Ablasskommissaren* ('indulgence commissioners'). A precise definition of the term is elusive, not least because the status and responsibilities of such individuals varied considerably: for all the sweeping powers that he enjoyed in 1474, Rangoni was less an *Ablasskommissar* than a high-level diplomat, a trusted agent of Pope and king. The most we can say is that certain people involved in promoting the crusade have left traces of exceptional expertise, less as hands-on preachers in the mould of Capistrano and the others examined in the previous chapter, than as managers of the process of assembling and transferring funds for the crusade. Arguably, the earliest example is Mariano de Senis, whom Calixtus sent to Croatia, Hungary, Serbia, and Bosnia in 1457 to raise men and money. He was allowed to assemble a team of two or three others, and Calixtus referred specifically to Paul of Ragusa and

---

[18] *AR*, no 19621.
[19] See Schneider, *Peraudi*, 103, note 3 for the way it was managed by Perault.
[20] *Acta Bosnae*, 259, no 1086.   [21] *BF*, NS2.261–3, no 619, at 262.
[22] Ibid. 260–1, no 618.   [23] e.g. ibid. 706, no 1410.   [24] *BF*, NS3.711–12, no 1419.

Nicholas of Srebrenica.[25] In 1459 Mariano was largely responsible for liaison with King Stephen of Bosnia, preaching the cross, collecting money, and checking whether *crucesignati* were fit for purpose, removing the crosses from those who were not. He had other, typical privileges that included channelling towards the crusade unclear legacies (*legata incerta*) and fines imposed on usurers and other 'unjust profits'.[26] One biographer claimed that Mariano signed many of his audience with the cross.[27] But a more convincing candidate in terms of both range and volume of activity is Marinus de Fregeno, whose career was described in detail by Klaus Voigt.[28] Marinus, who seems to have originated from Fergino near Spoleto,[29] received his first crusade commission in 1457, covering Denmark, Sweden, Norway, and northern Germany.[30] He returned to the north in 1459, and his energetic work in Sweden is reflected in the numerous indulgence letters that he issued there. He had quarrels with various secular rulers as well as with the *curia*, which in 1465 instituted a manhunt for him;[31] but he was rehabilitated, and in 1471 packed off again to preach the crusade in the north.[32] In 1478 Marinus was appointed to the Pomeranian see of Kammin but its chapter deposed him in 1481 on the grounds of greed, and he died the following year.[33]

Marinus is interesting in part because his service to the crusade spanned two decades, bridging the worlds of Calixtus III and Pius II on the one hand, and Sixtus IV on the other. In a number of respects he also prefigured Perault. He was an abrasive, controversial, probably venal individual, but also energetic and capable: he enjoyed the confidence of Christian I of Denmark, who hoped to use the crusade as leverage to enforce his rule in Sweden.[34] In two decades Marinus raised over 18,000 florins for the struggle against the Turks, an impressive return when one takes into account the region's economic profile. His success can be attributed in part to the preparatory work that he undertook for his visits and the knowledge that he accumulated about his audience. We have already witnessed him entering into specific detail in 1472 about the way the Turks were threatening Germany,[35] and in the same letter he instructed the bishop of Lübeck to ensure that the new indulgences were publicized by the secular clergy in advance of Marinus's own arrival, so that the faithful were primed about them. The arrival of a papal nuncio, he reminded the Danish town of Ribe in 1474, was akin to that of Christ. His emphasis in both letters on the clergy's duty to save souls and on the heavy responsibility they would carry if they failed to rise to that task, may indicate that Marinus

---

[25] *AM* 13.9–13.   [26] Ibid. 138–40.
[27] Dionisio Pulinari, *Cronache dei Frati Minori della provincia di Toscana*, ed. S. Mencherini (Arezzo, 1913), 269–70.
[28] Voigt, 'Kollektor', *passim*.   [29] Ibid. 158, note 21.   [30] *DS,* 411–19, nos 1262–8.
[31] Ibid. 501–3, nos 1359–60.   [32] Ibid. 537–50, nos 1405–10.
[33] M. Wehrmann, 'Bischof Marinus von Kammin (1479–1482). Ein Italiener auf dem Kamminer Bischofsstuhle', *Baltische Studien*, ns 18 (1914), 118–60.
[34] For details see Jensen, *Denmark, ad indicem*, esp. 83–103; Klaus Voigt, *Italienische Berichte aus dem spätmittelalterlichen Deutschland. Von Francesco Petrarca zu Andrea de' Franceschi (1333–1492)* (Stuttgart, 1973), 186–8 provides a handy *resumé*.
[35] Above, ch 2, at note 32.

expected resistance, which he was fully prepared to quash.[36] Most importantly, Marinus was observant. Probably in 1479 he wrote a *Descriptio provinciarum Alamanorum*, a detailed *tour d'horizon* of the contemporary German principalities and cities. He pulled no punches about the behaviour of certain rulers, and his concluding remarks about religious and social customs in Germany were astute as well as colourful. Hence: Germans took their religion seriously, attending mass daily, and kneeling or standing throughout. Strolling around the church, sampling different sermons, and joking were all anathema to them. They regarded people who neglected to fast rigorously as hardly worthy of the name of Christian, though this was less true of southern Germany. Italians had to be careful how they behaved, because while Germans warmed to charming and lively people, they did not like joking or word play for the sake of it. Praising them for their good qualities, especially honesty, religious zeal, cleverness, prudence, and maturity, was a more sure way to win them over than threats. In almost every religious order they esteemed the Observant branch rather than the Conventual one.[37] There was much more, and it reflects the fact that by this point, success for prototypical *Ablasskommissaren* like Marinus depended on weighing up their audience as well as having an attractive sheaf of privileges in their luggage and a worthy cause to promote. It is a text that one can easily imagine Perault producing and it is regrettable that he did not write something similar.

There is no evidence that Marinus wrote his *Descriptio* for his crusade preachers or that any of them profited from it.[38] But by 1479 those charged with the management of preaching had for some time been producing guides for their agents, and these form a rich source of information both for the process of crusade preaching and for the way in which the privileges available to the faithful were meant to be interpreted and communicated.[39] Two are worth noting for the pre-Perault period. The first, which has attracted a good deal of attention not least due to its author's fame, is the set of instructions that Bessarion compiled for his preachers in Venice and its *terraferma* in August 1463.[40] Bessarion's instructions are valuable evidence for two different reasons. In the first place, the opening section, which suggests themes to be developed in the preaching of the indulgences, is one of the best examples of how new motifs derived from the humanist approach towards crusading were integrated with more traditional rhetoric.[41] Secondly, but equally importantly, the instructions form a remarkably detailed guide to procedural issues.

---

[36] *DS*, 549–50, no 1410 (Lübeck); Jensen, *Denmark*, 110 (Ribe).

[37] Voigt, 'Kollektor', 199–202; id., *Berichte*, 191–3.

[38] Voigt, 'Kollektor', 169–72, argues convincingly that the recipient was Cardinal Auxias de Podio, sent as legate to the Nürnberg diet of 1479.

[39] For good English examples see Robert Swanson, 'Crusade Administration in Fifteenth-Century England: Regulations for the Distribution of Indulgences in 1489', *Historical Research*, 84 (2011), 183–8; id., 'Preaching Crusade in Fifteenth-Century England: Instructions for the Administration of the Anti-Hussite Crusade of 1429 in the Diocese of Canterbury', *Crusades*, forthcoming.

[40] Mohler, ed., 'Instruktion'.

[41] In this respect it is instructive to compare Bessarion's 1463 instructions with his 1459 Mantua oration: *Anecdota veneta*, 276–83.

They include the text not just of the liturgical formulae that were to be used when absolving the penitent, but also the letters to be given them, with variant wording based on their going in person (with or without taking the cross),[42] and despatching surrogates. This detail extends to the use of thread to sew a cross made of red silk or cotton to the chest of each *crucesignandus*. Yet this particular detail establishes the atypical nature of Bessarion's approach, for the vast majority of crusade preaching had by this point moved away from personal participation or even surrogacy towards donations of money or goods. In fact, the volume of detail relating to taking the cross establishes Bessarion's text as rather archaic in its approach. Although, as we have seen, it accorded with the Pope's own encouragement of personal service in 1463–4, it was at odds not just with more general trends but also with Venetian policy regarding the management of its war against the Turks, which is strange given that on most issues Bessarion's thinking was so closely in tune with that of the city's patriciate.

The second guide was issued by Angelo Carletti, one of the most effective Observant preachers of the crusade. Carletti was appointed 'apostolic nuncio and commissioner for the preaching of the crusade' to recover Otranto in December 1480.[43] To assist his agents he wrote and printed a 'declaration or interpretation', passing on the results of his own discussion with Pope Sixtus.[44] Even though the crusade had come closer to home, making it easier for individuals to take the cross to fight, we are in a different world from the one that generated Bessarion's 1463 text. The list of points concerns itself with precisely when, how, and under what terms the indulgences and its associated privileges could be granted. For example, a date should be set in each area covered, by which a contribution should normally be made; but latecomers had until the octave of Corpus Christ to make their payment. Furthermore, preachers should specify a date, such as Easter, by which confession must be made in order to enjoy the indulgence. On the incessantly vexatious issue of whether absolution could be bestowed from sins so serious that they were normally reserved for the Pope's court, the ruling was that the penitent could be absolved from these by a chosen confessor on one occasion only, whereas they could be absolved from non-reserved sins 'as often and whenever they want, so that they never again have to go to the bishop on any matter'. This seems to have been regarded as creating an open season for recidivist usury, for Carletti ruled that in such cases repeated absolution was not allowed. Attention was also given to the storing of collected money. For centuries the standard procedure had been the use of chests equipped with multiple locks, to discourage fraud; but if this technique did not guarantee security, the proceeds could be entrusted to reliable individuals, provided detailed accounts were kept. These and the text's many other rulings afford a clear picture of a conscientious preacher setting out guidelines that would be comprehensive, workable, and pastorally sound.

---

[42] Presumably 'hii qui non sumunt crucem et vadunt' are substitutes.
[43] *BF*, NS2.684, no 1367.
[44] Viora, 'Angelo Carletti', with text at 326–9.

When Carletti and his team were preaching their indulgences for Otranto, the most famous *Ablasskommissar* was already starting to make his mark. Raymond Perault was born in 1435 at Surgères in the diocese of Saintes. He achieved his doctorate in theology at the Sorbonne and in 1476 was appointed dean of Saintes Cathedral. In the same year he was commissioned to preach indulgences with the twin goals of restoring the cathedral's fabric and supporting the crusade. Such a division of profits was a typical Sixtine tactic: a way to persuade local agencies to release at least some of the collected cash or, as in this case, an incentive to apply to the administration of indulgences a zeal for the cause that otherwise might have been in short supply. If the latter consideration shaped Sixtus's approach in 1476 it was ironic because, over the course of the quarter century that followed his appointment, Perault showed himself more committed to crusading than any of the Popes whom he served. The Saintes indulgence, which lasted until 1488, was notable as the first occasion when indulgences were preached for the dead, at least outside the special circumstances of Iberia. Perault showed skill in interpreting this innovation; his talent was recognized and his star began to rise. He went to Rome as protonotary in 1482 and in 1486 embarked on his first tour of the empire preaching the crusade, which was now detached from the needs of Saintes. Perault became a familiar figure in Germany and he won the trust of Frederick III, who in 1488 appointed him procurator and orator for imperial business at the *curia*. In 1491 he was given the Carinthian see of Gurk, an appropriate choice for a crusading enthusiast, and the bestowal of the cardinal's hat two years later was a concession to Frederick. Perault's origins and political neutrality qualified him to act as a bridge-builder between France and the empire, but he could achieve nothing in this regard in the atmosphere of ubiquitous distrust that followed Charles VIII's descent into Italy in 1494. He was both repelled by and isolated at the court of Alexander VI. His third legation to Germany, in 1501–4, was his last preaching tour and we shall see that it was plagued by tensions created by the interaction of major currents of political contention. Nonetheless, Perault's management of crusade indulgences during this legation is remarkably well documented and, overall, the volume of evidence at our disposal for his involvement in crusade preaching from the 1480s onwards makes it possible to assess his profile and contribution as *Ablasskommissar*.[45]

As long ago as 1882 Johannes Schneider, the first student of Perault's activities, advanced the claim that 'with him a new phase begins in the character of indulgences'. Schneider's verdict was upheld in 1900 by the leading historian of

---

[45] The core studies on Perault remain Schneider, *Peraudi*; Nikolaus Paulus, 'Raimund Peraudi als Ablaßkommissar', *Historisches Jahrbuch* 21 (1900), 645–82. Among more recent contributions see in particular Francis Rapp, 'Un contemporain d'Alexandre VI Borgia, le cardinal Raymond Péraud (1435–1505)', *Académie des inscriptions et belles-lettres, comptes rendus*, (1994), 665–77; and the bibliography listed in Falk Eisermann, 'The Indulgence as a Media Event: Developments in Communication through Broadsides in the Fifteenth Century', in *PNTM*, 309–30, revised and updated version of his 'Der Ablaß als Medienereignis. Kommunikationswandel durch Einblattdrucke im 15. Jahrhundert. Mit einer Auswahlbibliographie', in Rudolf Suntrup and Jan R. Veenstra, eds, *Tradition and Innovation in an Era of Change* (Frankfurt a.-Main, 2001), 99–128, at 325, note 45.

indulgences, Nikolaus Paulus, and more recently affirmed by Bernd Moeller, another distinguished student of the pre-Reformation system that Perault did so much to create.[46] When all due qualifications are made about the organic, incremental nature of changes in such a field, Perault does appear to merit this rare unanimity on the part of those who have studied the subject. Why then was he so important? Two explanations stand out: first, Perault's clarification and exposition, making full use of the printing press, of the range of benefits to be derived from indulgences; and, secondly, the performance technique which he advocated, employed, and popularized. Together they created a 'package' that contemporaries, admirers and critics alike, came to associate with Perault, and which was adopted by others in the decades that ensued. Among Perault's prolific output, a cornerstone text was the *summaria declaratio,* which he initially had printed to elucidate the Saintes indulgence.[47] Its most significant section explained what became known as the 'four graces' that each recipient gained. These were the Jubilee indulgence; the extension of that indulgence to the deceased; the right of recipients to choose their own confessors; and the eligibility of recipients and their family (both living and dead) to benefit from the full range of the Church's intercessory work.[48] The main point about the third concession was that it could be enshrined in a 'confessional letter' (*confessionale*). This stated the beneficiary's right to confess to, be absolved by, and receive the indulgence from a confessor of their choice on two occasions, the second being their (anticipated) deathbed. *Confessionalia* were effectively bonds that could be traded in at a point selected by the recipient. This eliminated the logjam of having to hear multiple confessions at the point of delivery. They could be printed in the tens of thousands,[49] with blank spaces left for the names of recipients, thereby speeding up the whole administrative process.[50] And, as Falk Eisermann pointed out, it was presumably because of the need for durability that the vast majority of known copies were printed on vellum.[51]

---

[46] For references see Housley, 'Indulgences', 286.
[47] e.g. *DS,* 653–62, no 1521 (*c.* 1489). For Perault and printing, see Eisermann, 'Indulgence', 325–30.
[48] e.g. *DS,* 663–4, no 1522 (6 January 1490, Uppsala: its recipients were 'devoti in Christo Olavus Petri cum uxore sua Ingeborgh'). The text is worth giving in full: 'ultra jubileum et alias indulgentias gratias et facultates quas Christifideles ipsi obtinere possunt visitando ecclesias per nos aut commissarios nostros deputandas ac si visitassent basilicas Urbis tempore jubilei prout in litteris apostolicis desuper confectis plenius continetur, quod possint eligere confessorem ydoneum secularem vel regularem qui semel in vita ab omnibus et singulis suis peccatis excessibus criminibus et delictis etiam sedi apostolice generaliter vel specialiter reservatis absolutionem plenissimam impendet. Ab aliis vero eidem sedi non reservatis vita eis comite totiens quotiens absolvere et in mortis articulo ac etiam totiens quotiens de eorum morte dubitatur etiam si tunc eos decedere non contingat plenissimam omnium peccatorum suorum remissionem eis impartiri valeat. Indulsit etiam sanctissimus dominus noster motu suo proprio omnes et singulos Christifideles huiusmodi ac eorum parentes et benefactores defunctos qui cum caritate decesserunt in omnibus precibus, suffragiis, missis, elemosinis, ieiuniis, orationibus, disciplinis, et ceteris omnibus spiritualibus bonis que fiunt et fieri poterunt in tota universali sacrosancta Christi ecclesia militante et omnibus membris eiusdem imperpetuum participes fieri.'
[49] e.g. ibid. 668–75, no 1529, at 670 (20,000 copies). See also Eisermann, 'Indulgence', 327 and note 50.
[50] e.g. the British Library text published in Housley, 'Indulgences', 306–7.
[51] Eisermann, 'Indulgence', 326.

What Perault did with this system was most clearly described and justified by his lieutenant (*Unterkommissar*) Johannes von Paltz (c. 1444–1511), the Augustinian preacher and theologian.[52] In 1490 Perault appointed Paltz to administer the indulgence in Thuringia, Meißen, Saxony, and Brandenburg. He served again in 1501. Following his first period of service Paltz wrote a bulky treatise on indulgences, *Coelifodina* (*The mine of heaven*), to which he added a *Supplementum* that was published in 1504.[53] As Berndt Hamm, the doyen of Paltz studies, put it, Paltz became very familiar with Peraultian practices both as theorist and as practitioner.[54] There is no evidence that he was concerned by the Turkish threat, as Perault certainly was. For Paltz, the purpose of indulgences was saving souls: 'Experience has taught us that when such massive grace is present, a preacher can achieve more with the people in a short time than he could otherwise in twenty years.'[55] He was convinced of the good fortune of his contemporaries, living as they did in the 'happy times of plenary indulgences', and he derived his colourful title *Coelifodina* from a comparison between indulgences and the silver mined from the Erzgebirge at Schneeberg in Saxony, which he saw being done when he preached there in 1490. 'For just as gold can be extracted from a gold mine and silver from a silver mine, as I once had occasion to observe at the Erzgebirge, where they are abundant, so divine grace, more precious than either, is extracted from the mine of heaven.'[56] It was an effective metaphor, with some of the resonance of those coined to describe crusading indulgences by preachers like St Bernard and Humbert of Romans. The *Supplementum*, in which Paltz responded to criticism of indulgences, was enlivened by a woodcut depicting a metaphor with a similarly contemporary edge: the fortress of faith (sc. Tower of David) was being assailed by the armies of hell, whom its angelic defenders repelled with cannon fire.[57] The real weapons deployed by Satan's host were more insidious because they destroyed belief, but to all of them Paltz set out his replies at length.

Mixed in with Paltz's theological argumentation we find much detail about the way Perault and, to a lesser extent, his *Unterkommissaren* operated, and it is consistent with the specifics that we encounter in the evidence bequeathed to the urban centres on which they focused, including Bremen, Brunswick, Erfurt, Frankfurt, Halle, and Nürnberg.[58] Their objective was to make a strong impression, or as Perault and Paltz would undoubtedly have viewed it, to communicate to audiences that were extremely familiar with indulgences the unique character of what they

---

[52] Hamm, *Frömmigkeitstheologie*.
[53] Johannes von Paltz, *Werke, 1: Coelifodina*, ed. Christoph Burger and Friedhelm Stasch, Spätmittelalter und Reformation. Texte und Untersuchungen, 2 (Berlin and New York, 1983); id., *Supplementum*.
[54] Hamm, *Frömmigkeitstheologie*, 85.
[55] Ibid. 91, note 360.   [56] Ibid. 89 note 343.
[57] Paltz, *Supplementum*, 76, based on Paltz's description at 17.
[58] See in particular the important studies by Andreas Röpcke, 'Geld und Gewissen. Raimund Peraudi und die Ablaßverkündung in Norddeutschland am Ausgang des Mittelalters', *Bremisches Jahrbuch*, 71 (1992), 43–80, and Thomas Vogtherr, 'Kardinal Raimund Peraudi als Ablaßprediger in Braunschweig (1488 und 1503)', *Braunschweigisches Jahrbuch für Landesgeschichte*, 77 (1996), 151–80. Paulus, 'Peraudi', 660, 666, covers Erfurt. Fundamental still is Schneider, *Peraudi*, 97–110.

brought with them.[59] This entailed a good deal of preparation for and management of the visit. Descriptions of Perault's visits to Bremen and Brunswick in 1503 presuppose close liaison with the civic and ecclesiastical authorities to enliven processions and services through church bells, musical instruments, choirs, improvised outdoor platforms, and richly coloured fabrics.[60] The result was truly a multi-media event that attracted crowds numbering many thousands.[61] In a sense this is no more than one would expect: lavish spectacle and display were ingrained in late medieval religion, especially in urban settings, and Perault was a cardinal, whose friendship was worth cultivating. What seems to have been Perault's unique imprint (Paltz twice uses the verb *innovare*),[62] was the installation in the cathedral or principal church, immediately in front of the high altar, of an imposing wooden cross. Its summit held a crown of thorns and over the crossbeam were hung two red silk banners depicting the papal arms, bulls of indulgence, and the switch and scourge: traditional tokens of penance.

This cross remained the focus of devotional activity throughout the visit, and Paltz described in intricate detail the liturgy that Perault devised for its erection, daily veneration, and deposition.[63] Paltz characterized its role with theological precision. The cross stood for papal authority but it also acted as a sort of spiritual lightning rod, the channel through which the accumulated merits and prayers that underpinned the doctrine of indulgences radiated outwards to penitent sinners: 'A distinctive stream makes its way down to this church from heaven, formed from the good deeds and prayers of all those people from whom indulgences derive their origin.' For that reason it was 'more efficacious than all other crosses'.[64] Together with six other designated churches, the church hosting the cross formed a devotional circuit modelled on Rome's basilicas. Provided they were physically capable, the faithful were expected to visit each church and recite the Lord's Prayer there three times, displaying their penitence through their clothing and behaviour.[65] Perault's cross was therefore instrumental in importing into even such a late and highly evolved phase of crusade promotion an element of the devotional ethos that had made up the warp and weft of earlier crusading. Surviving evidence for collective penitence at Nürnberg in 1489, Halle in 1502, and Bremen in 1503, puts living tissue on the dry bones of the papal bulls and commissarial *summariae*.[66] The confessors, who were recruited locally, were usually kept very busy.[67] One does not need to accept at face value everything that Paltz says about Perault's approach to

---

[59] For the German urban milieu encountered by Perault and his agents see the essays by Bob Scribner listed in the bibliography.
[60] Description in Housley, 'Indulgences', 292–4.
[61] According to Contarini, up to 20,000 in the Rhineland: *AR*, no 16201.
[62] Paltz, *Supplementum*, 5, 7.
[63] Ibid. 79–82 ('modus inthronizandi', 'modus observandi', 'modus depositionis').
[64] Ibid. 7.
[65] The physically incapable were allowed to carry out this obligation at 7 altars within the church that held the cross.
[66] See Housley, 'Indulgences', 296–7.
[67] They were distinguished by their white rods of office and their numbers were adjusted to the size of the town, 43 at Nürnberg, 25 at Erfurt, and just 15 at Hof: Schneider, *Peraudi*, 100.

perceive that, when robustly managed, this could be an effective addition to standard penitential practices.

But even on Perault's (or Paltz's) own terms, the system had its flaws. Writing to Paltz in May 1502 to thank him for his 'learned...and elegant book called *Coelifodina*', the cardinal expressed his regret that he did not have a Paltz for every region in his legatine zone.[68] This was not just a courteous preface to a request to send copies to those same regions. Surviving letters that Perault wrote to the ecclesiastical and civil authorities at Utrecht between 1502 and 1504 highlight his discontent with numerous aspects of the administration of indulgences during his third German legation.[69] The first letter (August 1502) was his response to the refusal of the dean and chapter to allow the preaching to take place at all. Local clergy could hardly be expected to welcome the arrival of an *Unterkommissar*. The preaching of the crusade (*cruciata universalis*) did not only place their own indulgences in suspension, thereby imperilling their finances,[70] but through the *confessionalia* it excluded them from the penitential circuit for years if not decades to come. The Utrecht cathedral clergy put forward various arguments to justify their resistance, all of which Perault quickly and irritably dismissed, and in the face of his persistence they had no option but to comply. That said, a postscript in this letter reveals the cardinal's awareness that his own moral position had been placed in danger ('should there be grumbling') by the ruling by the *Reichsregiment* that a full third of the proceeds were to be handed over to him to cover the expenses of preaching and collection.[71] Not that this was new: as Perault pointed out on another occasion, Nicholas of Cusa had been granted a third from the collection of the 1450 Jubilee.[72] An entire network of agencies had to be created to preach the indulgence and Perault had no income dedicated to this; he had to borrow the money for all immediate expenses.[73] The persistence with which he applied himself to collecting his third is striking,[74] but he was driven by indebtedness and the desire to get back to Rome;[75] in fact, in March 1502 he proposed only to draw on the proceeds of the (lesser) *confessionalia* chests and not to touch the money stored in the Jubilee chests.[76] Still, Perault's attentiveness to his own needs was a gift not just to the system's critics, but to any sceptical contemporary, and Maximilian found it handy during his dispute

---

[68] Paltz, *Supplementum*, 77.
[69] For the background see Charles M.A. Caspers, 'Indulgences in the Low Countries, c. 1300– c. 1520', in *PNTM*, 65–99.
[70] Around one half of the cost of building Utrecht Cathedral was met from indulgences: ibid. 72.
[71] *Codex documentorum*, 421, no 290. For the legate's agreement with the *Reichsregiment*, see *AR*, no 15605.
[72] Mehring, 'Peraudi', 342, note 3.
[73] Biblioteca Apostolica Vaticana, Palat IV. 1229 (5), printed open letter (n.d.), at 11–12. It did not help that Perault had rejected levying a tenth in favour of concentrating on indulgences: even if resisted, the tenth was easier to collect and yielded quicker results.
[74] e.g. *AR*, no 21035 (arrangements for conversion of the specie).
[75] Perault's income as cardinal was one of the lowest in the college: see *AR*, no 5134, and for comparisons Setton, *Papacy*, 2.528–30.
[76] *AR*, no 19635. This important text was unknown to Schneider and Mehring. The latter's treatment of the complex issue of Perault's third, 'Peraudi', 346–50, is balanced.

with the legate.[77] In the summer of 1503 the legate felt it necessary to print a substantial and cogently argued text justifying the grant of the third.[78] When Perault claimed that he came to Lübeck to save souls, one observer commented that it did not stop him leaving with a few thousand of the town's florins.[79] The link between donation and indulgence was undisguised, indeed the great cross was raised directly above the collection chest; and of course it was justified in terms of the Turkish threat. But suspicion of a personal profit motive would not go away.

All of Perault's letters to Utrecht depict a system that was inherently vulnerable to abuse. He conceded in the August 1502 letter that the allocation of a third to expenses constituted a temptation to the greedy.[80] Four months later he requested the city's burgomaster and consuls to keep the proceeds of preaching secure, once expenses had been disbursed. He complained about the lavish life style of his *Unterkommissaren*.[81] In a letter to the imperial estates in March 1503 he went further, accusing his commissioners of having consumed the full third in some dioceses 'because of their excessive expenses and luxurious ways'; their greed knew no bounds.[82] A third Utrecht letter, written in January 1504 to the dean and chapter, elaborated on the shortcomings of the *Unterkommissaren*. Perault was now trying to assemble as much of his third as he could to pay for his return journey to Rome, and he found precious little of it left. It had been spent on salaries claimed by the commissioners, payments for bell ringers, reimbursement for alleged damage, and faked expenses. The guilty individuals had defrauded their Saviour, His Church, the empire, and their fellow Christians who were suffering 'the frightful massacres perpetrated by the Turks'. They should remember that they were not dealing with false pardoners whom it was their praiseworthy custom to round up and flog, but with an accredited legate of the Holy See. The recipients of this veritable Jeremiad were to expedite the despatch of as much money as they could find from the third and, given some of the phraseology used, and the stance they had earlier adopted towards the preaching, it seems likely that their own hands were not entirely clean.[83]

Such epistolary torpedoes raise obvious issues, and unfortunately the evidence is too patchy, anecdotal, and tendentious to address them as fully as one would like to. In the first place, what was the definition of honest or moderate expenses ('honestis... expensis', 'expensae... moderate factae')?[84] It is possible that behind Perault's assertions of bottomless greed and endless avarice lie the bills of the bell ringers, carpenters, caterers, musicians, notaries, printers, and numerous others who made these 'multi-media events' possible. When the crusade was preached in the Toulousain in 1517–18 (possibly for the last time in France), its administration ate up slightly more than a quarter of the proceeds, with payments being made for just such expenses: the man who carried the banner of the crusade received 13*l*., while 72s. were spent on dinner for the people who witnessed the counting of the money placed in the main chest in the church of St Etiènne.[85] As far as we can gauge, crusade preaching and

---

[77] *AR*, no 17880.   [78] Mehring, 'Peraudi', 406–8.   [79] Röpcke, 'Geld', 53.
[80] *Codex documentorum*, 421, no 290.   [81] Ibid. 425, no 293.
[82] Paulus, 'Peraudi', 681, note 1 (= *AR*, no 20353).   [83] *Codex documentorum*, 437–42, no 307.
[84] Ibid. 425, no 293.   [85] See Housley, 'Indulgences', 290–2, for details.

collection had always been costly and the Peraultian system, which was drawn-out, labour-intensive, and showy, was unusually expensive to operate. Unsurprisingly, Perault himself emphasized its cost when justifying his third: he had to hire 'commissioners... secretaries, messengers, printers, confessors etc [sic]'; they all cost money and 'it is fitting... that he who serves the altar should live of the altar'.[86] It is possible that *Unterkommissaren* found that local elites (such as the cathedral clergy at Utrecht) also presented their bills, albeit in a more roundabout fashion than the providers of material goods and services; Perault would not have been aware of this because in his case, as a cardinal, the potential flow of benefits was reversed. Although Perault was very careful about whom he chose to be his *Unterkommissaren*,[87] it is likely that at least some of his appointments proved to be mistakes, and this was even more so one tier down, in their selection of confessors. There were many of these, they were not closely supervised, they were local people who might well know their penitents, and there was no guidance on the amount of money to be paid; if fraud did occur at this level, the money would be unaccountable because it would never have reached the chests. It is interesting that in 1501 the *Reichsregiment* tried to control the behaviour of the confessors in respect of the *confessionalia*, by insisting that the agreed format be rigorously applied and placing a limit on the number of beneficiaries for each.[88] Such suspicion is likely to indicate a propensity towards fraud, but it is improvable. The temptation to blame disappointing returns on the corruption of collectors was understandably strong.[89] In the pre-Perault period, when Popes complained about their preachers and collectors, the latter were often able to establish their innocence. Marinus de Fregeno is an instructive example: we have seen that in 1465 he was being pursued across northern Europe.[90] The most we can conclude is that it would have been surprising if there were not some losses due to fraud, given the loopholes in procedures and our knowledge of corruption in this period;[91] and that there is no more justification for accepting as reality Perault's despairing denunciation of his underlings' behaviour than there is for subscribing to Paltz's rose-tinted view of the 'happy times of plenary indulgences'.

6.2 POPULARITY AND RETURNS

By the time of Perault indulgence campaigns on the scale associated with crusading programmes polarized opinions and generated heated debate.[92] In September 1482

---

[86] Mehring, 'Peraudi', 406–8, at 407.
[87] In his appointment of Perault in December 1488 the Pope laid heavy emphasis on the need for probity in the personnel whom he selected: *DS*, 640–8, no 1513.
[88] *AR*, no 15834.
[89] Sixtus IV had two of his leading collectors, Heinrich Institoris and Quirin Martini, investigated in 1482: Schlecht, *Zamometić*, 1.137–8.
[90] See *DS*, 504–5, no 1362, for his spirited defence of his actions.
[91] For a suspicion of fraud being practised see *AR*, no 12773. For one well-informed lobbyist's concerns see Feliciangeli, 'Le proposte', 48, 50.
[92] See Paulus, *Geschichte*, chs 18, 20, 470–500, 516–33, and for excellent recent surveys Moeller, 'Die letzten Ablaßkampagnen'; Winterhager, 'Ablaßkritik', *passim*.

Sixtus IV wrote about 'the many people who dare to condemn and criticize the granting and decree of indulgences and the crusade'.[93] In a printed broadside in March 1502 Perault took action against the 'grousers, grumblers, gainsayers, and backbiters' who were everywhere endangering souls by impeding the work of his preachers. To date, he wrote, he had handled the opposition 'with fatherly forbearance', but the time had come for a tougher response, and they were to be solemnly excommunicated.[94] Usually the critics remain anonymous, but occasionally we find out who they were. In August 1488 Jacques d'Apelteren, a canon of Utrecht, had a notarial act drawn up to document his preaching of the crusade during Perault's second imperial legation. He commented on one Abbode, rector at Wageningen in Gelderland, who had preached openly that 'this business of most holy indulgences is trickery pure and simple, a deceitful way of squeezing money out of the common people'. Abbode was so convincing that his parishioners would not allow the collection chest to be taken away.[95] We have seen that Paltz set himself the task of answering such accusations, which he attributed to the devil, and he divided Satan's hosts into five categories. Two of them were described in terms of their *modus operandi*. There was the *exercitus excaecationis*, the army of demons that 'blinded' the faithful to preaching, and the host of *recidivatio*, which undid the wholesome work of indulgences by inducing the Christian to sin again. More interesting in the context of criticism are the other three. First, there was *annihilatio*, which denied the efficacy of indulgences. Then there was *denigratio*, which questioned the motivation of the Pope in granting them (*pia fraus*). Finally, *desperatio* worked on the reflective penitent's doubt that they were worthy of receiving the indulgence.[96]

The response to preaching could be unpredictable, as a cluster of examples from northern and central Italy shows. In January 1456 Calixtus III claimed to be overjoyed at reports of Alessandria's enthusiastic response to crusade preaching there.[97] When Pius II's crusade was preached a few years later the people of Recanati allegedly displayed similar enthusiasm,[98] but Brescia, at least according to Cristoforo da Soldo, showed a distinct lack of interest even though the crusade was preached there by the celebrity, Roberto Caracciolo.[99] Sometimes the explanation for a lacklustre response is not hard to identify. The Genoese, who in 1456 had responded generously to indulgences promoted for the defence of their fellow citizens at Caffa, showed little enthusiasm for an expedition that many contemporaries saw as

---

[93] *BF*, NS3.830–1, no 1632.
[94] Otto Clemen, ed., 'Ein offener Brief Raimund Peraudis', *Zeitschrift für Kirchengeschichte*, 20 (1900), 442–4.
[95] Paul Fredericq, ed., 'Les comptes des indulgences en 1488 et en 1517–1519 dans le diocèse d'Utrecht', *Mémoires couronnés et autres mémoires publiés par l'Académie royale des sciences, des lettres et des beaux-arts de Belgique*, 59 (1899–1900), 1–80, at 20–2.
[96] See the summary by Hamm, *Frömmigkeitstheologie*, 124–8.
[97] *Monumenta Alexandrina: codex qui Liber crucis nuncupatur*, ed. Francisco Gasparolo (Rome, 1889), 176–7, no 130.
[98] *Bullarium Franciscanum, Supplementum*, 687, no 1480; but the letter reflects the difficulties Pius faced in February 1464 and he could be clutching at straws.
[99] Cristoforo da Soldo, *La cronaca*, 144.

serving Venetian interests.[100] This market volatility renders generalization hazardous, but critiques of indulgences on the basis that it was wrong to deploy the crusade against the Turks rarely appear in the sources. What seems to have caused more difficulty was Paltz's *denigratio*, not least because it appeared to be confirmed by such anomalies, to put it no more strongly, as the issuing of indulgences that suspended the content of existing *confessionalia*.[101] The association of indulgences with papal acquisitiveness had become a commonplace. Also detrimental to response was the saturated market, which generated what Wilhelm Winterhager aptly characterized as 'indulgence fatigue' (*Ablassmüdigkeit*).[102] In a perceptive despatch to Alexander VI in January 1498 the legate Leonello Chiericati reported on the activity at Innsbruck of individuals who were allegedly administering indulgences on behalf of Rome's Hospital of the Holy Spirit. Their technique was hard to fault: indeed it was up to the standards of Perault and had earned them considerable sums. The Pope needed to bear in mind that if he intended to use the upcoming Jubilee for the cause of a crusade there would be little left following the success of such groups. It was no wonder pilgrimage to Rome was falling off: why go to Rome when it came to you?[103] In this instance the bulls being used were fake and contained absurdities, but even in the case of *bona fide* campaigns like those instituted by Sixtus IV, and Perault's legations, one can detect a number of trends setting in that over the long-term inevitably told against good financial returns.

The first trend was that the more streamlined the business was made, the more its goal appeared to be financial profit, and this could only encourage *denigratio*, which in turn eroded response. Perault's stream of interpretative broadsides may therefore have been counterproductive. This was ironic, because clarity and efficiency were certainly preferable to the confusion that had beset Sixtus's preaching for Rhodes and Otranto, necessitating his letter of September 1482 in favour of the hospital of St Anthony at Vienna. Secondly, crusade preachers were increasingly isolated and unpopular. The authority that had sent them was both far off and suspected, and the local elites resented their presence; indeed their activities threatened the community's devotional cohesion.[104] It is hardly surprising that the Observants became reluctant to get involved.[105] The reason why Perault had to borrow to fund his preaching in 1501 was, he complained, because nobody was willing to spend a penny to help.[106] Too many social groups, clerical and lay, elite and popular, were coming to see the administration of indulgences on behalf of the crusade as intrusive, exploitative, and grubby. Highlighting the Turkish peril should have helped to counterbalance this, but beyond areas that were directly threatened by naval landings or *akinji* raids it was still perceived as remote. Winterhager has suggested that one reason why the Teutonic Order enjoyed notable

---

[100] Jacques Heers, 'La vente des indulgences pour la Croisade, à Gênes et en Lunigiana, en 1456', *Miscellanea storica ligure*, 3 (1963), 71–101, repr. in his *Société et économie à Gênes (XIVe–XVe siècles)* (London, 1979), esp. 72.
[101] Winterhager, 'Ablaßkritik', 38.   [102] Ibid. 33.   [103] *AR*, no 5724.
[104] A point well made by Caspers, 'Indulgences', 91–9.
[105] Compare Winterhager, 'Ablaßkritik', 41.
[106] Biblioteca Apostolica Vaticana, Palat IV. 1229 (5), printed open letter (n.d.), at 12.

success in promoting its Livonian indulgence in 1503–6 and again in 1507–10 was that it managed to dress it up in 'an ingenious propaganda in nationalist colours, directed against the menacing threat that the Muscovites posed from the east'.[107] If he is correct then the contrast is striking, because this too was a Jubilee indulgence, so the argument that Perault and his *Unterkommissaren* were unable to emphasize the military cause because their liturgical formulae stressed individual penitence loses its force. It is possible that so much money raised for the crusade had gone astray in the past that preachers considered it unwise to dwell on the cause, preferring to focus on the spiritual benefits that each recipient stood to gain; but that is hypothesis.[108] What we are left with is a growing gulf in perception, from around 1480 onwards, between the war and its chief support mechanism, one that is hard to explain.

Receptivity was shaped by a number of contextual factors and, as Perault's last preaching campaign shows, the explanatory patterns that they yield are not clearcut. Winterhager has emphasized that Germany was suffering considerable strains: poor harvests in 1500, 1501, and 1503 caused shortages and high prices; there were outbreaks of plague and the new and terrifying disease of syphilis.[109] The abbot of Sponheim, Johannes Trithemius, recorded the direct impact of the poor economic situation on Perault's preaching at Mainz in March 1502: 'Because of the people's want, they responded slowly and late. But in the course of time their devotion increased, and in various places a large sum of money was deposited in the Jubilee chests.'[110] Trithemius does not say what triggered this delayed surge of interest at Mainz, but while his entry references only poverty, atrocious weather, severe mortality affecting people and animals, and plague, there was an accompanying religious background that could have played a part. It was described at some length in the preamble to Maximilian's manifesto on behalf of his *societas sancti Georgii* in November 1503. The thousands of deaths from syphilis, a clear sign of God's wrath; the meteorite (*Donnerstein*) which had fallen near Ensisheim in 1492, prefiguring Maximilian's victory over the French at Salins;[111] the exhortations of the anorexic maid of Augsburg, Anna Lamalitlin; and the outbreak of miraculous appearances of the cross, were all listed as signs that the time was right to promote the crusade, the alleged rationale for establishing the *societas*.[112] It is very likely that

---

[107] Winterhager, 'Ablaßkritik', 25. See also Leonid Arbusow, 'Die Beziehungen des Deutschen Ordens zum Ablasshandel seit dem 15. Jahrhundert', *Mitteilungen aus dem Gebiete der Geschichte Liv-, Ehst-, und Kurland*, 20 (1910), 367–457.

[108] It is true that the Turks do not feature much in Paltz's substantial texts, but his focus was on the character of the indulgence, not the cause that its proceeds would support. A parallel would be the model sermons that survive from the thirteenth century, which concentrate on the redemptive power of the cross rather than the threat to the Holy Land. For sermons delivered at Nürnberg at the start of Perault's legation that focused in part on the Turkish threat see *AK*, no 15584.

[109] Winterhager, 'Ablaßkritik', 51–2.

[110] 'Chronicon Trithemii Sponheimense', in *Johannis Trithemii Spanheimensis... opera historica*, 1 vol. in 2 pts (Frankfurt, 1601), 236–435, at 416.

[111] Dieter Wuttke, 'Sebastian Brant und Maximilian I. Eine Studie zu Brants Donnerstein-Flugblatt des Jahres 1492', in Otto Herding and Robert Stupperich, eds, *Die Humanisten in ihrer politischen und sozialen Umwelt* (Boppard, 1976), 141–7.

[112] *Volumen*, 214–17. For the miraculous crosses see above, ch 2, at notes 5–6.

Maximilian's advisers were pressing into service features of the devotional landscape that they believed had over the course of the last two years inclined contemporaries to respond favourably to Perault's preaching. If this was the case then it illustrated a central demand paradox of indulgences: that the ability to give was greater at times of economic prosperity, but the urge to give was stimulated by a collective penitential ethos that was typically generated by economic distress and social disruption.

The atypical character of indulgences in terms of demand and supply analysis is reflected in their pricing. The fact that there was no alternative to allowing the poor, who could contribute nothing, to pray rather than pay, made indulgences different from any other marketed product.[113] In the case of those who did possess material resources, two popular approaches were to set a sliding scale,[114] and to call for the donation of a week's household expenses.[115] In one grant for the defence of Caffa in 1463 donors were given the choice of giving a straight cash sum (ten florins) or a percentage of their income (1 per cent) or possessions (5 per cent).[116] *Gradiente domino*, Alexander VI's crusade bull of May 1500, which was based on his Jubilee, set the donation expected as a quarter of the estimated costs of a visit to Rome lasting fifteen days,[117] but when Perault preached in Germany his agreement with the *Reichsregiment* specified a week's household expenses.[118] In many cases this should have proved lucrative: in December 1501 Zaccaria Contarini was mystified about why the collection chest at Vienna was found to hold just 600 florins when there were many people who ought to have paid between ten and fifty florins a head.[119] In such shifts of approach towards the question of pricing we see the papal *curia*, its agents, and others trying to achieve a balance between practicalities, profit, and pastoral or governmental concerns; and the difficulty of identifying a clear trend shows that it was no easy task. The price set for *confessionalia* was generally lower. Perault's September 1501 agreement with the *Reichsregiment* specified a charge of one Rhenish florin for three such letters.[120]

It was common practice to accept goods instead of specie,[121] though the result is seldom as clearly visible as at Genoa in 1456, when the detailed inventory enabled the economic historian, Jacques Heers, to offer an exemplary analysis of its profile and implications.[122] Heers discovered that the goods donated fell into four categories: animals (a stallion, mules, and asses); canvas, woollen, cotton, and linen cloth; arms and armour; and items such as rings with a high precious metal content. It might be thought that this practice added an unnecessary complication to a process that was cumbersome enough already, but, as Heers showed, the variety of small change in circulation that found its way into the chests posed issues of conversion that had to be managed in any case; so disposing of donated goods as well

---

[113] *BF*, NS2.623–4, no 1203 (1464); *DS*, 665, no 1525 (1490).
[114] Ibid. 543–5, no 1407 (1472: from 5 to 0.5 fl.).   [115] *BF*, NS2.639, no 1230 (1464).
[116] *Vetera monumenta Slavorum*, 464, no 657.   [117] *VMH*, 2.547–50, no 731.
[118] *AR*, no 15605.   [119] Ibid. no 12773.   [120] Ibid. no 15605.
[121] e.g. *AM*, 13.10, 60; *BF*, NS2. 216, no 429, 224, no 448; *DS*, 409, no 1259, 489–91, no 1345, 668–75, no 1529, at 669, 671.
[122] Heers, 'La vente', *passim*.

may not have complicated the process unduly. He was able to identify the purchaser of some of the goods, a Genoese merchant called Giovanni Piccamiglio, who bought cloth, clothing, some casks of wine, and a full suit of armour.[123] That said, occasional references do show that the diversity of coins could place the system under strain.[124] We should not assume that it was standard procedure to place donated goods on the market. A Lübeck chronicler wrote *à propos* of Marinus de Fregeno that he accepted anything, 'old copper, pewter, iron ore, old kettles, everything that could be made into money',[125] and at the end of 1463 money and goods raised by Marinus were alike entrusted to an agent of the Rucellai trading company for onwards despatch to Rome.[126] The absence of instructions at any level about how to deal with these donated goods is puzzling (how *did* collectors know how to proceed?), as well as creating an obstacle to our knowledge.[127]

Predicting returns was not just difficult but frequently an exercise heavy with political overtones, and this makes it unwise to place much confidence in what contemporaries thought (or said they thought) would be the outcome. When Matthias Corvinus complained to the Pope in January 1476 that the grant of the Jubilee indulgence would not pay for ten soldiers for a year, thereby implying that it was worth less than 500 florins, his estimate was probably not meant to be taken literally; it was a dramatic way of saying that a more solid and dependable source of income was required to take the war forward.[128] The fierce exchanges that characterized the final stage of Perault's last legation had the opposite effect on estimates, driving them upwards as Perault made wild claims for what he could have achieved if he had only been allowed to carry out his brief fully: well over a million florins late in 1503, two million early in 1504.[129] Less polemically inspired estimates of what had been donated, located in Venetian sources, are 300,000 and 400,000 florins.[130] The first of these figures is probably the most robust that we possess. It derived from Perault's own vice-legate, Bishop Thomas Malumbra of Curzola, when he came to Venice in October 1502 to promote an alliance with Maximilian, and represents a hard-headed appraisal of what had been donated. Matthias's approach to the subject of indulgences was usually more canny and attentive to detail than his dismissive 1476 letter would suggest. In April 1481 he wanted lands that had come under his control in the archdiocese of Salzburg to be included in the grant that had been made him. He argued that, whereas Hungary

---

[123] Heers pointed out (ibid. 78) that the weight of armour made it inherently less manageable than items such as table linen and silver jewellery.
[124] e.g. *MDE*, 2.262, no 182. [125] Jensen, *Denmark*, 95. [126] *DS*, 489–91, no 1345.
[127] In 1481 Sixtus IV referred to 'bona et res in pecuniam numeratam redacta', but how was this done? Schlecht, *Zamometić*, 2.113, no 100.
[128] *MCH*, 104–8, no 81, at 106.
[129] Mehring, 'Peraudi', 384, 402 (having to cut short his preaching had cost the crusade 'plus quam de uno milione florenorum'). The implication is that Perault thought he had raised somewhat under one million fl.
[130] Sanuto, *I diarii*, 4.374 (= *AR*, no 20019; 300,000 Rh. fl., October 1502), 694–7 (= *AR*, no 20250; 400,000 fl., February 1503). *AR*, no 16461, reports 200,000 Rh. fl. (May 1502). One complication is that not all figures specify which florin is being used; by 1500 the Rhenish florin had lost about 20 per cent of its value compared with the Florentine florin or Venetian ducat.

was financially exhausted by the struggle against the Turks, and had suffered heavily from the plague, his new German 'subjects' were better placed to contribute.[131] A few weeks later the king complained about changes to the provisions in the bulls granted: the removal of the clause entitling beneficiaries to a second indulgence on the point of death would be detrimental to take-up, which was already affected by the simultaneous marketing of the indulgence for Rhodes.[132] But despite the king's readiness to engage in such fine tuning, there seems to have been no attempt to apply Perault's intensive marketing techniques to Hungary, perhaps because it lacked the degree of urbanization that facilitated the legate's approach in Germany and the Low Countries.[133] It was Perault's usual practice to draw the line at preaching to fewer than 500 communicants.[134]

Ideally, we would work not from estimates, either prospective or retrospective, but from actual returns. But this can only be done with confidence when the sums were accurately logged at the point of final delivery. We have two such sets of figures for preaching by the Franciscans under Calixtus III and Sixtus IV, and although selective in character they are reasonably revealing. For Calixtus they represent receipts issued for preaching in Italy between January 1456 and June 1458. The highest figure is 862 florins (Bartolomeo da Colle, 27 February 1456), and five others reach 500 florins or more.[135] Such sums were useful, but, set against the Pope's naval expenses, they were of no more than supplementary value. An Observant called Antonio de Alberto, who had preached the crusade at Ragusa in Eugenius IV's time, was accused of defrauding the *curia* of 50,000 florins, though this sounds like wishful thinking.[136] One can see why Pius II showed such pessimism on occasion about the potential of indulgences, and made such a determined effort at Mantua and afterwards to move the burden of crusade funding to a tax basis. Using indulgences primarily as a sweetener to induce communities to pay had great advantages but, as we have seen, it foundered in the face of resistance. Receipts for payments logged between July 1481 and July 1484, many of them in the chest kept in the church of the Aracoeli on Rome's Capitoline Hill, show us what was achieved through the more systematic procedures instituted by Sixtus, above all by associating crusade with Jubilee. The figures are more impressive, including nine of 1,000 florins or more and three payments totalling over 14,000 florins on a single day, 14 August 1481.[137] Given that these figures represent

---

[131] *MKL*, 2.122, no 69.

[132] Ibid. 139–44, no 79, at 141–2. The king soon decided not to bother pressing on this issue: ibid. 161–2, no 93.

[133] Tom Scott and Bob Scribner, 'Urban Networks', in Bob Scribner, ed., *Germany. A New Social and Economic History, vol. 1, 1450–1630* (London, 1996), 113–43. Though for Hungary see above at note 17.

[134] Paulus, *Geschichte*, 217 (Perault sanctions preaching in communities of around 500 communicants, 8 November 1502, as a concession to the Advent season).

[135] Cenci, ed., 'Documenta...1447–1458', 245–59 (Bartolomeo da Colle at 247).

[136] *BF*, NS2.341–2, no 648: he was able to prove that the proceeds had all gone towards Calixtus's naval expenses.

[137] Caesar Cenci, ed., 'Documenta Vaticana ad Franciscales spectantia, ann. 1476–1481', *Archivum Franciscanum historicum*, 96 (2003), 85–127; id., ed., 'Documenta Vaticana ad Franciscales spectantia, ann. 1482–1484', *Archivum Franciscanum historicum*, 97 (2004), 133–58.

payments after deductions of a third or more had been made to local churches and rulers to secure their assent or assistance, the data for 1481–4 confirms that receipts had increased since Calixtus's time. It is possible to confirm the general conclusions reached on the subject of returns by Paulus almost a century ago: that Sixtus was one of three Popes (the others being Boniface IX and Leo X) who put maximum effort into increasing returns; but that it is unrealistic to form precise assessments of gains because of the many problems of interpretation surrounding the figures that we possess.[138]

With this in mind, we can return to Perault's preaching in 1501–3. Thomas Malumbra's figure of 300,000 florins can most readily be assessed using two approaches, one 'micro' or local and the other 'macro' or imperial. The first is best approached through the returns that were recorded for individual urban centres, while the second works with our knowledge of the costs of warfare under Maximilian, and the other revenues that were at his disposal. Together, they should enable us to gauge whether a state-of-the-art preaching campaign like that organized and run by Perault, and celebrated by Paltz, came near to meeting the costs of a major crusade. Winterhager's analysis of the 1501–3 yields led to mixed results: taking the examples of Nürnberg, Frankfurt am Main, and Strasbourg, he pointed out that the gains in 1501–3 were smaller than those of 1488–9 in the case of the first two towns, and better in that of the third. What was more striking was a comparison of such figures with those for the Mainz indulgence of 1517. This revealed a drastic slump; by the time of Luther's theses the balance-sheet from indulgences was 'effectively profitless' once expenses had been deducted. This conclusion, based on figures, is in line with the dominant trend in criticism highlighted by Winterhager, to the effect that the view of indulgences as *pia fraus* had been absorbed by the population at large. So Luther's claim to be reflecting what was said in workshop and tavern ('the incisive points made by layfolk') was not far-fetched. Whatever our conclusion on Perault's returns, by his last years indulgences were passing or had already passed their high-water mark in terms of profitability.[139] Whether or not this would have been the case had a large-scale crusade materialized from Perault's preaching campaigns of 1488–9 or 1501–3 is a moot point.

One of the most impressive returns in 1501–3 was that of Bremen, where 6,740 florins were counted following a week's visit by Perault in May 1503. In his analysis of the well-documented preaching at Bremen, Andreas Röpcke set this figure in context: it was the sum needed to hire 150 doctors for a year, or to pay for 100 good horses.[140] Granted that Bremen was one of the larger German towns, its proceeds almost equalled the combined donations at two other major centres, Nürnberg (4,500 florins) and Strasbourg (2,285 florins). It is fruitless to enquire

---

[138] Paulus, *Geschichte*, ch. 17, 450–69, and see too Winterhager, 'Ablaßkritik', 25 note 44 on methodological issues. For the relationship between indulgences and the collecting of regular dues see Schuchard, *Kollektoren*.

[139] Winterhager, 'Ablaßkritik', 22–34, and cf. 11 note 13 on 1518, 12–17 on Luther's rapport with popular feeling. I do not think the evidence supports Winterhager's argument on 24 that the slide downwards in *perception* started following the campaign of 1488–9 rather than that of 1501–3.

[140] Röpcke, 'Geld', 64–5.

why the people of Bremen and its hinterland proved so receptive to Perault. More instructive is a simple extrapolation using its generous response. In order to reach the million florins referred to by Perault late in 1503, the legate and his team would have had to achieve 150 comparable success stories. But the point about Bremen is that it proved exceptional, and in the whole of Germany there were only eighty-five towns that contained more than 5,000 inhabitants.[141] Adding Austria, the Low Countries, Livonia, and Denmark would undoubtedly have helped,[142] and we have observed the effort that Perault invested in getting the indulgences preached in the populous diocese of Utrecht. There exists a comparatively low figure of 15,725 florins for electoral Saxony,[143] and (not surprising given their exposure to Turkish attack) a more impressive estimate of 40,000 florins for Maximilian's *Erbländer*.[144] On the basis of these figures, and those that we have for such towns as Braunschweig, Bremen, Nürnberg, Ratzeburg, Regensburg, Speyer, and Strasbourg, Perault's million looks increasingly implausible, while even Malumbra's 300,000 florins (which presupposed fifty Bremens) seems optimistic. By way of comparison, the preaching for Livonia in 1503–10 raised at least 61,000 florins, and possibly 85,000.[145] It does not seem likely that Perault could have reached more than three times the higher of those figures.

The 'macro' side of the picture is the use to which this money would be put and other sources from which Maximilian's warfare was funded. We are fortunate to possess a document that addresses both issues. It was drawn up in April 1504 to detail anticipated income and recruitment for a three-month campaign in the war of the Landshut succession, a conflict that coincidentally signalled the end of residual hopes that the emperor-elect might go on crusade. The army comprised 5,450 horse and 28,200 foot, made up of a large number of contingents, accompanied by artillery 'as substantial and fine as you could hope for'. There was no provision for naval support, but that does not detract from the value of the text as a yardstick because imperial participation in a crusade would have taken place in alliance with Venice, which would have handled the naval component. The income amounted to 471,000 Rhenish florins and 1,000 oxen, the animals being a contribution in kind promised by the king of Hungary. As we would expect from Maximilian's reign, the majority was derived from the provinces of Austria and the Low Countries, but 50,000 florins would be taken from Perault's indulgence money.[146] At first sight this text seems to indicate the feasibility of a substantial imperial army raised for a crusade being funded largely from indulgence receipts. After all, Malumbra's 300,000 florins would have provided about three-fifths of the operational cost of this force, and Perault always applied the logic that hearing about a crusading army's campaigning would increase future donations, providing the income for the second and subsequent years. To this it could be objected that

---

[141] Scott and Scribner, 'Urban networks', esp. 116, 122–3 (map 5.1).
[142] In texts that he had printed towards the end of 1503 Perault referred to his plan to travel 'usque ad Daciam et Livoniam' preaching the crusade: Mehring, 'Peraudi', 401–6, no 7, at 401.
[143] *AR*, no 21035.   [144] Ibid. nos 16336, 17046.   [145] Winterhager, 'Ablaßkritik', 25.
[146] *AR*, no 18598. The wage rates were clearly those set out in the Augsburg *Abschied* of 1500, 8 fl. a month for horse and 4 for foot, *AR*, no 14407, para. 65.

there remained a considerable funding shortfall, not least because any crusade would last a lot longer than three months. So when Maximilian dismissed as inadequate a French offer of a 400,000 or 500,000 franc subsidy for a crusade, during negotiations in 1502, he was not simply playing politics.[147]

That said, an equally imposing consideration about funding revolves around Maximilian's financial dilemma as emperor-elect and his political outlook. Towards the end of a scholarly career spent largely studying Maximilian's reign, Hermann Wiesflecker summed up these associated issues well. In the first place, he estimated that the sultan enjoyed tax revenues fifty times those of the emperor-elect.[148] The reason was that the empire lacked any taxation base: in Chapter 4, we witnessed Maximilian attempting to deploy crusading ideas to institute just such a base at Worms in 1495 and Augsburg in 1500. As Wiesflecker observed,[149] Maximilian was prepared to spend fourteen weeks at the diet of Worms in 1495 at a time of diplomatic crisis, trying to get the *Gemeiner Pfennig* accepted. The fact that he could extract no more than around 50,000 florins a year from his German subjects meant that he was constantly struggling to meet his military outgoings.[150] Penury was a hallmark of his reign; everything had to be done on credit or free of charge, and a Venetian envoy dubbed him 'king empty-pockets' (*rè pochi danari*).[151] It is almost certain that for Maximilian indulgences were ersatz taxes, a way to escape from his dependence on revenues collected in his hard-pressed Austrian and Burgundian territories.[152] Moreover, he held a holistic view of his imperial responsibilities. This entailed equating the French with the Turks in terms of the threat that they posed, and viewing the recovery of his lost Italian lands ('Italia, quae mea est') as on a par with the defence of the Austrian *Erbländer*.

It is possible to be over-generous towards Maximilian: more than anything else, Perault's indulgence money was a way of plugging gaps, replacing the million florins that he had received as subsidies from Milan before the French occupied it in 1500, or complementing the silver mined in Tirol (a literal rendering of Paltz's metaphor). But there was conviction as well as accountancy at work. In much the same way that the Germans thought they were subsidizing Rome, Maximilian was convinced that he was subsidizing them. In an address delivered at the diet of Constance in 1507 and disseminated as a broadside throughout Germany, he maintained that he had spent ten million florins on imperial business and got just one million back.[153] Indulgences were a way to get the Germans to pay their fair share. Hence his proposal at Augsburg in 1500 that the priesthood should exhort people to pay the Common Penny, which would be collected through chests placed in churches; indulgences provided the means to achieve the same end via voluntary

---

[147] *AR*, no 19620.
[148] Wiesflecker, *Maximilian I.*, 128. This is a very useful summary of his great work, *Kaiser Maximilian I*. For treatment of Maximilian's finances see ibid., 5.563–611.
[149] Wiesflecker, *Maximilian I.*, 93.   [150] Ibid. 349.   [151] Ibid. 350.
[152] Ibid. 287. See also id., *Kaiser Maximilian I.*, 3.41 ('eine Art Ersatz für die Reichssteuer'), 86; Alfred Schröcker, 'Maximilians I. Auffassung vom Königtum und das ständische Reich. Beobachtungen an ungedruckten Quellen italienischer Herkunft', *QFIAB*, 50 (1971), 181–204.
[153] Wiesflecker, *Maximilian I.*, 153–4, and see too 196 (Augsburg, 1518).

means. This would allow Maximilian to engage with the grand ambitions that his impecunious father had always avoided and which his own more expansive character found irresistible. This included the crusade, though it was not high on the agenda.[154]

6.3 CONTROL AND RETENTION

A notarial instrument drawn up on 15 July 1502 at Strasbourg gives us a finely detailed snapshot of the point of transition represented by the opening of Perault's collection chests. Two chests had been positioned in the cathedral: a large one locked by four keys for indulgence money and a smaller one, secured by three keys, for *confessionalia* payments. They were carried to the town's *Pfennigturm* and opened on 4 July by the three clerics who were authorized to act by Perault and the *Reichsregiment*: the dean, Hoyer von Mühlingen, the cathedral schoolmaster, Heinrich von Henneberg, and one Andreas Hartmann. The trio proceeded in the presence of witnesses acting on behalf of the bishop and the city. The various currencies were sorted and counted, and on the following day converted into Rhenish florins, totalling 2,285. The two-thirds that belonged to Pope and empire—1,523 florins—were assigned for safe keeping to the city's deputies, with the explicit assent of the three agents. Of the 761 florins due to Perault, 300 were immediately set aside for outgoings, and a further 161 were handed over to Perault's agent on 15 July. The remaining 300 were placed, pending Perault's instructions, together with the 1,523 florins in the smaller chest. Its three keys were entrusted to Henneberg, Mühlingen, and a group of individuals acting for the city. The city's deputies affirmed to the notary that the 1,523 florins would only be handed over at the demand of the Pope or the empire.[155] There is no reason to consider the Strasbourg procedure atypical. Throughout most of the empire, money donated for the crusade was handled with proper circumspection, and responsibility for its future disposal became bound up with the honour of self-respecting urban elites. We shall see that this was most conspicuously the case at Cologne.

Some leakage through theft was always predictable, and nowhere more so than in the wilder parts of Germany, where public order was notoriously fragile. At the end of 1463 a Halberstadt dean called Tiderius Blok was given the unwelcome job of investigating the plundering in 1462 of money and goods collected by Marinus de Fregeno and en route to Rome. Far from being social outcasts, the robbers were headed by members of Braunschweig's roguish ducal dynasty, who justified their actions by reference to an ongoing feud with Lüneburg. They had been anathematized and excommunicated during the 1463 Holy Thursday reading of *In coena*

---

[154] Ibid. 365–75, esp. 370–1, 374, and for a more detailed narrative, id., *Kaiser Maximilian I.*, 3.144–63. Thomas A. Brady, 'Imperial Destinies: A New Biography of the Emperor Maximilian I', *Journal of Modern History*, 62 (1990), 298–314, offers a lively and sympathetic English summary of Wiesflecker's thesis.
[155] *AR*, no 19864.

domini, but this had proved ineffective.[156] A more curious incident involving Marinus was his 'losing' (*amisisti*) a bag containing specie, silver rings and golden rods (the precious metals are revealing) to the value of 3,243 Rhenish florins. The loss occurred when the preacher fell seriously ill on the road from Wismar to Lübeck. The bag ended up in the hands of Duke Heinrich of Mecklenburg, and in March 1464 the bishops of Lübeck and Ratzeburg were instructed by Pius II to exert pressure on the duke and the town council of Grevesmühlen to get it back.[157] Marinus's own indirect commentary on these incidents can be found in his remarks about the ducal houses of Braunschweig and Mecklenburg in his *Descriptio provinciarum Alamanorum*. In the circumstances they are notably restrained. On Frederick of Braunschweig he commented: 'He is a stormy individual, with habits more suited to a robber than a prince, manly though, and a skilful and cautious military commander.' And on the three co-dukes of Mecklenburg: 'These dukes do not know the meaning of peace, and they are constantly attacking the lands of their neighbours. I really do not know what I can say in their favour, except that their soldiers are very good at fighting and robbing.'[158]

The difference between outright pillaging of this kind and the grant of an agreed share of the proceeds of preaching lay in propriety. It was enshrined in Calixtus III's diplomatic response to Francesco Sforza's opposition to tax collection and preaching by Caracciolo in April 1457: the clear implication was that Sforza would get the money, or the bulk of it, eventually but he had to go through the right process.[159] The same realism underpinned Calixtus's advice to Caracciolo a few weeks later about managing resistance to paying the tenth on the part of the clergy. Sforza had warned the Pope of the danger that Caracciolo's unyielding insistence on collecting the tax would create an alliance between the clergy and the populace. His dramatic posting of threatened sanctions on all of Milan's church doors had been counterproductive, generating a wave of sympathy for the clergy among the population at large that bordered on rebellion.[160] Caracciolo responded by moderating his actions.[161] In a contest between clergy and populace on the one hand (with the duke affecting neutrality but probably working behind the scenes to encourage recalcitrance), and Pope and collector on the other, there could only be one outcome. But there was always a *quid pro quo* and, in Caracciolo's own case, it was ducal lobbying of Calixtus immediately after this exchange for his appointment as vicar-general of his order.[162] Amid the maelstrom of sectional interests that alternated between conflict and coalition, Calixtus had to steer a course that not only advanced his crusade but offered hope of gathering the financial resources required for success. With less noble intent, Chiericati advised Alexander VI in 1498 to fend off German demands for Church reform by breaking up the alliance of the princes with the German bishops.[163]

---

[156] *DS,* 489–91, no 1345.
[157] Ibid. 493–4, no 1349. Reiterated by Paul II in October: ibid. 500, no 1357.
[158] Voigt, 'Kollektor', 188, lines 226–9, p. 189, lines 259–60. See also ibid.161–2.
[159] Bastanzio, *Fra Roberto,* 271–2, no 28.   [160] Ibid. 272, no 29.
[161] Ibid. 273–4, no 31.   [162] Ibid. 274, no 32.   [163] *AR,* no 6539.

The scenario in Milan in 1457, or for that matter in Braunschweig in 1462, was complex enough, but neither matched the tangled web that awaited Perault when he crossed the Alps on his final legation in 1501.[164] In addition to setting up and monitoring a structure for the twin processes of preaching and collection, he had to manage a number of separate but related political issues. In the first place, he had to break free of Alexander's ground plan for the crusade, which the Pope set out in his instructions of October 1500. Certain elements of this, in particular Alexander's own participation, were not simply unrealistic but bizarre. Others, like the proposal that the proceeds of indulgences should be exported from Germany, were probably designed to hamstring effective action.[165] Perault had to create an alternative *modus operandi* that would serve the genuine purposes of a crusade: naturally, he emphasized his own identification, as bishop of a Carinthian see, with the empire and its embattled frontier, but more importantly he stressed that German money would be used only for German crusading, a standpoint that was attractive but far from easy to maintain.[166] It is unsurprising that Perault chose to work closely with Venice, which for much of his legation was still at war with the sultan and desperate to secure imperial assistance. But the Damocles sword always hung over his head of being recalled to Rome, either because Alexander saw his interests being undercut or because Maximilian demanded it.[167] Secondly, Perault was dealing with an emperor-elect whose own commitment to crusade, while arguably more genuine than Alexander's, was so tied up with other items on a long list of goals that in practice it was no more likely to produce results. Perault's response to this was to stick rigidly to the principle that none of the proceeds of his preaching should be diverted, even if this meant that no crusade took place. But the situation in the empire went far beyond the aspirations and needs of Maximilian. A full-scale constitutional crisis was in progress, caused by the clash over imperial reform and executive powers between Maximilian and the empire's administrative agencies (*Reichsregiment*) headed by his arch-chancellor, the archbishop of Mainz Berthold von Henneberg.[168] Berthold and his colleagues were deeply suspicious of Perault as a legate, but they sensed his potential as a means of maintaining pressure on Maximilian for radical change. They were also receptive to the idea of Church reform, which was widely seen as complementing the reform of the empire.[169] Perault's position was therefore paradoxical. His marketing techniques were radically new, among other things making full use of the new technology of printing, but his view of the crusading purpose that they served was highly traditional: it was an altruistic and unifying ideal that went hand in glove with peace between Christians. He was not duplicitous when he told the Venetians that he owed allegiance not to any individual or lobby but to God and his faith.[170] But his authority rested on a Pope whom he despised, and

---

[164] For a detailed narrative of events see Wiesflecker, *Kaiser Maximilian I.*, vol. 3, esp. 39–58.
[165] *AR*, nos 14472–4; Setton, *Papacy*, 2.526–32.   [166] *AR*, no 14717.
[167] Ibid. no 16104.   [168] For the key issues and events see Brady, *German Histories*, 114–21.
[169] This is well explored by Brady, ibid. pt 2.   [170] *AR*, no 12590.

he needed the support of an emperor-elect whose motives he distrusted, and whose political enemies he was driven to embrace.[171]

It is helpful to divide Perault's negotiation of this minefield into three phases. The first lasted from his appointment in October 1500 to his agreement with the *Reichsregiment* on how he would operate in September 1501. This delay of almost a year sprang largely from the negative response to the very idea of a papal legate, springing above all from fears of specie again being exported to Rome. In a set of demands to be presented to the Pope in January 1501 the *Reichsregiment* made its views on this crystal clear.[172] At this point, even Maximilian, who construed Alexander's crusade as a camouflaged anti-Habsburg coalition, saw nothing to be gained from allowing Perault into Germany; at the end of 1500 rumours even circulated that the emperor-elect was planning to appeal to popular prejudices by seizing Church revenues under cover of the crusade.[173] Barred from entry, Perault did not waste the six expensive months that he lingered at Rovereto, south of Trent. He conducted a veritable charm offensive to convince the imperial elites that his intentions were good and that no money would be exported. Maximilian was the first to be won over, no doubt because he saw the possibility of financial gain.[174] Persuading the *Reichsregiment* was tougher work, and Perault's letter to the diet assembled at Nürnberg on 31 July 1501 reveals as much about his irritation as his rhetorical skills.[175] Echoing Bessarion's orations to the imperial diets forty-one years previously, Perault painted a grim picture of the threat facing not just the Austrian lands but Germany at large.[176] Aware of the absence of any financial underpinning for the work of the *Reichsregiment*, many delegates at the Nürnberg diet were probably persuaded to yield less by Perault's arguments than by the hope that the *Reichsregiment* might secure some of the collected money.[177] Agreement was reached on 11 September and the terms incorporated into the official summary (*Abschied*) of the diet's proceedings three days later. At the administrative level, the clauses of the Nürnberg concordat were thorough enough. Representatives of the *Reichsregiment* would act as watchdogs, consenting to the appointment of *Ablasskommissaren* and confessors, holding keys to the collection chests, and accompanying Perault throughout his travels. The contributions expected for indulgence and confessional letters were set, to prevent abuses but possibly also with an eye to leaving sufficient capital for taxation. Together with Maximilian, the *Reichsregiment* would sanction the disposal of the proceeds (aside from Perault's third), which should only be used for a crusade. There should be another diet as soon as

---

[171] For the impact of the political scenario see Peter Schmid, 'Der päpstliche Legat Raimund Peraudi und die Reichsversammlungen der Jahre 1501–1503. Zum Prozeß der Entfremdung zwischen Reich und Rom in der Regierungszeit König Maximilians I.', in *RK*, 65–88.

[172] *AR*, no 14848.

[173] Sanuto, *I diarii*, 3.1158, 1252 (= *AR*, nos 14707, 14727). On this initial hostility see also Schmid, 'Der päpstliche Legat', 66–71.

[174] *AR*, no 15558.

[175] Wiesflecker's characterization (*Kaiser Maximilian I.*, 3.42) is astute: 'Es war ein Meisterwerk der Kreuzzugsagitation von packender Sprachgewalt und aufrüttelnder, treffsicherer Kritik der Schwächen des Reiches.'

[176] Kraus, *Reichsregiment*, 226–35.

[177] *AR*, no 15573a. Schmid, 'Der päpstliche Legat', p. 80, note 58, is sceptical on this point.

possible to make arrangements for a campaign. Together with some clauses that were added on 29 December, these provisions must have seemed watertight, provided the *Reichsregiment* presented a strong front against Maximilian's attempts at subversion, and itself remained faithful to the crusading cause.[178]

Phase two of Perault's legation lasted from September 1501 to early in 1503, by which point peace between Venice and Hungary on the one hand, and the sultan on the other, made it clear that no crusade would come about.[179] The existence of these potential allies, one of whom was clamouring for support, and the accumulation of donated money in collection chests, constituted the scenario's two most positive features: the conundrum facing Perault was how to bring them together. Throughout the autumn of 1501 the despatches of the envoy Zaccaria Contarini afford an extraordinarily rich view of the unfolding situation and in particular of Perault's outlook. The legate followed up the Nürnberg *Abschied* with a general summons to all the empire's estates to send envoys to the diet scheduled to meet in Frankfurt on 25 November, so that troop movements could be initiated during the winter months to join forces with the ships provided by the Venetians and others in the spring of 1502.[180] Optimistic by nature, Perault was capable of declaring that his indulgences would provide all the men and money needed.[181] At the same time, however, he harboured no illusions about the political obstacles to success. He was aware that Alexander was working ceaselessly to derail peace negotiations between Maximilian and Louis XII: to Perault the *sine qua non* for a crusade, but in Alexander's eyes a serious threat to the balance of power in Italy. On 9 November Contarini reported Perault laughing about a report that the Pope blamed his legate for the progress reached in the recent peace talks at Trent, regretting the day that he sent him to Germany.[182] He could not always be so even-tempered in his response to Alexander's extraordinary double-dealing. A few days earlier he had denounced Cesare Borgia to Contarini as a 'son of perdition', expressing the view that Alexander and his offspring were worse than the sultan, because Bayezid II at least adhered to his chosen moral code.[183] The situation north of the Alps afforded little more reason for hope. Maximilian was wedded to his grandiose programme of *Romzug*, coronation, and crusade. This stood no chance of being funded by the Frankfurt diet. In a report written on 11 November Contarini painted a portrait of a deeply frustrated Perault. The legate despaired of Maximilian's chameleon tendencies (*inconstantia et mutabilita*) and explained at length his reasons for believing that he had in the past secretly colluded with the Turks. His enthusiasm for the crusade was all show, intended only to milk money out of his subjects. It was hardly surprising that his own father had despaired of him and that the German princes hated him.[184] The Frankfurt diet did not even meet, and although preaching continued, by the close of 1501 the organizational programme agreed at Nürnberg in September had stalled.

---

[178] *AR*, nos 15605, 15610, 15834; Schmid, 'Der päpstliche Legat', pp. 77–8.
[179] Sanuto, *I diarii*, 4.879–84 (= *AR*, no 20283).
[180] Ibid. no 15612.   [181] Ibid. no 12625.
[182] Ibid. no 12667.   [183] Ibid. no 12602.   [184] Ibid. no 12671.

The gist of the problem was that while the *Reichsregiment* had proved helpful in setting up a system that offered hope that the indulgence proceeds could be kept safe, it could not provide military leadership: everybody agreed that this was Maximilian's role. The emperor-elect was quick to jump to the defence of his right to command the united forces of Christendom, especially when it was being challenged by the French king;[185] his unsought exclusion from the leadership of an imperial expedition would be tantamount to deposition.[186] In Chapter 4 we noted Perault's suggestions in 1502 that he himself would lead the empire's *crucesignati*, and that the collected money would be dispensed to recruits at the local level. Both ideas were impracticable, the first probably no more than a tactical gambit. But in any case, what was the guarantee that Germany's princes would behave any better than Maximilian? Like him they faced the heavy costs of warfare and building projects.[187] Given that Maximilian's involvement could not be avoided, it would be best to control it. This was the gist of Contarini's clever suggestion to the doge in January 1502 that, while drip-feeding money to Maximilian was a waste of time, Venice could take over the task of paying his troops directly, thereby ensuring their service.[188] There were clear advantages to this approach, given that Maximilian's response to the Turkish threat to his Austrian lands was the mobilization of some men and artillery there in the winter and spring of 1501–2.[189] But Contarini's idea does not seem to have been pursued, perhaps because the republic could not shoulder the additional expense: it was already subsidizing Hungary and had made it clear to Maximilian that there would be no more money for him.[190]

Arguably, the best way to square Maximilian's immediate need for cash with the concerns of Perault and the *Reichsregiment* about its exclusive use for crusading purposes was a phased release of the indulgence money. There was a consensus that just as the diversion of crusading funds caused disillusionment, so reports of military activity would create a virtuous circle; people would give more generously (so more souls would be saved) if they heard about a campaign.[191] The problem with implementing this approach was threefold. In the first place, nobody knew how much money had been donated: hence there was logic (though not necessarily sincerity) behind Maximilian's demand that the chests should be opened and the cash counted and then put back.[192] Secondly, the use that Maximilian was already making of the proceeds of the Austrian indulgence chests, which he had been opening since autumn 1501,[193] showed that the emperor-elect needed the money not to engage in future warfare but to pay existing debts, many of them incurred for day-to-day costs like bills for accommodation.[194] This was the advantage of the suggestions advanced by Contarini and Perault for direct payment; it was common

---

[185] Sanuto, *I diarii*, 3.435–8 (= *AR*, no 14160); Wiesflecker, *Maximilian I.*, 2.160.
[186] Schmid, 'Der päpstliche Legat', 73 note 28.
[187] Cf. Wiesflecker, *Maximilian I.*, 3.51.   [188] *AR*, no 15976.
[189] e.g. ibid. nos 15961, 16150, 16557 (reporting rumours that the musters were only for show).
[190] Ibid. nos 12625, 15936, 15943.   [191] Ibid. nos 15841, 16011.
[192] Ibid., nos 16336, 16692.   [193] e.g. ibid. no 12773 (Vienna).
[194] Ibid. no 16201 (Salzburg). For later uses of *Erbländer* proceeds see ibid. nos 17523, 17589, 17608, 17634, 17652, 20797, 17916.

knowledge that bringing the debt-laden ruler into the financial loop was a recipe for inactivity. Thirdly, Maximilian's sprawling view of what crusade entailed did not help: before the Turks could be fought he must go to Rome, be crowned, and set in train the reform of the Church, quite apart from any attempt to recover Milan from the French or subjugate the Swiss. What might have been a way forward in the limited context of frontier defence became much more problematic when Maximilian's imperial status and obligations came into play.[195] This is clear from the call to arms that Maximilian issued in July 1502, in which the frame of reference moved seamlessly from the Turks to the French, national honour and prestige rubbing shoulders with danger among the reasons for going to war.[196]

This summons, and the one that preceded it in January, constituted one of two prominent tactics that Maximilian deployed against Perault and the *Reichsregiment* to make them agree to hand over the contents of the chests in 1501–3. Contrary to what one might suppose given Maximilian's past history, propagating the image of an impending imperial crusade had its advantages. Perault was susceptible to it not just because of his optimistic nature, which many interpreted as dangerous naivety, but also because it incorporated the reform of the Church; delaying action against the Turks might be a price worth paying to clean the Augean stables of the Borgia court. Naturally, he disapproved of Maximilian's habit of equating the French with the Turks, but he hoped to remove that element of the programme through diplomacy.[197] As for the empire's elites, the pressure to which they could be subjected is exemplified by the speech that Maximilian delivered, partly in person, at the meeting of the Swabian league held at Ulm in early July 1502. In this bravura performance Maximilian painted an apocalyptic picture of the empire under attack from without and within. He denounced the rebel peasants (*Bundschuh*), their Swiss inciters, Louis XII, and Berthold. He claimed that there was a nefarious alliance of interests (France, Alexander VI, and the *Reichsregiment*) that aimed at ending 700 years of German imperial rule and replacing it with French control over Germany and Italy. Confronted by this deadly coalition, all that Maximilian had to work with was 100,000 ducats, plus his own blood and life.[198] The Turks played such a marginal role in this oratorical display that one historian, picking up on the suspicions of Perault and other contemporaries, believed that Maximilian had in mind an alliance with the sultan to carve up Italy.[199] But promoting the 'imperilled empire' theme assisted Maximilian's demand to enjoy access to the contents of the indulgence chests. For if circumstances were as grim as he painted them, the need to rally to the Habsburg flag pushed into the background not just suspicions about Maximilian's centralizing ambitions but also past experience of his volatility. The crusade might be associated with Maximilian's costly expansionism (not least because he insisted on yoking it to the *Romzug*), but the defence of

---

[195] For this distinction see ibid. no 16011.   [196] Ibid. no 16725.   [197] Ibid. no 16598.
[198] *Urkunden zur Geschichte des schwäbischen Bundes (1488–1533)*, ed. K. Klüpfel, pt 1: 1488–1506 (Stuttgart, 1846), 469–72.
[199] Wiesflecker drily commented that nothing was less likely ('nichts wäre unwahrscheinlicher als dies'): *Maximilian I.*, 3.20.

the *Reich* was another matter. And ceding him the indulgence proceeds was a more palatable way of demonstrating loyalty than reviving the unpopular Common Penny. There was a lot to be said for paying lip service to the emperor-elect's crusade programme, even if one continued to be sceptical about it.

The second tactic that Maximilian deployed, mainly against Perault, was pressure pure and simple. This had worked in 1491 and presumably he saw no reason why it should not again. We know the details of his bullying largely because of Perault's whistle-blowing campaign of early 1504, in which he placed in the public domain key documents testifying to it. The emperor-elect's unsubtle mixture of promises and threats clearly took their toll on the aged, sick, and isolated man, who had as much need as Maximilian to gain access to the money to meet his outgoings: for the emperor-elect tried to impose the line that if he could not get at the proceeds then neither would Perault.[200] But the legate refused to move from his position that the proceeds must be used specifically and visibly (*sichtiglich*) for a campaign against the Turks,[201] rather than sinking into the bottomless ocean of Maximilian's financial outgoings. The very suggestion that this could happen would be disastrous. In May 1502 he told Maximilian that if he acceded to his request for the handover of the money (as opposed to its counting and preservation *in situ*), 'never again could a single florin be raised anywhere in his legatine zone, which would entail irreparable damage for the crusade as well as infamy for the emperor-elect and legate'; the latter because people would inevitably attribute the change of approach to a clandestine agreement between the two. Perault's feelings on the subject were so strong that he returned to the theme at the close of his letter: handover would not just endanger the safety of Perault and his *Ablasskommissaren* but also spell the end of the crusade in Germany: 'There would be no point in talking any more about crusade or Jubilee in Germany.'[202] In another printed text he cited a string of biblical passages testifying to the divine punishment of rulers who acted unjustly by pillaging goods 'acquired through the sweat and work of the poor' and dedicated to God's work.[203] And towards the end of 1503 he retrospectively returned to the subject, once again in print. There was nothing, not 'the favour, fear, love, prayer, offer, or threats of any living being', that would make him yield to Maximilian's demands. He would rather die than betray people who had given up their daily bread and that of their dependants 'for the salvation of their souls and the protection of the faith'.[204] He was being somewhat melodramatic because Maximilian had no intention of creating another Beckett, though he did toy with the idea of placing Perault under lock and key.[205]

In maintaining this defensive stance the provisions of the Nürnberg concordat of 1501 had a vital role to play, and this made Perault's dependence on Berthold

---

[200] Mehring, 'Peraudi', 401–6, no 7, at 404.   [201] *AR*, no 19865.
[202] Mehring, 'Peraudi', 398–401, no 6, at 399, para. 6, 401, para.11.
[203] Biblioteca Apostolica Vaticana, Palat IV. 1229 (5), printed open letter (n.d.), at 1–9.
[204] Mehring, 'Peraudi', 401–6, no 7, at 402–3.
[205] In September 1502, according to a Contarini despatch: *AR*, no 16875. See ibid. no 14724 for Perault's earlier view of himself as another Beckett.

von Henneberg more pronounced. The affirmation of the Nürnberg concordat by Berthold's assembly of electoral princes at Gelnhausen in June 1502 was a boost to Perault's morale at a very trying time. It is tempting to view Perault forming an overt alliance with the cause of the *Reichsregiment*, but Peter Schmid has convincingly argued the case for Perault carefully keeping his distance from the quagmire of the constitutional conflict.[206] Both he and Berthold must have realized that the support of a papal legate would not help the *Reichsregiment*'s domestic programme of reform, even if this particular legate enjoyed such a strong reputation for backing Church reform that Berthold and his supporters lobbied for his election as Pope after Pius III's death in October 1503.[207] Distance and the speedy election of Julius II just fourteen days after Pius's demise wrecked Perault's chances, and (as in the case of Bessarion's failure to secure election in 1471) it is a matter for speculation whether the crusade would have prospered had its most prominent supporter become Pope.[208] As it was, by the close of 1502 the fate of the indulgence proceeds had become perilously reliant on the *Reichsregiment*, and this was problematic because Berthold proved unable to translate discontent with the current regime and ruler into a positive programme of action. Early in November Maximilian had to dismiss the troops he had painstakingly gathered in Austria because he could not pay them, which was a roundabout tribute to Perault's powers of resistance;[209] but a *Sondertagung* held under the auspices of the *Reichsregiment* at Würzburg later that month was only patchily attended. The *Reichsregiment* was abolished and the government of the empire (such as it was) reverted to Maximilian's control.[210] Berthold died in 1504, though by then he had ceased to be a major problem for Maximilian.

Perault's legation entered its third phase when Venice and Hungary agreed peace terms with the Turks early in 1503. It was perhaps awareness of this impending peace that caused a consistory to greet with amused laughter (*piacevolezza*) the latest proposal from Maximilian to lead a broad-based crusade.[211] Despite this development, Perault showed no clear signs of losing heart: indeed at the end of 1502, when the imminence of peace was apparent, he lobbied successfully to get his legation extended for a further year. He continued to preach as energetically and convincingly as in 1502; it was in May 1503, for example, that he achieved his strikingly successful outcome at Bremen. But a change of emphasis can be detected, notably an increasing focus on securing the proceeds of his own third. His legation ended in October 1503, and in his letters to Utrecht a few weeks later he can be viewed offering his own judgement on his achievements. On 15 December he commented that far from spending his time 'silently, inactively, and fruitlessly', he had worked for the salvation of many and the benefit of all, referring in particular to his peacemaking between Lübeck and the king of Denmark.[212] On 1 January

---

[206] Schmid, 'Der päpstliche Legat', 84, 86.
[207] *AR*, no 20740; Wiesflecker, *Maximilian I.*, 3.36.   [208] Setton, *Papacy*, 3.7–10.
[209] Wiesflecker, *Maximilian I.*, 3.157.   [210] Ibid. 29–30.
[211] *Dispacci di Antonio Giustinian*, ed. P. Villari, 3 vols (Florence, 1876), 1.402–4, no 291 (= *AR*, no 20273).
[212] *Codex documentorum*, 431–2, no 303.

1504 he was more expansive. He wrote that the goals of his legation had been to save as many souls as possible, restore peace in Germany, and 'bring into being (in so far as we could) a genuine expedition against the most wicked Turks'.[213] The qualification is revealing. It is possible that Perault really believed that achieving two goals out of three was a reasonable outcome, and a comparison might be drawn with St Bernard's famous apologia for the Second Crusade. But knowing the amount of effort Perault had invested into creating a crusade, it is hard not to detect bitterness in the remark. For when he wrote these two letters Perault was aware that he had lost the battle to keep the indulgence proceeds safe. In October 1503 he warned Louis XII of France to expect an attack by troops who were being paid with the money.[214] According to Contarini, the opening of chests in the Rhineland for accounting purposes had caused proceeds to start going astray as early as the autumn of 1502.[215] At the end of August 1503, in the wake of Alexander VI's death, Maximilian's envoy at the papal court suggested that he might use the excuse of an expedition to Rome to purge the Church to lay his hands more openly on the money sitting in the chests.[216] But Maximilian soon thought of an approach that was more congenial to him, and when Perault wrote his letters to Utrecht at the turn of 1503/4 he would certainly have heard news of Maximilian's recent and most dangerous assault on the Nürnberg provisions for keeping the indulgence money secure.

This took the form of a relaunch of his *societas sancti Georgii*. It is hard not to admire the devious cunning with which Maximilian brushed down his old idea and refashioned it to subvert the Nürnberg concordat. Anybody who enrolled in this 'worthwhile and praiseworthy society or confraternity' would be expected to accompany him on crusade for a year. The expedition had the familiar shape of a grand campaign that would follow his coronation at Rome, which was scheduled for early in 1504. It would be both the enactment of his role as Christendom's commander-in-chief and an apotheosis of his self-image as a Christian knight; so resistance to it would be unchristian and ignoble as well as treasonable. It was alleged that envoys had been despatched to various Christian kings and nations to secure their support. Men who enrolled in the society would be expected to provide 50 per cent of their own wages, or be sponsored in traditional crusading style by their friends and relatives. The other 50 per cent would originate in the Perault indulgence money. The proposal shared some features with the one that Perault had suggested in May 1502, but it was placed within a more chivalric context and, crucially, it involved spending the indulgence money from the start. For anybody familiar with Maximilian's reputation, this was the most troubling aspect of the plan. Nor would their fears have been allayed by the proposal that the 50 per cent of the wage bill originating with recruits or their sponsors should be assigned to Maximilian's bankers, the Welser and Fugger of Augsburg, who would disburse it as wages on a quarterly basis, on ember days.

---

[213] Ibid. 437–42, no 307, at 440.   [214] Sanuto, *I diarii*, 5.202 (= *AR*, no 20702).
[215] *AR*, no 16957.   [216] Ibid. no 20636.

The rationale for this was that the volunteers would otherwise fritter it away on dicing and whores.[217]

As so often with Maximilian's schemes, it is tempting but not entirely safe to regard this deployment of the society of St George as a confidence trick.[218] The confraternity was publicized at Augsburg on 12 November 1503 with an excitable and eclectic manifesto. Suspicions about the society's real purpose are aroused rather than assuaged by the manifesto's focus on the Turks because this ran counter to Maximilian's usual approach and, for that reason, looks brazenly tactical. The claim was made that in recent years no fewer than 90,000 Christians had suffered death or enslavement at their hands, in lands that stretched from Poland to the Peloponnese. Admittedly, on the same day that the manifesto was issued the Venetian envoy, Alvise Mocenigo, wrote about concrete plans for recruitment and funding.[219] That Maximilian intended to pay his troops from the collected crusade money is unquestionable. Mocenigo referred to hopes to make use of 170,000 florins from this source, and a month later the heaviest of pressure was exerted on the representatives of the Swabian league meeting at Ulm to hand over the indulgence money. It worked.[220] To help press home his case, Maximilian had made his ceremonial entry to Ulm on 8 December dressed in the confraternity's uniform,[221] and from this point until the spring of 1504 he continued to promote the *societas* vigorously.[222] Throughout these months he was planning for an Italian expedition, and he only abandoned these hopes when it proved impossible to avoid getting drawn into the war of the Landshut succession. There is a distinction to be drawn between Maximilian's undoubted use of the society of St George as a battering ram to break through the defences guarding the collection chests, and an inherently duplicitous approach towards crusade. The confraternity never got anywhere, and it is unlikely that Maximilian expected it to; it had served its purpose and could be allowed to lie dormant until the next time plans for a *Romzug*/crusade surfaced, which was in 1507–8.[223] But that does not mean that the cause it was revived to promote was without any substance; it was just that the substance was *sui generis*, possibly clear only to Maximilian.[224]

Numerous texts exist relating to the opening of the indulgence chests from mid-December 1503 onwards, and to the assignment of their contents to settle Maximilian's various expenses and repay his creditors.[225] It remains to examine the reactions to this process of the three key individuals and groups affected: the Pope, Perault, and the Germans. Alexander VI had acted decently on the German indulgence money, though he would have given it away in exchange for Maximilian's

---

[217] *Volumen*, 214–17 (= *AR*, no 17881). The services of the Welser and Fugger had been used since 1501 for indulgence proceeds collected in the *Erbländer*: Wiesflecker, *Maximilian I.*, 3.42.
[218] According to the Augsburg manifesto the society was Maximilian's response to lobbying by six named princes and nobles, so unless this was camouflage it is possible that the initiative did not originate as a tactic, but was shaped into one.
[219] *AR*, no 17909.   [220] Ibid. nos 17976–7.
[221] Wiesflecker, *Maximilian I.*, 3.37, 57, 161.   [222] *AR*, nos 18329, 18449.
[223] Wiesflecker-Friedhuber, 'Maximilian I.', 547–8.
[224] *Waghalsig* (reckless) is the word used by Wiesflecker, *Maximilian I.*, 3.150.
[225] For example, *AR*, nos 17990–1, 18033, 18056, 18071–2, 18116–18, 18172, 18254, 18329.

backing for Borgia dynastic ambitions if the cardinals had allowed him to.[226] Early in 1504, however, Pope Julius II sanctioned Maximilian's policy of collection in order to secure imperial assistance against Venetian encroachments in Romagna. Securing Romagna in the wake of Cesare Borgia's aborted state-building was bolted onto the Turkish crusade as an essential preliminary measure. In May Julius instructed his nuncio Mariano Bartholini to investigate how much money there was and where it was located: Perault, he added, would be able to advise.[227] It was ironic that money raised for the sake of a cause that Venice had vigorously promoted was now directed against the republic itself. The mustering of troops in southern Austria had made the Venetians nervous even when Maximilian talked about a crusade;[228] now their purpose was not in doubt. And it must have been particularly galling for the former legate to be expected to play a role in the handover of the specie to Maximilian. We do not know what, if any, view he held about Julius's war in Romagna, but the cornerstone of his approach had been that money raised through his preaching must be used for the anti-Ottoman crusade alone. This had been explicitly stated in 1500 as a condition for Perault's taking on the legation,[229] and even lobbying for the use of some of the proceeds to assist the Teutonic Order to defend Livonia against the Russians, which was a cause of direct relevance to the empire, had proved fruitless.[230] The Pope's change of policy at this late stage could be expected to bring serious consequences. It is not surprising that in his legatine report in consistory, in January 1505, Perault warned that there would be a revolt against Rome in Germany unless something was urgently done to mend relations.[231]

As Perault's consistorial prophecy shows, having succeeded as crusade preacher and failed as crusade promoter, the former legate took on a third role in 1504–5 as publicist. This was evidenced above all in the flow of printed *Flugschriften* with which, in the early months of 1504, he attempted both to bolster resistance to Maximilian's assault on his collection chests, and to make clear the consequences of surrender for the guilty parties and the crusading cause. Despite personal appeals like that to Duke Ulrich of Württemberg,[232] he did not manage to stem the flood of surrender, though as we saw in the previous chapter, his efforts annoyed Maximilian enough for him to make efforts to end the flow of printed material. The fact was that Perault's position was always fragile, given the approaches that were adopted towards the crusading cause by Pope and emperor-elect. His own record was clean and he did all that was humanly possible, but he lacked a supporting apparatus in terms of individuals and resources. Whatever our judgement on the efficiency and probity of Perault's preaching and collecting infrastructure, its remit was limited. Even Capistrano, whose exploits Perault aspired to emulate, had

---

[226] Ibid. nos 17099–17100.   [227] Ibid. no 21140 and see also nos 21139, 21141.
[228] cf. ibid. no 16104.   [229] Ibid. no 14474.   [230] Ibid. nos 19595, 19866, 19885.
[231] Schneider, *Peraudi*, 94. Generally see Hartmut Boockmann, 'Das 15. Jahrhundert und die Reformation', in Boockmann, ed., *Kirche und Gesellschaft im Heiligen Römischen Reich des 15. und 16. Jahrhunderts* (Göttingen, 1994), 9–25; Meuthen, 'Reiche'.
[232] *AR*, no 21038.

relied in 1456 on the backing of Juan Carvajal and Pope Calixtus (witness his earlier complaints about Nicholas V's shortcomings). In a memorandum written for Alexander VI shortly before Perault's appointment in 1500, his fellow cardinal and ardent crusade lobbyist, Stefano Taleazzi, recommended that

> In order to avoid confusion, and the suspicion that the money will be frittered away, as has proved to be the case in the past when the crusade was preached, the Pope, secular lords, bishops, and popular representatives should set up in every lordship a treasury (*camera*) together with its attendant personnel. In line with agreed procedures, all [crusade money] would be collected and stored there, for transportation to the treasuries located in Hungary, Italy and elsewhere; and later [taken] from them to the armies, wherever they are situated, as their victories carry them forward. In this way, when the armies need money, the means will exist to quickly supply it.[233]

The creation of this closely knit but independent network of financial agencies dedicated to serving the crusade was a pipedream; even Taleazzi conceded that there was 'a massive amount of work and effort involved in it all'. The real world provided Perault with nothing but the *Reichsregiment*, which was proving insufficient thanks to that body's limitations even before its abolition. The resulting 'confusion', as Taleazzi put it in his memorandum, was a polite way of describing the outcome of Perault's labours. His dilemma was illuminated by the postscript to his legation. After concluding his series of *Flugschriften* at Strasbourg, he made his way in the summer of 1504 to Basel and from there to Lucerne. The latter was an unexpected destination given that his crusade preaching had received probably its coolest reception among the *Eidgenossen*,[234] but Perault's brief now was to bring the Swiss into alliance with the Pope. The episode evinces Perault's lack of independent authority; he had no choice but to do what he was told and make the best of the situation. Because of this, it is hard to take issue with Wiesflecker's judgement that the crusading aspect of Perault's legation was hopeless from the start, for which reason, given the purity of his dedication to fighting the Turks, his fate was tragic.[235]

As for the Germans, their reaction to Maximilian's seizure of the chests took the form of distaste and occasional resistance. There were recorded expressions of chagrin at what was being done, as in the cases of the 'heavy-hearted' Hans Ungelter, who reluctantly voted for capitulation on behalf of Esslingen at Ulm in December 1503,[236] and Otto Sturm, who reported back to Strasbourg a month later that there was no alternative, and they must make a virtue of necessity.[237] Maximilian's practice of issuing guarantees to local authorities that he would shield them against repercussions implies that the handover was performed unwillingly.[238] There was enough resistance to provoke a general warning, issued on 6 March 1504, claiming

---

[233] Feliciangeli, 'Le proposte', 47–8 and see too 53. Taleazzi's proposed system of financial management was so ambitious that it even aimed to provide pensions for the dependents of dead combatants: ibid. 49.

[234] Preaching was permitted at only three locations: *AR*, no 19636.

[235] Wiesflecker, *Maximilian I.*, 3.57–8: 'Daher war seine Mission von Anfang an aussichtslos und sein Ende tragisch'.

[236] *AR*, no. 17976.   [237] *AR*, no 20909.   [238] *AR*, nos 20909, 18115, 18688, 18737.

that the assignment of the cash to imperial agents enjoyed papal support and reminding dissidents that they were Maximilian's subjects, not Perault's.[239] At the end of that month the bishop of Eichstätt was still refusing to cooperate.[240] There was much discontent at Constance, where in June the bishop favoured surrender to Maximilian, but his cathedral chapter insisted on its opposition being recorded in the presence of a notary and witnesses.[241] Given that in May 1502 Perault had described the existence of strong support for the crusade at Cologne, it is particularly interesting to find this city opposing the handover. In a letter to the burgomaster and council in July 1504 their envoy to Maximilian, Heinrich Slebusch, reported at length on a bruising encounter in which Slebusch, admittedly according to his own account, stood his ground courageously, even waylaying Maximilian when he was about to go hunting. But when Slebusch reminded the monarch of his clear obligations under the 1501 Nürnberg concordat, Maximilian dismissed the concordat as the product of a priestly cabal and made it clear that he would only back Cologne's civic authorities in their dispute with the city's archbishop if they gave way on the chests.[242] Faced with such tactics, and lacking any coordination, the cluster of localized complaints could get nowhere. Maximilian secured the funds that he needed to persevere with wars that eventually came to nothing while the Turks, their objectives in Greece achieved, turned to their eastern front.[243] At the end of his reign, at the diet of Augsburg in 1518, Maximilian would again hope to find in indulgences the financial means to pursue his endgame of leading a great crusade against the Turks, only to abandon the idea once it became clear that the profits were not worth having.[244] The price that he paid for his behaviour in 1503–4 was not the rejection of his power characteristic of the *Bundschuh* or the Swiss, against whom he had directed his call to arms at Ulm in 1502, but a subtler and broader erosion of confidence in his assertions and trust in his authority.

[239] *AR*, no 18334.   [240] *AR*, no 18459.   [241] *AR*, no 21181.
[242] *AR*, no 18999. Maximilian had already mortgaged the Cologne proceeds: ibid. no 17698.
[243] The outcome was later caustically summarized by the Swiss historian Valerius Anshelm, *Die Berner-Chronik*, ed. Historischer Verein des Kantons Bern, 2 vols (Bern, 1884–6), 342–3 (= *AR*, no 19636).
[244] Winterhager, 'Ablaßkritik', 10–12, esp. note 13.

7
Conclusion

In Chapter 62 of his *Epitome rerum Germanicarum*, published at Strasbourg in 1505, the Alsatian, Jacob Wimpfeling, exhorted Germany's princes to take up arms against the Turks on three grounds: *gloria, Christus,* and *salus patriae*.[1] Wimpfeling referred to orations delivered at imperial diets since 1454 by Aeneas Sylvius Piccolomini, John Bessarion, and Giannantonio Campano, and these fellow humanists would certainly have felt at home with his tripartite evaluation of the grounds for combating the Turks. Since the fall of Constantinople it had played a crucial role in shaping not just the ideological construction of a future crusade but also the way in which past crusaders were depicted; Benedetto Accolti had Godfrey of Bouillon refer to 'Christ's religion, the massacre of our people, and the desire for fame' as the forces that had brought the first crusaders to Antioch.[2] Synergizing such different values was not without its challenges, intellectual and practical alike. The absorption of classical themes into crusading ideas that underpinned the motivating value attributed by humanists to glory was not easily squared with the Church's traditional emphasis on penance and its reluctance to promote an intentionality that might encourage hubris and greed.[3] Nonetheless, the balance sheet of the humanist contribution to crusading ideology was positive and the term 'Renaissance crusading' should no longer be regarded as an oxymoron. Defence of the homeland (*salus patriae*) was a natural reaction to the unprecedented Islamic threat to home and hearth. The challenge was how to make a worldview that tended to be local or regional promote an all-inclusive Christian response. Among the obstacles were the ebbing away of papal and imperial authority, and a sense of detachment from the fate of fellow Christians living on the frontier, indeed *Schadenfreude* when it came to losses incurred by one particularly unpopular *antemurale* state. Charity ('the massacre of our people') certainly helped but was insufficient. Devotion (Wimpfeling's *Christus*) presented fewer problems of a core nature, for there is much evidence testifying to the continuing appeal of religious warfare to many contemporaries.[4] The difficulty in this case was deciding how best to mobilize zeal and penitence. The last years of Giovanni da Capistrano and Raymond Perault offered outstanding examples of the two main choices: personal service and financial donation. The difficulties that both men had to contend with are very well documented, and the fact that the outcome was a triumph in

---

[1] Mertens, '"Europa, id est patria"', at 45–7, 55.   [2] Accolti, *De bello*, 570–1, at 570.
[3] Accolti made Adhemar of Puy tackle this conundrum head on: ibid. 584–6, at 585.
[4] Housley, *Religious Warfare*.

Capistrano's case and a failure in Perault's is due in large measure to Mehmed II's mismanagement of his campaign in 1456. As always in the history of crusading, the problem was how to translate religious convictions into effective military activity. This had never been easy, nor should we read too much into contemporary awe at Ottoman war-making prowess: it was only the contemporary counterpart to the demographic imbalance faced by their ancestors in defending the kingdom of Jerusalem.

The burden of initiative, and to a large extent direction, lay with the papal court and its agencies. When Constantinople fell Eugenius IV had already reclaimed crusading's various instruments for a reunified papacy, putting in place a range of policies (in particular co-operation with *antemurale* states, proactive legates, naval contributions, and organized preaching) that could be applied to the new strategic situation once a Pope had been elected who possessed the will and energy that were called for. The turbulence of the 1460s enabled George Podiebrad to stage an attempt to hijack the crusade, but even the interest of an exceptionally anti-papal French court did not allow his project to gain traction. Nobody else mounted an open challenge to papal authority, though it was constantly ignored, circumvented, and criticized.[5] When Perault defended the sole right of the Pope to launch crusades, he was responding to a peculiarly elusive opposition, one which saw little to be gained from stepping openly into the ring. He was also representing a Pope of a very different timbre from Calixtus III and Pius II. It is tempting to see everything changing after 1494, when the longstanding volatility of Italian politics was translated onto a broader, European stage. There is no doubt that under Alexander VI papal policy towards the Turks was characterized by duplicity and contradictions: perhaps his most audacious comment was that since Louis XII had occupied so much of Italy, he should start to pull his weight in defending it against the Turks.[6] But this tendency to make the crusade serve Italian, indeed dynastic, goals had been almost as fully present under Sixtus IV. In particular, Sixtus's handling of the Turkish capture of Otranto in 1480–1 was deeply politicized.

Substantial shifts in political culture are notoriously hard to pin down, and it is useful to establish two points. The first is that, given the costly naval contributions that Sixtus and Alexander made towards the struggle against the Turks, it is inaccurate to say that either 'neglected' the Turkish issue. It is easier to defend Sixtus than Alexander: his inconsistent, self-defeating bellicosity in Italy was balanced by an ambitious and imaginative anti-Turkish policy, which he pursued with vigour.[7] The second point is that Calixtus III and Pius II took very seriously opposition to their authority stemming from Christians, whether it was the *condottiere*, Jacopo Piccinino,[8] the lord, Everso dell'Anguillara or the king, George Podiebrad. In the

---

[5] The parallel with responses to papal trading bans is striking: see Stantchev, *Embargo*, ch. 6.
[6] *AR*, no 14160, writing to Louis in June 1500.
[7] As Schlecht pointed out, *Zamometić*, 1.148–70, the surviving instructions that Sixtus IV gave to his nuncios are unprecedentedly detailed, reflecting both his strengths and weaknesses.
[8] Miguel Navarro Sorni, ed., 'Breves del papa Calixto III en el "Archivio di Stato" de Milán. (Año 1455)', *Anthologica annua*, 44 (1997), 675–734, no 23, at 711–12.

autumn of 1463 Pius debated with his cardinals whether to postpone his crusade against the Turks in order to deal first with Everso. It was no easy task to dissuade him from doing so.[9] To that extent there was deep continuity of policy between these two Popes and Calixtus's nephew, Alexander. Defence of the lands of the papal state against attack from without or within, and the promotion of military action against rulers and groups holding heretical beliefs came close to enjoying automatic priority over the crusade against the Turks. As Sixtus IV expressed it, 'the dignity of the apostolic see, the universal Church, and the faith can be destroyed more easily by internal foes than by external unbelievers'.[10] Having said that, what occurred in the papal court's management of its crusading policy between the 1450s and 1490s looks like more than a change of emphasis or a shift in priorities. It formed part of a broader mutation in ethos, one described as 'Italian politicisation, increasingly princely style, financial corruption, family favouritism and luxury'.[11] In crusading terms, this meant that the Turks became accepted as a feature of the military and diplomatic landscape rather than being viewed as an alien intruder to be expelled.[12] When Sixtus IV, Innocent VIII, and Alexander VI addressed the Turkish question they did so without the sense of mission and urgency that had characterized the efforts of Calixtus and Pius, and the impressive team of lobbyists and enthusiasts that accumulated during their reigns. The 1450s and early 1460s constituted a remarkable period of focused and largely selfless effort in which there was a strong correlation between stated goals and actual aims. More than 500 years later one can still be moved by Bessarion's remark to Pius II in November 1463 that news of the Pope's public announcement that he would be setting out against the Turks next spring was the happiest moment of his life.[13]

Arguably, such a mood could not persist indefinitely (in this instance it seems to have passed within a year), and in recent years historians have shown more patience for the retrenchment and redirection of energies that marked Paul II's crusading efforts. But it is instructive to compare the situation in 1464 with that in 1481, particularly since both scenarios were fully documented by contemporaries who were well placed to observe what was going on. In 1464 Pius II pursued his determination to participate in an overseas expedition to the point of his death at Ancona. In the autumn of 1481, once Otranto had been recovered following Mehmed II's death, Sixtus wound down operations, notwithstanding his public declaration that his galleys would seize Valona (Vlorë) and carry the war into Albania.[14] When all due allowance is made for the problems of naval logistics and

[9] Ammannati Piccolomini, *Lettere*, 2.815–25, no 187.
[10] Schlecht, *Zamometić*, 2.58, no 39.
[11] D.S. Chambers, *Popes, Cardinals and War: The Military Church in Renaissance and Early Modern Europe* (London, 2006), 77. The author does not make it clear whether he subscribes to this view.
[12] See Bülent Ari, 'Early Ottoman Diplomacy: Ad Hoc Period', in A. Nuri Yurdusev, ed., *Ottoman Diplomacy: Conventional or Unconventional?* (Basingstoke, 2004), 36–65; Halil Inalcik, 'A Case Study in Renaissance Diplomacy: The Agreement between Innocent VIII and Bayezid II on Djem Sultan', ibid. 66–88.
[13] Mohler, *Bessarion*, 3.525.
[14] Pastor, *History*, 4.345–7, 518–19. *BF*, NS3.766–8, no 1516, is the key statement on the Pope's plan to carry on with the war.

communications, the contrast between the two approaches remains striking.[15] Sixtus, or rather his nephew, Girolamo Riario, had other priorities. Crusade preaching continued, but this too was hastily shut down when Sixtus's policies provoked a complex crisis in the spring of 1482. In the late 1490s a crusade enthusiast like Perault found himself effectively running a one-man show to promote the crusade in Germany, arguably good training for the situation that he would have to manage as legate a couple of years later. It was not only because Perault was regarded as being a diehard Francophile,[16] or favoured reform, that he had to operate wholly outside the papal circle. A man of the stamp of Leonello Chiericati, who practised duplicity during his activity in Germany, was more at ease with Alexander's goals and methods than Perault was. In fact, it is tempting to regard Perault as a relic from the earlier period of crusading zeal. He compared himself to Capistrano and was well aware of the approach that Pius had taken towards the crusade at Mantua. Pius's project of 1463–4 represented the last opportunity for a crusade that would be directed in the fullest sense by a Pope, while Perault's legation in 1501–4 was the last chance for a crusade that would be operating as a truly international venture. Like Pius and unlike Alexander (except notionally), Perault saw a crusade as by definition the expression of Christian unity, the programmatic counterpart and diplomatic sequel to peace between Christendom's monarchs.

It was Perault who put the finishing touches to the identification of crusade with the systematic promotion of indulgences. This was undoubtedly the period's most significant development, but in terms of facilitating a crusade the results were mixed. The chief benefit was that it offered the potential for modernizing the practice of crusading, bringing devotion into line with the military practices of the day, with their emphasis on professional combatants but more importantly massive supplies of money. It is striking how large a place continued to be held by both volunteering and surrogate service, and further research into this would be revealing, particularly in respect of other crusading theatres and the operations of the Military Orders at Rhodes and along the Baltic. But the overall trend towards donations is undeniable, and it was facilitated and rewarded on a scale never experienced before. It was possible for committed commentators like Johannes von Paltz to argue that nobody lost out: the minds of contemporaries were concentrated on penitence, the Turkish threat to the faith was driven back, souls were saved in the heartlands and both lives and souls at the frontiers. But this was to disregard the corrosive effect of abuses in the way indulgences were promoted, the vulnerability of the proceeds to raids by individuals and groups across the entire political and ecclesiastical spectrum, and the fact that the most zealously publicized indulgences could not provide sufficient money for even a medium-sized campaign. Earlier commentators like Marino Sanudo Torsello, who had addressed funding issues following the loss of Acre in 1291, would have recognized the dilemma all too clearly. Perault and his predecessors made more substantive progress than Sanudo and his generation had, but the

---

[15] Setton, *Papacy*, 2.371–3, esp. note 34, documents the difficulties.
[16] 'Lilium habens in corde suo', as Burchard put it in 1494: *Liber*, 1.541 (= *AR*, no 3171).

evidence suggests that they could not make good the funding shortfall. Moreover, in their strident attempts to do so, they gave the promotion of crusading a bad name in the eyes of many reflective observers, culminating in the clinically dismissive analysis offered by Erasmus a few years later.[17] The net effect was a credibility gap, and a vicious circle of diminishing returns in all senses.

The paradox of crusade was that while its enormous complications were obvious to all, not least the Popes, association with it did bring kudos, political advantage and, thanks to the efforts of men like Perault, financial value. It is the approach of the two leading *antemurale* states that illuminates this best. When they were at war with the Turks, Venice and Hungary eloquently proclaimed the ideals of crusade and were capable of fighting with courage and persistence. This was above all true of Venice in its exhausting war of 1463–79, when it made at least fourteen approaches to the papal *curia* for a full implementation of the trading embargo against the sultanate.[18] Much of the period's most resounding crusading rhetoric and argumentation emanated from Venice and Buda, where the new humanist *topoi* were quickly assimilated. But when not at war with the Turks both powers became clever at avoiding commitments and adroit in justifying their stance. This was the case, notably, with Venice during the congress of Mantua and it applied to Matthias Corvinus for most of his reign after the disappointments of 1464. Their apparent hypocrisy made historians like Pastor indignant, but the intrinsic logic of their position is hard to counter.[19] Crusading derived most of its cutting edge from the agreement of states like Venice and Hungary to work together on the issue, and in such coalitions we can detect the vigour that would come to characterize the naval leagues under whose organizational shell crusading persisted into the late sixteenth century. Pius II came closest to success when he worked with the grain of this approach, which achieved one of Wimpfeling's goals, *salus patriae*; and Pius's successors attempted to do the same, with varying degrees of sincerity and less success. Nothing could beat self-interest as an engine for action. It meant that state-building, the period's most important political trend, was working for crusade instead of against it; and although it was a retreat from the broad-based crusade that had been Pius's goal at Mantua, he managed to give it an ersatz inclusivity by encouraging volunteers from other states.

In the decades either side of 1500, crusading was at its most vigorous when it was absorbed into the pronouncements, policies, and mechanisms of governments.[20] This process was complemented by, and dovetailed with, liturgical persistence, a continuing appeal within chivalric culture, and curiosity about the crusading past,

---

[17] Norman Housley, 'A Necessary Evil? Erasmus, the Crusade, and War against the Turks', in John France and William G. Zajac, eds, *The Crusades and their Sources: Essays Presented to Bernard Hamilton* (Aldershot, 1998), 259–79.

[18] See Stantchev, Embargo, Part 2, and his '*Devedo*: The Venetian Response to Sultan Mehmed II in the Venetian-Ottoman Conflict of 1462–79', *Mediterranean Studies*, 19 (2010), 43–66.

[19] The contrasting views of Pastor and Picotti on Venetian policy were noted in ch. 3. Picotti's more nuanced and sympathetic interpretation of the republic's attitude towards the crusade is currently gaining ground through the work of such scholars as Michael Carr and Stefan Stantchev.

[20] For further development of this argument see my 'Crusading and State-Building'.

especially when viewed through humanist lenses. We should finish by briefly considering what it meant for the enemy. It is far from easy to assess the impact on the Ottoman Turks of the crusade planning and activity that took place in the five decades following 1453. The view has been advanced that ceaseless talk of crusading stimulated Ottoman aggression as pre-emptive action against 'papal calls for the total extirpation of Islam and its adherents [and] projects to expel the Turks from their hard-won home in Asia Minor'.[21] It is possible that individual campaigns were prompted or their timing advanced by such fears, but the evidence needs to be set out fully. As a general thesis both the established dynamic of Ottoman expansion and the reactive character of so much crusading tell against it. The use of Djem as a deterrent rather than as an aggressive weapon was indicative of a preference for living with the *status quo* if it could somehow be arranged. The Renaissance Popes have much to answer for, but in the light of our existing knowledge it is unfair to place responsibility for the sultanate's conquests at their door. The period's most conspicuous feature is the failure to bring about any general crusade, whether it was the projected follow-up to victory at Belgrade in 1456 and Otranto in 1481, the programmes that Pius devised at Mantua in 1459 and launched in 1464, or the many plans that never got beyond the meeting rooms of diets and assemblies. They remain historical 'might have beens',[22] though useful as evidence for Christian strategic ideas and appreciation of Ottoman strengths and weaknesses, and revealing about evolving perceptions of the Orthodox and the sultanate's Islamic foes.

On the other hand, we should not ignore the range of military activity that *did* occur under the aegis of crusade, in particular naval raids in the eastern Mediterranean, campaigning in the Peloponnese and the Danube basin, and the sponsorship of Iskanderbeg. Balanced assessment is rendered difficult, *inter alia*, by the fact that we rely heavily on tendentious reports that exaggerated both defeats (to secure support) and successes (to justify past backing). But historians have started to give this fighting the attention it deserves, and the results to date are mixed. Stefan Stantchev has passed a critical verdict on Venice's waging of its war of 1463–79, in which Mehmed achieved his run of successes with much less investment than the republic put into its many defeats.[23] By contrast, Dan Mureşan has argued that the net effect of Christian operations along the Danube frontier, in Albania, and even at distant Caffa, was to deny Mehmed II the access he sought to the Adriatic, Italy, and his ultimate goal, Rome.[24] It is apparent that more work needs to be done, but while the possibility exists that contemporaries judged themselves too severely, it is likely that they would have found that meagre consolation. As a mechanism for dealing with the Ottoman threat the crusading programme failed, and its impact and significance are to be located not at the frontier but within the lands that it was supposed to protect.

---

[21] Ryder, *Alfonso*, 295. The supporting reference is to ch. 4 of Stanford Shaw's *History of the Ottoman Empire*, vol. 1, which comprises a general account of Ottoman history from 1451 to 1566.
[22] The same can be said of the unsuccessful lobbying for the election as pope of Bessarion in 1471 and Perault in 1503.
[23] Stantchev, *Embargo*, pt 2.   [24] Mureşan, 'La croisade'.

Bibliography

UNPUBLISHED SOURCE

Biblioteca Apostolica Vaticana, Palat IV. 1229 (5)

PRIMARY SOURCES

[Toponyms are listed under the individual's first name]

Accolti, Benedetto, *De bello a christianis contra barbaros gesto*, Recueil des historiens des croisades, Historiens occidentaux, 5 (Paris, 1895), 529–620.

Acta Albaniae Vaticana. Res Albaniae saeculorum XIV et XV atque cruciatam spectantia, ed. Ignatius Parrino, Studi e testi, 266 (Città del Vaticano, 1971).

Acta Bosnae potissimum ecclesiastica, ed. Euzebije Fermendžin (Zagreb, 1892).

Aeneae Silvii Piccolomini Senensis opera inedita, ed. Josephus Cugnoni (Rome, 1883; facs. edn, Farnborough, 1968).

Ammannati Piccolomini, Jacopo, *Commentarii*, in Frankfurt 1614 edn of Pope Pius II's *Commentarii*.

—— *Lettere (1444–1479)*, ed. Paolo Cherubini, 3 vols, Pubblicazioni degli Archivi di Stato, Fonti XXV (Rome, 1997).

Anecdota litteraria ex MSS codicibus eruta, ed. J. C. Amaduteus and G. L. Bianconius, 4 vols (Rome, 1773–83).

Anecdota veneta nunc primum collecta ac notis illustrata, ed. Joannes Baptista Maria Contareni OP, vol. 1 (Venice, 1757).

Annales ecclesiastici, ed. O. Raynaldus and G. D. Mansi, vols 9–10 (Lucca, 1752–3).

Annales minorum, 3rd edn, accuratissima auctior et emendatior ad exemplar editionis Josephi Mariae Fonseca ab Ebora, 25 vols (Quaracchi, 1931–5).

Annales regum Hungariae, ed. Georg Pray, 5 vols (Vienna, 1764–70).

Anshelm, Valerius, *Die Berner-Chronik*, ed. Historischer Verein des Kantons Bern, 2 vols (Bern, 1884–6).

Ausgewählte Regesten des Kaiserreiches unter Maximilian I., 1493–1519, ed. Hermann Wiesflecker and others, 4 vols in 7 pts so far (Vienna, 1990–).

Bartolomeo da Giano, 'Epistola de crudelitate Turcarum', in *PG*, 158.1055–68.

B. Bernardini Aquilani Chronica fratrum minorum Observantiae, ed. L. Lemmens (Rome, 1902).

Bessarion, 'Ad principes Italiae de Christianorum clade in Chalcide Eubœæ...orationes', in *PG*, 161.641–76.

Bughetti, Benvenuto, ed., 'Documenta inedita de S. Bernardino Senensi O.F.M. (1430–1445)', *Archivum Franciscanum historicum*, 29 (1936), 478–500.

Bullarium Franciscanum, nova series, ed. Joseph M. Pou y Marti and Caesar Cenci, vols 2–4, (Quaracchi and Rome, 1939–90).

Bullarium Franciscanum, Supplementum, ed. Caesar Cenci, vol. 1 (Rome, 2002).

Burchard, Johann, *Liber notarum*, ed. Enrico Celani, 2 vols, RISNS 32, pt 1.

Carteggi diplomatici fra Milano Sforzesca e la Borgogna, ed. E. Sestan, 2 vols, Fonti per la storia d'Italia, 140–1(Rome, 1985–7).

Cenci, Caesar, ed., 'Documenta Vaticana ad Franciscales spectantia, ann. 1447–1458', *Archivum Franciscanum historicum*, 93 (2000), 217–59.
Cenci, Caesar, ed., 'Documenta Vaticana ad Franciscales spectantia, ann. 1476–1481', *Archivum Franciscanum historicum*, 96 (2003), 85–127.
Cenci, Caesar, ed., 'Documenta Vaticana ad Franciscales spectantia, ann. 1482–1484', *Archivum Franciscanum historicum*, 97 (2004), 133–58.
Cent-dix lettres grecques de François Filelfe, ed. Émile Legrand (Paris, 1892).
'Chronicon Trithemii Sponheimense', in *Johannis Trithemii Spanheimensis… opera historica*, 1 vol. in 2 pts (Frankfurt, 1601), 236–435.
Die Chroniken der niederrheinischen Städte. Cöln, vol. 3, ed. Historische Commission bei der königl. Academie der Wissenschaften, Die Chroniken der deutschen Städte vom 14. bis ins 16. Jahrhundert, 14 (Leipzig, 1877).
Die Chroniken der niedersächsichen Städte. Lübeck, vol. 4, ed. Historische Commission bei der königl. Academie der Wissenschaften, Die Chroniken der deutschen Städte vom 14. bis ins 16. Jahrhundert, 30 (Leipzig, 1910).
Die Chroniken der niedersächsichen Städte. Magdeburg, vol. 1, ed. Historische Commission bei der königl. Academie der Wissenschaften, Die Chroniken der deutschen Städte vom 14. bis ins 16. Jahrhundert, 7 (Leipzig, 1869).
Clemen, Otto, ed., 'Ein offener Brief Raimund Peraudis', *Zeitschrift für Kirchengeschichte*, 20 (1900), 442–4.
Codex diplomaticus partium regno Hungariae adnexarum, ed. L. Thallóczy and A. Antal, vol. 2 (Budapest, 1907).
Codex documentorum sacratissimarum indulgentiarum Neerlandicarum, ed. Paul Fredericq (The Hague, 1922).
Codex epistolaris saeculi decimi quinti, ed. A Sokołowski and others, 3 vols (Cracow, 1876–94).
Corpus chronicorum bononensium, RISNS 18, pt 1.
Cristoforo da Soldo, *La cronaca*, ed. G. Brizzolara, RISNS 21, pt 3.
Cristoforo da Varese, 'Vita S. Joannis a Capistrano', in *AS Oct*, 491–541.
Crivelli, Lodrisio, *De expeditione Pii papae II*, ed. G.C. Zimolo, RISNS 33, pt 5.
Cronica gestorum ac factorum memorabilium civitatis Bononie, ed. A. Sorbelli, RISNS 23, pt 2.
The Crusades against Heretics in Bohemia, 1418–1437, tr. Thomas Fudge (Aldershot, 2002).
The Crusade of Varna, 1443–45, tr. Colin Imber (Aldershot, 2006).
Della historia di Bologna parte terza del R.P.M. Cherubino Ghirardacci, ed. A. Sorbelli, RISNS 33, pt 1.
Deutsche Reichstagsakten unter Kaiser Friedrich III., fünfte Abteilung, erste Hälfte 1453–1454, ed. Helmut Weigel and Henny Grüneisen, Deutsche Reichstagsakten, 19.1 (Göttingen, 1969).
Deutsche Reichstagsakten unter Maximilian I. Erster Band. Reichstag zu Frankfurt 1486, ed. Heinz Angermeier, Deutsche Reichstagsakten, mittlere Reihe, 1 (Göttingen, 1989).
Deutsche Reichstagsakten unter Maximilian I. Fünfter Band. Reichstag zu Worms 1495, ed. Heinz Angermeier, 3 vols in 2 pts, Deutsche Reichstagsakten, mittlere Reihe, 5 (Göttingen, 1981).
Deutsche Reichstagsakten unter Maximilian I. Sechster Band. Reichstage von Lindau, Worms und Freiburg 1496–1498, ed. Heinz Gollwitzer, Deutsche Reichstagsakten, mittlere Reihe, 6 (Göttingen, 1979).
Deutsche Reichstagsakten unter Maximilian I. Zweiter Band. Reichstag zu Nürnberg 1487, ed. Reinhard Seyboth, 2 vols, Deutsche Reichstagsakten, mittlere Reihe, 2 (Göttingen, 2001).

Diary of an Embassy from King George of Bohemia to King Louis XI. of France in 1464, ed. and tr. A.H. Wratislaw (London, 1871).
Diplomatarium svecanum, appendix, Acta pontificum svecica, I, Acta cameralia, vol. II ann. MCCCLXXI–MCDXCII, ed. L.L. Bååth (Stockholm, 1957).
Dispacci di Antonio Giustinian, ed. P. Villari, 3 vols (Florence, 1876).
Długosz, Jan, *Annals* (= *Annales seu cronicae incliti regni Poloniae*), tr. Maurice Michael, with a commentary by Paul Smith (Chichester, 1997).
Ebendorfer, Thomas, *Chronica Austriae*, ed. Alphons Lhotsky, MGH SRG nova series, XIII (Berlin/Zürich, 1967).
——*Chronica regum Romanorum*, ed. Harald Zimmermann, pt 2, MGH SRG nova series, XVIII (Hannover, 2003).
Epistolae pontificiae ad concilium Florentinum spectantes, pt 3, ed. George Hofmann (Rome, 1946).
Festa, Giovanni Battista, ed., 'Cinque lettere intorno alla vita e alla morte di S. Giovanni da Capestrano', *Bullettino della R. Deputazione Abruzzese di storia patria*, serie 3, 2 (1911), 7–58.
Foucard, C., ed., 'Fonti di storia napoletana nell'Archivio di Stato in Modena. Otranto nel 1480 e nel 1481', *Archivio storico per le province napoletane*, 6 (1881), 74–176.
Fredericq, Paul, ed., 'Les comptes des indulgences en 1488 et en 1517–1519 dans le diocèse d'Utrecht', *Mémoires couronnés et autres mémoires publiés par l'Académie royale des sciences, des lettres et des beaux-arts de Belgique*, 59 (1899–1900), 1–80.
Giovanni da Tagliacozzo, 'Relatio de victoria Belgradensi', in *AM*, 12.750–96.
Glassberger, Nicholas, *Chronica*, Analecta Franciscana, 2 (Quaracchi, 1887).
Hamburgische Chroniken in niedersächsicher Sprache, ed. J.M. Lappenberg (Hamburg, 1861).
Des Heiligen römischen Reichs Teutscher Nation Reichs Tags Theatrum... 1440 bis 1493, ed. Johann Joachim Müller (Jena, 1713).
Hungary as 'Propugnaculum' of Western Christianity: Documents from the Vatican Secret Archives (ca. 1214–1606), ed. Edgár Artner and others, (Budapest and Rome, 2004).
Johannes de Thurocz, *Chronica Hungarorum*, ed. Elisabeth Galántai and Julius Kristó, 2 vols, Bibliotheca scriptorum medii recentisque aevorum, series nova, 7, 9, (Budapest, 1985–8).
Johannes von Paltz, *Werke, 1: Coelifodina*, ed. Christoph Burger and Friedhelm Stasch, Spätmittelalter und Reformation. Texte und Untersuchungen, 2 (Berlin and New York, 1983).
——*Werke, 2: Supplementum Coelifodinae*, ed. Berndt Hamm, Spätmittelalter und Reformation. Texte und Untersuchungen, 3 (Berlin and New York, 1983).
Kaiser und Reich: Verfassungsgeschichte des Heiligen Römischen Reiches Deutscher Nation vom Beginn des 12. Jahrhunderts bis zur Jahre 1806 in Dokumenten, ed. Arno Buschmann, vol. 1, 2nd edn (Baden-Baden, 1994).
The Laws of the Medieval Kingdom of Hungary, Volume 3, 1458–1490, ed. and tr. János M. Bak and others (Los Angeles Calif., 1996).
Levi, Guido, ed., 'Diario Nepesino di Antonio Lotieri de Pisano (1459–1468)', *Archivio della R. Società romana di storia patria*, 7 (1884), 115–82.
Il 'Liber brevium' di Callisto III. La crociata, l'Albania e Skanderbeg, ed. Matteo Sciambra and others (Palermo, 1968).
Lorenzo de' Medici, *Lettere, V (1480–1481)*, ed. Michael Mallett (Florence, 1989).
Magyar Diplomacziai Emlékek. Mátyás Király Korából 1458–1490, ed. Nagy Iván and Nyáry Albert, Monumenta Hungariae Historica, acta extra, 4–7 (Budapest, 1875–8).

Mandeville, *Travels*, tr. C.W.R.D. Moseley (London, 1983).
Marino Sanudo Torsello, *The Book of the Secrets of the Faithful of the Cross*, tr. Peter Lock (Farnham, 2011).
Mathiae Corvini Hungariae regis epistolae ad Romanos pontifices datae et ab eis acceptae 1458–1490 (*Mátyás Király levelezése a Római pápákkal*), Monumenta Vaticana Hungariae, series 1, 6 (Budapest, 1891).
Matthew Paris, *Chronica maiora*, ed. H. R. Luard, 7 vols, Rolls Series, 57 (London, 1890).
Mátyás Király Levelei. Külügyi Osztály, ed. Vilmos Fraknói, 2 vols (Budapest, 1893–5).
Mémoires de messire Philippe de Comines, ed. Abbé Lenglet de Fresnoy, vol. 2 (London and Paris, 1747).
Mihailović, Konstantin, *Memoirs of a Janissary*, tr. Benjamin Stolz (Ann Arbor, 1975).
'Memorandum/Propositum Antonii Marini Gracianopolitiani ad procedendum magnanime contra Turcum', ed. František Šmahel in 'Antoine Marini de Grenoble et son *Mémorandum* sur la nécessité d'une alliance anti-turque', in *La noblesse et la croisade à la fin du Moyen Âge (France, Bourgogne, Bohême)*, ed. Martin Nejedlý and Jaroslav Svátek (Toulouse, 2009), 205–31, at 216–31.
Mohler, Ludwig, ed., 'Bessarions Instruktion für die Kreuzzugspredigt in Venedig (1463)', *Römische Quartalschrift*, 35 (1927), 337–49.
Monumenta Alexandrina: codex qui Liber crucis nuncupatur, ed. Francisco Gasparolo (Rome, 1889).
Monumenta conciliorum generalium seculi decimi quinti, ed. Kaiserliche Akademie der Wissenschaften in Wien, 3 vols (Vienna, 1857–86).
Monumenta historica Boemiae, ed. Gelasius Dobner, 6 vols (Prague, 1764–85).
Nauclerus, D. Iohannes, *Chronica...ab initio mundi usque ad annum Christi nati M. CCCCC* (Cologne, 1579).
Navarro Sorni, Miguel, ed., 'Breves del papa Calixto III en el "Archivio di Stato" de Milán. (Año 1455)', *Anthologica annua*, 44 (1997), 675–734.
Niccolò da Fara, 'Vita clarissimi viri fratris Joannis de Capistrano', in *AS Oct*, 439–83.
Niccolò della Tuccia, 'Cronaca di Viterbo', in *Cronache e statuti della città di Viterbo*, ed. Ignazio Ciampi, Documenti di storia italiana, 5 (Florence, 1872), 1–272.
Notes et extraits pour servir à l'histoire des croisades au XVe siècle, ed. Nicolai Iorga, 6 series (Paris and Bucharest, 1899–1916).
Opera inedita Aeneae Silvii Piccolomini Senensis, ed. Josephus Cugnoni (Rome, 1883; facs. edn, Farnborough, 1968).
Pannonius, Andreas, 'Libellus de virtutibus Matthiae Corvino dedicatus', in *Irodalomtörténeti Emlékek*, 1 (Budapest, 1886), 1–133.
Péllisier, L., ed., 'Documents sur la première année du règne de Louis XII tirés des Archives de Milan', *Bulletin historique et philologique du Comité des trauvaux historiques et scientifiques* (1890), 47–124.
Peter Eschenloer's...Geschichten der Stadt Breslau, ed. J.G. Kunisch, 2 vols (Breslau, 1827–8).
Philippe de Mézières, *Une Epistre lamentable et consolatoire*, ed. Philippe Contamine and Jacques Paviot (Paris, 2008).
Piccolomini, Aeneas Sylvius, *Der Briefwechsel. III. Abteilung: Briefe als Bischof von Siena, vol. 1 (1450–1454)*, ed. Rudolf Wolkan (Vienna, 1918).
—— *Opera omnia* (Basel, 1571; facs. edn, Frankfurt a. M., 1967).
—— *Epistola ad Mahomatem II*, ed., with translation and notes, Albert R. Baca (New York, 1990).

―― *De Europa*, ed. Adrian van Heck, Studi e testi, 398 (Città del Vaticano, 2001).
―― 'De ritu, situ, moribus et conditione Germaniae, descriptio', in his *Opera omnia*, 1034–86.
Pii II Commentarii rerum memorabilium que temporibus suis contigerunt, ed. Adrian van Heck, 2 vols, Studi e testi, 312–13 (Città del Vaticano, 1984).
Pii II orationes, ed. Joannes Dominicus Mansi, 3 vols (Lucca, 1755–9).
Pius II, *Commentaries*, ed. and tr. Margaret Meserve and Marcello Simonetta, I Tatti Renaissance Library, 12 (Cambridge, Mass., 2003–).
Priuli, Girolamo, *I diarii*, ed. A. Segre, RISNS 24/3, vol. 1.
Pulinari, Dionisio, *Cronache dei Frati Minori della provincia di Toscana*, ed. S. Mencherini (Arezzo, 1913).
Rabelais, François, *Gargantua and Pantagruel*, tr. J.M. Cohen (London, 1955).
Regestum Observantiae Cismontanae (1464–1488), Analecta Franciscana, 12 (Grottaferrata, 1983).
Rutebeuf, *Œuvres complètes*, ed. Edmond Faral and Julia Bastin, vol. 1 (Paris, 1959).
Sacrorum conciliorum nova et amplissima collectio, ed. G. D. Mansi, vols 32, 35 (Paris, 1902).
Sammlung der Reichs-Abschiede, ed. Johann Jacob Schmauss, vol. 1 (Frankfurt a. M., 1747).
Sánchez de Arévalo, Rodrigo, 'Historiae Hispanicae partes quatuor', in *Hispaniae illustratae seu rerum urbiumque Hispaniae... scriptores varii*, ed. Andreas Schott, 4 vols (Frankfurt, 1603–8), 1.121–246.
Sanuto, Marino, *I diarii*, ed. R. Fulin and others, 58 vols (Venice, 1879–1903).
Schefer, C., ed., 'Le discours du voyage d'oultremer au très victorieux roi Charles VII, prononcé, en 1452, par Jean Germain, évêque de Chalon', *Revue de l'Orient latin*, 5 (1895), 303–42.
Selecta iuris et historiarum, ed. H. C. Senckenberg, 6 vols (Frankfurt, 1734–43).
Sigismondo de' Conti, da Foligno, *Le storie de' suoi tempi dal 1475 al 1510*, 2 vols (Rome, 1883).
Simoneta, Johannes, *Rerum gestarum Francisci Sfortiae Commentarii*, ed. G. Soranzo, RISNS 21, pt 2.
Testi inediti e poco noti sulla caduta di Costantinopoli, ed. Agostino Pertusi (Bologna, 1983).
Theuerdank, facs. of 1517 edn (Cologne, 2003).
Thuróczy, János, *Chronicle of the Hungarians*, tr. Frank Martello, Indiana University Uralic and Altaic Series,155 (Bloomington Ind., 1991).
'Tractatus pacis toti Christianitati fiendae', ed. Jiři Kejř in *The Universal Peace Organization of King George of Bohemia: A Fifteenth Century Plan for World Peace 1462/1464* (London, 1964), 71–80, English tr. 83–92.
Turcica: Die europäische Türkendrucke des XVI. Jahrhunderts, I. Bd, MDI–MDL, ed. Carl Göllner (Bucharest, 1961).
Gli umanisti e la guerra otrantina. Testi dei secoli XV e XVI, ed. Lucia Gualdo Rosa and others (Bari, 1982).
Ungedruckte Akten zur Geschichte der Päpste vornehmlich im XV., XVI. und XVII. Jahrhundert, erster Band: 1376–1464, ed. Ludwig Pastor (Freiburg i.-Breisgau, 1904).
Urkunden zur Geschichte des schwäbischen Bundes (1488–1533), ed. K. Klüpfel, pt 1: 1488–1506 (Stuttgart, 1846).
Venice: A Documentary History, 1450–1630, ed. David Chambers and Brian Pullan (Oxford, 1992).

Vetera monumenta historica Hungariam sacram illustrantia, ed. Augustin Theiner, 2 vols (Rome, 1859–60).

Vetera monumenta Poloniae et Lithuaniae gentiumque finitimarum historiam illustrantia, ed. Augustin Theiner, 4 vols (Rome, 1986–4).

Vetera monumenta Slavorum meridionalium historiam illustrantia, ed. Augustin Theiner, vol. 1 (Rome, 1863).

Le Vite di Pio II di Giovanni Antonio Campano e Bartolomeo Platina, ed. Giulio C. Zimolo, RISNS 3, pt 3.

Volumen rerum germanicarum novum libri V, ed. Johannes Philippus Datt (Ulm, 1698).

Zafarana, Zelina, ed., 'Per la storia religiosa di Firenze nel Quattrocento: una raccolta privata di prediche', *Studi medievali*, serie 3, 9 (1968), 1017–113.

SECONDARY SOURCES

Ait, Ivana, 'Un aspetto del salariato a Roma nel XV secolo: La *fabrica galearum* sulle rive del Tevere (1457–58)', in *Cultura e società nell'Italia medievale: Studi per Paolo Brezzi*, Istituto storico italiano per il Medio Evo, studi storici, fasc. 184–7, vol. 1 (Roma, 1988), 7–25.

Albanese, Gabriella, 'La storiografia umanistica e l'avanzata turca: dalla caduta di Costantinopoli alla conquista di Otranto', in *CTO*, 1.319–52.

Andrić, Stanko, *The Miracles of St John Capistran* (Budapest, 2000).

Angermeier, Heinz, 'Der Wormser Reichstag 1495—ein europäisches Ereignis', *Historische Zeitschrift*, 261 (1995), 739–68.

Annas, Gabriele, *Hoftag—Gemeiner Tag—Reichstag. Studien zur strukturellen Entwicklung deutscher Reichsversammlungen des späten Mittelalters (1349–1471)*, 2 vols (Göttingen, 2004).

Arbusow, Leonid, 'Die Beziehungen des Deutschen Ordens zum Ablasshandel seit dem 15. Jahrhundert', *Mitteilungen aus dem Gebiete der Geschichte Liv-, Ehst-, und Kurland*, 20 (1910), 367–457.

Ari, Bülent, 'Early Ottoman Diplomacy: Ad Hoc Period', in A. Nuri Yurdusev, ed., *Ottoman Diplomacy: Conventional or Unconventional?* (Basingstoke, 2004), 36–65.

Babinger, Franz, *Mehmed the Conqueror and his Time*, ed. William C. Hickman, tr. Ralph Manheim (Princeton, 1978).

Bak, János M., 'The Price of War and Peace in Late Medieval Hungary', in Brian Patrick McGuire, ed., *War and Peace in the Middle Ages* (Copenhagen, 1987), 161–78.

Baldi, Barbara, 'Enea Silvio Piccolomini e il *De Europa*: umanesimo, religione e politica', *Archivio storico italiano*, 598 (2003), 619–83.

—— *Pio II e le trasformazioni dell'Europa cristiana* (Milan, 2006).

—— 'La corrispondenza di Enea Silvio Piccolomini dal 1431 al 1454. La maturazione di un'esperienza fra politica e cultura', in Isabella Lazzarini, ed., *I confini della lettera. Pratiche epistolari e reti di communicazione nell'Italia tardomedievale* (Florence, 2009), = *Reti Medievali Rivista*, 10, 1–22.

—— 'Il problema turco dalla caduta di Costantinopoli (1453) alla morte di Pio II (1464)', in *CTO*, 1.55–76.

Bárány, Attila, 'Matthias's European Diplomacy in the 1480s', in *ML*, 363–92.

Bastanzio, S.E., *Fra Roberto Caracciolo. Predicatore del secolo XV, vescovo di Aquino e Lecce (†1495)* (Isola del Liri, 1947).

Benziger, Wolfram, *Zur Theorie von Krieg und Frieden in der italienischen Renaissance. Die Disputatio de pace et bello zwischen Bartolomeo Platina und Rodrigo Sánchez de Arévalo und andere anläßlich der Pax Paolina (Rom 1468) entstandene Schriften* (Frankfurt a.-Main, 1996).

Berend, Nora, *At the Gate of Christendom: Jews, Muslims and 'Pagans' in Medieval Hungary, c. 1000–c. 1300* (Cambridge, 2001).

Bianca, Concetta, *Da Bisanzio a Roma. Studi sul cardinale Bessarione* (Rome, 1999).

Birnbaum, Marianna D., *Janus Pannonius, Poet and Politician* (Zagreb, 1981).

Bisaha, Nancy, 'Pope Pius II's Letter to Sultan Mehmed II: A Reexamination', *Crusades* 1 (2002), 183–200.

—— *Creating East and West: Renaissance Humanists and the Ottoman Turks* (Philadelphia, 2004).

—— 'Pope Pius II and the Crusade', in *CFC*, 39–52, 188–91.

Black, Robert, *Benedetto Accolti and the Florentine Renaissance* (Cambridge, 1985).

Blusch, J., 'Enea Silvio Piccolomini und Giannantonio Campano: Die unterschiedlichen Darstellungsprinzipien in ihren Türkenreden', *Humanistica Lovaniensia*, 28 (1979), 78–138.

Boockmann, Hartmut, 'Das 15. Jahrhundert und die Reformation', in Hartmut Boockmann, ed., *Kirche und Gesellschaft im Heiligen Römischen Reich des 15. und 16. Jahrhunderts* (Göttingen, 1994), 9–25.

Borosy, András, 'The *Militia Portalis* in Hungary before 1526', in *FHR*, 63–80.

Brady, Thomas A., 'Imperial Destinies: A New Biography of the Emperor Maximilian I', *Journal of Modern History*, 62 (1990), 298–314.

—— *German Histories in the Age of Reformations, 1400–1650* (Cambridge, 2009).

Bryer, Anthony, 'Ludovico da Bologna and the Georgian and Anatolian Embassy of 1460–1461', *Bedi Kartlisa*, 19–20 (1965), 178–98.

Carl, Doris, 'Franziskanischer Märtyrerkult als Kreuzzugspropaganda an der Kanzel von Benedetto da Maiano in Santa Croce in Florenz', *Mitteilungen des kunsthistorischen Institutes in Florenz*, 39 (1995), 69–91.

Caselli, G., *Studi su S. Giacomo della Marca pubblicati in occasione del II. centenario della sua canonizzazione*, 2 vols (Ascoli Piceno, 1926).

Caspers, Charles M. A., 'Indulgences in the Low Countries, c. 1300–c. 1520', in *PNTM*, 65–99.

Cassandro, Michele, 'I banchieri pontifici nel XV secolo', in Sergio Gensini, ed., *Roma capitale (1447–1527)* (Pisa, 1994), 207–34.

Chambers, D.S., *Popes, Cardinals and War: The Military Church in Renaissance and Early Modern Europe* (London, 2006).

Christensen, Stephen Turk, 'The Heathen Order of Battle', in Stephen Turk Christensen, ed., *Violence and the Absolutist State: Studies in European and Ottoman History* (Copenhagen, 1990), 75–135.

Covini, Maria Nadia, *L'esercito del duca. Organizzazione militare e istituzioni al tempo degli Sforza (1450–1480)* (Rome, 1998).

Dall'Oco, Sondra, ' "Mantuam ivimus... non audiverunt Christiani vocem pastoris". Fede, politica e retorica nelle "orazioni" e nelle "reazioni" mantovane', in *SP*, 503–15.

Damian, Iulian Mihai, 'La *Depositeria della Crociata (1463–1490)* e i sussidi dei pontefici romani a Mattia Corvino', *AIRCRUV*, 8 (2006), 135–52.

—— 'La disfatta di Solgat (Crimea) e i suoi echi nei trattati d'arte militare rinascimentale', *Ephemeris* (forthcoming).

—— 'Sub crucis vexillo: il re e la crociata', in *Between Worlds* (forthcoming).

D'Avray, David, 'Printing, Mass Communication, and Religious Reformation: the Middle Ages and After', in Julia Crick and Alexandra Walsham, eds, *The Uses of Script and Print, 1300–1700* (Cambridge, 2004), 50–70.

De Guasconibus, P., 'S. Bernardino predicatore delle indulgenze per la crociata', *Bolletino senese di storia patria*, 2 (1895), 130–6.

Delumeau, Jean, *L'Alun de Rome XVe–XIXe siècle* (Paris, 1962).

Eisermann, Falk, 'The Indulgence as a Media Event: Developments in Communication through Broadsides in the Fifteenth Century', in *PNTM*, 309–30, revised and updated version of his 'Der Ablaß als Medienereignis. Kommunikationswandel durch Einblattdrucke im 15. Jahrhundert. Mit einer Auswahlbibliographie', in Rudolf Suntrup and Jan R. Veenstra, eds, *Tradition and Innovation in an Era of Change* (Frankfurt a.-Main, 2001), 99–128.

Engel, Pál, *The Realm of St Stephen: A History of Medieval Hungary, 895–1526*, tr. Tamás Pálosfalvi (London, 2001).

Esch, Arnold, 'Pio II e il congresso di Mantova', in *SP*, 1–14.

Feliciangeli, Bernardino, 'Le proposte per la guerra contro i Turchi presentate da Stefano Taleazzi vescovo di Torcello a papa Alessandro VI', *Archivio della R. Società Romana di storia patria*, 40 (1917), 5–63.

Fossati, Felice, 'Milano e una fallita alleanza contro i Turchi', *Archivio storico lombardo*, 3rd ser., 16 (1901), 49–95.

Frauenholz, Eugen von, *Das Heerwesen in der Zeit des freien Soldnertums, zweiter Teil: Das Heerwesen des Reiches in der Landsknechtszeit* (Munich, 1937).

Fubini, Riccardo, 'Diplomacy and Government in the Italian City-States of the Fifteenth Century (Florence and Venice)', in Daniela Frigo, ed., *Politics and Diplomacy in Early Modern Italy: The Structure of Diplomatic Practice, 1450–1800* (Cambridge, 2000), 25–48.

Fügedi, Erik, 'Two Kinds of Enemies—Two Kinds of Ideology: The Hungarian-Turkish Wars in the Fifteenth Century', in Brian Patrick McGuire, ed., *War and Peace in the Middle Ages* (Copenhagen, 1987), 146–60.

Füssel, Stephan, *Emperor Maximilian and the Media of his Day: The Theuerdank of 1517, a Cultural-Historical Introduction* (Cologne, 2003).

—— 'Die Funktionalisierung der "Türkenfurcht" in der Propaganda Kaiser Maximilians I.', in *OEEH*, 9–30.

Gecser, Ottó, 'Itinerant Preaching in Late Medieval Central Europe: St John Capistran in Wrocław', *Medieval Sermon Studies*, 47 (2003), 5–20.

—— 'Preaching and Publicness: St John of Capestrano and the Making of his Charisma North of the Alps', in Katherine L. Jansen and Miri Rubin, eds, *Charisma and Religious Authority: Jewish, Christian, and Muslim Preaching, 1200–1500* (Turnhout, 2010), 145–59.

Ghinato, Alberto, 'La predicazione francescana nella vita religiosa e sociale del Quattrocento', *Picenum seraphicum*, 10 (1973), 24–98.

Göllner, Carl, *Turcica, III. Band, Die Türkenfrage in der öffentlichen Meinung Europas im 16. Jahrhundert* (Bucharest and Baden-Baden, 1978).

Goñi Gaztambide, José, *Historia de la Bula de la cruzada en España* (Vitoria, 1958).

Gottlob, Adolf, *Aus der Camera apostolica des 15. Jahrhunderts. Ein Beitrag zur Geschichte des päpstlichen Finanzwesens und des endenden Mittelalters* (Innsbruck, 1889).

Guglielmotti, Alberto, *Storia della marina pontificia*, vol. 2 (Rome, 1886).

Guilmartin, John F., 'Ideology and Conflict: The Wars of the Ottoman Empire, 1453–1606', in Robert I. Rotberg and Theodore K. Rabb, eds, *The Origin and Prevention of Major Wars* (Cambridge, 1989), 149–75.

Gunn, Steven, David Grummitt and Hans Cools, 'War and the State in Early Modern Europe: Widening the Debate', *War in History*, 15 (2008), 371–88.

Györkös, Attila, 'La guerre des Pazzi et les relations franco-hongroises (1478–1481)', in *ML*, 393–404.
Halecki, Oscar, 'Sixte IV et la Chrétienté orientale', in *Mélanges Eugène Tisserant, vol. II. Orient chrétien, première partie*, Studi e testi, 232 (Città del Vaticano, 1964), 241–64.
Hamilton, Bernard, 'The Ottomans, the Humanists and the Holy House of Loreto', *Renaissance and Modern Studies*, 31 (1987), 1–19.
Hamm, Berndt, *Frömmigkeitstheologie am Anfang des 16. Jahrhunderts. Studien zu Johannes von Paltz und seinem Umkreis* (Tübingen, 1982).
Hankins, James, 'Renaissance Crusaders: Humanist Crusade Literature in the Age of Mehmed II', *Dumbarton Oaks Papers*, 49 (1995), 111–207.
Harris, Jonathan, *Greek Emigrés in the West 1400–1520* (Camberley, 1995).
Heath, Michael J., *Crusading Commonplaces: La Noue, Lucinge and Rhetoric against the Turks* (Geneva, 1986).
Heers, Jacques, 'La vente des indulgences pour la Croisade, à Gênes et en Lunigiana, en 1456', *Miscellanea storica ligure*, 3 (1963), 71–101, repr. in his *Société et économie à Gênes (XIVe—XVe siècles)* (London, 1979).
Held, Joseph, *Hunyadi: Legend and Reality* (New York, 1985).
Helmrath, Johannes, 'The German *Reichstage* and the Crusade', in *CFC*, 53–69, 191–203.
—— 'Pius II. und die Türken', in *ETR*, 79–137.
Heymann, Frederick G., *George of Bohemia: King of Heretics* (Princeton, 1965).
Hofer, Johannes 'Der Sieger von Belgrad 1456', *Historisches Jahrbuch*, 51 (1931), 163–212.
——, *Johannes Kapistran: Ein Leben im Kampf um die Reform der Kirche*, 2 vols (rev. repr., Heidelberg, 1964–5).
Housley, Norman, *The Avignon Papacy and the Crusades, 1305–1378* (Oxford, 1986).
—— *The Later Crusades, 1274–1580: From Lyons to Alcazar* (Oxford, 1992).
—— 'Crusading as Social Revolt: The Hungarian Peasant Uprising of 1514', *Journal of Ecclesiastical History*, 49 (1998), 1–28.
—— 'A Necessary Evil? Erasmus, the Crusade, and War against the Turks', in John France and William G. Zajac, eds, *The Crusades and their Sources: Essays Presented to Bernard Hamilton* (Aldershot, 1998), 259–79.
—— *Religious Warfare in Europe, 1400–1536* (Oxford, 2002).
—— 'Crusading and State-Building in the Middle Ages', in Peter Hoppenbrouwers and others, eds, *Power and Persuasion: Essays on the Art of State Building in Honour of W.P. Blockmans* (Turnhout, 2010), 291–308.
—— 'Pope Pius II and Crusading', *Crusades*, 11 (2012), forthcoming.
—— 'Crusading and the Danube', in Alexandru Simon, ed., *The Danube in the Middle Ages* (New York, 2012), 117–39.
—— 'Crusading and Interreligious Contacts in the Eastern Mediterranean: The Religious, Diplomatic and Juridical Frameworks', in conference proceedings, *Slavery and the Slave Trade in the Eastern Mediterranean 11th to 15th Centuries*, forthcoming.
—— 'Giovanni da Capistrano and the Crusade of 1456', in *CFC*, 94–115, 215–24.
—— 'Indulgences for crusading, 1417–1517', in *PNTM*, 277–307.
—— 'Matthias Corvinus and crusading', in *Between Worlds IV: Matthias Corvinus and His Time*, forthcoming.
—— '*Robur imperii*: Mobilizing Imperial Resources for the Crusade against the Turks, 1453–1503', in *Partir en croisade à la fin du moyen âge: financement et logistique*, ed. Daniel Baloup, forthcoming.

Hughes, Diane Owen, 'Distinguishing Signs: Ear-rings, Jews and Franciscan Rhetoric in the Italian Renaissance City', *Past and Present*, 112 (1986), 3–59.
Imber, Colin, *The Ottoman Empire 1300–1481* (Istanbul, 1990).
—— *The Ottoman Empire, 1300–1650: The Structure of Power* (Basingstoke, 2002).
Inalcik, Halil, 'A Case Study in Renaissance Diplomacy: The Agreement between Innocent VIII and Bayezid II on Djem Sultan', in A. Nuri Yurdusev, ed., *Ottoman Diplomacy: Conventional or Unconventional?* (Basingstoke, 2004), 66–88.
Isenmann, Eberhard, 'The Holy Roman Empire in the Middle Ages', in Richard Bonney, ed., *The Rise of the Fiscal State in Europe, c. 1200–1815* (Oxford, 1999), 243–80.
Izbicki, Thomas M., 'A New Copy of Rodrigo Sánchez de Arévalo's Commentary on the Bull "Ezechielis" of Pope Pius II', *Revista española de teologia*, 41 (1981), 465–7.
Jászay, Magda, 'Venezia e Mattia Corvino', in Sante Graciotti and Cesare Vasoli, eds, *Italia e Ungheria all'epoca dell'umanesimo corviniano* (Florence, 1994), 3–17.
Jensen, Janus Møller, *Denmark and the Crusades 1400–1650* (Leiden and Boston, 2007).
Kafadar, Cemal, *Between Two Worlds: The Construction of the Ottoman State* (Berkeley Calif., 1995).
Kejř, Jiří, 'Manuscrits, éditions et traductions du projet', in Václav Vaněček, ed., *Cultus pacis* (Prague, 1966), 75–82.
Kienzle, Beverly Mayne, 'Medieval Sermons and Their Performance: Theory and Record', in Carolyn Muessig, ed., *Preacher, Sermon and Audience in the Middle Ages* (Leiden, 2002), 89–124.
Klaniczay, Tibor, 'Hungary', in Roy Porter and Mikuláš Teich, eds, *The Renaissance in National Context* (Cambridge, 1992), 164–79.
Knoll, Paul W., 'Poland as *antemurale Christianitatis* in the Late Middle Ages', *Catholic Historical Review*, 60 (1974), 381–401.
Koller, Heinrich, 'Der St. Georgs-Ritterorden Kaiser Friedrichs III.', in Josef Fleckenstein and Manfred Hellmann, eds, *Die geistlichen Ritterorden Europas* (Sigmaringen, 1980), 417–29.
Kosztolnyik, Z. J., 'Some Hungarian Theologians in the Late Renaissance', *Church History*, 57 (1988), 5–18.
Kraus, Victor Felix von, *Das Nürnberger Reichsregiment, Gründung und Verfall, 1500–1502* (Innsbruck, 1883).
Kruse, Holger, Werner Paravicini, and Andreas Ranft, eds, *Ritterorden und Adelsgesellschaften im spätmittelalterlichen Deutschland. Ein systematisches Verzeichnis* (Frankfurt a.-M., 1991).
Kurelac, Miroslav, 'Croatia and Central Europe during the Renaissance and Reformation', in *CLMAR*, 41–62.
Lacroix, Jean, 'I *Commentarii* di Pio II fra storia e diaristica', in Luisa Rotondi Secchi Tarugi, ed., *Pio II e la cultura del suo tempo* (Milano, 1991), 133–49.
Ladero Quesada, Miguel Angel, *Castilla y la conquista del reino de Granada* (Valladolid, 1967).
Landi, Aldo, *Concilio e papato nel Rinascimento (1449–1516): Un problema irrisolto* (Turin, 1997).
Lassalmonie, Jean-François, 'Louis XI, Georges de Poděbrady et la croisade', in *NC*, 185–203.
Lechat, Robert, 'Lettres de Jean de Tagliacozzo sur le siège de Belgrade et la mort de S. Jean de Capistran', *Analecta Bollandiana*, 39 (1921), 139–51.
Lemaitre, Nicole, 'La Papauté de la Renaissance entre mythes et réalités', in Florence Alazard and Frank la Brasca, eds, *La Papauté à la Renaissance* (Paris, 2007), 13–34.

Linder, Amnon, *Raising Arms: Liturgy in the Struggle to Liberate Jerusalem in the Late Middle Ages* (Turnhout, 2003).
Lindkvist, Thomas, 'Crusades and Crusading Ideology in the Political History of Sweden, 1140–1500', in *Crusade and Conversion on the Baltic Frontier 1150–1500*, ed. Alan V. Murray (Aldershot, 2001), 119–30.
Mallett, Michael, *The Borgias: The Rise and Fall of a Renaissance Dynasty* (London, 1969).
—— 'Preparations for War in Florence and Venice in the Second Half of the Fifteenth Century', in *Florence and Venice: Comparisons and Relations, vol. 1: Quattrocento* (Florence, 1979), 149–64.
—— 'Diplomacy and War in Later Fifteenth-Century Italy', *Proceedings of the British Academy*, 67 (1981), 267–88.
—— 'Condottieri and Captains in Renaissance Italy', in D.J.B. Trim, ed., *The Chivalric Ethos and the Development of Military Professionalism* (Leiden and Boston, 2003), 67–88.
—— 'Venezia, i Turchi e il papato dopo la pace di Lodi', in *SP*, 237–46.
—— and John R. Hale, *The Military Organization of a Renaissance State: Venice, c. 1400–1617* (Cambridge, 1984).
Manselli, Raoul, 'Il cardinale Bessarione contro il pericolo turco e l'Italia', *Miscellanea francescana*, 73 (1973), 314–26.
Markgraf, Hermann, 'Ueber Georgs von Podiebrad Project eines christlichen Fürstenbundes zur Vertreibung der Türken aus Europa und Herstellung des allgemeinen Friedens innerhalb der Christenheit', *Historische Zeitschrift*, 21 (1869), 245–304.
Martels, Zweder von, '"More Matter and Less Art". Aeneas Silvius Piccolomini and the Delicate Balance between Eloquent Words and Deeds', in *Pius II*, 205–27.
Märtl, Claudia, 'Donatellos Judith—Ein Denkmal der Türkenkriegspropaganda des 15. Jahrhunderts?', in *OEEH*, 53–95.
Mehring, Gebhard, 'Kardinal Raimund Peraudi als Ablaßkommissar in Deutschland 1500–1504 und sein Verhältnis zu Maximilian I.', in *Forschungen und Versuche zur Geschichte des Mittelalters und der Neuzeit. Festschrift Dietrich Schäfer* (Jena, 1915), 334–409.
Mertens, Dieter, '"Europa, id est patria, domus propria, sedes nostra…" Zu Funktionen und Überlieferung lateinischer Türkenreden im 15. Jahrhundert', in Franz-Reiner Erkens, ed., *Europa und die osmanische Expansion im ausgehenden Mittelalter*, Zeitschrift für historische Forschung, Beiheft 20 (Berlin, 1997), 39–57.
—— '*Claromontani passagii exemplum*: Papst Urban II. und der erste Kreuzzug in der Türkenkriegspropaganda des Renaissance-Humanismus', in *ETR*, 65–78.
Meserve, Margaret 'Patronage and Propaganda at the First Paris Press: Guillaume Fichet and the First Edition of Bessarion's Orations against the Turks', *Papers of the Bibliographical Society of America*, 97 (2003), 521–88.
—— 'News from Negroponte: Politics, Popular Opinion and Information Exchange in the First Decade of the Italian Press', *Renaissance Quarterly*, 59 (2006), 440–80.
—— *Empires of Islam in Renaissance Historical Thought* (Cambridge, Mass., 2008).
Meuthen, Erich 'Der Fall von Konstantinopel und der lateinische Westen', *Historische Zeitschrift*, 237 (1983), 1–35.
—— 'Ein "deutscher" Freundeskreis an der römischen Kurie in der Mitte des 15. Jahrhunderts. Von Cesarini bis zu den Piccolomini', *Annuarium Historiae Conciliorum*, 27/28 (1995/96), 487–542.
—— 'Reiche, Kirchen und Kurie im späteren Mittelalter', *Historische Zeitschrift*, 265 (1997), 597–637.

Moeller, Bernd, 'Die letzten Ablaßkampagnen. Der Widerspruch Luthers gegen den Ablaß in seinem geschichtlichen Zusammenhang', in Hartmut Boockmann and others, eds, *Lebenslehren und Weltentwürfe im Übergang vom Mittelalter zur Neuzeit. Politik—Bildung—Naturkunde—Theologie* (Göttingen, 1989), 539–67.

—— 'Die frühe Reformation als Kommunikationsprozeß', in Hartmut Boockmann, ed., *Kirche und Gesellschaft im Heiligen Römischen Reich des 15. und 16. Jahrhunderts* (Göttingen, 1994), 148–64.

Mohler, Ludwig, *Kardinal Bessarion als Theologe, Humanist und Staatsmann. Funde und Forschungen,* 3 vols (Paderborn, 1923–42).

Monfasani, John, 'Bessarion latinus', *Rinascimento*, 2nd ser., 21 (1981), 165–209.

Moorman, John, *A History of the Franciscan Order from its Origins to the Year 1517* (Oxford, 1968).

Morris, Colin, *The Sepulchre of Christ and the Medieval West: From the Beginning to 1600* (Oxford, 2005).

Mureşan, Dan Ioan, 'Girolamo Lando, titulaire du patriarcat de Constantinople (1474–1497), et son rôle dans la politique orientale du Saint-Siège', *AIRCRUV*, 8 (2006), 153–258.

—— 'La croisade en projets. Plans présentés au Grand Quartier Général de la croisade—le Collège des cardinaux', forthcoming.

—— 'Les *Oraisons contre les Turcs* de Bessarion: propagande de la croisade au *Große Christentag* de Ratisbonne (1471)', forthcoming.

Murphey, Rhoads, 'Ottoman Military Organisation in South-Eastern Europe, c. 1420–1720', in Tallett and Trim, eds, *European Warfare*, 135–58.

Nehring, Karl, *Matthias Corvinus, Kaiser Friedrich III. und das Reich. Zum hunyadisch-habsburgischen Gegensatz im Donauraum* (Munich, 1975).

Nejedlý, Martin, 'Promouvoir une alliance anti-turque, éviter une croisade anti-hussite: un noble tchèque en mission diplomatique. Le témoignage de l'écuyer Jaroslav sur l'ambassade à Louis XI en 1464', in *NC*, 163–84.

Niccoli, Ottavia, *Prophecy and People in Renaissance Italy*, tr. L. G. Cochrane (Princeton, 1990).

Norman, Corrie E., 'The Social History of Preaching: Italy', in Larissa Taylor, ed., *Preachers and People in the Reformations and Early Modern Period* (Boston and Leiden, 2003), 125–91.

Nowakowska, Natalia, 'Poland and the Crusade in the Reign of King Jan Olbracht, 1492–1501', in *CFC*, 128–47, 227–31.

Odložilík, Otakar, *The Hussite King: Bohemia in European Affairs 1440–1471* (New Brunswick, N.J., 1965).

Orlando, Ermanno, 'Venezia e la conquista turca di Otranto (1480–1481). Incroci, responsabilità, equivoci negli equilibri europei', in *CTO*, 1.177–209.

Ortalli, Gherado, '*Europa-christianitas*. Tra Giorgio di Trebisonda e Enea Silvio Piccolomini', in Giancarlo Andenna and Hubert Houben, eds, *Mediterraneo, mezzogiorno, Europa. Studi in onore di Cosimo Damiano Fonseca*, 2 vols (Bari, 2004), 2.783–97.

Partner, Peter, 'Papal Financial Policy in the Renaissance and Counter-Reformation', *Past & Present*, 88 (1980), 17–62.

Pastor, Ludwig, *The History of the Popes*, Engl. tr., vols 2–6, 5th/7th edns (London, 1949–50).

Paulus, Nikolaus, 'Raimund Peraudi als Ablaßkommissar', *Historisches Jahrbuch*, 21 (1900), 645–82.

—— *Geschichte des Ablasses am Ausgange des Mittelalters* (Paderborn, 1923) = *Geschichte des Ablasses im Mittelalter*, vol. 3.

Paviot, Jacques, *Les ducs de Bourgogne, la croisade et l'Orient (fin XIVe siècle–XVe siècle)* (Paris, 2003).
Pellegrini, Marco, 'A Turning-Point in the History of the Factional System in the Sacred College: The Power of Pope and Cardinals in the Age of Alexander VI', in Gianvittorio Signorotto and Maria Antonietta Visceglia, eds, *Court and Politics in Papal Rome, 1492–1700* (Cambridge, 2002), 8–30.
Pepper, Simon, 'Fortress and Fleet: The Defence of Venice's Mainland Greek Colonies in the Late Fifteenth Century', in David S. Chambers and others, eds, *War, Culture and Society in Renaissance Venice: Essays in Honour of John Hale* (London and Rio Grande, 1993), 29–55.
Pertusi, Agostino, 'Le notizie sulla organizzazione amministrativa e militare dei Turchi nello "Strategicon adversus Turcos" di Lampo Birago (c. 1453–1455)', *Studi sul medioevo cristiano offerti a Raffaello Morghen*, 2 vols (Rome, 1974), 2.669–700.
Petersohn, Jürgen, *Kaiserlicher Gesandter und Kurienbischof, Andreas Jamometić am Hof Papst Sixtus' IV (1478–1481): Aufschlüsse aus neuen Quellen* (Hannover, 2004).
Petrovich, Michael B., 'The Croatian Humanists and the Ottoman Peril', *Balkan Studies*, 20 (1979), 257–73.
Piana, Celestino, 'Nunzi apostolici nella regione Emiliana per le crociate del 1455 e 1481', *Archivum Franciscanum historicum*, 50 (1957), 195–211.
Picotti, Giovanni Battista, *La dieta di Mantova e la politica de' Veneziani* (Trent, 1912; facs. edn, Trent, 1996).
Plösch, Josef, 'Der St. Georgsritterorden und Maximilians I. Türkenpläne von 1493/94', in Helmut J. Mezler-Andelberg, ed., *Festschrift Karl Eder zum siebzigsten Geburtstag* (Innsbruck, 1959), 33–56.
Polecritti, Cynthia, *Preaching Peace in Renaissance Italy: Bernardino of Siena and his Audience* (Washington D.C., 2000).
Poumarède, Géraud, *Pour en finir avec la croisade: Mythes et réalités de la lutte contre les Turcs aux XVIe et XVIIe siècles* (Paris, 2004).
Powicke, Maurice, *The Thirteenth Century 1216–1307*, The Oxford History of England, 4, 2nd edn (Oxford, 1962).
Pozzi, Mario, 'La struttura epica dei *Commentari*', in Luisa Rotondi Secchi Tarugi, ed., *Pio II e la cultura del suo tempo* (Milan, 1991), 151–62.
Rando, Daniela, 'Antitürkendiskurs und antijüdische Stereotypen: Formen der Propaganda im 15. Jahrhundert am Beispiel Trient, in *OEEH*, 31–52.
Rapp, Francis, 'Un contemporain d'Alexandre VI Borgia, le cardinal Raymond Péraud (1435–1505)', *Académie des inscriptions et belles-lettres, comptes rendus*, (1994), 665–77.
—— 'La fin décevante d'une campagne d'indulgences: le cardinal Péraud à Strasbourg (1504)', in Jean Kerhervé and Albert Rigaudière, eds, *Finances, pouvoirs et mémoire: Mélanges offerts à Jean Favier* (Paris, 1999), 578–86.
Raukar, Tomislav, 'Croatia within Europe', in *CLMAR*, 7–38.
Rázsó, Gyula, 'Una strana alleanza. Alcuni pensieri sulla storia militare e politica dell'alleanza contro i Turchi (1440–1464)', in Vittore Branca, ed., *Venezia e Ungheria nel Rinascimento* (Florence, 1973), 79–100.
—— 'Hungarian Strategy against the Ottomans (1365–1526)', in *XXII. Kongress der Internationalen Kommission für Militärgeschichte: Acta 22* (Vienna, 1997), 226–37.
—— 'Military Reforms in the Fifteenth Century', in László Veszprémy and Béla K. Király, eds, *A Millennium of Hungarian Military History* (New York, 2002), 54–82.
—— 'The Mercenary Army of King Matthias Corvinus', in *FHR*, 125–40.
Reeves, Marjorie, ed., *Prophetic Rome in the High Renaissance Period* (Oxford, 1992).

Riley-Smith, Jonathan, 'Crusading as an Act of Love', *History*, 65 (1980), 177–92.
Robertson, Ian, 'Pietro Barbo-Paul II: *Zentilhomo de Uenecia e Pontifico*', in David S. Chambers and others, eds, *War, Culture and Society in Renaissance Venice: Essays in Honour of John Hale* (London and Rio Grande, 1993), 147–72.
Roemer, H. R., 'The Türkmen Dynasties', in *The Cambridge History of Iran, vol. 6: The Timurid and Safavid Periods*, ed. Peter Jackson and Laurence Lockhart (Cambridge, 1986), 147–88.
Ronchey, Silvia, 'Malatesta/Paleologhi. Un'alleanza dinastica per rifondare Bisanzio nel quindicesimo secolo', *Byzantinische Zeitschrift*, 93 (2000), 521–67.
—— *L'Enigma di Piero. L'ultimo bizantino e la crociata fantasma nella rivelazione di un grande quadro* (Milan, 2006).
Röpcke, Andreas, 'Geld und Gewissen. Raimund Peraudi und die Ablaßverkündung in Norddeutschland am Ausgang des Mittelalters', *Bremisches Jahrbuch*, 71 (1992), 43–80.
Rubinstein, Nicolai, 'Italian Reactions to Terraferma Expansion in the Fifteenth Century', in John R. Hale, ed., *Renaissance Venice* (London, 1973), 197–217.
Rusconi, Roberto, 'Giovanni da Capestrano: Iconografia di un predicatore nell'Europa del'400', *Venezie Francescane*, 6 (1989), 31–60.
Russell, Jocelyne G., 'The Humanists Converge: The Congress of Mantua (1459)', in her *Diplomats at Work: Three Renaissance Studies* (Stroud and Wolfeboro Falls N.H., 1992), 51–93.
Ryder, Alan, 'The Eastern Policy of Alfonso the Magnanimous', *Atti della Accademia Pontaniana* (1979), 7–25.
—— *Alfonso the Magnanimous: King of Aragon, Naples and Sicily 1396–1458* (Oxford, 1990).
Šanjek, Franjo, 'The Church and Christianity', in *CLMAR*, 227–58.
Schlecht, Joseph, *Andrea Zamometić und der Basler Konzilsversuch vom Jahre 1482*, 2 vols (Paderborn, 1903).
Schmid, Peter, 'Der päpstliche Legat Raimund Peraudi und die Reichsversammlungen der Jahre 1501–1503. Zum Prozeß der Entfremdung zwischen Reich und Rom in der Regierungszeit König Maximilians I.', in *RK*, 65–88.
Schmitt, Oliver Jens, 'Skanderbeg als neuer Alexander. Antikerezeption im spätmittelalterlichen Albanien', in *OEEH*, 123–44.
Schneider, Johannes, *Die kirchliche und politische Wirksamkeit des Legaten Raimund Peraudi (1486–1505)* (Halle, 1882).
Schröcker, Alfred, 'Maximilians I. Auffassung vom Königtum und das ständische Reich. Beobachtungen an ungedruckten Quellen italienischer Herkunft', *QFIAB*, 50 (1971), 181–204.
Schuchard, Christiane, *Die päpstlichen Kollektoren im späten Mittelalter* (Tübingen, 2000).
Schuhmann, Günther, 'Kardinal Bessarion in Nürnberg', *Jahrbuch für Fränkische Landesforschung*, 34/35 (1975), 447–65.
Schwoebel, Robert, *The Shadow of the Crescent: The Renaissance Image of the Turk (1453–1517)* (Nieuwkoop, 1967).
Scott, Tom and Bob Scribner, 'Urban Networks', in Bob Scribner, ed., *Germany. A New Social and Economic History, vol. 1, 1450–1630* (London, 1996), 113–43.
Scribner, Robert W., 'Communities and the Nature of Power', in his *Germany: A New Social and Economic History, vol. 1, 1450–1630* (London, 1996), 291–325.
—— 'Anticlericalism and the Cities', in his *Religion and Culture in Germany (1400–1800)*, ed. Lyndal Roper (Leiden, 2001), 149–71.

—— 'Perceptions of the Sacred in Germany at the End of the Middle Ages', in his *Religion and Culture in Germany (1400–1800)*, ed. Lyndal Roper (Leiden, 2001), 85–103.
Setton, Kenneth M., *The Papacy and the Levant (1204–1571)*, 4 vols (Philadelphia, 1976–84).
Shaw, Christine, 'The Papal Court as a Centre of Diplomacy from the Peace of Lodi to the Council of Trent', in Florence Alazard and Frank la Brasca, eds, *La Papauté à la Renaissance* (Paris, 2007), 621–38.
Silver, Larry, *Marketing Maximilian: The Visual Ideology of a Holy Roman Emperor* (Princeton and Oxford, 2008).
Simon, Alexandru, 'The Use of the "Gate of Christendom". Hungary's Mathias Corvinus and Moldavia's Stephen the Great, Politics in the late 1400s', *Quaderni della Casa Romena*, 3 (2004), 205–24.
—— 'The Hungarian Means of the Relations between the Habsburgs and Moldavia at the End of the 15th Century, *AIRCRUV*, 8 (2006), 259–96.
—— 'Anti-Ottoman Warfare and Crusader Propaganda in 1474: New Evidence from the Archives of Milan', *Revue roumaine d'histoire*, 46 (2007), 25–39.
—— 'Antonio Bonfini's *Valachorum regulus*: Matthias Corvinus, Transylvania and Stephen the Great', in *Between Worlds [I], Stephen the Great, Matthias Corvinus and their Time*, ed. László Koszta and others (Cluj-Napoca, 2007), 209–26.
—— 'The Arms of the Cross: The Christian Politics of Stephen the Great and Matthias Corvinus', in *Between Worlds [I], Stephen the Great, Matthias Corvinus and their Time*, ed. László Koszta and others (Cluj-Napoca, 2007), 45–86.
—— 'The Limits of the Moldavian Crusade (1474, 1484)', *AIRCRUV*, 9 (2007), 273–326.
—— 'The Walachians between Crusader Crisis and Imperial Gifts (mid 1400' and early 1500')', *AIRCRUV*, 9 (2007), 141–94.
—— 'The Ottoman-Hungarian Crisis of 1484: Diplomacy and Warfare in Matthias Corvinus' Local and Regional Politics', in *ML*, 405–36.
—— and Cristian Luca, 'Documentary Perspectives on Stephen the Great and Matthias Corvinus', *Transylvanian Review*, 17 (2008), 85–114.
Simonetta, Marcello, 'Pius II and Francesco Sforza. The History of Two Allies', in *Pius II*, 147–70.
Šmahel, František, 'Antoine Marini de Grenoble et son *Mémorandum* sur la nécessité d'une alliance anti-turque', in *NC*, 205–31.
Somaini, Francesco, 'La curia romana e la crisi di Otranto', in *CTO*, 1.211–62.
Soranzo, Giovanni, 'Sigismondo Pandolfo Malatesta in Morea e le vicende del suo dominio', *Atti e memorie della r. deputazione di storia patria per le provincie di Romagna*, ser. 4, 8 (1917–18), 211–80.
Stantchev, Stefan, '*Devedo*: The Venetian Response to Sultan Mehmed II in the Venetian-Ottoman Conflict of 1462–79', *Mediterranean Studies*, 19 (2010), 43–66.
Stein, Henri, 'Un diplomate bourguignon du XVe siècle: Antoine Haneron', *Bibliothèque de l'École des chartes*, 98 (1937), 282–348.
Stieber, Joachim W., *Pope Eugenius IV, the Council of Basel and the Secular and Ecclesiastical Authorities in the Empire: the Conflict over Supreme Authority and Power in the Church* (Leiden, 1978).
Studt, Birgit, *Papst Martin V. (1417–1431) und die Kirchenreform in Deutschland* (Cologne, 2004).
Swanson, Robert, 'Crusade Administration in Fifteenth-Century England: Regulations for the Distribution of Indulgences in 1489', *Historical Research*, 84 (2011), 183–8.

Swanson, Robert, 'Preaching Crusade in Fifteenth-Century England: Instructions for the Administration of the Anti-Hussite Crusade of 1429 in the Diocese of Canterbury', *Crusades*, forthcoming.
Szakály, Ferenc, 'Das Bauerntum und die Kämpfe gegen die Türken bzw. gegen Habsburg in Ungarn im 16.–17. Jahrhundert', in Gusztáv Heckenast, ed., *Aus der Geschichte der ostmitteleuropäischen Bauernbewegungen im 16.– 17. Jahrhundert* (Budapest, 1977), 251–66.
—— 'The Hungarian-Croatian Border Defense System and its Collapse', in *FHR*, 141–58.
Szűcs, Jenő, 'Die Ideologie des Bauernkrieges', in his *Nation und Geschichte: Studien* (Budapest, 1981), 329–78.
—— 'Die Nation in historischer Sicht und der nationale Aspekt der Geschichte', in his *Nation und Geschichte: Studien* (Budapest, 1981), 11–160.
Tallett, Frank, and D.J.B. Trim, eds, *European Warfare, 1350–1750* (Cambridge, 2010).
Tambora, Angelo, 'Problema turco e avamposto polacco fra Quattrocento e Cinquecento', in Vittore Branca and Sante Graciotti, eds, *Italia, Venezia e Polonia tra Medio Evo e Età Moderna* (Firenze, 1980), 531–49.
Tateo, Francesco, 'Letterati e guerrieri di fronte al pericolo turco', in his *Chierici e feudatari del Mezzogiorno* (Bari, 1984), 21–68.
Teke, Szuzsanna, 'Rapporti diplomatici tra Mattia Corvino e gli stati italiani', in Sante Graciotti and Cesare Vasoli, eds, *Italia e Ungheria all'epoca dell'umanesimo corviniano* (Florence, 1994), 19–36.
Thiriet, Freddy, *La Romanie vénitienne au Moyen Âge. Le développement et l'exploitation du domaine colonial vénitien (XIIe–XVe siècles)* (Paris, 1959).
Toews, John B., 'The View of Empire in Aeneas Sylvius Piccolomini (Pope Pius II)', *Traditio*, 24 (1968), 471–87.
Trame, Richard H., *Rodrigo Sánchez de Arévalo, 1404–1470: Spanish Diplomat and Champion of the Papacy* (Washington D.C., 1958).
Vast, Henri, *Le cardinal Bessarion (1403–1472). Étude sur la Chrétienté et la Renaissance vers le milieu du XVe siècle* (Paris, 1878).
Vatin, Nicolas, 'L'Affaire Djem (1481–1495)', in *Le Banquet du faisan*, ed. Marie-Therèse Caron and Denis Clauzel (Arras, 1997), 85–96.
—— *Sultan Djem. Un prince ottoman dans l'Europe du XVe siècle* (Ankara, 1997).
Veszprémy, László, 'The State and Military Affairs in East-Central Europe, 1380–c. 1520s', in Tallett and Trim, eds, *European Warfare*, 96–109.
Vicko Lisičar, Lopud, 'Program Dubrovačkoga senata za doček Pape Pija II (1464)', *Croatia sacra*, 5 (1933), 97–109.
Viora, Mario, 'Angelo Carletti da Chivasso e la crociata contro i Turchi del 1480–81', *Studi Francescani*, ns. 22 (1925), 319–40.
Vogtherr, Thomas, 'Kardinal Raimund Peraudi als Ablaßprediger in Braunschweig (1488 und 1503)', *Braunschweigisches Jahrbuch für Landesgeschichte*, 77 (1996), 151–80.
—— '"Wenn hinten, weit, in der Turkei…". Die Türken in der spätmittelalterlichen Stadtchronistik Norddeutschlands', in Franz-Reiner Erkens, ed., *Europa und die osmanische Expansion im ausgehenden Mittelalter*, Zeitschrift für historische Forschung, Beiheft 20 (Berlin, 1997), 103–25.
Voigt, Klaus, 'Der Kollektor Marinus de Fregeno und seine *"Descriptio provinciarum Alamanorum"*, *QFIAB*, 68 (1968), 148–206.
—— *Italienische Berichte aus dem spätmittelalterlichen Deutschland. Von Francesco Petrarca zu Andrea de' Franceschi (1333–1492)* (Stuttgart, 1973).

Walsham, Alexandra and Julia Crick, 'Introduction: Script, Print, and History', in their *The Uses of Script and Print, 1300–1700* (Cambridge, 2004), 1–26.
Webb, Diana M., 'Italians and Others: some Quattrocento Views of Nationality and the Church', in Stuart Mews, ed., *Religion and National Identity* (Oxford, 1982), 243–60.
Weber, Benjamin, 'La croisade impossible: Étude sur les relations entre Sixte IV et Mathias Corvin (1471–1484)', in Bernard Doumerc and Christophe Picard, eds, *Byzance et ses périphéries. Hommage à Alain Ducellier* (Toulouse, 2004), 309–21.
—— 'Conversion, croisade et œcuménisme à la fin du Moyen-âge: encore sur la lettre de Pie II à Mehmed II', *Crusades* 7 (2008), 181–99.
Wehrmann, M., 'Bischof Marinus von Kammin (1479–1482). Ein Italiener auf dem Kamminer Bischofsstuhle', *Baltische Studien*, ns 18 (1914), 118–60.
Wiesflecker, Hermann, *Kaiser Maximilian I. Das Reich, Österreich und Europa an der Wende zur Neuzeit*, 5 vols (Munich and Vienna, 1971–86).
—— *Maximilian I. Die Fundamente des habsburgischen Weltreiches* (Vienna and Munich, 1991).
Wiesflecker-Friedhuber, Inge, 'Maximilian I. und der St. Georgs-Ritterorden. Zur Frage seiner Ordenszugehörigkeit', *Forschungen zur Landes- und Kirchengeschichte. Festschrift Helmut J. Mezler-Andelberg zum 65. Geburtstag* (Graz, 1988), 543–54.
Winterhager, Wilhelm Ernst, 'Ablaßkritik als Indikator historischen Wandels vor 1517: Ein Beitrag zu Voraussetzungen und Einordnung der Reformation', *Archiv für Reformationsgeschichte*, 90 (1999), 6–71.
Wolff, Helmut, 'Päpstliche Legaten auf Reichstagen des 15. Jahrhunderts', in *RK*, 25–40.
Worcester, Thomas, 'Catholic Sermons', in Larissa Taylor, ed., *Preachers and People in the Reformations and Early Modern Period* (Boston and Leiden, 2003), 3–33.
Wuttke, Dieter, 'Sebastian Brant und Maximilian I. Eine Studie zu Brants Donnerstein-Flugblatt des Jahres 1492', in Otto Herding and Robert Stupperich, eds, *Die Humanisten in ihrer politischen und sozialen Umwelt* (Boppard, 1976), 141–7.

UNPUBLISHED THESES

Stantchev, Stefan, *Embargo: The Origins of an Idea and the Implications of a Policy in Europe and the Mediterranean, ca. 1100–ca. 1500*, University of Michigan, 2009.
Weber, Benjamin, *Lutter contre les Turcs. Les formes nouvelles de la croisade pontificale au XVe siècle*, Université Toulouse II Le Mirail, 2009.

Index

Toponyms are listed under the individual's first name. Notes are marked with n.

Abbode (rector at Wageningen, Gelderland) 188
Ablasskommissaren (indulgence commissioners) 177, 181, 200, 204
Accolti, Benedetto 163, 211
Act of Nrem 29
Adhemar of Le Puy, Bishop 163
akinjis (Turkish raiders) 21, 25
Akkerman 41
Albania 28, 47, 49, 86, 115, 123, 146
Albert, bishop of Lübeck 24, 104
Alberto da Sarteano 27, 29, 146
Albrecht of Bavaria, Duke 172–3
Alexander the Great 63
Alexander III, Pope 72
Alexander of Lithuania, Grand Prince 72
Alexander VI, Pope 18, 29, 53–60, 55 n.211, 66–8, 67 n.28, 72, 82, 84, 86–7, 99, 105–6, 130–2, 166, 171, 181, 189, 191, 198–201, 206–9, 212–14
Alfonso V (The Magnanimous), king of Aragon 64, 66–7, 73–4, 77, 108
Alfonso, duke of Calabria 146
Aliprandi, Pietro 48
alum discovery 133–4
Amedeo of Savoy 170
Anatolia 29
Ancona 37, 40, 75, 97–9, 101, 121–4, 138, 140–1, 213
Andrew, St. 163–4
Angelo da Bolsena 138–9, 141
antemurale thinking 40–1, 43, 45–9, 50–2, 77–8, 86, 92, 110, 117, 119, 129, 154, 159, 211–12
Antioch 24, 163
Antonio de Alberto 193, 193 n.136
Antonio de Montefalcone 138
Antonio de Mugnano 142
Aracoeli, church of (Rome) 143, 193
Arnulf, Patriarch 163
Augsburg 206
Augustinians 170, 173, 183
Austria 24, 35, 39, 42, 81, 200, 202, 208; *see also under individual rulers*
Auxias de Podio, Cardinal 24
Avlona, Albania 23, 213

Baldi, Barbara 22, 59, 75–6, 76 n.28, 85, 85 n.125, 120–1
Baptista de Levante 137–8, 140
Barbo, Cardinal Marco 52, 54
Bartholini, Mariano 208

Bartolomeo da Camerino 142, 142 n.67, 145 n.99, 146
Bartolomeo da Colle 138
Bartolomeo da Giano 29, 146, 153
Basel Compacts (1436) 51, 56
Bayezid II, Sultan 18, 34, 42, 46, 54, 70–1, 91, 201
Beatrice of Aragon 91
Beaufort, Henry 82
Belgrade 26–8, 30, 41, 43–4, 47, 103, 109, 111–14, 118, 139, 151, 153, 157–8, 216
Benedetto da Maiano 144–5, 159
Bernardino da Feltre 158
Bernardino da Siena 150, 158
Bernard of Kotor, Bishop 153
Bernard, St. 170, 183, 206
Bernhardin of Ingolstadt 107
Berthold von Henneberg 38, 125, 199, 205
Bessarion, Cardinal John
  alternatives to papal authority 51–2
  Catholic Europe 35, 39
  Christianity and Islam 20–3, 20 n.14, 21 n.16, 25
  communication 136, 146, 149, 153–4, 156, 162, 164–5, 168–70
  crusading/conclusions 179–80, 179 n.41, 200, 211, 213
  Holy Land/Orthodox Christians 30–2, 34
  recruitment/finance 100–1, 134
  strategy 64, 78–80, 82–4, 82 n.99, 92
Bianca Maria Sforza, duchess of Milan 101
Birago, Lampo 22, 71, 102
Birnbaum, Marianna 41, 43
Blok, Tiderius 197
Bohemia 51–2, 56, 92, 177
Bohemund of Taranto/Antioch 26, 163
Boniface IX, Pope 194
Borgia, Cesare 201, 208
Borso d'Este, duke of Ferrara 168
Bosnia 23, 31, 41, 49, 75, 81, 86–7, 90, 115, 120, 137, 139
Branda da Castiglione 156
Brankovics, George 108
Brant, Sebastian 172
Braunschweig 195
Bremen 195
Brežice (Rann) 105
Brindisi 47
Bruneck (Brunico) 24
Buda diet (1456) 110
Bulgaria 29, 34

Burgundy 58, 75–6, 78, 88, 94, 120;
  see also under individual rulers
Byzantine Empire 40

Caffa 32
Calixtus III, Pope
  administration of crusade indulgences 177–8, 188, 193, 198, 209
  Catholic Europe 35, 37–8
  communication 136, 138–44, 139 n.33, 146–7, 146 n.107, 148–9
  conclusions 212–13
  criticism/challenges 41, 47, 51, 55
  Holy Land and the Orthodox Christians 25, 27–8, 30–1
  recruitment/finance 103, 108–9, 114–15, 119, 128–31, 133, 133 n.212
  strategy/mobilization/control 66–8, 67 n.25, 72–4, 97
Campano, Giovanni Antonio 39–40, 81, 81 n.96, 123, 163
'Capistrano's shears' 148
Caracciolo, Roberto (da Lecce) 129–30, 138, 147, 149–50, 156, 188, 198
Carbone, Ludovico 168–9
Carinthia (Kärnten) 37, 44, 104, 181, 199
Carl, Doris 144
Carletti da Chivasso, Angelo 141–2, 145–6, 180–1
Carmelites 170
Carniola (Krain) 24, 44, 46, 104–5
Carthusians 170
Carvajal, Cardinal Juan 37, 51, 67, 73–4, 83–4, 109–14, 110 n.51, 113 n.76, 114–16, 122, 148, 209
Cesarini, Cardinal Giuliano 29, 31, 156
Charlemagne 19
Charles the Bold, duke of Burgundy 170
Charles VII, king of France 106
Charles VIII, king of France 53–5, 60, 70, 99, 105, 181
Cherubino da Spoleto 139
Chiericati, Leonello, bishop of Concordia 47, 54–5, 54 n.202, 81, 84, 99, 99 n.213, 166, 189, 198, 214
Christian I, king of Denmark 178
Christianity
  blow inflicted on 18
  crusading commercial ban 128
  defence of 43–4
  goal of the Turks 25, 64
  need to attend to its own defence 71
  neutrality of 68, 68 n.29
  retreat to a corner of the world 22
Cistercians 170
Clement VI, Pope 22, 24
Clement V, Pope 38
Coelifodina (The mine of heaven) (Paltz) 183
Cogimur iubente altissimo bull 95

College of Cardinals 54
Colleoni, Bartolomeo 92, 92 n.161
Cologne 125, 210
Commentarii (Pius II) 160, 164
Common Penny tax (*Gemeine Pfennig*) 132, 196
Conrad III, king of Germany 37
Constantine, king of Georgia 29
Constantinople
  fall of (1453) 18, 21, 21–4, 30, 66, 73, 81, 124, 138, 148, 153, 156, 159, 166, 211
  and Perault's promotion of crusade 55
  planned recovery of 27–8
  Turkish threat to 153
Constantinopolitana clades (Piccolomini), 159–61, 164
Contarini, Zaccaria 55, 65, 191, 201–2, 206
Conventuals, Franciscan 147, 152, 179
Cosimo de' Medici 166
Cremona 149
Crete 168
Cristoforo da Soldo 176, 188
Cristoforo da Varese 153–4, 158
Crivelli, Carlo 158
Croatia 12, 14, 24–5, 42, 44–5, 47 n.167, 48, 52, 53 n.193, 62, 65, 71, 73 n.57, 83, 91 n.157, 104, 113, 144, 177
cross (Perault), 184
crucesignati, see crusaders
crusade
  almost entirely expunged from Marini's text 57
  anti-Ottoman 24–6, 29
  Calixtus III's indulgences for 35
  communication 135–45
  goal of 22
  Maximilian's unspecified commitment to 60, 60 n.234
  'national' (Hungarian, in 1526) 118
  papal *curia* and 71–2, 71 n.47
  paradox of 215
  plans for a *Romzug* 207
  preaching 214
  promoted by Maximilian in 1503 19
  stalled momentum of 51
  Venetian support for 36–7, 86
crusade commission 88
crusaders 107–10, 108 n.39, 112–17, 112 n.67, 119–24, 127, 155–7, 155 n.172, 180, 202
Crusades
  First (1095–9) 26, 119, 124, 160–1, 163, 211
  Second (1145–9) 37, 124, 170, 206
  Third (1189–92) 35, 37, 124
  Fifth (1217–29) 19
crusading
  core spiritual benefit 175
  and Germany 126
  ideology 37, 125
  leagues 85

'Renaissance crusading' 211
taxation 127–34, 127 n.169, 130 n.189, 140, 140 n.53, 196
Crusading Commonplaces (Heath) 165
Cum bellum hodie (Pius II) 97, 160–1, 164
Cum hiis superioribus bull 138
Cum salvator noster (Bessarion) 162
Czechs 42; *see also* Bohemia

Dalmatia 87
De Europa (Pius II) 22–3
De imperio Cn. Pompei (Cicero) 159
Denmark 142, 178, 195, 205
depositeria della crociata 32, 133–4
De remediis afflictae Ecclesiae (Arévalo) 35
Déschamps, Gerard 101–2, 119
Descriptio provinciarum Alamanorum (Marinus de Fregeno) 198
Dieter von Isenburg, archbishop-elector of Mainz 59
Djem Sultan 22, 46, 69–71, 70 n.41, 83, 91, 166, 216
Długosz, Jan 42, 148, 148 n.121, 156
Dominicans 170, 175
Dracul, Vlad 62
Dürer, Albrecht 171–2

Ebendorfer, Thomas 154
Ecclesiam Christi bull 78, 119–20, 125
Ecclesiastica (Erasmus) 147
Edward IV, king of England 169
Egypt 52
Eichstätt, bishop of 210
Eisermann, Falk 182
Emerich von Kemel 142–4
Engel, Pál 42
England 129; *see also under individual rulers*
Epitome rerum Germanicarum (Wimpfeling) 211
Erasmus, Desiderius 147
Erzgebirge 183
Ethiopia 27, 68
Etsi ecclesia Christi bull 18, 72–3, 127–8
Euboea 69
Eugenius III, Pope 72, 161
Eugenius IV, Pope 27, 29, 29 n.59, 72, 76, 136, 146, 193, 212
European assembly proposal 56
Everso dell'Anguillara 212–13
Execrabilis decree 59
Ezechielis propheta bull 96, 98, 120, 123, 130, 164, 166–7

Feast of the Pheasant (1454) 106, 119
Feast of the Transfiguration 152
Federico da Montefeltro 95
Ferdinand, king of Aragon 99
Ferrante, king of Naples 93–6
Ferrara 47

Fichet, Guillaume 168–70
Filelfo, Francesco 166, 166 n.226
Finland 32
Flagellation of Christ, The (Piero della Francesca) 31
Florence 85, 88–9, 92, 94, 145, 163, 175
Florence, council of (1439) 29
Flugschriften (Perault) 172–3, 208–9
Foscarini, Lodovico 77
Fossati, Felice 94
France 38, 40, 49, 53–4, 59, 76, 82, 84, 94, 129, 162, 203; *see also under individual rulers*
Francesco de Carbonibus 138–9, 139 n.39, 140–1
Francesco da Toledo 98
Franciscans 136, 138, 142, 145, 147–9, 152, 157, 170, 193; *see also* Conventuals, Observants
Franco-Bohemian coalition (1463–4) 59
Frankfurt 38, 183, 194, 201
Frankfurt diet (1454) 73, 79–80, 107, 107 n.36, 150 n.132, 159–60
Frederick of Braunschweig, duke 198
Frederick III, Holy Roman Emperor 41–2, 45–6, 52–3, 59–60, 79, 81, 91, 104, 111, 159, 169, 181
Freiburg diet (1498) 55
Friuli 23
Fubini, Riccardo 75
Füssel, Stephan 171
Fugger bankers 206

Gabriel de Paly 137
Gargantua (Rabelais) 64
Gaztambide, Jose Goñi 174
Gecser, Ottó 150, 156
Gedük Ahmed Pasha 93
Geiler von Kaysersberg 172
Georg of Chiemsee, Bishop 39–40, 144, 144 n.93
George of Trebizond 169
Germany 24, 33, 38–40, 54–5, 58, 76–84, 117, 123–5, 129–30, 143–4, 156, 179, 190–1, 193, 196, 200–3, 206–11; *see also under individual rulers*
Ghinato, Alberto 150
Giovanni da Capistrano
 antemurale states 43
 Catholic Europe 37
 communication 136–9, 145–8, 150–9, 151 n.140, 153 n.153, 156 n.186, 158 n.194, 159 n.199, 161
 conclusions 209–12, 214
 the Holy Land 27, 30
 indulgences 176–7, 176 n.12, 208
 recruitment 103, 107–13, 115–16, 118–20, 118 n.116, 123–5
 strategy 63, 67, 73, 75, 97

Giovanni da Castiglione 114, 160
Giovanni da Napoli 138, 175
Giovanni da Tagliacozzo 30, 102–3, 111–13, 116, 118, 148, 151–3, 155, 157–8
Glassberger, Nicholas 144
Gniezno, archbishop of 143
Godfrey of Bouillon 26, 62, 163, 211
Golden Fleece, Burgundian Order 60
Göllner, Carl 170
Gonzaga, Cardinal Francesco 92
Gonzaga, Lodovico 75
Gradiente domino bull 191
Granada, fall of (1492) 174
Great Schism 71, 74
Greece 29, 92, 146, 156
Guglielmotti, Alberto 124
Guillaume d'Estouteville, Cardinal 122

Hamm, Berndt 183
Hankins, James 166
Hannibal 63
Hartmann, Andreas 197
Heath, Michael J. 165, 165 n.225
Heers, Jacques 191–2, 192 n.123
Heimburg, Gregor 59, 130
Heinrich, duke of Mecklenburg 198
Heinrich von Henneberg 197
Helmrath, Johannes 24, 159
Henry VI, king of England 78
Hofer, Johannes 111–13, 156–7
Holy Land
  military needs of 35, 43
  recovery of 27–8, 135
Holy Roman Empire 56, 72, 127, 127 n.168, 132; *see also under individual rulers*
Hospital of the Holy Spirit, Rome 189
Hospital of St Anthony, Vienna 177, 189
Hoyer von Mühlingen 197
Hughes, Hector 106
humanism 24–5
Humbert of Romans 183
Hungarian Orthodox 31
Hungary 25–6, 29–31, 34–5, 37, 40–7, 47 n.167, 49, 50–1, 55–8, 62–6, 75–80, 82, 84–7, 91, 96, 101–4, 107–9, 113–15, 117–20, 123–6, 137, 139, 153–5, 159, 176, 192–3, 202, 205, 215; *see also under individual rulers*
Hunyadi, Janos 26–7, 37, 43, 48, 62–4, 106, 108–14, 111 nn.59/61, 112 n.72, 118, 137, 148, 152, 155, 155 n.175, 159, 159 n.198
Hunyadi, Ladislaus 114, 117–18
Hussites 56–7, 82, 82 n.98, 132, 146, 156, 159

Iberia 28
Illyria 90
In calumniatorem Platonis (George of Trebizond) 169
In coena domini bull 37, 128, 134

Innocent III, Pope 71–2, 161, 171
Innocent VIII, Pope 46, 70, 72, 83, 99, 129, 174, 213
Institutio oratoria (Quintilian) 163
Instrumentum in causa defensionis fidei (1459) 75
Isenmann, Eberhard 81
Isidore, Cardinal 70
Isvalies, Cardinal Pietro 86–7
Italian-Hungarian axis 88
Italian league 85
Italy 38, 54–5, 60, 63, 88, 92, 116, 203, 212
Ivan III (The Great) 32

Jacques d'Apelteren 188
Jacques du Clerc 106
Jacopo de Mezzanica 139–40
Jacopo delle Marche 74, 100–1, 136–7, 137 n.11, 146–52, 154, 158
Jajce, siege of (1463), 43, 101
Jamometić, Andrija 52–3, 144
janissaries (Turkish troops) 21, 103
Jaroslav's diary 58
Jerusalem 27, 29
Jews 128, 156, 164
Johannes de Curte 140
Johannes de Horne 18–19
Johannes von Paltz 39, 183–5, 187–90, 190 n.108, 194, 214
John Albert, king of Poland 42
Jubilee indulgence 175, 177, 182, 185, 190, 192–3, 204
Julius Caesar 63
Julius II, Pope 47, 56, 173, 205, 208

Kalteisen, Heinrich 107
Kammin, (Pomeranian see) 178
Kastriote, George (Iskanderbeg) 43, 49, 73
Kilia 41
Knights of St John 69–70, 73, 142, 172
Kosovo, battle of (1448) 62

Ladislas V, king of Hungary 21, 30, 80, 107–9, 111, 114–15, 117, 117 n.111, 127
Lamalitlin, Anna 190
Lamento di Negroponte 167
Lando, Girolamo 30, 34, 51–3, 122–3
Landshut succession, war of (1504) 195
Leo X, Pope 194
Lesbos 65
Letter to Mehmed (Pius II) 20
Libellus de virtutibus Mathiae Corvino dedicatus (Pannonius) 119
Liber secretorum fidelium crucis (Torsello) 102
Linder, Amnon 38
Lithuania 32–4
Livonia 195
Livonian indulgence 190
Lodi, Peace of (1454) 74, 85

Lolli, Goro 98
Lombardy 85
Long March (1443) 29, 41–2, 63
Lorenzo da Palermo 137–8, 138 n.20, 140
Lorenzo de' Medici 52–3, 94–6, 145, 145 nn.97/8
Louis IX, king of France 170
Louis XI, king of France 55, 58, 70, 90, 93–4, 121
Louis XII, king of France 59, 129, 201, 203, 206, 212
Low Countries 8 n.31, 193
Lübeck 36, 122, 124, 186, 192, 198, 205
Lübeck, bishop of 178
Ludwig of Bavaria, duke 169
Luther, Martin 173, 194
Lyon, councils at (1245/1274) 27

Maccabees 154–5
Mair, Martin 39, 56
Malatesta, Cleope 31
Malatesta, Sigismondo 51, 85, 123
Mallett, Michael 85
Malumbra, Bishop Thomas 192, 194–5
Mamluk-Ottoman alliance 68
Mamluks 27, 68, 71
Mansi, Bishop Pietro 83
Mantua, congress of 38, 49–50, 59, 75, 78–80, 82–3, 87–8, 97–8, 101, 103, 105–6, 117–20, 124, 128, 161–2, 164, 215
Marcana, bishop of 175, 175 n.8
Marco da Bologna 136, 138
Mariano da Firenze 137
Mariano de Senis 139, 177–8
Marini, Antoine 56–8, 128–9
Marinus de Fregeno 24, 178–9, 179 n.38, 187, 192, 197–8
Marrakesh 145
Martin V, Pope 50, 148
Matteo da Reggio 138, 141
Matthias I (Corvinus), king of Hungary 23, 34, 41–6, 49–52, 51 n.187, 61, 63, 69–70, 78, 82, 82 n.100, 84, 87–93, 87 n.133, 90 n.146, 95–6, 104, 107, 109, 114–15, 117–19, 121, 137, 146, 192–3, 215
Maximilian, Holy Roman Emperor 19, 32, 36–9, 44, 48–9, 53–5, 59–61, 60 n.234, 64–5, 68, 81–2, 99, 102, 104–5, 125–7, 129, 132–3, 171–3, 172 n.261, 177, 185–6, 190–210, 210 n.242
Maynus, Jason 171
Mehmed II, Sultan
  besieges Belgrade 30, 103, 108–9, 111, 212
  captures Negroponte 92–3, 167
  captures Otranto 95, 143, 213
  conquers Bosnia 120
  conquers Constantinople 124
  nature of the threat posed 18–22, 49, 56, 78, 146, 158
  threat to Hungary 41–4, 46, 63, 80, 89
  threat to Peloponnese 75, 101–3
  and Turkish pretenders 69–70
  war against Venice 33, 149, 216
Mehring, Gebhard 172
Meserve, Margaret 25, 69, 165, 167–8
Meuthen, Erich 39
Michelozzi, Niccolò 96
Mihailović, Konstantin 34, 41–2
Milan 85, 88, 92, 94, 99, 102–3, 129, 132
Millstatt, Carinthia 104
Missa contra Turcos (Bernard of Kotor) 153
Mistra, siege of (1464) 123
Mocenigo, Alvise 207
Modon 47
Moeller, Bernd 182
Mohács, battle of (1526) 118
Mohammed 28, 152
Moldavia 32–3, 46–7, 66
Molinet, Jean 19
Moorman, John 150
Moors 174
Moravia 41
Moreuil, Lord of 105
Moro, Doge Cristoforo 121–2
Morris, Colin 72
Möttling, county of 104–5
Multa quidem (Bessarion) 162
Murad II, Sultan 30
Mureşan, Dan 25, 33, 52, 168–9
Muscovy 32, 68
Muslims 37, 103
Mytilene 28, 115

Name of Jesus (YHS) 150, 152, 156
Naples 66, 89, 91–4
naval warfare 67–9, 67 n.28
Negroponte 19–25, 32, 47, 49, 52, 54, 69, 73, 75, 81, 92, 165, 167–8, 170, 176
Niccolò da Fara 154
Nicholas of Cusa 185
Nicholas of Srebrenica 178
Nicholas V, Pope 18, 22, 71–4, 79, 95, 102–3, 127, 133, 138, 148, 209
Nicopolis, battle of (1396) 26
Nomen Iesu, see Name of Jesus (YHS)
North Africa 170
Norway 145 n.99, 178
Nürnberg 195
Nürnberg concordat 200–1, 204–5

Observants, Franciscan 136–8, 140–5, 146–59, 155 n.177, 164, 179–80, 189, 193
Oddi, Francesco, bishop of Assisi 111
Olomouc fresco (1468) 118, 159

Orationes ad principes christianos contra Turcos (Bessarion) 52, 165–6, 168–9
Order of the Garter 104–5
Order of the Holy Sepulchre 19
Order of St George 59–60, 104–5
Order of St John 104
Orsini, Giordano 156
Orsini, Orso of Theano 43
Otranto 19, 23–4, 33, 44, 48, 54, 75, 94–6, 95 n.188, 142–3, 145, 177, 180–1, 213
Ottone del Carretto 59
Owen Hughes, Diane 156

Palaeologina, Maria Assanina 32
Palaeologos dynasty 31–2
Palaiologos, Thomas 31, 100
Palaiologos, Zoe (Sophie) 31–2
Palmieri, Matteo 166
Pamplona 170
Pannonius, Andreas 46, 119
Pannonius, Janus 41–3
passagium 29
Pastor, Ludwig 67, 76
Paul II, Pope 51–2, 70, 73, 88–92, 90 n.146, 91 n.154, 92 n.163, 104, 137, 153, 169, 213
Paul of Ragusa 177
Paulus, Nikolaus 182, 194, 194 n.138
Pazzi conspiracy 144
Peloponnese, the 23, 31, 49, 75, 80, 90, 101, 103, 112, 123, 146
Pentancius, Felix 62–3, 63 n.3, 71
Perault, Cardinal Raymond
 alternatives to papal authority 53–6, 53 n.195, 54 n.199, 55 n.211, 56 n.213
 antemurale states 47
 Catholic Europe 35–6, 39
 communication 171–3
 conclusions 211–15
 indulgences 174–5, 179, 181–9, 182 n.48, 185 n.73, 187 n.87, 190–5, 193 n.134, 195 nn.42/3, 197–210, 204 n.205
 recruitment/finance 102, 125–7
 strategy 65, 71, 79, 82
Perotti, Niccolò 164
Peter the Hermit 170
Peter, St. 163–4
Petrovaradin agreement (1463) 87
Petrus de Thomasiis 115–16
Philip (The Good), duke of Burgundy 74, 78, 96, 98, 105–6, 106 nn.29/30, 107, 119, 121, 127, 131, 170
Philip of Mézières 64
Piccamiglio, Giovanni 192
Piccinino, Jacopo 51, 98, 212
Piccolomini, Aeneas Sylvius 24–5, 24 n.34, 30, 72–4, 72 n.50, 107, 115, 119, 159–62, 164, 166, 211; *see also* Pius II, Pope

Piccolomini, Cardinal Francesco 39–40, 83–4, 98, 144
Piccolomini, Jacopo Ammannati 84, 98, 115–16, 123, 137
Picotti, Giovanni Battista 75–7
Picrochole, King 64, 64 n.12
Piero della Francesca 31
Pietro da Camerino 142, 142 n.67, 146
Pius II, Pope
 alternatives to papal authority 51–2, 56, 58–9
 antemurale states 46, 49, 49 n.176
 Catholic Europe 34–40, 37 n.99
 Christianity and Islam 20, 22–3
 communication 136–8, 141, 146, 149, 160–6, 161 n.207
 conclusions 212–16
 the Holy Land 26, 28–9, 31
 indulgences 178, 188, 188 n.98, 193, 198, 205
 recruitment/finance 100–1, 103–4, 103 n.17, 117, 119–25, 121 n.135, 123 n.150, 127–8, 130–3
 strategy 66–70, 72, 73 n.59, 74–8, 76 n.68, 83–5, 85 n.124, 87–90, 94, 96–9
Platina, Bartolomeo 123
Plösch, Josef 105
Podiebrad, George, king of Bohemia 32, 50–1, 56, 58–9, 61, 91, 120–1, 128–9, 212
Poland 32–4, 40 n.121, 42, 55–6, 142
Polecritti, Cynthia 150
Powicke, F. M., 135
printing 167–73
prophecy of the dragon 18

Quesada, Miguel Ladero 174

Rabelais, François 64, 64 n.12
Ragusa 122, 139, 146, 175, 175 n.9, 193
Rangoni, Cardinal Gabriele 34, 43–4, 93, 96, 176–7
Rapp, Francis 173
Ratzeburg 195
Regensburg 38, 195
Regensburg (1454 diet) 79, 106, 106 n.30, 107, 110, 132, 160, 175 n.6
Regensburg (1471 diet) 13, 39, 169
Reichsregiment 38, 71, 125–6, 132, 171, 185, 187, 191, 197, 199–203, 205, 209
Relatio de victoria Belgradensi (Tagliacozzo) 151–2, 154, 157
René, duke of Anjou 76
respublica Christiana 34, 39, 99, 125, 130, 130 n.187
Revelation, chs 12–13 18
Rhodes 143, 193
Riario, Girolamo 95, 214
Romagna 92, 208
Rome 18–19, 33, 47, 50, 52, 55, 61, 67–8, 71–2, 93, 118, 122, 164, 176, 181, 189
Rome agreement (1463) 87

Rome congress (1490) 13–14, 83
Ronchey, Silvia 31
Röpcke, Andreas 194
Rubinstein, Nicolai 48
Rucellai trading company 192
Rusconi, Roberto 158
Russell, Jocelyne 75–6
Russia 32
Rutebeuf 35
Ryder, Alan 66

Šabac 44
S. Pietro di Camerino, church 158
Saladin tithe 35
San Bernardino da Siena 136
Sánchez de Arévalo, Rodrigo 35, 46, 97–9, 122, 164–5
Sansone, Francesco 145
Saxons 123, 123 n.148
Schmid, Peter 205
Schneider, Johannes 181–2, 181 n.45
Septimo iam exacto mense (Pius II) 162
Serbia 30, 139, 146
Setton, Kenneth 66–7, 71 n.46
Severi da Bologna, Lodovico 68, 68 n.33
Sforza, Bianca 176–7
Sforza, Francesco 36, 47–9, 59, 77, 85, 110, 113–14, 116, 122, 146, 149, 198
Sforza, Gian Galeazzo 142
Shaw, Christine 83
Sicily 138
Sigismund, duke of Tyrol 59, 146
Silver, Larry 171
Simon, Alexandru 33
Simon of Lalaing 106
sipahis (Turkish troops) 21
Sixtus IV, Pope 19, 24, 32–5, 43–7, 52–4, 66–7, 69, 72, 82, 82 nn.104/5, 84, 91–6, 95 n.178, 98–9, 131–4, 137–8, 142–5, 144 n.91, 150, 169, 174–8, 180–1, 187–9, 187 n.89, 193–4, 212–14, 212 n.7, 213 n.14
Slebusch, Heinrich 210
Smederevo 44
societas Iesu 102
societas sancti Georgii (Society of St George) 59, 60, 102, 119, 127, 133, 173, 190, 206–7
Somaini, Francesco 94
'Spanish syndrome' 28
Speyer 195
Stantchev, Stefan 216
Stephen III of Moldavia 32–4, 42, 62, 92
Stephen Thomas, king of Bosnia 115, 178
Strasbourg 172–3, 194–5, 197, 209, 211
Strategicon (Birago) 71
Studt, Birgit 156
Sture, Sten 32
Sturm, Otto 209

Styria 24, 44–6
summaria declaratio (Perault) 182
Super securitate Italiae bull 93
Supplementum (Paltz) 183
Suscepturi hodie (Pius II) 96–7
Swabian league 203, 207
Sweden 8 n.31, 32, 145 n.99, 176–8
Szilágyi, Michael 111–12, 114–15, 118
Szűcs, Jeno 118

Tacitus 39
Taleazzi, Stefano 56, 56 n.214, 127, 129, 209, 209 n.233
Tatars of the Golden Horde 67, 71, 102
Teutonic Order 104, 159, 189, 208
Theodore II of Mistra 31
Theuerdank (Maximilian) 171
Thuróczy, János 111, 118
tithing, of children by Turks (*devshirme*) 25
Todeschini-Piccolomini, Francesco 81
Torsello, Marino Sanudo 102, 214
Tractatus pacis (Marini) 57–8, 67
Travels (Mandeville) 154
Trevisan, Cardinal Lodovico 67
Trithemius, Johannes, abbot of Sponheim 190
turchetto (little Turk) 70
Turcica, genre 170
Turks, the
 advance 166
 aggression of 87
 appointment of commander of expedition against 92
 army in Apulia 94–5
 association with barbarism 25–6
 and Belgrade 103, 115, 151–3, 216
 blockade of the Danube 112–13, 113 n.75
 capture of Otranto 23–4, 48, 98–9, 146–7, 212–13, 216
 conquests 22, 38, 41–6
 crusade against 119, 165, 172, 175, 211, 213, 216, 216 n.21
 defeat of at Belgrade, in 1456, 155
 defence of important river crossings against, in 1469 104
 and the eastern front 210
 failure of Christendom's rulers 154
 fall of Negroponte 167–8, 170, 176
 fundamental reorganization proposal to answer threat of 57
 and Hungary 42, 159, 193, 205
 image of 18–20
 importance of resistance 162–3
 intended attack on Valona 143
 massacres by 186
 Maximilian's call to arms against (1502) 125
 no enemies in the east 71
 papal policy towards 50, 212
 Paul II's policy towards 51, 90

Turks, the (*cont.*)
  peace with Venice 96
  plans for using Venetian naval power against 66
  Polish invasion 34
  Pope Sixtus a friend of 52–3
  preparing a mighty fleet in 1482 143
  presented a common threat 74–5
  pressure on Hungary and Poland 55, 86, 91
  retreat into Serbia 116
  routes to strike at Ottoman power 62–3
  sailing vessels to fight 137–8
  sieges of 1440/1456 41
  threat of 28, 35–6, 36 n.94, 82, 121, 135
  threat to Germany 178
  threat to Lesbos 65
  troops of 21
  and Venice 47–8, 77, 77 n.78, 81, 89, 205; *see also under individual sultans*

Ugolini, Baccio 53
Ulrich of Cilli 108, 114, 117
Ulrich, duke of Württemberg 208
Ungelter, Hans 209
Unterkommissaren, for indulgence preaching 187, 190
Urban II, Pope 37, 72, 161, 163
Utrecht Cathedral 185–6, 185 n.70
Uzun Hassan 22, 32, 66, 68–71, 91

Valdarfer, Christophorus 168
Varna, battle of (1444) 26, 29–30, 62, 102, 108
Vaslui, battle of (1475) 33, 42
Vast, Henri 101, 101 n.3

Vatin, Nicolas 70
Veneto-Hungarian alliance 88
Veneto-Ottoman war 120
Veneto-Turkish peace 94
Venice 36–7, 41, 45–9, 48 n.171, 50–2, 57–8, 64–70, 73–8, 81, 85–7, 87–96, 87 n.131, 91 n.157, 99, 102–3, 120–5, 129, 131, 168, 173, 176, 205, 215–16, 215 n.19
Vicenza, Ludovico da 138
Vienne, council at (1311–12) 28
Vila, Ch. 141
Vinzenz of Aggsbach 25
Vitéz, János 41–2
Vlorë, Appollonia, *see* Avlona, Albania
Vogtherr, Thomas 122
Voigt, Klaus 178
Vrhbosna (Sarajevo) 45

Weber, Benjamin 76
Welser bankers 206
Wiener Neustadt 42, 104
Wiener Neustadt diet (1455) 79–80, 95, 107–8
Wiesflecker, Hermann 196, 209
Wimpfeling, Jacob 211, 215
Winterhager, Wilhelm 189–90, 194, 194 n.139
Wladislas I, king of Hungary 29, 41
Wladislas II, king of Hungary 42, 62, 129, 129 n.182
Worms diet (1495) 60, 132

Xerxes 63

Zemun (Semlin) 112–13, 122
zimmis 30